FROMMERS

COMPREHENSIVE TRAVEL GUIDE

VIRGINIA '92-'93

by Rena Bulkin,
Gloria S. McDarrah, and
Fred W. McDarrah

PRENTICE HALL TRAVEL

NEW YORK • LONDON • TORONTO • SYDNEY • TOKYO • SINGAPORE

FROMMER BOOKS

Published by Prentice Hall General Reference
A division of Simon & Schuster Inc.
15 Columbus Circle
New York, NY 10023

ISBN 0-13-334632-3
ISSN 1058-4943

Design by Robert Bull Design
Maps by Geografix Inc.

Manufactured in the United States of America

FROMMER'S VIRGINIA '92-'93

Editor-in-Chief: Marilyn Wood
Senior Editor: Judith de Rubini
Editors: Alice Fellows, Paige Hughes, Theodore Stavrou
Assistant Editors: Suzanne Arkin, Peter Katucki, Lisa Renaud
Managing Editor: Leanne Coupe

CONTENTS

LIST OF MAPS

INVITATION TO THE READERS

In researching this book, we have come across many wonderful establishments, the best of which we have included here. We're sure that many of you will also come across appealing hotels, inns, restaurants, guesthouses, shops, and attractions. Please don't keep them to yourself. Share your experiences, especially if you want to comment on places that we have covered in this edition that have changed for the worse. You can address your letters to us:

Rena Bulkin, Gloria McDarrah, and Fred McDarrah
Frommer's Virginia '92–'93
c/o Prentice Hall Travel
15 Columbus Circle
New York, NY 10023

A DISCLAIMER

Readers are advised that prices fluctuate in the course of time and travel information changes under the impact of the varied and volatile factors that affect the travel industry. The authors and publisher cannot be held responsible for the experiences of readers while traveling. Readers are invited to write to the publisher with ideas, comments, and suggestions for future editions.

SAFETY ADVISORY

Whenever you're traveling in an unfamiliar city or country, stay alert. Be aware of your immediate surroundings. Wear a moneybelt and keep a close eye on your possessions. Be particularly careful with cameras, purses, and wallets, all favorite targets of thieves and pickpockets.

CHAPTER 1

GETTING TO KNOW VIRGINIA

No state in the nation can equal the Commonwealth of Virginia in its role as the cradle of the American republic. America originated at Jamestown and grew along the banks of the Rappahannock, the Potomac, and the James rivers. Spurred on by Virginia leaders like Patrick Henry, whose ringing denunciation of the Stamp Act inspired all 13 Colonies, the desire for American independence grew strong. A Tidewater planter, George Mason, wrote a Bill of Rights, and Virginia aristocrat Thomas Jefferson gave voice to this revolutionary philosophy in the ringing phrases of the Declaration of Independence. And the mantle of responsibility for leading the new nation in its struggle for freedom and its first years as a republic fell on the most famous of all Virginians, George Washington.

With monuments and sites marking more than three centuries of American history, Virginia today is a pioneer in the field of historic preservation. Its landmarks and historic places, including its battlefields, are carefully restored and maintained, and its gem of an 18th-century restoration, Williamsburg, enjoys international renown.

While Virginia's place in U.S. history may first bring you to the Old Dominion, the commonwealth's natural beauty will lure you back again and again. From the pristine beaches of the Eastern Shore to the forests and highlands of western Virginia, visitors will find boundless opportunities for hiking, freshwater and ocean fishing, swimming, boating, sailing, and skiing. America's favorite scenic routes—the Skyline Drive and Blue Ridge Parkway—traverse the Shenandoah Valley and southwestern highlands.

To this appealing mix of living history and outdoor fun, add a vibrant cultural scene with the nation's oldest repertory theater company, major art and science museums, a growing wine industry, and a culinary spectrum that ranges from Virginia ham to Chincoteague oysters. And that's not to mention the theme parks, the steeplechase race meets in Hunt Country, the opportunities to sample farm life, or the nation's premier spa hotel (The Homestead).

For any traveler setting out to explore America, Virginia is a wonderful place to start.

1. GEOGRAPHY & HISTORY

GEOGRAPHY

Virginia is shaped like a triangle, with the base resting on the North Carolina and Tennessee borders. To the west are Kentucky and West Virginia; Maryland is to the

✔ WHAT'S SPECIAL ABOUT VIRGINIA

Accommodations
☐ Numerous B&Bs, charming country inns, and renowned multifacility resorts like The Homestead and The Tides.

Architectural Highlights
☐ Jefferson's Palladian-style Monticello home, the University of Virginia, and the state capitol, leading examples of his architectural genius.
☐ Kenmore, in Fredericksburg, 18th-century manor of Betty (Washington) and Fielding Lewis with its exquisite dining room, rated one of the 100 most beautiful rooms in America.

Battlefields
☐ Civil War sites like Manassas, Chancellorsville, Richmond, Petersburg, and Appomattox, as well as Yorktown, where Cornwallis surrendered, ending the Revolutionary War, all with historically interesting battlefield tours involving scenic drives and walks through fields and woods.

Black History Sites
☐ Birthplace of noted educator and author Booker T. Washington; homes of poet Anne Spencer, in Lynchburg, and the first woman bank president, Maggie L. Walker, in Richmond's Jackson Ward.

Cemeteries
☐ Arlington National Cemetery, the national shrine, site of the Tomb of the Unknown Soldier, and graves of many noted Americans.
☐ Hollywood Cemetery, Richmond, a typically Victorian parklike setting for graves of Presidents Monroe and Tyler, six Virginia governors, Jefferson Davis, and other notables.

Historic Towns
☐ Old Town Alexandria and Fredericksburg, with many preserved and restored homes and buildings associated with Washington, Lee, and Jefferson, among others.
☐ Williamsburg, brilliantly restored 18th-century capital.
☐ Jamestown, site of the first English colony in the New World.

Historic Plantations
☐ Washington's beloved Mount Vernon, George Mason's Gunston Hall, and the magnificent Carter's Grove, among many classic 18th-century estates.

Museums
☐ Chrysler Museum, in Norfolk, one of the great art museums in the U.S.
☐ Virginia Museum of Fine Art, Richmond, with the largest collection of Fabergé objets d'art outside the U.S.S.R.

Natural Wonders
☐ Tidewater and Eastern Shore beaches.
☐ The Blue Ridge Mountains and their spectacular caverns.
☐ Natural Bridge limestone formation near Lexington.

Scenic Drives
☐ Skyline Drive through Shenandoah National Park and the Blue Ridge Parkway through the George Washington National Forest, arguably the most beautiful routes in the country.
☐ The 17.6-mile Chesapeake Bay Bridge-Tunnel, an engineering marvel and a superb drive between Eastern Shore and the Virginia Beach/Norfolk area.

north. The Potomac River, Chesapeake Bay, and Atlantic Ocean form the watery eastern boundary.

Along the eastern coast the **Tidewater** or coastal plain is dominated by four

VIRGINIA

0 — 30 ml / 51 km

MARYLAND

Baltimore

Washington, D.C.

Alexandria

Arlington

Mount Vernon

Fredericksburg

Potomac River

Chincoteague

Chesapeake Bay

Yorktown

James River

Williamstown

Jamestown

Norfolk

Newport News

Virginia Beach

RICHMOND

Petersburg

Appomattox

Charlottesville

Lynchburg

Front Royal

Winchester

Hagerstown

Cumberland

George Washington National Forest

Luray

Shenandoah National Park

New Market

Staunton

Warm Springs

Hot Springs

Lexington

WEST VIRGINIA

Morgantown

Parkersburg

Charleston

Blacksburg

Roanoke

Pulaski

Danville

Abingdon

KENTUCKY

15

17

17

360

64

295

95

95

1

460

360

29

81

81

220

79

79

77

81

81

17

rivers—the Potomac, Rappahannock, York, and James—that empty into the Chesapeake. These rivers divide the Tidewater into three peninsulas, or necks, that end in a series of harbors, the largest of which is Hampton Roads.

The **Piedmont,** central Virginia, includes Richmond, Charlottesville, and Lynchburg. This is farm country that gently rises to meet the foothills of the **Blue Ridge Mountains.** The series of valleys called collectively the **Valley of Virginia** (including the noted Shenandoah) extends the length of the state, from the Potomac in the north to Tennessee in the south. The **Appalachian Plateau** and **Virginia Allegheny Mountains** are at the southern and western borders.

REGIONS IN BRIEF

Arlington, Alexandria, and Hunt Country Just across the Potomac from Washington, D.C., is Arlington National Cemetery. Historic Alexandria, centered around Old Town, offers fascinating daytime walks as well as lively nighttime entertainment and good restaurants. Beyond are the beautiful Potomac plantations, including Mount Vernon. In Virginia's Hunt Country, sightseers can enjoy Virginia's traditional historic inns and fine restaurants. Farther south is Manassas, site of the first major battle of the Civil War.

Fredericksburg and the Northern Neck The quaint cobblestone streets and historic houses of Fredericksburg recall America's first heroes—Washington, James Monroe, John Paul Jones—as does the quiet Northern Neck farmland, where stand the birthplaces of Washington and Robert E. Lee. Military buffs love to explore Fredericksburg's Civil War battlefields.

Charlottesville and Lynchburg This is "Mr. Jefferson's country." Visit his magnificent estate, Monticello, and his retreat at Poplar Grove, and the University of Virginia, which he designed. Area wineries offer tours. Based in Lynchburg, you can visit Appomattox Court House, where Lee surrendered to Grant, and Patrick Henry's final home at Red Hill.

Shenandoah Valley and Virginia Highlands Virginia's most striking scenery is along the Skyline Drive through Shenandoah National Park, and its southern continuation, the Blue Ridge Parkway. Historic towns dot the countryside along this long strip through western Virginia from Front Royal to the North Carolina border. Nearby are the famous mineral waters of Warm Springs and Hot Springs; historic Lexington, where Robert E. Lee spent his last years; and Roanoke, largest city of the Valley. Acres of untouched forest, waterfalls, and quiet streams lure visitors to the Virginia Highlands and the pretty village of Abingdon.

Richmond The state capital has few rivals among U.S. cities for its wealth of historic associations, among them, St. John's Church, where Patrick Henry made his famous "Liberty or Death" speech. Fine arts and science museums, cafés, lively

IMPRESSIONS

To be a Virginian, either by birth, marriage, adoption, or even on one's mother's side, is an introduction to any state in the union, a passport to any foreign country, and a benediction from the almighty God.
—ANONYMOUS

Carry me back to old Virginny, There's where the cotton and the corn and taters grow.
—JAMES A. BLAND, 1875

concerts, and theater add to Richmond's cosmopolitan ambience. Military buffs can tour the Richmond and Petersburg battlefield sites.

Colonial Williamsburg, Yorktown, and Jamestown   This is known as coastal Virginia's Historic Triangle. Colonial Williamsburg, in its 173 acres, re-creates Virginia's Colonial capital. Yorktown commemorates the last, victorious battle of the American Revolution. And Jamestown is where America's first permanent English settlers arrived, in 1607.

Norfolk, Virginia Beach, and the Eastern Shore   The great port of Tidewater Virginia includes cosmopolitan Norfolk and Virginia Beach with its white sandy beach, boardwalk, and nearby historic homes. And the Chesapeake Bay Bridge-Tunnel links Norfolk to the Eastern Shore, an unspoiled sanctuary noted for the Assateague Wildlife Refuge and dotted with small fishing villages.

HISTORY

Virginia's history begins on April 26, 1607, when 104 English men and boys arrived at Cape Henry on the Virginia coast after a 4-month voyage aboard three small ships—the *Susan Constant,* the *Godspeed,* and the *Discovery.* The expedition—an attempt to compete with profitable Spanish encroachments in the New World—was sponsored by the Virginia Company of London and supported by King James I.

A MODEST BEGINNING

The travelers were lured by promises of wealth. Upon arrival they were heartened to find, if not streets paved with gold, an abundance of fish and game. However, the settlers' optimism was short-lived. The very day of their arrival they were attacked by Indians. Fleeing Cape Henry, they started searching for a site that offered greater protection from the Spanish and the Indians. On May 13 the band of English adventurers moored their ships at Jamestown in "six fathom water" and the next day "set to worke about the fortification." Unfortunately, the group's lack of qualifications for the tasks before them soon emerged. Most were gentlemen, unaccustomed to work of any kind, and had little inclination or aptitude for it. None of the rest was equipped for survival in a primeval wilderness. As one on-the-scene chronicler described it, "a world of miseries ensewed." An unfamiliar climate, contaminated water, famine, disease, and Indian attacks claimed their victims, and by autumn only 50 remained alive.

The Tidewater Indians were ambivalent to the new arrivals. When Capt. John Smith tried to barter for corn and grain, the Indians took him prisoner and carried him to Chief Powhatan. According to legend, they would have killed him, but Powhatan's daughter, Pocahontas, interceded and saved his life. However, Smith was not much of a diplomat in dealing with natives; he helped sow seeds of

DATELINE

- **1607**   First permanent English settlement in New World established at Jamestown.
- **1612**   John Rolfe begins cultivation of tobacco for export.
- **1619**   House of Burgesses—first representative legislative body in New World—meets in Jamestown. First Africans arrive at Jamestown; sold as indentured servants.
- **1624**   Virginia becomes a royal colony.
- **1652**   Burgesses affirm only they have right to elect officers of Virginia colony.
- **1682**   Tobacco riots protest falling crop prices.
- **1699**   Virginia's government moves to Williamsburg.
- **1754**   French and Indian War begins as George Wash-
(continues)

dissension that would result in centuries of hostility between Indians and European settlers.

In 1613, John Rolfe (who later married Pocahontas) brought from the New World a new aromatic tobacco that proved popular in England. The settlers had discovered not the glittery gold they expected, but the "golden weed" that would be the foundation of Virginia's fortunes.

The year 1619 was marked by several important happenings: The Virginia Company sent a shipload of 90 women to suitors who paid their transportation costs; 22 burgesses were elected to set up the first legislative body in the New World; and 20 Africans arrived in a Dutch ship to work as indentured servants, a precursor of slavery.

In 1699 the capital of the colony was moved from Jamestown, which had suffered a disastrous fire, to Williamsburg, and it was from Williamsburg that some of the first strong protests were lodged against Parliament by Colonial patriots.

COLONIAL LIFE

By the mid-18th century, the growth of vast tobacco plantations along Tidewater Virginia's rivers brought with it a concurrent increase in the importation of slaves from Africa as the base for the "plantation economy."

The French and Indian War in the 1750s proved to be a training ground for America's Revolutionary forces. When the French built outposts in territory claimed by Virginia, Governor Dinwoody sent George Washington to protect Virginia's claims. In the field Washington acquitted himself with honor, and after General Braddock's defeat, he was appointed commander-in-chief of Virginia's army on the frontier.

UNREST GROWS

Expenses from the war and economic hardships led the British to increase taxes in the Colonies, and protests in Virginia and Massachusetts escalated. The 1765 Stamp Act met with general resistance. Patrick Henry inspired the Virginia General Assembly to pass the Virginia Resolves, setting forth Colonial rights according to constitutional principles. The young orator exclaimed, "If this be treason, make the most of it." The Stamp Act was repealed in 1766, but the Revenue Acts of 1767, which included the hated tax on tea, exacerbated tensions.

Ties among the Colonies were strengthened when Virginia's Burgesses, led by Richard Henry Lee, created a standing committee to communicate their problems in dealing with England to similar committees in the other colonies. When the Boston Post Bill closed that harbor in punishment for the Boston Tea Party, the Virginia Assembly moved swiftly. Although Governor Dunmore had dissolved the legislature, they met at Raleigh Tavern and recommended that a general congress be held annually.

Virginia sent seven representatives to the First Continental Congress in 1774, among them Lee, Patrick Henry, and George Washington.

The following year, Patrick Henry made a fiery plea for arming Virginia's militia. He concluded his argument in these now-familiar words, "Is life so dear or peace so sweet as to be purchased at the price of chains and slavery? Forbid it, Almighty God! I know not what course others may take, but, as for me, give me liberty, or give me death!"

Later in 1775, upon hearing news of the battles of Lexington and Concord, the Second Continental Congress in Philadelphia voted to make the conflict near Boston a Colony-wide confrontation and chose Washington as commander of the Continental Army. War had begun.

BIRTH OF THE NATION

On June 12, 1776, the Virginia Convention, meeting in Williamsburg, adopted George Mason's Bill of Rights and instructed Virginia's delegates to the Continental Congress to propose independence for the Colonies. Mason's revolutionary document stated that "all power is vested in, and consequently derived from, the people," and that "all men are created free and independent, and have certain inherent rights . . . : among which are the enjoyment of life and liberty, with the means of acquiring and possessing property . . ." He also firmly upheld the right of trial by jury, freedom of the press, and the right of all people to freedom of religion. When the Congress meeting in Philadelphia adopted Thomas Jefferson's Declaration of Independence (based on Mason's bill) on July 4, 1776, the United States of America was born.

The Revolution was a bloody 7-year conflict marked by many staggering defeats for the patriots. Historians believe that it was only the superb leadership and pertinacity of Gen. George Washington that inspired the Continental Army (a ragtag group of farmers, laborers, backwoodsmen, and merchants) to continue so long in the face of overwhelming odds.

VICTORY AT YORKTOWN

Although many Virginians were in Washington's army, it was not until the war's final years that the state became a major battleground. The turning point came in March 1781, when British General Lord Cornwallis established a base at the York River.

Two weeks after Cornwallis settled into Yorktown for the winter, General Washington received word from the French admiral, the Comte de Grasse, that he was taking his squadron to the Chesapeake and that his men and ships were at Washington's disposal through October 15. "I shall be obliged to you," wrote de Grasse, "if you will employ me promptly and effectually during that time." After conferring with the Comte de Rochambeau, commander of

DATELINE

- **1789** Washington inaugurated as first President. Virginia cedes area to U.S. for seat of government.
- **1801** Thomas Jefferson inaugurated President.
- **1803** Jefferson sends James Monroe to France for purchase of Louisiana Territory.
- **1809** James Madison inaugurated President.
- **1814** President and Dolley Madison flee to Virginia as British enter Washington.
- **1831** Nat Turner's slave rebellion.
- **1832** House of Delegates bill to abolish slavery in Virginia loses by seven votes.
- **1859** John Brown hanged after failed raid on Harper's Ferry Arsenal.
- **1861** Richmond chosen Confederate capital. First battle of Manassas.
- **1862** First ironclad ships, *Monitor* and *Merrimac*, battle in Hampton Roads harbor. Confederate victories at Second Manassas, Fredericksburg.
- **1863** Stonewall Jackson fatally wounded at Chancellorsville.
- **1864** Confeder-
  (continues)

DATELINE

acy wins Battle of the Wilderness at Spotsylvania Court House near Fredericksburg. Grant's siege of Petersburg begins.
- **1865** Richmond evacuated. Lee surrenders at Appomattox.
- **1867** Virginia put under military rule of Reconstruction Act. Confederate President Jefferson Davis imprisoned for treason in Fort Monroe.
- **1870** Virginia readmitted to Union.
- **1900** Legislature passes "Jim Crow" segregation laws.
- **1902** Poll tax in new state constitution effectively keeps blacks from voting.
- **1913** Woodrow Wilson inaugurated President.
- **1917** Wilson leads America into war against Germany. Growth of Hampton Roads naval and military installations.
- **1954** Supreme Court school integration ruling leads to school closings to avoid compliance with law.
- **1989** L. Douglas Wilder, nation's first black governor, takes office in Richmond.

the French troops in America, Washington decided to march 450 miles to Virginia with the object of defeating Cornwallis.

Meanwhile, on September 5, 1781, a fleet of 19 British ships under Admiral Thomas Graves appeared at the entrance to Chesapeake Bay with the aim of reinforcing Cornwallis's Yorktown entrenchment. They were met by 24 French ships under de Grasse. Though the battle ended in a stalemate, Graves was forced to return to New York to repair his ships. The French remained to block further British reinforcements or the possibility of their escape by water, while the French and American armies under Washington neared Yorktown to block aid or escape by land.

The siege began on September 28 when 17,000 men under Washington occupied a line encircling the town. The allied army, spread out in camps extending 6 miles, dug siege lines, and bombarded the redcoats with heavy cannonfire. British defeat was inevitable. On October 17, a cease-fire was called and a British officer was led to American lines, where he requested an armistice. Although the war was not officially over until the Treaty of Paris was signed 2 years later, Cornwallis's defeat effectively marked the colonists' victory.

FRAMING THE CONSTITUTION

The new nation's governmental powers were weak, resting on the inadequate provisions of the Articles of Confederation. To remedy the situation, a Constitutional Convention met in Philadelphia, and Washington was elected president of the Convention. He and fellow Virginian James Madison fought to have the new Constitution include a Bill of Rights and gradual abolition of the slave trade. Although both measures were defeated, the two Virginians voted to adopt the Constitution, feeling that its faults could be amended later.

In 1788 Virginia became the 10th state to ratify the Constitution, and by 1791 the first 10 amendments—the Bill of Rights—had been added. Madison was author of the first 9 amendments, Richard Henry Lee the 10th.

THE COUNTRY'S EARLY VIRGINIAN PRESIDENTS

Washington was elected President under the new Constitution and took office on April 30, 1789.

As third President of the United States, Jefferson nearly doubled the size of the country by purchasing the Louisiana Territory from the French.

James Madison took office as President in 1809. Unable to maintain Jefferson's peace-keeping efforts in the face of continued provocations by England, Madison was swayed by the popular demand for armed response, and in 1812 Congress declared war. Although some coastal plantations were attacked by British warships, the only suffering Virginia witnessed was the burning of nearby Washington, D.C.

James Monroe followed, having already served Virginia and the nation in many capacities. During his two terms as president the nation pushed westward, and he faced the first struggle over the slavery question (which resulted in the Missouri Compromise), established the Monroe Doctrine, and settled the nation's boundary with Canada.

A NATION DIVIDES

It was not long before the United States became a nation divided. The issues were states' rights, slavery, and the conflicting goals of an industrial North and an agricultural South. In 1859 John Brown and his small band of followers raided the arsenal at Harper's Ferry (now West Virginia) to obtain arms for a slave revolt he hoped to instigate. Brown was captured and hanged. In the North his execution rallied support for the abolitionist cause; in the South people shuddered at the threat of a slave revolt.

The election of 1860 had been crucial. The Republicans nominated Abraham Lincoln, whom the South vowed it would not accept; but the Democrats split and Lincoln was elected. Seven states seceded—Texas, Louisiana, South Carolina, Alabama, Georgia, Florida, and Mississippi. At his inauguration Lincoln declared, "In your hands, my dissatisfied fellow countrymen, and not in mine, is the momentous issue of civil war. You can have no oath registered in heaven to destroy the government, while I have the solemn one to preserve, protect, and defend it."

On April 12, 1861, guns sounded at Fort Sumter in Charleston harbor. Secession had become war.

CIVIL WAR

First Manassas, July 21, 1861

In May 1861, the Confederate capital was transferred to Richmond, only 100 miles from Washington. Virginia was doomed to become the first major battleground of the Civil War. The first of six heavy offensives by the North against Richmond was decisively repulsed on July 21, 1861, at the battle of First Manassas (Bull Run). Union Gen. Irvin McDowell's 35,000 ill-trained federal volunteers marched southward to the cry "Onward to Richmond," and the following Union attacks were successful. Later, however, a stonewall-like stand by the Virginia Brigade of Gen. Thomas J. Jackson swept McDowell's forces back to Washington. In addition to the victory, the South had found a new hero—"Stonewall" Jackson. Total casualties in this first major engagement of the war: 4,828 men! It was now apparent that this would be a long and bitter conflict.

The Peninsula Campaign

The second major offensive against Richmond, the Peninsula Campaign, devised by Union Gen. George B. McClellan, was the setting for the most famous naval engagement in the western hemisphere. On March 9, 1862, two ironclad vessels, the U.S.S. *Monitor* and the C.S.S. *Virginia* (formerly the *Merrimac*) pounded each other with cannon. Although the battle was a draw, the advent of ironclad warships heralded a new era in naval history.

Two months later Yorktown was reduced to rubble and the Union army advanced up the peninsula. The Confederates retreated until they were only 9 miles from Richmond. At that point they fought, and the Confederate leader, General Johnson, was badly wounded. Robert E. Lee, grandson of Colonial patriot Richard Henry Lee,

❓ DID YOU KNOW . . . ?

- The only brothers to sign the Declaration of Independence were Richard Henry and Francis Lightfoot Lee.
- Norfolk's innovative recycling program created "Mount Trashmore," a mountain of trash now a children's playground.
- Robert E. Lee's faithful horse Traveller is buried just outside the general's crypt on the campus of Washington and Lee University in Lexington.
- More Americans lost their lives in the Civil War than in World Wars I and II combined.
- Over 60% of the Civil War was fought in Virginia.
- Stonewall Jackson acquired his nickname in the first Battle of Manassas, when General Bee, marveling at his persistence in standing his ground, exclaimed, "There stands Jackson, like a stone wall!"
- Playwright George Bernard Shaw, when paid a ham by the Barter Theatre, returned it for spinach because he was a vegetarian.
- There are more miles of trout streams than roads in Virginia.
- Woodrow Wilson was the first southerner to become President since the Civil War.
- The world's largest office building (the Pentagon) is located in Arlington. It contains more than 6.5 million square feet of space and almost 18 miles of corridors.
- Virginia's motto, SIC SEMPER TYRANNUS, translated from the Latin means "Thus Always to Tyrants."
- Eight U.S. Presidents were born in Virginia: George Washington, Thomas Jefferson, James Madison, James Monroe, both William Henry and Benjamin Harrison, John Tyler, and Woodrow Wilson.
- The Norfolk Naval Base is the world's largest naval facility.

(continues)

was appointed head of the army of Virginia. Personally opposed to secession, Lee had sadly resigned his commission in the U.S. Army when Virginia joined the Confederacy, saying, "My heart is broken, but I cannot raise my sword against Virginia." In a series of victories beginning on June 26, 1862, Lee finally defeated the Union armies. Richmond had again been saved.

Second Manassas, Fredericksburg, and Chancellorsville, 1862–63

The third Union drive against Richmond was repulsed at Manassas, where Gen. Robert E. Lee secured his place in history by soundly defeating 70,000 Union troops under Gen. John Pope with a Confederate army of 55,000 men in 3 days. On December 13, 1862, Gen. Ambrose Burnside, newly chosen head of the Army of the Potomac, crossed the Rappahannock and struck Fredericksburg while Lee's army was scattered in northern Virginia. The Federal advance was so slow that by the time the Union armies moved, Lee's forces were firmly entrenched in the hills south of the city. Burnside was unsuccessful and the fourth Union drive against Richmond was turned back.

General Joseph Hooker took command of the Union army early in 1863, and, once again, Federal forces attempted to take Richmond. Fighting raged for 4 days. The Union army retreated, and the fifth drive on Richmond had failed. But Lee's victory was costly. In addition to heavy casualties, Stonewall Jackson was wounded by his own troops and died of complications resulting from the amputation of his arm. Without Jackson, Lee began his second invasion of the North, which would end in the small Pennsylvania town of Gettysburg.

A War of Attrition

In March 1864 Grant was put in command of all Federal armies. His plan for victory called for "a war of attrition," total unrelenting warfare that would put constant pressure on all points of the Confederacy. The first great confrontation between Lee and Grant, the Battle of the Wilderness, resulted in a Confederate victory, but the South's casualties were high, 11,400. The Richmond campaign was the heaviest fighting of the Civil War. Three times Grant tried and failed to interpose his forces between Lee and Richmond. More than 80,000 men were killed and wounded.

DID YOU KNOW . . . ?

- One of the Seven Natural Wonders of the World, Natural Bridge, just south of Lexington, is 215 feet (17 stories) high.
- Christ Church, built by Robert "King" Carter on the Northern Neck, is the finest example of untouched Colonial church architecture in the U.S. Still exactly as it was when it was built, it has no heat or electricity.
- National observance of Memorial Day began after the Civil War in Petersburg, when a group of schoolgirls decorated the graves of Confederate soldiers.
- Luray Caverns has the only "Stalacpipe Organ" in the world. The instrument utilizes rock formations to produce symphonic music.
- Virginia was named for Queen Elizabeth I of England, the Virgin Queen.
- Eight states—Illinois, Indiana, Kentucky, Michigan, Minnesota, Ohio, West Virginia, and Wisconsin—were formed from Virginia territory.
- Smoking is not allowed on tours of the Philip Morris Manufacturing Center.
- There is a life-size bronze statue honoring black tap dancer Bill "Bojangles" Robinson in the Jackson Ward neighborhood of Richmond where he grew up.

Laying Siege to Petersburg, June 1864–April 1865

Still determined, Grant secretly moved his army across the James River toward Petersburg, an important rail junction south of Richmond. Improvised Southern forces managed to hold the city until Lee arrived. Grant then resorted to ever-tightening siege operations. Blocked in his trenches, Lee could not leave Grant's front. To do so would be to abandon Petersburg and Richmond. Subject to hunger and exposure, the Confederate will to resist began to wane and periodic skirmishes further weakened Confederate morale.

Lee, hoping to divert Grant's attention, dispatched a small army under Jubal Early to the menaced Shenandoah Valley. Grant instructed Union Gen. Philip Sheridan: "The Shenandoah is to be so devastated that crows flying across it for the balance of the season will have to bring their own provender." The second valley campaign resulted in the destruction of Early's army and the Shenandoah Valley.

Last Days of the War

Back in Petersburg, Grant's attrition strategy was succeeding. For the army of Northern Virginia the 10-month siege of that city meant physical hardship, disease, filth, dwindling morale, and tedious waiting for the inevitable onslaught. It came on April 1, 1865, when Federal forces smashed through weakened Confederate lines at Five Forks; Petersburg fell and Richmond was occupied by Federal forces. Lee's last hope was to rendezvous with Joe Johnson's army, which was retreating through North Carolina before Sherman's advance. However, on April 8 the vanguard of Grant's army succeeded in reaching Appomattox Court House ahead of Lee, thus blocking the Confederates' last escape route.

On April 9, 1865, the Civil War ended in Virginia at Appomattox in Wilbur McLean's farmhouse. Grant, so uncompromising in war, proved compassionate in peace. All Confederate soldiers were permitted to return home on parole, cavalrymen could keep their horses, and officers to retain their sidearms. Rations were provided at once for the destitute Southerners. Accepting these generous terms, Lee surrendered his 28,000 soldiers, the ragged remnants of the once-mighty Army of Northern Virginia. Lee's farewell was moving in its simplicity: "I earnestly pray that a merciful God will extend to you his blessing and protection. With an unceasing admiration of your constancy and devotion to your country, and a grateful remembrance of your kind and generous consideration for myself, I bid you all an affectionate farewell."

RECOVERY & RENEWAL

To a state devastated by a conflict that pitted brother against brother, recovery was slow. Besides the physical and psychological damages of the conflict, the Reconstruction era brought Virginia under Federal military control until 1870.

However, by the turn of the century, Virginia's economic growth was characterized by new railroad lines connecting remote country areas in the west with urban centers. Factories were bringing more people to the cities, and the economy, once based entirely on agriculture, now had a growing industrial base. The great ports enjoyed growing importance as steamship traffic carried an increasing volume of commercial freight. During this period the great scholar, author, and educator, Booker T. Washington, who had been born in slavery, studied at Virginia's Hampton Institute and achieved fame as an advisor to Presidents.

Another Virginian, Woodrow Wilson, was inaugurated President in 1913. Although noted for his peace-loving ideals, Wilson saw the entry of the U.S. into World War I in 1917. War brought prosperity to Virginia with new factories and munitions plants and the expansion of military-training camps throughout the state.

In the years after the war, the Byrd family, prominent in Virginia Tidewater plantation society since the 1600s, dominated the state's politics. World War II brought a population explosion, with men and women of the armed forces flocking to northern Virginia suburbs near Washington, D.C., and the port area of Hampton Roads. Many of these people stayed after the war, and by 1955 the major part of Virginia's population was urban dwelling. Today the state's population is more than five million.

VIRGINIA TODAY

Although John Rolfe's tobacco is still an important crop, farm income in Virginia is also based on the apple orchards of the Shenandoah Valley; livestock, dairying, and poultry-raising in the Piedmont; and the state's famous Smithfield hams and peanuts from the Tidewater country. Industry continues to grow as well, notably in the manufacturing of clothes, chemicals, furniture, and transportation equipment.

For today's Virginians, the memory of the state's past still exerts its influence, as it surely must in towns where descendants of America's first patriots still live and where the homes, monuments, and battlefields that shaped the country's history comprise their daily landscape. But Virginians look ahead, past their historical treasures, to an exciting future, as cities undergo dramatic downtown renewals and scenic mountains and beach resorts become vacation meccas for visitors to the Old Dominion.

2. RECOMMENDED BOOKS, FILMS, RECORDS & VIDEOS

BOOKS
BIOGRAPHY

Mary Chesnut's Civil War, C. Van Woodward, ed. (Yale University Press, 1982). Pulitzer Prize–winning autobiography.
Thomas Jefferson: An Intimate Portrait, Fawn M. Brodie (Norton, 1974).
Jefferson and His Times, Dumas Malone (6 vols.; Little, Brown, 1948–81).
Lee, Douglas Southall Freeman (4 vols., 1935; abridged 1-vol. edition, Macmillan, 1985).

Up from Slavery, Booker T. Washington (1903; reprinted by Doubleday, 1963).
George Washington, Douglas Southall Freeman (7 vols., 1948–57; abridged 1-vol. edition, Macmillan, 1985).

NOVELS

Adams, Richard. *Traveller* (Dell, 1989). About General Lee's horse.
Bontemps, Arna. *Black Thunder* (1936; reprinted, Beacon, 1968). Based on Gabriel Prosser's slave uprising in Richmond in 1800.
Cather, Willa. *Sapphira and the Slave Girl* (1940; reprinted by Vintage, 1975).
Crane, Stephen. *Red Badge of Courage* (1895; Bantam, 1981).
Glasgow, Ellen. *The Voice of the People* (1900; Irvington, 1972).
Styron, William. *The Confessions of Nat Turner* (1967; Bantam, 1981).

HISTORY

Dabney, Virginius. *Virginia, The New Dominion* (University Press of Virginia, 1971).
Foote, Shelby. *The Civil War* (3 vols., 1963–74; Vintage, 3 vols., 1986).
Ward, Geoffrey C., with Ric Burns and Ken Burns. *The Civil War* (Knopf, 1990).
———. *Witness to Appomattox* (Harper Perennial, 1989).

GENERAL

Dillard, Annie. *Pilgrim at Tinker Creek* (Harper & Row, 1974).
Hume, Ivor Noel. *Martin's Hundred* (Knopf, 1982).
Jefferson, Thomas. *Notes on the State of Virginia* (1787; reprinted by Norton, 1982).
Loth, Calder. *The Virginia Landmarks Register* (3rd ed.; University Press of Virginia, 1986).
Peters, Margaret T., comp. *A Guidebook to Virginia's Historical Markers* (University Press of Virginia, 1985).

FILMS

Trail of the Lonesome Pine (1937), with Fred MacMurray, Henry Fonda, and Sylvia Sidney.
Brother Rat (1938), with Jane Wyman and Ronald Reagan, depicting cadet life at VMI.
Dirty Dancing (1987), with Jennifer Grey and Patrick Swayze; filmed at Mountain Lake Resort.
Silence of the Lambs (1990), with Jodie Foster and Anthony Hopkins; filmed at Quantico, Va.

RECORDS

"The Civil War: Its Music and Its Sounds," Philip's Mercury (1991).
"Original Sound-track Recordings: The Civil War," Elektra Nonesuch (1991).

VIDEOS

"The Civil War" PBS Series, Time-Life.
"Virginia's Civil War Parks," Finley-Holiday.

CHAPTER 2

PLANNING YOUR TRIP

This chapter is devoted to the where, when, and how of your trip to Virginia. Whether you plan to stay a day, a week, 2 weeks, or longer, there are many choices you'll need to make *before* leaving home. All this, and more, in the sections that follow.

1. SOURCES OF TOURIST INFORMATION

One of the best sources is the **Virginia Division of Tourism,** 1021 East Cary Street, Richmond, VA 23219 (tel. 804/786-4484). Write or call them for: a comprehensive 140-page guide to the state, a calendar of events, a state highway map, brochures, and a campground directory. Or visit one of their Welcome Centers where knowledgeable staffers are on hand to answer questions and help plan travel routes. The **Welcome Centers** are located in: Bracey, I-85 at the North Carolina border (tel. 804/689-2295); Bristol, I-81 at the Tennessee border (tel. 703/466-2932); Clearbrook, I-81 at the West Virginia border (tel. 703/667-0758); Covington, I-64 at the West Virginia border (tel. 703/559-3010); New Church, U.S. 13 at the Maryland border (tel. 804/824-5000); Fredericksburg, I-95 south (tel. 703/786-8344); Lambsburg, I-77 north (tel. 703/755-3931); Manassas, I-66 west (tel. 703/361-2134); Rocky Gap, I-77 south (tel. 703/928-1873); and Skippers, I-95 north (tel. 804/634-4113).

Other excellent sources are local convention and visitors bureaus, which are listed in the appropriate chapters.

2. WHEN TO GO

THE CLIMATE

Virginia's temperate climate is a delight year round. The state enjoys four distinct seasons, with some variations in temperature from the warmer, more humid coastal areas to the cooler, dryer climate in the mountains. Wintertime snows are pretty much confined to northern Virginia and the Blue Ridge Mountains. In summer, extremely hot spells are short-lived. Spring and autumn are long seasons, and in terms of natural beauty and heavenly climate, they're optimum times to visit. Annual rainfall averages 46 inches; annual snowfall, 18 inches.

VIRGINIA'S AVERAGE TEMPERATURES

	Jan	Feb	Mar	Apr	May	June	July	Aug	Sept	Oct	Nov	Dec
High	44	46	56	68	75	84	90	88	81	69	57	47
Low	26	27	38	45	54	62	66	65	59	48	39	28

VIRGINIA CALENDAR OF EVENTS

JANUARY

☐ **Lee Birthday Celebrations,** Alexandria. Period music, house tours at Lee-Fendall House and Lee's Boyhood Home. 4th Sunday.

FEBRUARY

☐ **Antiques Forum,** Williamsburg. Lectures and workshops on 18th-century life. 1st week.
☐ **Maymont Flower and Garden Show,** Richmond. A breath of spring in February. Landscape exhibits, vendors, speakers. Early February.

✪ ALEXANDRIA'S GEORGE WASHINGTON BIRTHDAY

EVENTS   Black tie or colonial costume dinner Saturday evening, followed by birthnight ball at Gadsby's Tavern, where George and Martha Washington attended balls in 1798 and 1799. On Sunday, Revolutionary War encampment at Fort Ward, featuring a skirmish between British and Colonial uniformed troops. Parade on Monday.
Where: Alexandria. When: Washington's Birthday weekend. How: Phone 703/838-4200 for information.

☐ **Washington's Birthday Celebration,** Williamsburg. Special themed tours, Palace Ball, military review. Washington's Birthday weekend.
☐ **Presidents' Day Celebration,** Fredericksburg. Monday of Washington's Birthday weekend. Reduced rates at attractions.
☐ **Mount Vernon Open House,** Mount Vernon. Wreath-laying, fife and drum corps performance. Monday of Washington's Birthday weekend.

MARCH

☐ **Mid-Atlantic Wildfowl Festival, Virginia Beach.** Carvers, artists, exhibitors with decoys, photos, art, and artifacts for sale. 1st weekend.
☐ **James Madison's Birthday,** Montpelier. Ceremony at cemetery, reception at house. March 16.
☐ **Trout Season Opening Day.** You may think the whole state had grabbed a rod

and reel if you stop at one of the scenic roadside streams. Valid license required; State Game & Inland Fisheries Dept. (tel. 804/346-1000). March 16.

☐ **Patrick Henry Speech Reenactment,** St. John's Church, Richmond. "Give me liberty or give me death," he said here. Closest Sunday to March 23.

APRIL

✪ BARTER THEATRE SEASON OPENING *America's oldest running repertory company presents comedies, drama, children's theater.*
Where: Abingdon. **When:** April to November. **How:** Subscription- or single-ticket sales at box office (tel. toll free 800/368-3240).

✪ INTERNATIONAL AZALEA FESTIVAL *A salute to NATO countries. The brilliant beauty of azaleas in bloom is backdrop for ceremonies in the Norfolk Botanic Garden attendant on crowning a queen who reigns at a parade and other festivities. Also a military display that includes an air show, visiting of ships, and aircraft ground exhibits.*
Where: Norfolk. **When:** 2nd to 3rd week in April. **How:** Most events free. Phone 804/622-2312 for information.

☐ **Dogwood Festival,** Charlottesville. The peak of the blossoming season; sale of dogwood trees, concerts, quilt show, athletic events. Last 2 weeks.

☐ **Fairfax Steeplechase Races,** Leesburg. Six to nine races over jumps at Belmont Plantation (tel. toll free 800/752-6118). Late April.

✪ HISTORIC GARDEN WEEK IN VIRGINIA *The event of the year—a statewide celebration, with tours of the grounds and gardens of some 200 Virginia landmarks, including plantations and other sites open only during this week.*
Where: Statewide. **When:** Last full week of April. **How:** The Garden Club of Virginia, 12 East Franklin Street, Richmond, VA 23219 (tel. 804/644-7776 or 804/643-7141), publishes a free guide with detailed information; send $1 for postage.

☐ **Thomas Jefferson Birthday Commemoration,** Monticello, Charlottesville. Wreath-laying ceremony at gravesite, fife and drum corps, speaker. April 13.

✪ STRAWBERRY HILL RACES *Steeplechase event, with carriage promenade.*
Where: Fair Grounds, Richmond. **When:** Mid-April. **How:** Phone 804/228-3238 for advance tickets.

MAY

✪ SHENANDOAH APPLE BLOSSOM FESTIVAL *Acres of orchards in blossom throughout the valley, plus 5 days of music, band competitions, parades, coronation of queen, foot races, arts and crafts sale, midway amusements, and carnival, celebrity grand marshal.*
Where: Winchester. **When:** Usually 1st weekend. **How:** Many events free; contact Festival, 5 North Cameron Street, Winchester, VA 22601 (tel. 703/662-3863).

☐ **Seafood Festival,** Tom's Cove, Chincoteague. All you can eat—a seafood-lover's dream come true. Must have tickets in advance from Eastern Shore

Chamber of Commerce, P.O. Drawer R, Milfa, VA (tel. 804/787-2460). 1st weekend.

☐ **George Mason Day,** Gunston Hall, Lorton. All-day celebration with music and costumed role-players portraying his daily life and concern for the Bill of Rights. May 5.

☐ **Jamestown Landing Day,** Jamestown. Militia presentations and sailing demonstrations to celebrate the first settlers. Early May.

☐ **New Market Battlefield Historical Park,** New Market. Reenactment of battle. 2nd Sunday.

☐ **Mother's Day Pageant,** Fredericksburg. A skit portraying George Washington's last visit to his mother is performed at Mary Washington's cottage. Mother's Day, early May.

☐ **New Market Day,** VMI Campus, Lexington. Annual roll call for cadets who died in the battle. May 15.

☐ **Oatlands Sheepdog Trials.** Dogs compete in sheep-herding contests. Crafts, food, house and garden tours. Late May.

✪ *VIRGINIA HUNT COUNTRY STABLE TOUR* *A unique opportunity to view prestigious horse farms and private estates.*
Where: Loudoun County. *When:* Late May. *How:* Ticket information at Trinity Church, Upperville (near Middleburg) (tel. 703/592-3711).

JUNE

☐ **Great Rappahannock Whitewater Canoe Race,** Fredericksburg. Challenging 4.5-mile race; registration 8 to 10am (tel. 703/371-5085). Early June.

☐ **Harborfest,** Norfolk. Tall ships, sailboat races, air shows, military demonstrations, fireworks. 1st weekend.

☐ **Boardwalk Art Show,** Virginia Beach. Works in all media, between 18th Street and 30th Street along the boardwalk. Mid-June.

✪ *JAMES RIVER BATEAU FESTIVAL* *Boat race to Richmond. Music at the riverfront, foot races, games, historic crafts exhibits and demonstrations. The 8-day festival moves along the James, stopping each night at a historic town along the 200-year-old river route.*
Where: Lynchburg. *When:* 2nd to 3rd week in June. *How:* Contact the Festival at P.O. Box 60, Lynchburg, VA 24505 (tel. toll free 800/282-1786).

☐ **Anheuser Busch Golf Classic,** Williamsburg. PGA tour event featuring top professional golfers in competition, at Kingsmill Golf Course. Late June.

✪ *ASHLAWN-HIGHLAND SUMMER FESTIVAL* *James Monroe's home is the setting for opera, musicals, concerts, Saturday-morning family entertainment, Midsummer Eve dinner, and traditional bonfire finale.*
Where: Charlottesville. *When:* End of June to August. *How:* Tickets from the box office or in town (tel. 804/293-8000). To order a picnic supper at the festival, call 804/296-5496 before 12:30pm on the day of performance.

JULY

☐ **Happy Birthday USA,** Staunton. Free concert hosted by Statler Brothers in Gypsy Hill Park. July 4.

☐ **Independence Day Celebration,** Brookneal. Revolutionary War encampment at Patrick Henry's home, Red Hill. July 4.

☐ **Old-Fashioned 4th of July,** Richmond. Country activities—wagon rides, sack races, music—at Meadow Park Museum. July 4.
York County Celebration, Yorktown Victory Monument. July 4th.
Virginia Scottish Games, Alexandria. Celtic-theme festival; Highland dancing, bagpiping, fiddling competition, Scottish foods. 4th weekend.

✪ *PONY SWIM AND AUCTION* *Famous miniature ponies swim the Assateague Channel on Wednesday. Ponies later herded to carnival grounds and auctioned off. Return swim to Assateague on Friday.*
Where: Chincoteague Island. *When:* Begins last Wednesday in July.
How: Event is free. Get to Memorial Park, which overlooks the channel, early; phone 804/336-6519 for information.

☐ **Mountain Heritage Festival,** Shenandoah National Park, Skyland Lodge. Live entertainment, square dancing, craft demonstrations. Late July.
☐ **Virginia Highlands Festival,** Abingdon. Appalachian Mountain culture showcase for musicians, artists, writers. Antiques market, hot-air balloons. Late July.

AUGUST

☐ **Old Fiddlers' Convention,** Galax. One of the largest and oldest such conventions in the world. Phone 703/236-2184 for information. Early August.

✪ *AUGUST COURT DAYS* *Street fair celebrating opening of the Colonial Judicial Court. Craft booths, music, militia, street performers, reenactment, children's fair.*
Where: Leesburg. *When:* Mid-August. *How:* For ticket information, phone toll free 800/752-6118.

SEPTEMBER

☐ **Blue Ridge Highlands Scottish Games,** Roanoke. Pipe bands, folk-dance competitions, rugby, British car show, Scottish food. Labor Day Weekend.

✪ *SENIOR TIME* *A salute to senior citizens with special rates and extra-value programs at hotels and attractions, shops, etc.*
Where: Williamsburg. *When:* September 1 to 30. *How:* For details, call 804/220-7645.

✪ *ANNUAL INTERNATIONAL CHILDREN'S FESTIVAL* *A 3-day event with visual and performing artists from many nations. Performances, hands-on workshops, and children's entertainment.*
Where: Wolf Trap Farm Park, near Arlington. *When:* Labor Day Weekend. *How:* Purchase tickets at the box office, or call 702/642-0862.

☐ **State Fair of Virginia,** Richmond. Rides, entertainment, agricultural exhibits, pioneer farmstead, flower shows. 10 days in late September.

OCTOBER

☐ **Fall Race Meet,** Middleburg. Steeplechase races and hunter championships. Early October.
☐ **Oyster Festival,** Chincoteague. A feast of oysters, but for ticket-holders only (call 804/336-6161). Early October.

☐ **Waterford Homes Tour and Craft Exhibit,** Waterford Village. Early October. Tel. 703/882-3018 for tickets.

☐ **Yorktown Day.** British surrender in 1781 celebrated with parade, historic house tours, colonial music and dress, military drills. October 19.

DECEMBER

☐ **Grand Illumination,** Williamsburg. Gala opening of holiday season with fife and drum corps, illumination of buildings, caroling, dancing, fireworks. December.

☐ **Christmas Candlelight Tour,** Fredericksburg. Early December.

☐ **Christmas at Point of Honor,** Lynchburg. Early December.

☐ **Victorian Family Christmas,** Charlottesville. Early December.

☐ **Jamestown Christmas,** Jamestown. 2nd to 4th week.

☐ **Christmas in the Museums,** Petersburg. Mid-December.

☐ **First Night/Virginia,** Charlottesville. Parade, fireworks, music, drama, dance. New Year's Eve.

☐ **New Year's Eve in Festival Park,** Richmond.

3. WHAT TO PACK

The most important aspect of a traveler's wardrobe is comfort. It can get very unpleasant trekking around even the most fascinating attractions when your shoes hurt or your clothing is too warm. In summer especially, the ideal ensemble is sneakers, shorts, and a T-shirt—in other words, the least amount of clothing you can wear in public without causing a commotion. You might, however, wish to carry a light jacket or shawl, since interior spaces are frigidly air-conditioned.

In winter, you'll need a hat, coat, and boots, but don't get carried away—this isn't Alaska. A fold-up umbrella is always a good idea. Men should bring along a jacket and tie, as fancy restaurants often require them.

4. TIPS FOR THE DISABLED, SENIORS, FAMILIES & STUDENTS

FOR THE DISABLED

The *Virginia Travel Guide for the Disabled,* published by The Opening Door, Inc., Route 2 (Box 1805), Woodford, VA 22580 (tel. 804/633-6752), is a 300-page guide distributed free to persons with disabilities. Listings provide information on accessible hotels, restaurants, shops, and attractions.

Another source is the **Moss Rehabilitation Hospital,** 12th Street and Tabor Road, Philadelphia, PA 19141 (tel. 215/456-9600). For a nominal fee they'll send you a travel-accessibility package; there is no charge for brief phone inquiries or their general information sheet.

You may want to join a tour specifically for disabled visitors. These are offered by **Whole Person Tours,** P.O. Box 1084, Bayonne, NJ 07002-1084 (tel. 201/858-3400, or toll free 800/462-2237 outside New Jersey). Their bimonthly magazine for disabled travelers, *The Itinerary,* costs $10 per year.

For information about **Amtrak** services for disabled rail passengers, contact:

Access America, Office of Customer Relations, Amtrak, 60 Massachusetts Avenue NE, Washington, DC 20002 (tel. toll free 800/USA-RAIL, ask for Special Services to make arrangements; for Teletypewriter Services for the deaf 800/523-6590, 800/562-6960 in Pennsylvania). For a copy of *Amtrak's America: The Rail Travel Planner*, with information for the disabled, write to Amtrak Distribution Center, P.O. Box 7717, Itasca, IL 60143. **Greyhound/Trailways** publishes a brochure, "Helping Hand Services for the Handicapped"; to obtain a free copy, write Greyhound/Trailways, 901 Main Street, Dallas, TX 75202 (tel. 214/744-6500). The **National Park Service** (tel. 202/485-9666) issues "Golden Access Passports," admitting a disabled person and companion into a national park, forest, or wildlife refuge at no charge. The passports are obtainable at park entrances.

FOR SENIORS

Williamsburg has designated the month of September as "Senior Time," and special prices are offered by hotels, motels, B&Bs, campgrounds, restaurants, and rental-car companies.

The **American Association of Retired Persons (AARP),** 1909 K Street NW, Washington, DC 20049 (tel. 202/872-4700), offers members a "Purchase Privilege Program," for discounts on hotels, car rentals, air travel, and tours. The AARP Travel Service sponsors group worldwide tours and cruises; members must be 50 years or older. Even if you're not a member of any organization, always ask about senior discounts when making air or hotel reservations.

Check out **Elderhostel,** 80 Boylston Street, Boston, MA 02116 (617/426-7788), which sponsors vacations on college campuses. Participants must be 60 years of age or older; however, if two people go as a couple, only one person has to be of the required age.

The **National Park Service "Golden Age Passport"** will give any citizen or person who lives in the U.S. and is 62 or older free admittance to all national parks. Obtain this lifetime admission permit free at any Park Service property; proof of age is necessary.

FOR FAMILIES

Careful planning makes all the difference between a successful, enjoyable vacation and one that ends up with exhausted, irritable parents and cranky kids. Here are a few hints to help:

Get the kids involved. Let them, if they're old enough, write to the tourist offices for information and colorful brochures. Let them help plan the itinerary, and plot it together on a map. Carry a few simple games to relieve boredom in the car. Many Virginia hotels offer baby-sitting services and most resorts have children's programs.

For additional information, contact **Travel With Your Children,** 80 Eighth Avenue, New York, NY 10011 (tel. 212/206-0688). It's a resource center and publisher of a monthly newsletter for families with children of all ages called *Family Travel Times*. Subscriptions are $35 a year.

FOR STUDENTS

Use your high school or college ID to obtain an **International Student Identity Card (ISIC);** although it's not as widely recognized in the U.S. as it is abroad, it still delivers some savings. Obtain an ISIC from the **Council on International Educational Exchange,** 205 East 42nd Street, New York, NY 10017 (tel. 212/661-1414), and 312 Sutter Street, Room 407, San Francisco, CA 94108 (tel. 415/421-3473). Of course, your current student ID may well be all that's needed.

FROMMER'S COOL FOR KIDS:
TOP ATTRACTIONS

Virginia will bring history to life for your kids (and you, too) with myriad associations involving America's first heroes—Washington, Jefferson, Madison, Monroe, and Patrick Henry among them. Be sure to take them to **Mount Vernon, Monticello,** and **Ashlawn-Highland.** The first English settlement at **Jamestown** and the picturesque village of **Colonial Williamsburg,** which re-creates the daily life of earliest America with craft demonstrations, militia reviews, and tours designed especially for kids, are musts. **Civil War battlefield** tours portray crucial events with fascinating exhibits, scenic walks and drives, and multimedia programs.

OTHER ATTRACTIONS

Theme parks offer thrills and chills, not to mention food, fun, and entertainment at **King's Dominion; Busch Gardens, The Old Country;** and **Water Country USA.**

Roanoke's museums, especially the **Museum of Transportation,** with its railroad cars, and **Science Museum,** featuring all sorts of interactive exhibits, rate high with kids.

Richmond's **Children's Museum** and the **Science Museum of Virginia** will keep children enthralled with participatory activities and "touch me" exhibits.

Our family favorite is Virginia Beach's **Marine Science Museum,** where computers, exhibits, and the museum's own waterside setting explore the marine environment.

Kids will love an outing in one of Richmond's parks: **Maymont** offers a nature center, a carriage collection, a children's farm, and plenty of space for outdoor play.

Theater for young people is sponsored by **Theatre Virginia** in the Virginia Museum of Fine Arts, Richmond. Outdoor theater is appealing to kids of all ages, in Lexington the **Theatre at Lime Kiln** has folk music and other concerts as well as musicals that kids will enjoy.

After reading the story of the **wild ponies' swim across Assateague Channel** in *Misty of Chincoteague,* kids will adore a chance to see the action themselves. The wildlife refuge also offers hikes, nature programs, and a sandy beach.

5. GETTING THERE

BY PLANE

If you live in or near any major American city, chances are you can hop a flight to **Washington's National Airport** (tel. 703/685-8000), located in northern Virginia, midway between Arlington and Alexandria. International visitors will probably arrive at **Dulles International Airport** (tel. 703/471-7838), also in northern Virginia, about 25 miles west of the Potomac.

Domestic Carriers   The following are among the domestic carriers serving National: **American** (tel. toll free 800/433-7300), **Continental** (tel. toll free 800/525-0280), **Delta** (tel. toll free 800/221-1212), **TWA** (tel. toll free 800/221-2000), **United** (tel. toll free 800/241-6522), and **USAir** (tel. toll free 800/428-4322).

International Carriers   Among the international airlines serving Dulles are: **Aeroflot** (tel. 202/429-4922 in Washington, D.C.), **Air France** (tel. toll free 800/237-2747), **All Nippon Airways** (tel. toll free 800/2FLY-ANA), **British Airways** (tel. toll free 800/247-9297), and **Lufthansa** (tel. toll free 800/645-3880).

PLANE ECONOMICS

Wherever you're traveling from, always shop the different airlines and ask for the lowest fare. Check travel sections of local and national newspapers for special promotional fares or packages. Contact your travel agent (it doesn't cost anything) to find out all available options. The cheapest fares are usually advance-purchase, restricted deals (you may have to stay a minimum or maximum number of days, and return on a certain day).

BY TRAIN

Amtrak connects Virginia with most of the U.S. It operates the *Colonial* and the *Virginian* daily from Boston to Washington, D.C. Both trains stop at Alexandria, Fredericksburg, and Richmond; the *Colonial* goes on to Williamsburg and Newport News. From Newport News, Amtrak's Thruway Bus service is available trainside to Norfolk and Virginia Beach.

Call or write **Amtrak,** Union Station, 60 Massachusetts Avenue, Washington, DC 20002 (tel. toll free 800/USA-RAIL or 800/872-7245), for ticket and schedule information.

Washington's Union Station is a major connecting hub for Virginia cities. From Union Station (or National Airport), you can make the trip to Arlington or Alexandria via underground Metro.

BY BUS

Greyhound/Trailways (tel. toll free 800/531-5332) connects many of Virginia's cities and towns with the entire country.

BY CAR

Visitors arriving in Virginia by car from New York and points north and east do so via **I-95;** from western Maryland the major highway is **I-81.** Both these north-south highways traverse the length of the state. Major western entrance points are from West Virginia, **I-77** and **I-64.** In northern Virginia, **I-66** traverses the state east-west and connects I-95 to I-81. For more information about driving in Virginia, contact the **Virginia Department of Transportation,** Administrative Services Division, 1404 East Broad Street, Richmond, VA 23219.

6. GETTING AROUND

If at all possible, see Virginia by car. The highway system is excellent, with interstates paralleling many of the smaller routes, thus giving you the option of taking, say, the Skyline Drive for some of your trip, then switching over to nearby I-81 if time is short.

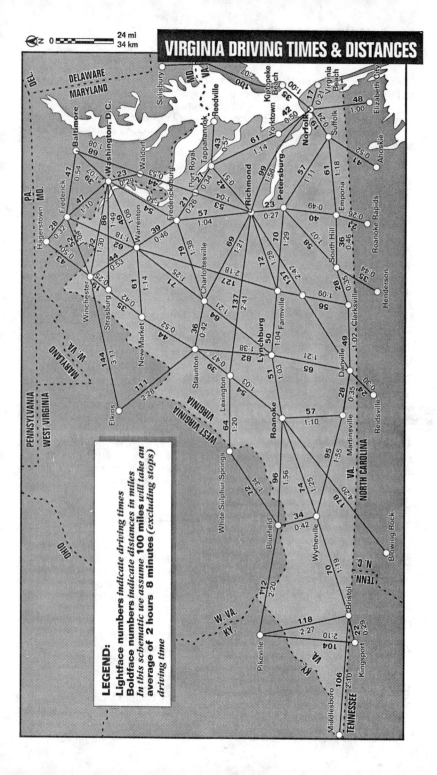

VIRGINIA DRIVING TIMES & DISTANCES

LEGEND:

Lightface numbers *indicate driving times*
Boldface numbers **indicate distances in miles**
In this schematic we assume 100 miles will take an average of 2 hours 8 minutes (excluding stops) driving time

BY PLANE

The major airports in northern Virginia are Dulles and National. Shenandoah Valley and the Virginia Highlands gateways are Roanoke Regional and Shenandoah Valley Regional airports. For central Virginia, Charlottesville, Lynchburg, and Richmond provide scheduled service. In the Hampton Roads/Tidewater area, service is provided by Norfolk and Patrick Henry (Newport News) airports. USAir is the airline with the most flights around the state.

BY BUS & TRAIN

Generally, you'll find bus service available between Virginia cities, and often there's train service as well. Both are listed in the individual city listings of this book.

BY CAR

Traveling by car in Virginia is our recommendation if at all possible. You'll have optimum flexibility to see the rural beauties of the state, including the plantations and Civil War battlefields. And, of course, two of the state's most scenic attractions, the Skyline Drive and Blue Ridge Parkway, are motoring destinations. The state maintains a highway helpline (tel. toll free 800/367-ROAD) for emergencies. A free state highway map is available from the Division of Tourism (see Section 1, "Sources of Tourist Information," above).

CAR RENTALS

Car-rental companies are listed in major city chapters.

SUGGESTED ITINERARIES

A grand tour of Virginia could take a month, which is almost impossible for the average visitor, so you'll have to choose where to go based on time, personal interests, and your pocketbook. Keep in mind that it's very easy to get around by car, and you can cover long distances easily via interstates, which link many of Virginia's scenic splendors.

IF YOU HAVE 4 DAYS (NORTHERN VIRGINIA)

Day 1: Spend a day in Arlington, seeing the National Cemetery and nearby attractions. Arlington is a good base if you're combining a visit to Washington, D.C., with northern Virginia sites. Otherwise, you might prefer to stay in Alexandria, which is smaller, has a more diversified selection of hotels, and is also a good center for exploring.

Day 2: Based in either Arlington or Alexandria, head for the major Alexandria attractions—Old Town's museums, historic houses, shops, and restaurants.

Day 3: Again based in Arlington or Alexandria, head south and east about 15 to 20 miles for a day trip to the Potomac plantations—Washington's beloved Mount Vernon and George Mason's Gunston Hall are the premier estates.

Day 4: Leave Arlington or Alexandria and head east to Manassas (about 30 miles). Visit the battlefield, then go north to Hunt Country (about 11 miles). Overnight in Middleburg or Leesburg, take a walking tour of downtown Leesburg, and see nearby plantations. Civil War buffs can take a 14-mile ride to Harper's Ferry Historic Park, scene of John Brown's raid.

IF YOU HAVE 5 DAYS (RICHMOND & TIDEWATER)

Day 1: Spend 1 full day and overnight in Fredericksburg; see Old Town. Visit Civil War battlefields.

Day 2: Head south 45 miles on I-95 to Richmond. Families can spend at least half a day at King's Dominion theme park, about halfway between the two cities. History buffs can go about 10 miles farther south on I-95, then head west for a tour of Scotchtown, Patrick Henry's plantation. If time allows, visit Richmond attractions. Overnight in Richmond.

Day 3: Spend the day in Richmond. Walk around the Court End district, stopping in at the Museum and White House of the Confederacy, the Valentine Museum, the John Marshall House, and the impressive State Capitol building designed by Jefferson, among other attractions. Civil War buffs may choose to go south on I-95 about 14 miles to see Petersburg Battlefield Park. Overnight in Richmond.

Day 4: Leave Richmond and take Route 5 east to Williamsburg, sightseeing along the way at one or more of the James River plantations. Overnight in Williamsburg.

Day 5: After you've explored Williamsburg's many attractions, you'll also want to see Jamestown and Yorktown, both within a 30-mile radius of Williamsburg. Two theme parks—Busch Gardens, The Old Country, and Water Country USA—are also within a few minutes of Williamsburg. This area, in itself, could occupy a week.

IF YOU HAVE 6 DAYS (CHARLOTTESVILLE, SKYLINE DRIVE & BLUE RIDGE PARKWAY)

Day 1: Starting at Winchester, the northernmost town of the Shenandoah Valley, see Middletown, Front Royal, and the Skyline Caverns. Overnight in one of the area's charming country inns or B&Bs.

Day 2: Follow the Skyline Drive south, enjoying the superb panoramic views of the Blue Ridge and the valley, to Route 211. Head west to visit New Market Battlefield and Luray Caverns. Overnight along the drive in Big Meadows or Skyland Lodge or nearby B&B.

Day 3: Continue south on Route 11, I-81, or the Skyline Drive (depending on your time frame) to Staunton and Charlottesville, a good overnight stop.

Day 4: You'll have a full day of sightseeing in Charlottesville—here you can see Jefferson's Monticello, Ashlawn-Highland, and the University of Virginia, among other sights. Overnight in Charlottesville.

Day 5: Continue south (Route 11, I-81, or the Blue Ridge Parkway) to Lexington. Spend part of the day exploring Lexington's historic sites, but save some time for a drive to Warm Springs on Route 39, over the Goshen Pass. If the budget allows, spend the night at The Homestead in Hot Springs; but there are also charming inns in nearby Warm Springs, or downtown Lexington.

Day 6: Continue south on the Blue Ridge Parkway, enjoying the beautiful scenery, to Roanoke, which has some of the best attractions for children in the state—including the Museum of Transportation and the Science Museum in Market Square.

Those with the time will want to explore the southwest highlands of Virginia, stopping off in the pretty village of Abingdon and exploring the mountain country.

CHAPTER 3

FOR FOREIGN VISITORS

1. PREPARING FOR YOUR TRIP

● **FAST FACTS: FOR THE FOREIGN TRAVELER**

This chapter provides international visitors with practical information to make their entry and stay as easy and trouble-free as possible.

1. PREPARING FOR YOUR TRIP

NECESSARY DOCUMENTS

Canadian citizens need only proof of Canadian residence to enter the United States. British, Dutch, French, German, Italian, Japanese, Swedish, and Swiss citizens need only a valid national (or EC) passport for holiday or business travel, provided their stay is 90 days or less and they enter the U.S. with a return ticket on an airline or cruise line that participates in the no-visa travel program.

Citizens of other countries will need two documents: a valid passport with an expiration date at least 6 months later than the scheduled end of the visit to the U.S.; and a tourist visa available at no charge from the nearest U.S. embassy or consulate. Visa application forms are available also at airline offices and from travel agents.

To obtain a visa, you must submit a completed application form (either in person or by mail) with a passport photograph attached. If you apply in person, you will usually get your visa at once, or within 24 hours at most. If you apply by mail, enclose a large, stamped, self-addressed envelope, and expect an average wait of 2 weeks.

The U.S. tourist visa (B-2) is supposed to be valid for 1 year, and for unlimited entries, but the U.S. consulate that gives you the visa will determine the length of stay for a multiple- or single-entry visa. Actually, there is some latitude here, and if you have a neat appearance and can give the address of a friend or relative in the U.S., you have an excellent chance of getting a longer permit if you want one.

MEDICAL REQUIREMENTS

You don't need any inoculations to enter the U.S., unless you are arriving from areas known to be experiencing a cholera, yellow fever, or other epidemic.

If you have any medical conditions requiring the use of special drugs or a syringe, it's important to carry with you a valid, signed prescription from your doctor.

TRAVEL INSURANCE (BAGGAGE, HEALTH & ACCIDENT)

In the U.S. all such insurance is voluntary; however, given the high cost of medical care in the States, we cannot too strongly advise every traveler to arrange for coverage before setting out. Coverage may also include loss or theft of your baggage, trip cancellation, and illness or injury costs. Travel insurance is sold through insurance companies, automobile clubs, travel agencies, and at many airports.

FAST FACTS: FOR THE FOREIGN TRAVELER

Automobile Organizations   The **American Automobile Association (AAA),** with national headquarters at 1000 AAA Drive, Heathrow, FL 32745 (tel. 407/444-7000), will supply maps, recommended routes, guidebooks, accident and bail-bond insurance, and emergency road service. Check the phone book for local offices. Membership ranges from $17 to $56, depending on which local office you join. Their emergency road service toll-free number is 800/336-4357. Foreign visitors should note that the AAA can provide a "Touring Permit" validating your driver's license. Some foreign auto clubs have reciprocal arrangements with AAA so their members can enjoy AAA services at no charge.

Business Hours   Public and private **offices** are usually open Monday through Friday from 9am to 5pm. **Banking** hours in Virginia are Monday through Thursday from 9am to 2pm and on Friday from 9am to 5pm. A few banks are open on Saturday morning until noon. Most **post offices** are open Monday through Friday from 8:30am to 5pm; some major offices are also open on Saturday from 10am to 1pm. **Store** hours are usually Monday through Friday from 10am to 6pm; some shopping centers operate 7 days a week, opening on Sunday from 1 to 6pm, and on weekdays staying open till 9pm. **Museum** hours vary widely; the norm for big cities is Monday through Saturday from 10am to 5pm and on Sunday from 1 to 5pm, though many are closed Monday.

Currency and Exchange   The U.S. monetary system has a decimal base: 1 dollar ($1) = 100 cents (100¢). The most common bills (all green) are the $1 ("a buck"), $5, $10, and $20 denominations. The coins you're most likely to receive and use are 1¢ (1 cent, or a penny), 5¢ (5 cents, or a nickel), 10¢ (10 cents, or a dime), 25¢ (25 cents, or a quarter), and 50¢ (50 cents, or a half dollar).

Customs   Every adult visitor may bring in, free of duty: 1 liter of wine or hard liquor; 200 cigarettes or 100 cigars (but *no* cigars from Cuba) or 3 pounds of smoking tobacco; and $400 worth of gifts. These exemptions are offered to travelers who spend at least 72 hours in the U.S. and who have not claimed them in the preceding 6 months. *Foodstuffs and plants are not allowed.* Sums larger than $10,000 in U.S. or foreign currency must be declared to Customs on entering or leaving. If you have a connecting flight, allow plenty of time for standing in line at Customs.

Drinking Laws   Every state has its own laws governing the sale of liquor. The only federal regulation restricts the consumption of liquor in public places to persons aged 21 or over. In Virginia many grocery and convenience stores sell beer and wine, but only state-controlled Alcoholic Beverage Control (ABC) stores are permitted to sell bottles of other kinds of liquor. Any licensed establishment (restaurant or bar) can sell drinks by the glass, but if you look younger than the legal age, be sure to have a photo ID handy to prove you're over 21.

Electricity   Electricity in the U.S. is 110–120 volts AC, compared to 220–240 in Europe. Small appliances of non-American manufacture need a plug adapted with two flat, parallel pins and a transformer to U.S. current.

Embassies   All foreign embassies are located in nearby Washington, D.C. Call 202/555-1212 for phone numbers.

Emergencies   Call **911** to get police or an ambulance or to report fire. U.S. **hospitals** have emergency rooms with special entrances where you will be admitted for quick assistance.

Holidays The following are legal national holidays when banks, government offices, many stores, schools, and some museums and restaurants are closed: January 1 (New Year's Day), third Monday in February (Presidents' Day), last Monday in May (Memorial Day), July 4 (Independence Day), first Monday in September (Labor Day), second Monday in October (Columbus Day), November 11 (Veterans Day/Armistice Day), fourth Thursday in November (Thanksgiving), and December 25 (Christmas).

The Tuesday following the first Monday in November is Election Day, a legal holiday in presidential-election years.

Mail You can receive mail at the main post office of the city or region where you expect to be. It should be addressed "c/o General Delivery," and must be picked up in person with proof of identity (passport, driver's license, credit card). U.S. mailboxes are found at intersections; they're blue with a red-and-white stripe.

Postage Within the U.S. it costs 19¢ to mail a postcard, 29¢ for a 1-ounce letter. Mail to Canada costs 30¢ for a postcard and 40¢ for a 1-ounce letter. A postcard to Europe, Australia, New Zealand, the Far East, South America, and elsewhere costs 40¢, while a letter is 50¢ for half an ounce and 95¢ for 1 ounce.

Safety Virginia is generally a safe state, especially in rural areas. However, whenever you're traveling in any unfamiliar city or country, stay alert. Be aware of your immediate surroundings. Avoid isolated locations such as parking lots after dark. Never carry on your person valuables like jewelry (leave it in the hotel safe) or large sums of cash (use traveler's checks instead).

Taxes Throughout the state of Virginia there is a 4.5% sales tax, and a hotel tax in addition to the general sales tax that varies widely from town to town. In most Virginia communities the hotel tax is 5%, which adds on a total tax of 9.5% to your hotel bill.

Telephone Pay phones in Virginia usually cost 25¢, exact change only. Telephones may be found on street corners, hotel lobbies, and shopping centers. For local directory assistance (information), call 411. For long-distance information, dial 1, then the appropriate area code and 555-1212.

Time Virginia is on eastern standard time, which is 3 hours later than on the U.S. West Coast and 5 hours earlier than Greenwich Mean Time. Virginia, like most of the rest of the U.S., observes daylight savings time; in late spring the clocks are turned ahead 1 hour and then are turned back again in the fall.

Tipping Hotels and restaurants in the U.S. don't usually include a service charge in their bills, so as a general rule, visitors should tip bellhops and doormen, as well as airport and railway porters, about $1 per bag; taxi drivers, 15% of the fare; servers in restaurants, 15% of the check.

Traveler's Checks and Credit Cards Traveler's checks in *dollars* are easily changed in banks, and are also accepted at most hotels, motels, stores, and restaurants. Sometimes passport or other photo identification is necessary.

When in the U.S., you may choose to do as many Americans do and pay with a credit card: VISA (BarclayCard in Britain, Chargex in Canada), MasterCard (EuroCard in Europe, Access in Britain, Diamond in Japan, etc.), American Express, Diners Club, and Carte Blanche, in descending order of acceptance. A credit card also serves as a deposit when you rent a car or as proof of identity.

Note: Foreign-exchange bureaus, so common in Europe, are nonexistent in the U.S. Exchange windows are found in the U.S. only at the largest airports.

Yellow Pages The *Yellow Pages* telephone directory lists local services, businesses, and industries by type, with an index at the back. It also includes city plans or detailed area maps, showing postal ZIP Codes and public transportation routes.

THE AMERICAN SYSTEM OF MEASUREMENTS

LENGTH

1 inch (in.)			=	2.54cm	
1 foot (ft.)	=	12 in.	=	30.48cm	= .305m
1 yard (yd.)	=	3 ft.			= .915m
1 mile	=	5,280 ft.			= 1.609km

To convert miles to kilometers, multiply the number of miles by 1.61. Also use to convert speeds from miles per hour (m.p.h.) to kilometers per hour (kmph).

To convert kilometers to miles, multiply the number of kilometers by .62. Also use to convert kmph to m.p.h.

CAPACITY

1 fluid ounce (fl. oz.)			=	.03 liters	
1 pint	=	16 fl. oz.	=	.47 liters	
1 quart	=	2 pints	=	.94 liters	
1 gallon (gal.)	=	4 quarts	=	3.79 liters	= .83 Imperial gal.

To convert U.S. gallons to liters, multiply the number of gallons by 3.79.

To convert liters to U.S. gallons, multiply the number of liters by .26.

To convert U.S. gallons to Imperial gallons, multiply the number of U.S. gallons by .83.

To convert Imperial gallons to U.S. gallons, multiply the number of Imperial gallons by 1.2.

WEIGHT

1 ounce (oz.)			=	28.35g	
1 pound (lb.)	=	16 oz.	=	453.6g	= .45kg
1 ton			=	2,000 lb. = 907kg	= .91 metric tons

To convert pounds to kilograms, multiply the number of pounds by .45.

To convert kilograms to pounds, multiply the number of kilograms by 2.2.

AREA

1 acre			=	.41ha	
1 square mile	=	640 acres	=	259ha	= 2.6km²

To convert acres to hectares, multiply the number of acres by .41.

To convert hectares to acres, multiply the number of hectares by 2.47.

To convert square miles to square kilometers, multiply the number of square miles by 2.6.

To convert square kilometers to square miles, multiply the number of square kilometers by .39.

TEMPERATURE

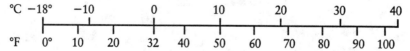

To convert degrees Fahrenheit to degrees Celsius, subtract 32 from °F, multiply by 5, then divide by 9 (example: 85°F − 32 × 5/9 = 29.4°C).

To convert degrees Celsius to degrees Fahrenheit, multiply °C by 9, divide by 5, and add 32 (example: 20°C × 9/5 + 32 = 68°F).

CHAPTER 4

ARLINGTON, ALEXANDRIA & HUNT COUNTRY

1. ARLINGTON
2. ALEXANDRIA
• WALKING TOUR: OLD TOWN ALEXANDRIA
3. HUNT COUNTRY

America's past and present meet in northern Virginia. Arlington, just across the Potomac from Washington, D.C., is very much in the international, cosmopolitan orbit of the capital. Yet in nearby Alexandria, the cobblestone streets of the 18th-century Old Town historic district still ring with the footsteps of George Washington, James Monroe, and Robert E. Lee. Just a few miles away, charming country inns nestle in the villages that dot Virginia's lovely Hunt Country.

---

1. ARLINGTON

Just across the Potomac River from Washington, D.C.;
100 miles N of Richmond

GETTING THERE **By Plane** Washington's **National Airport** (tel. 703/685-8000) is most conveniently located in Arlington. Ground transportation via Washington Flyer Airport shuttles (tel. 703/685-1400) operates daily from 6am to 10pm to locations in D.C. and northern Virginia. The same company also offers taxi and limousine service. The Washington Metrorail has a station at the airport.

Dulles International Airport (tel. 703/471-7838) is in northern Virginia, about 25 miles west of the Potomac bridges, and is used principally for international flights. Washington Flyer shuttles from Dulles will bring you to the West Falls Church Metro stop for just $5, from which you have access to all Metro route locations.

By Train Visitors arriving on Amtrak at Washington's **Union Station,** 50 Massachusetts Avenue NE (tel. 202/484-7540), can easily switch to the Metro stop there for a quick ride to Arlington.

By Bus **Greyhound/Trailways,** 3860 South Four Mile Run Drive, near South Walter Reed Drive (tel. 703/998-6312), has service directly to Arlington.

By Car From the north, **I-95** is the major highway to Arlington. Follow I-95 south to Exit 19, for Route 50W. Follow 50W (John Hanson Highway), which will turn into New York Avenue. Follow signs for I-395S/Virginia and cross the 14th Street Bridge, leaving Washington, D.C. In addition, **I-66** from the west, **U.S. 1, 29-211,** and the **George Washington Memorial Parkway** all pass through Arlington.

ESSENTIALS The **telephone area code** is 703. Contact the **Arlington Visitor Center,** 7335 18th Street South, Arlington, VA 22202 (tel. 703/358-5720), for information about events, maps, accommodations, restaurants, and answers to any questions about the area.

County Layout   Arlington is a county, following the south bank of the Potomac River, across from Washington, D.C. There are no cities in the county; its place names—Crystal City, Pentagon City to the south, Clarendon and Ballston to the west, and Rosslyn across from Georgetown—denote neighborhoods, not political entities.

Getting Around   Washington's Metrorail (underground rail) offers efficient transport in Arlington to Washington, D.C., National Airport, and Alexandria. Metrorail operates Monday through Friday from 5:30am to midnight, on Saturday from 8am to midnight, and on Sunday from 10am to midnight. For information, call 202/637-7000.

Easy access to Washington, D.C.'s tourist attractions is Arlington's lead card for travelers, although it is also home to northern Virginia's most popular historic site, Arlington National Cemetery, and the Pentagon.

Originally the land now comprising Arlington County was part of the territory ceded to form the nation's new capital district. Unneeded in the final planning, the land was returned to the state of Virginia in 1847.

The county was named to honor Arlington House, built by George Washington Parke Custis (see "What to See and Do," below). The beginnings of the national cemetery date from just after the first Battle of Bull Run, when some Union soldiers were buried here.

WHAT TO SEE & DO
ARLINGTON NATIONAL CEMETERY

Unless you're a hiking enthusiast, head for the ✪ **Arlington Cemetery Visitors Center** (tel. 703/692-0931) and purchase a **Tourmobile** ticket ($10 for adults, $5 for children age 3 to 11) that allows you to stop at all major sights and reboard when you're ready. Service is continuous and the narrated commentary is interesting.

For more than a century Arlington National Cemetery has been a cherished national shrine commemorating the lives given by members of the United States armed forces, but these grounds have always figured prominently in American history. In 1778 the "Arlington estate" was purchased by John Parke Custis, son of Martha Washington by her first marriage. Custis died during the siege of Yorktown, and his son, George Washington Parke Custis, inherited the estate and continued to develop it. He erected the Greek Revival **Custis-Lee mansion** (his daughter married Robert E. Lee), today known as Arlington House. The house and grounds were in Mrs. Lee's possession when the Civil War broke out, and the property was seized by the U.S. government. It was many years after the war, following lengthy litigation, that the Supreme Court ruled Robert E. Lee's son, George Washington Custis Lee, to be the rightful owner. In 1883 Lee sold the Arlington estate to the U.S. government for $150,000.

Today, the national cemetery's seemingly endless graves mark the mortal remains of the honored dead, the known and unknown, who served in conflicts from the Revolutionary War through the Persian Gulf War. Two Presidents, William Howard Taft and John F. Kennedy, are also interred here, as are Robert F. Kennedy, capital architect Pierre Charles L'Enfant, Rear Admiral Robert E. Peary, and many other notables. A more complete list is provided on a free map distributed at the Visitor Center.

Arlington National Cemetery is open to visitors daily April through September from 8am to 7pm, until 5pm the rest of the year.

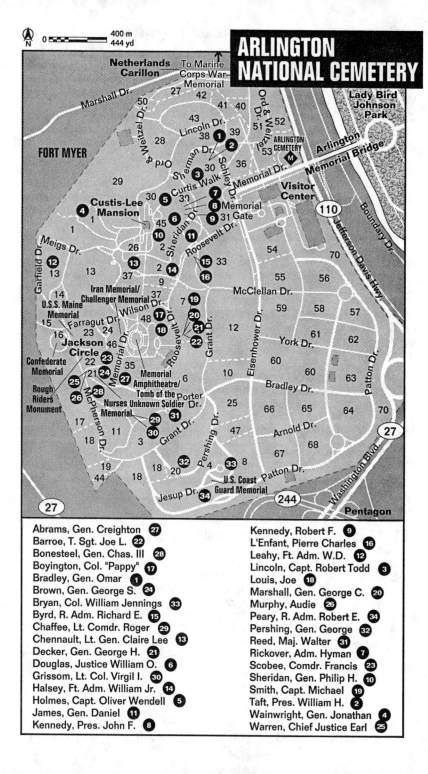

0 400 m / 444 yd

N

Netherlands Carillon

To Marine Corps War Memorial

Lady Bird Johnson Park

Marshall Dr.

FORT MYER

Custis-Lee Mansion

Lincoln Dr.

Sherman Dr.

Curtis Walk

Schley Dr.

Ord & Weitzel Dr.

Iser Dr.

ARLINGTON CEMETERY

Arlington Memorial Bridge

Memorial Dr.

Visitor Center

Memorial Gate

Sheridan Dr.

Roosevelt Dr.

Jefferson Davis Hwy

Boundary Dr.

110

Meigs Dr.

Garfield Dr.

U.S.S. Maine Memorial

Iran Memorial/ Challenger Memorial

Wilson Dr.

Farragut Dr.

Jackson Circle

Confederate Memorial

Rough Riders Monument

McPherson Dr.

Memorial Dr.

Memorial Amphitheatre/ Tomb of the Unknown Soldier

Nurses Memorial

Grant Dr.

Roosevelt Dr.

Grant Dr.

McClellan Dr.

Eisenhower Dr.

York Dr.

Bradley Dr.

Porter Dr.

Arnold Dr.

Patton Dr.

Pershing Dr.

Jesup Dr.

U.S. Coast Guard Memorial

Patton Dr.

Washington Blvd

27

244

Pentagon

27

Abrams, Gen. Creighton — 27
Barroe, T. Sgt. Joe L. — 22
Bonesteel, Gen. Chas. III — 28
Boyington, Col. "Pappy" — 17
Bradley, Gen. Omar — 1
Brown, Gen. George S. — 24
Bryan, Col. William Jennings — 33
Byrd, R. Adm. Richard E. — 15
Chaffee, Lt. Comdr. Roger — 29
Chennault, Lt. Gen. Claire Lee — 13
Decker, Gen. George H. — 21
Douglas, Justice William O. — 6
Grissom, Lt. Col. Virgil I. — 30
Halsey, Ft. Adm. William Jr. — 14
Holmes, Capt. Oliver Wendell — 5
James, Gen. Daniel — 11
Kennedy, Pres. John F. — 8

Kennedy, Robert F. — 9
L'Enfant, Pierre Charles — 16
Leahy, Ft. Adm. W.D. — 12
Lincoln, Capt. Robert Todd — 3
Louis, Joe — 18
Marshall, Gen. George C. — 20
Murphy, Audie — 26
Peary, R. Adm. Robert E. — 34
Pershing, Gen. George — 32
Reed, Maj. Walter — 31
Rickover, Adm. Hyman — 7
Scobee, Comdr. Francis — 23
Sheridan, Gen. Philip H. — 10
Smith, Capt. Michael — 19
Taft, Pres. William H. — 2
Wainwright, Gen. Jonathan — 4
Warren, Chief Justice Earl — 25

ARLINGTON HOUSE After it was acquired by the U.S. government in 1883, Arlington House was used for several decades as office space and living quarters for cemetery staff. In 1925, however, Congress empowered the secretary of war to restore the house to its pre–Civil War appearance and furnish it with original pieces (insofar as possible) and replicas. In 1955 Congress designated it a permanent memorial to Robert E. Lee. It was from this house that Lee received word of the dissolution of the Union and Virginia's secession. He left the next morning to offer his services to his state and never returned to the house.

There's a self-guided tour, and volunteers in period dress are on hand to give an introductory talk, hand out brochures, and answer questions. Servants' quarters and a small museum adjoin.

Admission is free. Open October to March, daily from 9:30am to 4:30pm; till 6pm April through September (closed Christmas and New Year's days).

JOHN F. KENNEDY & ROBERT F. KENNEDY GRAVESITES Just south of Arlington House, the gravesite monument to John F. Kennedy is marked by an eternal flame, and nearby, marked by a simple white cross, is the grave of Robert F. Kennedy. Looking north there's a spectacular view of the capital city across the river (during his presidency Kennedy once remarked of this spot, "I could stay here forever"). A few steps below the gravesite is a wall inscribed with JFK quotations, including the one he's most remembered for: "And so my fellow Americans, ask not what your country can do for you, ask what you can do for your country. My fellow citizens of the world, ask not what America will do for you, but what together we can do for the freedom of man."

THE TOMB OF THE UNKNOWN SOLDIER Watched over by America's most distinguished honor guard, the Tomb of the Unknown Soldier is a tribute to all soldiers who have given their lives for their country in war. The 50-ton white marble tomb rests above the remains of unidentified soldiers slain during World War I. World War II, Korean War, and Vietnam unknowns are in the crypts on the plaza in front of it. Plan your visit to coincide with the changing of the guard ceremony—an impressive ritual of rifle maneuvers, heel clickings, and military salutes. It takes place daily every hour on the hour October through March, every half hour the rest of the year.

Adjoining the tomb is the Greek Revival outdoor **Memorial Amphitheater,** used for special holiday services. Free Tourmobile transportation from the Visitor Center parking lot is provided on these occasions.

THE IWO JIMA STATUE

On the northern periphery of Arlington National Cemetery, just off Route 50, is the **U.S. Marine Corps War Memorial,** a symbol of the nation's esteem for the honored dead of the U.S. Marine Corps. The tribute is the Iwo Jima statue, recalling the marine invasion of Iwo Jima in February 1945 and the placing of a flag atop Mount Suribachi. News photographer Joe Rosenthal won a Pulitzer Prize for his photo of the flag-raising, and sculptor Felix W. de Weldon, then on duty, was moved to create a sculpture based on the scene Rosenthal had captured.

The Memorial grounds are used for military concerts and parades on Tuesday from 7 to 8:30pm in summer, and at all times many visitors picnic on the grass.

THE NETHERLANDS CARILLON

Near the Iwo Jima statue is the Netherlands Carillon, a gift from the people of Holland, with 49 bells, each carrying an emblem signifying a segment of Dutch society. For instance, the smallest bells represent Dutch youth. Verses cast on each bell were composed by poet Ben van Eysselsteijn. The carillon was officially dedicated on May 5, 1960, the 15th anniversary of the liberation of the Netherlands from the Nazis. The 127-foot-high open steel tower housing it stands on a plaza with steps guarded by two bronze lions. Some 15,000 tulip bulbs are planted on the surrounding grounds, a beautiful display in spring. Carillon concerts are presented from 2 to 4pm on Saturday and national holidays from April through September. Visitors are permitted into the tower after the carillonneur performs to enjoy spectacular views of Washington.

THE PENTAGON

Hawk or dove, you'll find it interesting to tour the Pentagon (tel. 703/695-1776), the immense five-sided headquarters of the American military establishment. Built during the early years of World War II, it's the world's largest office building, housing 24,000 employees and, for their convenience, it contains a complete indoor shopping mall. There are many mind-boggling statistics to underscore the vastness of the Pentagon— for example, the building contains enough phone cable to run halfway to the moon!

For almost 30 years the Pentagon was probably the only military ministry in the world completely open to the general public. However, Vietnam-era demonstrations and an actual bomb explosion in a fourth-floor washroom in 1972 changed all that. You can, however, take a free **tour** of certain corridors. The tour takes an hour and 20 minutes, and no reservation is necessary. Departure is from the Concourse area; the line forms near the Metro exit. In tourist season, avoid a long wait on line by arriving at 8:30am. Tours leave every half hour Monday through Friday between 9:30am and 3:30pm; closed on federal holidays.

The best way to get to the Pentagon is via Metrorail's Blue or Yellow Line. If you drive, take I-395 to Boundary Channel Drive North Parking Exit, and park in the E-1 lot on the left-hand side. It costs 25¢ an hour to park and shuttle buses make frequent runs to the Pentagon South Parking Area. From here, signs will direct you to the ticket window.

Note: You must bring a photo ID (a license or passport) to be admitted. You'll have to go through a metal detector and have your bags searched before the tour, so leave any articles that would arouse protective suspicion at the hotel. Also be aware that there are no food facilities or public rest rooms at the Pentagon.

WHERE TO STAY

Generally a room is easy to come by here, even at the last minute, except perhaps during the height of the summer season or during an occasional vast convention.

VERY EXPENSIVE

CRYSTAL GATEWAY MARRIOTT, 1700 Jefferson Davis Hwy., Arlington, VA 22202. Tel. 703/920-3230, or toll free 800/228-9290. Fax 703/685-0191. 700 rms, including 46 suites. A/C TV TEL **Metro:** Crystal City.

$ Rates: $185 single; $205 double; $190 and $210 respectively on the concierge level. Children under 18 stay free in parents' room. Weekend and other packages available. AE, CB, DC, DISC, MC, V. **Parking:** $10 a night.

Just 5 minutes from National Airport, and minutes—via on-site Metro—to downtown Washington, the Gateway is connected by a short passageway to a subterranean mall of some 75 shops, restaurants, and such facilities as a post office, Ticketron outlet, bank, and hair salon. This is a first-rate property, from its six-story atrium skylight lobby adorned with Oriental art objects to its lovely and spacious pastel-hued rooms. All guest rooms offer in-room movies and AM/FM radios.

The 16th floor is the concierge level, where a private lounge serves a complimentary breakfast and evening cocktails with hors d'oeuvres. A concierge is on duty, and additional in-room amenities include nightly turndown, bathroom scales, electric shoe polishers, and magazines.

Dining/Entertainment: Plushest of the hotel's three restaurants is the romantic Véronique's, noted for its classic French cuisine (entrees $17 to $24) served under the stars (there's a skylight). Not quite as posh is the Terrace, with cushioned wicker furnishings amid lush greenery. Overlooking the pool, it's open for all meals, serving American fare.

Light buffet fare (lunch and dinner) is featured at the Atrium Café. At the cocktail hour there's piano music in the lobby, and at night there's dancing at Crystal's.

Services: Room service (7am to midnight), nightly turndown on request, free newspaper delivery, concierge, complimentary airport shuttle, American Airlines desk.

Facilities: Indoor/outdoor pool, Jacuzzi, health spa with Universal equipment, saunas, nearby tennis and racquetball courts, business center, lobby gift shop plus Underground concourse shops.

RITZ-CARLTON, PENTAGON CITY, 1250 S. Hayes St., Arlington, VA 22202. Tel. 703/415-5000, or toll free 800/241-3333. Fax 703/415-5061. 345 rms, including 41 suites. A/C MINIBAR TV TEL **Metro:** Pentagon City.

$ **Rates:** $150–$190 single; $170–$210 double. Weekend and other packages available. AE, CB, DC, DISC, MC, V. **Parking:** $10 a night.

Across the street from the Pentagon, the Ritz-Carlton is in the upscale Fashion Centre retail-office complex. It's hard to believe that this very traditional-looking hostelry—decorated with massive polished china cabinets, graceful wing chairs, plush sofas, Oriental rugs, crystal sconces, and a $2.5-million collection of 18th- and 19th-century paintings and antiques—was built as late as 1990. The impeccable service also harks back to another era. Rooms are spacious and airy, with beautiful mahogany pieces (some have four-poster beds) and every amenity. The remote-control TV is concealed in an armoire. Amenities include plush terry bathrobes, marble bathrooms (with extra phone), hairdryer, and an in-room safe.

Guests on Club floors have a private lounge where complimentary breakfast, light lunch, afternoon tea, and hors d'oeuvres and cocktails are on tap. And Club guests also have a private concierge staff.

Dining/Entertainment: The hotel's highly acclaimed Sunday brunch is served in its premier dining room, the Ritz-Carlton Restaurant, a spacious venue with pink silk-covered walls and well-spaced tables set with Rosenthal china. At dinner it offers regional specialties such as roast duck in Virginia cherry-brandy sauce.

The less formal Grill evokes an English club, with a green marble mantel over the fireplace, equestrian-themed oil paintings and bronzes, and shaded table lamps and wall sconces. Afternoon tea is served daily in the Lobby Lounge.

Services: 24-hour room service, baby-sitting, bed turndown, complimentary shoeshine, complimentary airport shuttle, multilingual concierge staff.

Facilities: Fitness and exercise center, indoor pool and Jacuzzi, steam room, sauna, business center, gift shop.

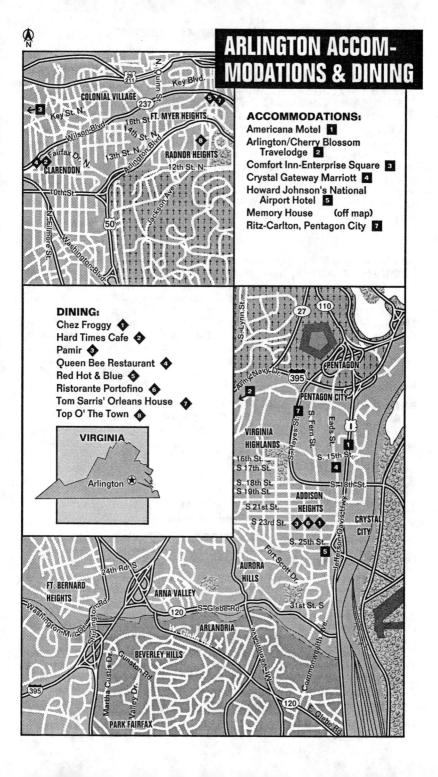

ARLINGTON ACCOM- MODATIONS & DINING

ACCOMMODATIONS:

Americana Motel **1**

Arlington/Cherry Blossom Travelodge **2**

Comfort Inn-Enterprise Square **3**

Crystal Gateway Marriott **4**

Howard Johnson's National Airport Hotel **5**

Memory House   (off map)

Ritz-Carlton, Pentagon City **7**

DINING:

Chez Froggy **1**

Hard Times Cafe **2**

Pamir **3**

Queen Bee Restaurant **4**

Red Hot & Blue **5**

Ristorante Portofino **6**

Tom Sarris' Orleans House **7**

Top O' The Town **8**

VIRGINIA

Arlington ☆

MODERATE

HOWARD JOHNSON'S NATIONAL AIRPORT HOTEL, 2650 Jefferson Davis Hwy., Arlington, VA 22202. Tel. 703/684-7200, or toll free 800/654-2000. 279 rms. A/C TV TEL **Metro:** Crystal City.

$ Rates: $80–$115 single; $85–$120 double. Weekend rates available. AE, DC, DISC, MC, V. **Parking:** Free.

Attractively decorated rooms and a good location convenient to the Metro and National Airport make this HoJo a good choice. Its first five floors are used for parking, so rooms are at least six stories up and many provide D.C. or Potomac views. Although the midweek rate is moderate to expensive, weekend prices are highly competitive, going down to $59. The restaurant is open daily from 6am to midnight, later on weekends. A pool and exercise room are on site, and there's free airport shuttle service.

BUDGET

AMERICANA MOTEL, 1400 Jefferson Davis Hwy., Arlington, VA 22202. Tel. 703/979-3772, or toll free 800/548-6261. 104 rms. A/C TV TEL **Metro:** Crystal City.

$ Rates: $60 single; $60–$65 double. Reduced weekend rates available. DC, DISC, MC, V. **Parking:** Free.

This modest well-located hotel is in Crystal City, a block from the Metro and Crystal Underground's numerous restaurants and shops. You'll find accommodations equipped with all standard motel features, and color schemes a pleasing mix of beige with mauve or cranberry. Complimentary coffee, orange juice, and doughnuts are served in the lobby each morning. Free shuttle service to National Airport is available from 7am to 10pm daily.

ARLINGTON/CHERRY BLOSSOM TRAVELODGE, 3030 Columbia Pike, Arlington, VA 22204. Tel. 703/521-5570, or toll free 800/255-3050. 76 rms. A/C TV TEL **Directions:** From I-395, take the Columbia Pike West exit.

$ Rates: $45–$65 single; $52–$72 double. Extra person $7. Children under 18 stay free in parents' room. AE, CB, DC, DISC, MC, V. **Parking:** Free.

Set back from the street so there's no traffic noise, this clean, well-run property offers standard guest rooms. Walls are white, carpets a rust color, and crewel-print spreads and matching draperies are a soft rust as well. An excellent Thai restaurant, Rincome, open from 11am to 11pm, adjoins the motel. Nearby on Columbia Pike are a number of fast-food restaurants.

COMFORT INN—ENTERPRISE SQUARE, 1211 N. Glebe Rd., Arlington, VA 22201. Tel. 703/247-3399, or toll free 800/228-5150. 126 rms. A/C TV TEL **Metro:** Ballston Metro (about half a mile away).

$ Rates: $69 single or double; $79 suite. Children under 18 stay free in parents' room. Weekend and other packages available. AE, CB, DC, DISC, MC, V. **Parking:** Free.

A small property housed in a three-story red-brick building, the Comfort Inn offers reasonable rates and a convenient location off I-66, at Washington Boulevard, just 10 minutes from National Airport. Rooms are exceptionally bright and spacious, decorated in shades of plum and mauve, with dark polished-wood furnishings and all the standard motel amenities. There's a lobby gift shop and an adjoining restaurant, Angelo's, that's open daily from 6:30am to 10:30pm.

A BED & BREAKFAST

MEMORY HOUSE, 6404 N. Washington Blvd., Arlington, VA 22205. Tel. 703/534-4607. 3 rms (none with bath). A/C TV TEL **Metro:** East Falls Church.

$ Rates (including continental breakfast): $65 single; $70 double. No credit cards. **Parking:** Free.

Memory House looks so traditionally Victorian that it could serve as a model of that era's architectural elements. Its clapboard and fish-scale-shingle facade is topped with iron cresting and surmounted by a stained-glass butterfly weathervane, front and side porches are adorned with gingerbread trim, and a pretty lawn surrounds the house. The owners spent many hours working to achieve such splendid results. Both Marlys and John McGrath took an active role in stripping paint, refinishing floors, and varnishing woodwork. Much of the old oak furniture was bought inexpensively and refinished by the McGraths. Prize-winning needlepoint, handworked by John, is displayed in several rooms. An expanded continental breakfast (oatmeal, fresh breads, fruit juice, coffee or tea) is served in the dining room.

WHERE TO DINE

If you have a taste for the exotic, you'll find plenty of choices in Arlington—the capital of ethnic cuisine for the entire Washington–northern Virginia area. Restaurants representing some 35 different nationalities are scattered throughout the county.

EXPENSIVE

TOP O' THE TOWN, 1414 N. 14th St., corner of N. Oak St. Tel. 703/525-9200.
   Cuisine: AMERICAN. **Reservations:** Recommended.
$ Prices: Appetizers $6.50–$8.95; entrees $13.95–$21. AE, CB, DC, MC, V.
   Open: Dinner only, Sun–Thurs 6–10pm, Fri–Sat 6–11pm.

This place is literally tops. Housed in the penthouse of a high-rise residential building, it affords sensational views of the Potomac bridges and the Washington skyline. The panorama at dusk is particularly lovely. The softly lit decor is rightfully minimalist (the view is the star), with candle lamps and fresh flowers on white tablecloths. A pianist provides a show-tune background to dinner.

You might begin with shrimp cocktail, oysters Rockefeller, cream of crabmeat soup, or a Caesar salad. Duck flambé with raspberry hoisin sauce; veal piccata sautéed in butter, white wine, and capers; and peppered salmon cooked with sherry and tarragon vinegar are sound entrees. And the steaks—chateaubriand bouquetière for two, filet mignon, steak Diane flambé—are house specialties. For dessert, bananas flambé or cherries jubilee finish dinner with a dramatic flourish. After dinner, head for the adjoining lounge for an after-dinner liqueur.

MODERATE

CHEZ FROGGY, 509 S. 23rd St. Tel. 703/979-7676.
   Cuisine: FRENCH. **Reservations:** Recommended. **Metro:** Crystal City.
$ Prices: Appetizers $5.95–$6.25; entrees $10.50–$19.50. CB, DC, MC, V.
   Open: Lunch Mon–Fri 11am–2pm; dinner Mon–Sat 5:30–10pm.

The food at this cozy bistro is maintained with consistency by chef Jean-Claude Lelan. The decor is pleasant but unpretentious, with lots of ceramic and glass frogs, large and small, scattered around to add a note of whimsy.

At dinner, appetizers of homemade duck mousse or a half dozen snails in garlic butter deserve consideration, as does a salad of fresh spinach and chèvre with almonds. Recommended entrees: fresh bay scallops sautéed with garlic and tomatoes, steamed salmon with fresh basil beurre blanc, and roast rack of lamb with garlic and thyme. Potatoes, assorted vegetables, French bread, and sweet butter accompany all entrees. Dessert offerings include profiteroles, chocolate mousse, and coupe Froggy (vanilla ice cream, fresh strawberries, whipped cream, and Curaçao). The lower-priced lunch menu adds salads and omelets.

RISTORANTE PORTOFINO, 526 S. 23rd St. Tel. 703/929-8200.

Cuisine: ITALIAN. **Reservations:** Recommended. **Metro:** Crystal City.
$ Prices: Appetizers $6.95; entrees $13.95–$18.95. AE, CB, DC, MC, V.
Open: Lunch Mon–Fri 11am–2pm; dinner daily 5–10pm.

A pretty downstairs garden room is just one of the dining spaces in this bustling Italian restaurant. The entrance is at the rear of the converted three-story residence, and you'll know when you hear the taped arias of such famous tenors as Enrico Caruso and Mario Lanza that you're in for a home-style Italian meal. The dinner offerings begin with some tasty specialties, including fried calamari, baked eggplant filled with ricotta cheese and served with creamy tomato sauce, and prosciutto with fresh mozzarella. Any of the pastas on the menu can be ordered in a half portion as an appetizer—linguine with green pesto sauce, fettuccine Alfredo, and spaghetti carbonara are just a few of the possibilities. Entrees include veal in all expected guises (parmigiana, piccata, marsala) and all nicely done, plus a good variety of chicken and fish dishes. The house special dessert is a wonderful rum cake with whipped cream, but there are fine alternatives, such as cannoli, zabaglione, and various gelati and liqueur concoctions.

INEXPENSIVE

HARD TIMES CAFE, 3028 Wilson Blvd. Tel. 703/528-2233.

Cuisine: TEX-MEX. **Metro:** Clarendon.
$ Prices: Entrees $3.95–$5.25. MC, V.
Open: Sun–Thurs 11am–10pm, Fri–Sat 11am–11pm.

A casual, laid-back hangout, the Hard Times Cafe is the kind of chili parlor you'd find in Texas. The bar is always crowded, there's country music on the jukebox, and the "bowls of red" are first rate. The Lone Star State decor features Texas flags, plus a longhorn steer hide and historic photos of the Old West on the walls. Seating is in roomy oak booths. The restaurant cooks up three styles of chili: Texas (ground chuck simmered with secret spices and *no* tomatoes), Cincinnati (with hot and sweet spices, including cinnamon), and vegetarian. All styles are served with homemade cornbread and beans—and cheese, onions, or spaghetti, which can be added at your request. Sandwiches, burgers, salads, and sides of onion rings and steak fries round out the offerings. Pecan pie is the logical dessert.

PAMIR, 561 S. 23rd St. Tel. 703/979-0777.

Cuisine: AFGHAN. **Metro:** Crystal City.
$ Prices: Entrees $7.95–$11.95; fixed-price dinner for two $28.50 or $32.50. AE, MC, V.
Open: Lunch Mon–Fri 11am–2pm; dinner Mon–Sat 5:30–11pm.

Afghan cuisine bears some resemblance to Indian food, so if you've enjoyed that spicy fare, you'll have some idea of what's cooking at this attractive and inexpensive storefront spot, shaded from passersby with a pretty lace curtain. What are some Afghan specialties? For starters you might have the dumplinglike aushak, filled with leeks, topped with yogurt and meat sauce, and sprinkled with mint. Well-seasoned kebabs of beef, lamb, or chicken are marinated in yogurt and garlic, then charcoal-broiled and served with rice, a small salad, and Afghan bread. If you're puzzled by the various choices, opt for one of the four complete dinners offered for two people, some of which come with a half carafe of wine.

QUEEN BEE RESTAURANT, 3181 Wilson Blvd. Tel. 703/527-3444.

Cuisine: VIETNAMESE. **Metro:** Clarendon.

$ **Prices:** Appetizers $2.50–$7.50; entrees $5.50–$7.50. MC, V.

Open: Daily 11am–10pm.

Some of the best Vietnamese food in Arlington can be found at this friendly and unpretentious eatery that's popular with locals. Etched-glass sconces provide soft lighting, and white tablecloths are plastic covered and set with red-and-gold paper place mats. Mirrors line one of the walls, adding an illusion of depth to the room. At lunch or dinner, start with the Queen Bee platter, a sampler of appetizers including a spring roll, shrimp tempura, charcoal-grilled pork, and house salad. Among the entrees, house specials include steamed rice-flour meat rolls and shrimp cakes. Chicken is prepared in several delicious ways—curried, in ginger sauce, or with lemon grass. Roast duck and quail are also stellar entrees. Vegetarians can choose a melange of vegetables sautéed in oyster sauce, or fresh tofu sautéed with tomato and scallions. Desserts are simple: lychee fruit, flambéed pineapple or bananas, or black-eyed beans with coconut milk.

RED HOT & BLUE, 1600 Wilson Blvd. Tel. 703/276-7430.

Cuisine: AMERICAN. **Metro:** Rosslyn.

$ **Prices:** Entrees $5.25–$16.45. MC, V.

Open: Mon–Fri 11am–11pm, Sat noon–11pm, Sun 1–10pm.

Winner of *Washingtonian* magazine's 1990 "50 Very Best Restaurants Award," Red Hot & Blue purveys what *Washington Post* food critic Phyllis Richman calls "barbecue worth waiting for." So join the line of hungry diners waiting for tables (no reservations) at this casual, fun-filled, high-energy eatery. Some of the crowd gravitates to the bar for frosted steins of cold beer under the jolly eye of a blue neon pig strumming a red guitar. The late Lee Atwater, chairman of the Republican National Committee, along with a group of Washingtonians transplanted from their native Memphis, opened the restaurant and named it for a hometown radio show. The decor is a jumpy black, white, and red, and seating is in banquettes and at small tables, jammed rather close together. But the food is just fine—ribs wet (with sauce) or dry (secret spices), barbecued beef brisket, smoked chicken and ham, and homemade trimmings like beans, cole slaw, potato salad, and fries. For dessert, the mouthwatering Karo pecan pie packs a sweet wallop.

TOM SARRIS' ORLEANS HOUSE, 1213 Wilson Blvd., Rosslyn. Tel. 703/524-2929.

Cuisine: AMERICAN. **Reservations:** Not accepted. **Metro:** Rosslyn.

$ **Prices:** Entrees $6.95–$12.95. AE, DC, MC, V.

Open: Mon–Fri 11am–11pm, Sat 4–11pm, Sun 4–10pm.

Sarris's place has been a local favorite for more than 30 years—and no wonder. A delicious roast prime rib of beef dinner can be had for $6.95! The menu also features steak and seafood, but the prime rib, which comes in three cuts—the above dinner portion (regular, ample for most appetites), Louis XIV ($10.95), and mammoth ($12.95)—is what draws the crowds. The meat is tender and well seasoned, served in its own juices. With it you get a baked potato and offerings from an exceptional salad bar that's decorated like a riverboat. Wine and other drinks are available. The restaurant is housed in an imposing white pseudo-antebellum building, trimmed in wrought iron. The interior resembles a New Orleans garden, with iron chairs and railings, leaded-glass fixtures, ceiling fans, hurricane lamps on every table, and fountains and foliage.

EVANS FARM INN, 1696 Chain Bridge Rd., McLean. Tel. 703/356-8000.

Cuisine: AMERICAN. **Directions:** From I-495, take Exit 11N; it's 2 miles east of Tyson's Corner (Rte. 7).

$ Prices: Entrees $8.25–$20.95; lunch buffet $9.95 ($7.25 for children under 6). AE, CB, DC, DISC, MC, V.
Open: Sun–Thurs noon–9pm, Fri–Sat noon–10pm; buffet lunch Mon–Sat noon–2:30pm.

A 40-acre working farm, complete with horses, goats, pigs, a donkey, and all sorts of fowl, is the setting for the charming Evans Farm Inn, an 18th-century-style building, erected in the 1950s with timbers, old bricks, and early glass salvaged from nearby colonial sites. The restaurant has large dining rooms, decorated with old farm implements, corner cupboards, carousel horses, and spinning wheels. Downstairs, the Sitting Duck Pub evokes an old Tudor inn with a dart board, Hogarth drawings, copper pitchers, and, in winter, a roaring fireplace. Also on the property is a cookhouse that displays colonial cooking items, a mill and mill pond, a country store and doll shop, and a large duck pond. There's a whole afternoon's entertainment here for a family.

The lunch buffet includes a trip to the bounteous salad bar, entree, vegetables, and home-baked bread. Dinner entrees, such as roast duckling, half a chicken, or sirloin steak, come with vegetables, spoon bread, and salad bar. The Evans Farm garden provides all the floral decorations and much of the produce used at the inn. On Friday and Saturday nights there's piano playing and singing in the pub.

SHOPPING

The suburban sprawl of Arlington is mall country.

FASHION CENTRE AT PENTAGON CITY, 1100 S. Hayes St., immediately south of the Pentagon. Tel. 703/415-2400.

Anchored by Macy's and Nordstrom's, this plush four-level shopping complex with more than 130 shops, restaurants, and services adjoins a Ritz-Carlton Hotel (see "Where to Stay," above). It features branches of Ann Taylor, Au Coton, Banana Republic, Brentano's, Scribner's, the Disney Store, Record World, Crabtree & Evelyn, Godiva Chocolates, Hoffritz, Laura Ashley, Villeroy & Boch (exquisite china), Victoria's Secret, Lane Bryant, The Limited, the Body Shop, and the Gap (also Gap Kids and Gap Accessories). Dining choices include a food court with 13 eateries. There is a six-screen movie theater, and parking is available in a six-level garage. Open Monday through Saturday from 10am to 9:30pm and on Sunday from noon to 6pm.
Metro: Pentagon City.

SPRINGFIELD MALL, at the intersection of I-95, I-395, and I-495, in Springfield, Va. Tel. 703/971-3600.

Located about 10 miles south of downtown D.C., this is one of the area's largest malls, with more than 230 shops, 20 restaurants, 10 movie theaters, and free parking for about 8,000 cars. Major stores include branches of Macy's, J.C. Penney, Raleigh's, Lane Bryant, Herman's Sporting Goods, W. Bell, and Montgomery Ward. You'll find over a dozen shoe stores and numerous shops selling clothing, gourmet food, health food, bridal wear, furniture, toys, books, gifts, cosmetics—you name it. Open Monday through Saturday from 10am to 9:30pm and on Sunday from noon to 5pm.
Directions: Take I-95 south to the Franconia exit and stay in the right-hand lane.

TYSONS CORNER CENTER, 1961 Chain Bridge Rd. at Rte. 7, McLean, Va. Tel. 703/893-9400.

Among the 230 shops here are five major department stores—Bloomingdale's, Nordstrom, Lord & Taylor, Hecht's, and Woodward & Lothrop. Other notable emporia include Laura Ashley, the Nature Company, Williams-Sonoma (kitchenware), The Limited, Disney Store, Banana Republic, Raleighs, Brooks Brothers,

F.A.O. Schwarz, Waldenbooks, Britches of Georgetown, Ann Taylor, Crabtree & Evelyn, Woolworth's and the Gap. There are 30 restaurants (running the gamut from Magic Pan to California Pizza Kitchen) and eight movie theaters. Open Monday through Saturday from 10am to 9:30pm and on Sunday from noon to 5pm. **Metro:** West Falls Church; shuttles run from there every half hour.

THE GALLERIA AT TYSONS II, 2001 International Dr., McLean, Va. Tel. 703/827-7700, or toll free 800/950-7467.

This plush three-level mall offers 120 shops, galleries, restaurants, and services. Anchored by three fine department stores—Macy's, Saks, and Neiman-Marcus—the Galleria also covers the whole shopping spectrum: shoes and clothing for the entire family, jewelry, electronics, home furnishings, gifts, and more. There are five full-service restaurants, as well as a lovely Garden Food Court. Open Monday through Saturday from 10am to 9:30pm and on Sunday from noon to 6pm. **Metro:** West Falls Church; shuttles run from there every half hour.

EVENING ENTERTAINMENT

The Crystal City Marriott and Ritz-Carlton have lounges offering entertainment on weekends. But the Arlington area is also home to the country's only national park devoted to the performing arts:

WOLF TRAP FARM PARK, 1624 Trap Rd., Vienna, Va. Tel. 703/255-1868.

You can buy tickets in advance for its star-studded summer season, from late May to the beginning of September. In recent years the Boston Pops, Bolshoi Opera, Moiseyev Dance Company, B. B. King, Judy Collins, Ray Charles, Willie Nelson, and Bill Cosby have performed here. Talk about eclectic! Performances are held in the 6,900-seat Filene Center II, about half of which is under the open sky.

Prices: Seats, $16–$75; lawn tickets, $12–$18. (You'd best arrive early; the lawn opens an hour prior to the performance. Bring a picnic dinner—everyone does.)

Metro: West Falls Church. Then take the Wolf Trap Express Shuttle ($3); buses run every 20 minutes from 6:20pm, including every 20 minutes after the performance, to no later than 11pm. **Directions:** Take I-495 to Exit 12W (Dulles Toll Road); stay on local exits (you'll see a sign) until you come to Wolf Trap.

2. ALEXANDRIA

5 miles S of Washington, D.C.;
95 miles N of Richmond; 2 miles S of Arlington

GETTING THERE   By Plane   Washington's **National Airport** (tel. 703/685-8000) is just 2 miles north of Alexandria. Washington's Metrorail (see below) provides easy transport to Alexandria. Also, Washington Flyer Shuttles (tel. 703/685-1400) has van, taxi, and limo service from the airport.

By Train   The Amtrak passenger **rail station** is at 110 Callahan Drive, near King Street (tel. 703/836-4339).

By Washington Metrorail   From Arlington or Washington, take the Yellow Line to the King Street station. From the station, board a DASH bus (70¢) to King and Fairfax—right to the door of the Visitors Center. Take a transfer, and you can board any DASH bus for 3 hours. It's a short ride from the station; in fact you could walk it, but better to save your feet for sightseeing.

By Car   Going south from Washington, take the scenic George Washington

Memorial Parkway, which will take you right into King Street, Alexandria's main street. Parking permits for visitors are free at the Visitors Center (see below). I-95 skirts Alexandria; if you're coming from the north, take the U.S. 1 exit into town.

Founded by a group of Scottish tobacco merchants, the seaport town of Alexandria came into being on a sunny day in July 1749 when a 60-acre tract of land was auctioned off in half-acre lots. Today the original 60 acres of lots in George Washington's hometown (also Robert E. Lee's) are the heart of Old Town, a multi-million-dollar urban-renewal historic district. As you stroll Old Town's brick sidewalks and cobblestone streets, you'll see more than 2,000 18th- and 19th-century buildings. You'll visit Gadsby's Tavern, where 2 centuries ago the men who created this nation discussed politics, freedom, and revolution over tankards of ale. You'll stand in the tavern's doorway where Washington reviewed his troops for the last time, visit Lee's boyhood home, and sit in the pews of Christ Church where both men worshipped.

In this "mother lode of Americana" the past is being ever-increasingly restored in an ongoing archeological and historical research program. And though the present is manifested by an abundance of quaint shops, boutiques, art galleries, and restaurants capitalizing on the volume of tourism, it's still easy to imagine yourself in Colonial times—to smell the fragrant tobacco; hear the rumbling of horse-drawn vehicles over cobblestone; envision the oxcarts piled with crates of chickens, country-cured ham, and casks of cheese and butter; and picture the bustling waterfront where fishermen brought in the daily catch and foreign vessels unloaded exotic cargo.

ORIENTATION

INFORMATION

The **Alexandria Convention & Visitors Bureau** at Ramsay House, 221 King Street, at Fairfax Street (tel. 703/838-4200; 703/838-5005 for 24-hour Alexandria events recording), is open daily from 9am to 5pm (closed Thanksgiving, Christmas, and New Year's days). Here you can pick up maps and brochures, find out about special events taking place during your visit, and get information about accommodations, restaurants, sights, shopping, and whatever else. If you came by car, get a free **3-day parking permit** here for gratis parking at any 2-hour meter for as many hours as you like.

Also available at Ramsay House: a **block ticket** for discounted admission to four historic Alexandria properties: Gadsby's Tavern, Lee's Boyhood Home, the Carlyle House, and the Lee-Fendall House. The ticket, which can also be purchased at any of the four buildings, costs $8 for adults, $3 for children 6 to 17; under 6, free.

Though it's easy to see Alexandria on your own, you may find your experience enhanced by a comprehensive walking tour. **Doorways to Old Virginia** (tel. 703/548-0100) offers tours daily at 11am ($3 per person). They leave from the Visitors Bureau at Ramsay House.

CITY LAYOUT

Alexandria is laid out in a simple grid system. Union to Lee Street is the 100 block, Lee to Fairfax the 200 block, and so on up. The cross streets (more or less going north and south) are divided north and south by King Street. King to Cameron is the 100 block north, Cameron to Queen the 200 block north, and so on. King to Prince is the 100 block south, etc.

As a glance at your walking-tour map later in this chapter will indicate, Old Town is contained within several blocks. Park your car for the day, don comfortable shoes, and start walking—it's the easiest way.

WHAT TO SEE & DO

Whenever you come, you're sure to run into some activity or other—a jazz festival, tea garden or tavern gambol, quilt exhibit, wine tasting, or organ recital. It's all part of Alexandria's *cead mile failte* (100,000 welcomes) to visitors.

Note: Many Alexandria attractions are closed on Monday. The Potomac plantations (described in Chapter 5) are just 14 miles south of Alexandria and most logically visited on day trips from it.

GADSBY'S TAVERN MUSEUM, 134 N. Royal St. Tel. 703/838-4242.

Alexandria was at the crossroads of Colonial America, and the center of life in Alexandria was Gadsby's Tavern. Consisting of two buildings—a tavern dating to about 1770 and the 1792 City Tavern and Hotel—it's named today for a memorable owner, Englishman John Gadsby, whose establishment was a "gentleman's tavern" renowned for elegance and comfort. The rooms have been restored to their 18th-century appearance. The second-floor ballroom with its musicians' gallery was the scene of Alexandria's most lavish parties, and since 1793 George Washington's birthday ball and banquet has been an annual tradition here.

Thirty-minute **tours** depart 15 minutes before and after the hour, with a final tour at 4:15pm. On Wednesday the final tour is at 1:30pm, and it's a special tour called Gadsby's Time Travels.

To cap off the experience, you can dine at Gadsby's Colonial-style restaurant (see "Where to Eat," below).

Admission: $3 adult, $1 children 6–17.

Open: Tues–Sat 10am–5pm, Sun 1–5pm.

BOYHOOD HOME OF ROBERT E. LEE, 607 Oronoco St. Tel. 703/548-8454.

Revolutionary cavalry hero Gen. "Light Horse Harry" Lee brought his wife, Ann Hill Carter, and five children to this early Federal-style mansion in 1812 when Robert, destined to become the Confederate military leader, was just 5 years old. A tour of the house, built in 1795, provides a glimpse into the gracious life-style of Alexandria's gentry. George Washington was an occasional guest of earlier occupants, Col. and Mrs. William Fitzhugh. In 1804 the Fitzhughs' daughter, Mary Lee, married Martha Washington's grandson, George Washington Parke Custis, in the drawing room. And the Custises' daughter married Robert E. Lee.

General Lafayette, a comrade-in-arms with Lee during the American Revolution, honored Ann Hill Carter Lee with a visit to the house in October of 1824. The drawing room today is called the Lafayette Room to commemorate that visit. The furnishings here today are of the Lee period but did not belong to the family.

Admission: $3 adults, $1 children 10–17, free for children under 10.

Open: Tours Mon–Sat 10am–3:30pm, Sun 1–3:30pm.

LEE-FENDALL HOUSE, 614 Oronoco St., at Washington St. Tel. 703/548-1789.

This handsome Greek Revival–style house is a veritable Lee family museum of furniture, heirlooms, and documents. Light Horse Harry Lee never actually lived here, though he was a frequent visitor, as was his good friend, George Washington. He did own the original lot, but sold it to Philip Richard Fendall (himself a Lee on his mother's side), who built the house in 1785.

Thirty-minute guided **tours** interpret the 1850s era of the home and provide insight into Victorian family life. You'll also see the Colonial garden with its magnolia and chestnut trees, roses, and boxwood-lined paths.

Admission: $3 adults, $1 children 10–17, free for children under 10.
Open: Tues–Sat 10am–3:45pm, Sun noon–3:45pm.

CARLYLE HOUSE, 121 N. Fairfax St. Tel. 703/549-2997.

Not only is Carlyle House regarded as one of Virginia's most architecturally impressive 18th-century houses, it also figured prominently in American history. Patterned after Scottish/English manor houses, it was completed in 1753 by Scottish merchant John Carlyle for his bride, Sara Fairfax of Belvoir, who hailed from one of Virginia's most prominent families.

When it was built, Carlyle House was a waterfront property with its own wharf. A social and political center, the house was visited by numerous great men of the time, George Washington among them. But its most important moment in history occurred in April 1755 when Maj. Gen. Edward Braddock, commander-in-chief of His Majesty's forces in North America, met with five colonial governors here and asked them to tax colonists to finance a campaign against the French and Indians. Colonial legislatures refused to comply, one of the first instances of serious friction between America and Britain. Nevertheless, Braddock made Carlyle House his headquarters during the campaign.

The house is furnished in period pieces and two of the original rooms—the large parlor and the adjacent study—have survived intact. An upstairs room houses an exhibit called "A Workman's View," that explains 18th-century construction methods with hand-hewn beams and hand-wrought nails. **Tours,** taking about 40 minutes, leave every half hour between 10am and 4:30pm.

Admission: $3 adults, $1 children 10–17, free for children under 10.
Open: Tues–Sat 10am–5pm, Sun noon–5pm.

CHRIST CHURCH, 118 N. Washington St., at Cameron St. Tel. 703/549-1450.

This sturdy red-brick English-style church, in continuous use since 1773, would be an important national landmark even if its two most distinguished members were not Washington and Lee. There have, of course, been many changes since Washington's day. The bell tower, church bell, galleries, and organ were added by the early 1800s, the "wineglass" pulpit in 1890. But much of what was changed later has since been unchanged. The pristine white interior with wood moldings and gold trim is colonially correct, though modern heating has obviated the need for charcoal braziers and hot bricks. And, for the most part, the original structure remains, including the hand-blown glass in the windows. The town has grown up around the building that was first called the "Church in the Woods" because of its rural setting.

Christ Church has had its historic moments. Washington and other early church members discussed revolution in the churchyard, and Robert E. Lee met here with Richmond representatives who offered him command of Virginia's army at the beginning of the Civil War. You can sit in the pew where George and Martha sat with her two Custis grandchildren, or in the Lee family pew. In 1987, the **Old Parish Hall** was completely restored to its original appearance; it now houses a gift shop. Do walk in the weathered graveyard, Alexandria's first and only burial ground until 1815. The remains of 34 Confederate soldiers are also interred here.

Admission: Free.
Open: Mon–Sat 9am–4pm, Sun 2–4:30pm.

STABLER-LEADBEATER APOTHECARY, 105–107 S. Fairfax St. Tel. 703/836-3713.

When it went out of business in 1933, this landmark drugstore was the second oldest in continuous operation in America. Run for five generations by the same family (beginning in 1792), its early patrons included Robert E. Lee (he purchased the paint for Arlington House here) and George Washington. Gothic Revival decorative elements and Victorian-style doors were added in the 1860s.

Today the apothecary shelves are lined with about 900 of the original hand-blown gold-leaf-labeled bottles (the most valuable collection of antique medicinal bottles in the U.S., actually), old scales stamped with the royal crown, patent medicines, and equipment for blood letting. Among the shop's documentary records are such as this 1802 epistle from Mount Vernon: "Mrs. Washington desires Mr. Stabler to send by the bearer a quart bottle of his best Castor Oil and the bill for it."

There's no tour, but a 10-minute recording guides you around the displays.
Admission: Free.
Open: Tues–Sat 10am–4pm, except lunchtime.

OLD PRESBYTERIAN MEETING HOUSE, 321 S. Fairfax St. Tel. 703/549-6670.

Presbyterian congregations have worshipped in Virginia since Jamestown days when the Rev. Alexander Whittaker converted Pocahontas. This brick church was established by Scottish pioneers in 1774. Though it wasn't George Washington's church, the Meeting House bell tolled continuously for 4 days after his death in December 1799, and memorial services were preached from the pulpit here by Presbyterian, Episcopal, and Methodist ministers.

Many famous Alexandrians are buried in the church graveyard—John and Sara Carlyle, Dr. James Craik (the surgeon who treated George Washington, dressed Lafayette's wounds at Brandywine, and ministered to the dying Braddock at Monongahela), and William Hunter, Jr., founder of the St. Andrew's Society of Scottish descendants (bagpipers pay homage to his grave the first Saturday of each December). It is also the site of a Tomb of an Unknown Revolutionary Soldier. The original parsonage, or manse, is still intact. There's no guided tour, but there are recorded narratives in the church and graveyard.
Admission: Free.
Open: Mon–Fri 9am–4pm, most Suns noon–4pm; services Sun at 8:30 and 11am.

THE ATHENAEUM, 201 Prince St., at Lee St. Tel. 703/548-0035.

A handsome Greek Revival building with a classic portico and unfluted Doric columns, the Athenaeum, is home to the Northern Virginia Fine Arts Association. Art exhibits here run the gamut from Matisse lithographs to shows of East Coast artists. The building dates from 1851, and originally contained the Bank of the Old Dominion. The bank's operations were interrupted by the Civil War when Yankee troops turned the building into a commissary.
Admission: Free (donations appreciated).
Open: Tues–Sat 10am–4pm, Sun 1–4pm. Gallery shows Sept–June.

THE LYCEUM, 201 S. Washington St. Tel. 703/838-4994.

Another Greek Revival building, the Lyceum is a museum focusing on Alexandria's history from colonial times through the 20th century. It features changing exhibits and an ongoing series of lectures, concerts, and films. An adjoining nonprofit shop carries 18th-century reproductions and crafts.

But even without its manifold offerings, the brick-and-stucco Lyceum itself merits a visit. Built in 1839, it was designed in the Doric temple style (with imposing white columns) to serve as a lecture, meeting, and concert hall. The first floor originally contained the Alexandria Library and various natural-science and historical exhibits. It was an important center of Alexandria's cultural life until the Civil War when Union forces took it over for use as a hospital.

Admission: Free.
Open: Daily 10am–5pm.

FORT WARD MUSEUM AND PARK, 4301 W. Braddock Rd. Tel. 703/ 838-4848.

A short drive from Old Town is a 45-acre museum, park, and historic site that takes you a leap forward in Alexandria history to the Civil War. The action here centers, as it did in the early 1860s, on an actual Union fort that Lincoln ordered erected to defend Washington, D.C. The Northwest Bastion has been restored, and six mounted guns (there were originally 36) face south waiting for trouble that in fact never came; the fort was not attacked.

Visitors can explore the fort and replicas of the Ceremonial Entrance Gate and an officer's hut. A museum on the premises houses Civil War memorabilia. **Tours** of the fort are given by guides in Union soldier costumes on selected Sundays.

There are picnic areas with barbecue grills in the woods surrounding the fort, and concerts are presented on selected evenings June through mid-September in the outdoor amphitheater.

Admission: Free.
Open: Park, daily 9am–sunset; museum, Tues–Sat 9am–5pm, Sun noon–5pm.
Directions: From Old Town, follow King Street west, go right on Kenwood Street, then left on West Braddock Road. Continue for three-quarters of a mile to the entrance on the right.

THE TORPEDO FACTORY, 105 N. Union St. Tel. 703/838-4565.

Studio space for some 175 artists and craftspeople, who create and sell their own works on the premises, is contained in this block-long, three-story building. Here you can see artists at work—potters, painters, print-makers, photographers, sculptors, and jewelers, among others.

In addition, on permanent display are exhibits on Alexandria history provided by **Alexandria Archaeology** (tel. 703/838-4399), headquartered here and engaged in extensive city research.

And the building itself is of historic interest. It's a converted torpedo shell-case factory built by the U.S. Navy in 1918 and operated as such through the early 1950s. Later, the Smithsonian used it to store various and sundry, including dinosaur bones.

Admission: Free.
Open: Daily 10am–5pm; special exhibit area, Tues–Thurs 10am–3pm, Fri–Sat 10am–5pm.

THE SCHOONER ALEXANDRIA, Waterfront Park. Tel. 703/549-7078.

The Alexandria Seaport Foundation, an organization devoted to maritime heritage, acquired the Scandinavian schooner *Alexandria* (formerly the *Lindø*) in 1983, and when it's in port (sometimes it's elsewhere participating in tall-ship festivals) it's docked at Waterfront Park. A red-sail Baltic trader vessel built in 1929, the ship was remodeled for passenger use in the 1970s.

Admission: Free (donations appreciated).
Open: Spring–fall Sat–Sun noon–5pm, when it's in port.

ALEXANDRIA WATERFRONT MUSEUM, 44 Canal Center Plaza, Level G-1. Tel. 703/838-4288.

In the early 19th century several prominent Alexandria businesspeople initiated a plan for the construction of a canal that would follow a 7-mile route along the Potomac River. Except for the Civil War years, during which trade was suspended, service on the canal continued until 1886. High maintenance costs, competition from the railroads, and the advent of steamboats contributed to the canal's decline, and, eventually, it was abandoned. In 1978 the remains of the canal's tide lock were discovered. Using historical maps and photographs, and the notebooks and drawings of the original engineers, archeologists excavated and then reconstructed the lock. The Alexandria Waterfront Museum, at TransPotomac Center, documents and interprets maritime and waterfront activities in and around the city during the canal's heyday.

Admission: Free.
Open: Tues–Fri 11am–4pm, Sat–Sun 1–4pm. **Closed:** Legal and religious hols and hol weekends (check before visiting).

BLACK HISTORY AND RESOURCE CENTER, 638 N. Alfred St. Tel. 703/838-4356.

In a 1940s building that originally housed the black community's first public library, the Black History and Resource Center exhibits historical objects, photographs, documents, and memorabilia relating to black Alexandrians from the 18th century forward. Besides the permanent collection, the museum presents rotating exhibits and offers walking tours.

Admission: Free.
Open: Tues–Sat 10am–3pm, Sun 1–4pm.

WALKING TOUR — Old Town Alexandria

Start: Ramsay House Visitors Center, King Street and Fairfax Street.
Finish: Torpedo Factory, Waterfront at Cameron Street.
Time: Allow approximately 2½ hours, not including museum and shopping stops.
Best Times: Anytime.
Worst Times: Monday, when many historic sites are closed.

You'll feel as though you've stepped back into the 18th century as you stroll Alexandria's brick-paved sidewalks, lined with Colonial residences, historic houses and churches, museums, shops, and restaurants. This walk ends at the waterfront, no longer a center of commercial shipping, but now home to a vibrant arts center along the Potomac riverfront park.

Begin your walk at the:

1. **Ramsay House Visitors Center,** 221 King Street, at Fairfax Street, in the heart of the Historic District. It's a historic structure itself, with a Dutch barn roof and a English garden. After perusing the wealth of information offered here about Alexandria, go north on Fairfax to:
2. **Carlyle House,** an elegant 1753 manor house set off from the street by a low wall. Continue north on Fairfax to the corner. Turn left on Cameron, past the back of the old city hall, to the red-brick buildings across Royal Street, known as:
3. **Gadsby's Tavern.** The original 18th-century tavern now houses a museum of 18th-century antiques, while the hotel portion is an Early American–style restaurant.

REFUELING STOP   If you're ready for lunch, the 18th-century atmosphere at Gadsby's Tavern is the perfect place for a sandwich or salad.

From here, continue west on Cameron Street to St. Asaph Street. Turn right onto it. At Queen Street, you can see:
4. **No. 523,** the smallest house in Alexandria. Continuing north on St. Asaph, you'll come to:
5. **Princess Street.** The cobblestones that pave the street are original; heavy

traffic is banned. One block farther north on St. Asaph, turn left at Oronoco Street. On your right is:

6. **Robert E. Lee's Boyhood Home,** where he lived before he went to West Point in 1825. Across Oronoco Street, at the corner of Washington, is the:

7. **Lee-Fendall House,** a gracious white clapboard residence that was home to several generations of Lees. Enter through a pretty Colonial garden. Head south on Washington, a busy commercial thoroughfare, to Queen Street and cross over to:

8. **Lloyd House,** a beautiful late Georgian residence (1797) that is now part of the Alexandria Library and houses a fascinating collection of old documents, books, and records on the city and state. From here, proceed south on Washington Street to the quiet graveyard entrance behind:

9. **Christ Church,** where the Washingtons and Lees worshiped. Leave by the front entrance, on Columbus Street, and turn left to King Street.

REFUELING STOP A cappuccino and pastry break at **10. Bread & Chocolate,** 611 King Street, is guaranteed to revive flagging spirits. Sandwiches and salads are also available at this casual spot.

From King Street, turn left on Alfred Street, to the:

11. **Friendship Veterans Fire Engine Association,** on South Alfred Street. This historic firehouse has an extensive collection of antique firefighting equipment. Turn left at the corner of Prince Street and proceed to Washington. At the corner is the Greek Revival:

12. **Lyceum,** built in 1839 as the city's first cultural center. Today it's a city historical museum. The museum shop has a lovely selection of crafts, silver, and other gift items. At the intersection of Washington and Prince stands:

13. **The Confederate Soldier,** a sadly dejected bronze figure, modeled after a figure in the painting *Appomattox* by John A. Elder. From here, continue walking east on Prince to Pitt Street, then turn left to King. You'll see the large open area called:

14. **Market Square,** along King Street from Royal to Fairfax, used as a town market since 1749. Today the market is held once a week, on Saturday. From here, turn right on Fairfax to the quaint:

15. **Stabler-Leadbeater Apothecary Shop,** housing a remarkable collection of early medical ware and hand-blown glass containers. Proceed south on Fairfax to Duke Street, to the:

16. **Old Presbyterian Meeting House,** the 18th-century church where George Washington's funeral sermons were preached in 1799. The graveyard has a marker commemorating the Unknown Soldier of the Revolutionary War. Retrace your steps back to Prince Street, and turn right. Between Fairfax Street and Lee Street you'll see:

17. **Gentry Row,** named for the local leaders who made their homes in these three-story town houses in the 18th and 19th centuries. At the corner of Prince and Lee is the:

18. **Atheneum,** a handsome Greek Revival structure that now houses contemporary art shows. Cross Lee Street to:

19. **Captain's Row,** a pretty cobblestone section of Prince Street. You're now in sight of the Potomac riverfront and may want to stroll down to the little waterfront park at the foot of Prince Street for a panoramic view of the river.

REFUELING STOP The **20. Deli on the Strand,** on Union Street between Prince and Duke, has delicious salads and sandwiches, to eat at picnic tables on their porch, or to carry out to the park.

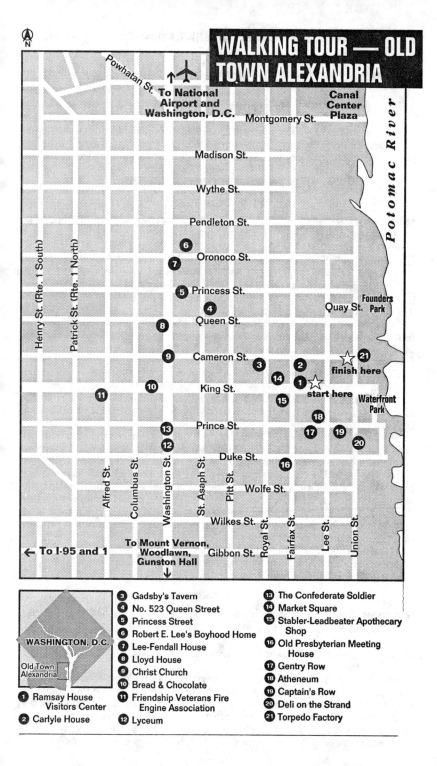

WALKING TOUR — OLD TOWN ALEXANDRIA

N

Potomac River

Powhatan St.

↑✈ **To National Airport and Washington, D.C.**

Montgomery St.

Canal Center Plaza

Madison St.

Wythe St.

Pendleton St.

Oronoco St.

Princess St.

Queen St.

Quay St.

Founders Park

Cameron St.

finish here ☆ ㉑

King St. ☆ **start here**

Waterfront Park

Prince St.

Duke St.

Wolfe St.

Wilkes St.

Gibbon St.

← **To I-95 and 1**

To Mount Vernon, Woodlawn, Gunston Hall ↓

Henry St. (Rte. 1 South)

Patrick St. (Rte. 1 North)

Alfred St.

Columbus St.

Washington St.

St. Asaph St.

Pitt St.

Royal St.

Fairfax St.

Lee St.

Union St.

WASHINGTON, D.C.

Old Town Alexandria

❶ Ramsay House Visitors Center

❷ Carlyle House

❸ Gadsby's Tavern
❹ No. 523 Queen Street
❺ Princess Street
❻ Robert E. Lee's Boyhood Home
❼ Lee-Fendall House
❽ Lloyd House
❾ Christ Church
❿ Bread & Chocolate
⓫ Friendship Veterans Fire Engine Association
⓬ Lyceum

⓭ The Confederate Soldier
⓮ Market Square
⓯ Stabler-Leadbeater Apothecary Shop
⓰ Old Presbyterian Meeting House
⓱ Gentry Row
⓲ Atheneum
⓳ Captain's Row
⓴ Deli on the Strand
㉑ Torpedo Factory

Continue north on Union Street to the:

21. Torpedo Factory, an arts-and-crafts center where studios and galleries are open to the public.

WHERE TO STAY

Within Alexandria's Old Town there are some choice accommodations—with prices that reflect the convenience of being in the city center. Outside the historic area there are interesting choices, too, with more hotels in the moderate to budget range.

OLD TOWN ACCOMMODATIONS

Very Expensive

MORRISON HOUSE, 116 S. Alfred St., Alexandria, VA 22314. Tel. 703/838-8000, or toll free 800/367-0800. Fax 703/684-6283. 45 rms, including 3 suites. A/C TV TEL

$ Rates: $165–$195 single or double; from $250 suite. Weekend and holiday packages available. AE, CB, DC, MC, V. **Parking:** $8 per night.

Designed after the grand manor houses of the Federal period, Morrison House, in the heart of Old Town, is enchanting from the moment you ascend the curving staircase to its white-columned portico where a butler greets guests at the door of the marble foyer. The residential-style lobby divides into a series of beautifully appointed, cozy rooms: a mahogany-paneled library, a formal parlor with silk brocade-upholstered sofas and chairs, and two intimate restaurants. Afternoon tea is served daily from the sideboard in the parlor.

Guest rooms are charmingly furnished in fine Federal-period reproductions including mahogany four-poster beds, brass chandeliers, and decorative fireplaces. In-room amenities include two phones, AM/FM radios, remote-control TVs housed in armoires, fresh flowers, and imported terry robes. The plush Italian marble baths are equipped with hairdryers.

Dining/Entertainment: The Club Room, open for dinner only, has a traditional English look, with antique prints on the walls and fresh bouquets of flowers on every table. Entrees ($19 to $22) include grilled swordfish, salmon, beef tenderloin, and rack of lamb. The Grill has an English clubby look, with burgundy leather chairs, brass chandeliers, and dark-green draperies. At lunch it offers soups, salads, and sandwiches such as crabcakes on a brioche. Dinner menus feature traditional American fare. The Grill bar, serving both restaurants, offers over 20 different wines and champagnes by the glass. Monday through Saturday a resident pianist performs on the baby grand in the lounge.

Services: 24-hour butler, concierge, and room service; indoor valet parking, complimentary shoeshine, free newspaper delivery, nightly turndown.

Facilities: Health club privileges at nearby facility.

Expensive

HOLIDAY INN OLD TOWN, 480 King St., Alexandria, VA 22314. Tel. 703/549-6080, or toll free 800/368-5047. Fax 703/549-6080, ext. 7777. 227 rms. A/C TV TEL

$ Rates: $99–$145. Weekend and other packages available. AE, CB, DC, DISC, MC, V. **Parking:** $5 per night.

A block from the Visitors Center, this six-story red-brick building, entered via a quiet brick courtyard, occupies an entire block. Coffee and tea are served throughout the day in an inviting lamp-lit lobby. Guest rooms are done up in various color schemes; they're vaguely Colonial in feel, many with green rugs, off-white patterned wallpaper, and dark furnishings. Rooms with king-size beds have small seating areas with couches and coffee tables; all rooms offer safes, hair dryers, and clock radios.

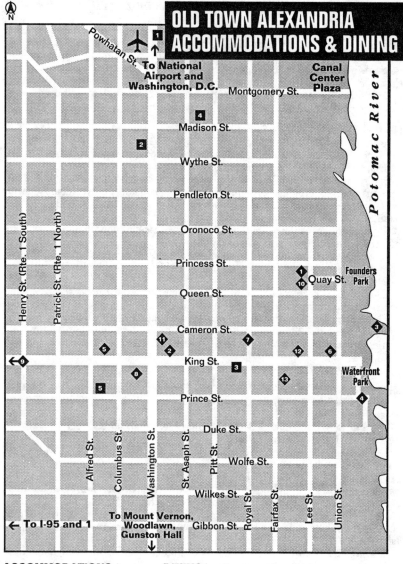

OLD TOWN ALEXANDRIA ACCOMMODATIONS & DINING

ACCOMMODATIONS:

Best Western Old Colony 1
Econo Lodge Old Town 2
Holiday Inn Old Town 3
Marriott Suites 4
Morrison House 5

DINING:

Bilbo Baggins 1
Bread and Chocolate 2
Chart House 3
Deli on the Strand 4
East Wind 5
Fish Market 6
Gadsby's Tavern 7

Geranio 8
Hard Times Cafe 9
La Bergerie 10
Le Refuge 11
Two–Nineteen 12
The Warehouse 13

Dining/Entertainment: 101 Royal Restaurant features American fare; Annabelle's, an intimate lounge off the courtyard, is open for afternoon and evening drinks and light snacks.

Services: Room service (7am to 10pm), turndown on request, concierge, airport shuttle.

Facilities: Heated indoor pool, sauna, gift shop. Guests may request complimentary exercise bike; outdoor bikes available.

MARRIOTT SUITES, 801 N. St. Asaph St., Alexandria, VA 22314. Tel. 703/836-4700, or toll free 800/228-9290. 249 suites. A/C MINIBAR TV TEL

$ Rates: $145 single or double. Weekend and holiday packages available. AE, CB, DC, DISC, MC, V. **Parking:** $4.50 per night.

This very hospitable, all-suite hotel provides a luxurious residential atmosphere. Each spacious suite has a full living room, with an extra phone on the desk (equipped with call waiting), a comfortable convertible sofa, and a big console TV (both TVs have remotes).

Bedrooms, set off from the living rooms by lace-curtained French doors, are furnished in traditional dark mahogany pieces. Most have king-size beds. They're decorated in a mauve/dusty rose/aqua color scheme, with pretty pale-gray floral-print bedspreads. Other in-room amenities: coffee makers, hairdryers, and clock radios.

Dining/Entertainment: Sheffield's restaurant features seafood specialties and lighter fare in a casual atmosphere.

Services: Room service (6:30am to 11pm), concierge, complimentary newspaper.

Facilities: Indoor pool, health club, Jacuzzi, gift shop.

Moderate

BEST WESTERN OLD COLONY, 625 First St., Alexandria, VA 22314. Tel. 703/548-6300, or toll free 800/528-1234. Fax 703/548-8032. 332 rms and suites. A/C TV TEL

$ Rates: $98–$108 single; $108–$118 double. Weekend and festival packages available. MC, V. **Parking:** Free.

Encompassing some 5 acres of beautifully landscaped property, this Best Western is a 10-minute stroll from the heart of Old Town. It's a rambling, three-story, red-brick building, the main section of which has arched windows and double chimneys that pay homage to Alexandria's past. Rooms are exceptionally spacious, many of them decorated in a dusty rose/blue/cream color scheme. Floral-print bedspreads, color-coordinated draperies, an easy chair with an ottoman (some rooms have a small couch), a work desk, and two armchairs complete the picture. Some rooms have Jacuzzis.

Dining/Entertainment: Traditions Restaurant, open for all meals, has a sleek, modern art deco look. A cocktail lounge/piano bar adjoins.

Services: Room service (6am to 11:30pm), free airport shuttle.

Facilities: Indoor/outdoor pool, health club, sauna, gift shop.

Budget

ECONO LODGE OLD TOWN, 700 N. Washington St., Alexandria, VA 22314. Tel. 703/836-5100, or toll free 800/446-6900. Fax 703/836-0732. 39 rms. A/C TV TEL

$ Rates: $40.95–$49.95 single; $44.95–$54.95 double. Extra person $5. AE, MC, V. **Parking:** Free.

Part of the well-run budget chain whose motto is "Spend a night, not a fortune," this two-story Econo Lodge is just a few blocks from the center of Old Town activity. It offers standard facilities in clean, good-sized rooms. Shuttle service to National Airport.

NEARBY ACCOMMODATIONS
Expensive

GUEST QUARTERS SUITE HOTEL, 100 S. Reynolds St., Alexandria, VA 22304. Tel. 703/370-9600, or toll free 800/424-2900. Fax 703/370-0467. 225 suites. A/C TV TEL **Directions:** From Old Town, follow Duke Street about 4 miles; turn left at South Reynolds Street.

$ Rates (including continental breakfast): $125–$185 single; $145–$185 double. Weekend and holiday packages available. AE, DC, MC, V. **Parking:** Free.

Designed to offer travelers the ultimate in homeyness and hospitality, this Guest Quarters property occupies a nine-story modern box on nicely landscaped grounds. Accommodations are spacious one- and two-bedroom suites decorated in soft pastel hues. Handsome contemporary furnishings—glass dining tables, leather-and-steel director's chairs, plush sofas, comfortable easy chairs, good-sized desks, and framed modern-art posters—are standard throughout. Both living rooms and bedrooms have TVs with remote control and telephones. Kitchens are fully equipped.

Dining/Entertainment: A continental breakfast is served in the Quarters Pub & Grille, also open for dinner during the week, lunch and dinner on weekends.

Services: Shuttle to King Street Metro.

Facilities: Outdoor pool, coin-op laundry.

Budget

COMFORT INN LANDMARK, 6254 Duke St., Alexandria, VA 22312. Tel. 703/642-3422, or toll free 800/228-5150. 148 rms. A/C TV TEL **Directions:** From Old Town, follow Duke Street past the Landmark Shopping Center.

$ Rates (including continental breakfast buffet): $45–$67 single or double. Children under 18 stay free in parents' room. Extra person $6. AE, CB, DC, DISC, MC, V. **Parking:** Free.

Accommodations here, exceptionally spacious for a budget hotel, are cheerful—warm oak pieces with green-and-mauve print spreads, green carpets, and mauve easy chairs. Watercolors of Asian landscapes adorn pristine white walls. Rooms with king-size beds have recliners and some also feature Jacuzzis. The executive floor has upgraded amenities, including in-room coffee makers and a complimentary morning newspaper. An outdoor pool is open seasonally.

BED & BREAKFAST ACCOMMODATIONS

Thirty private homes, all historic properties (1750–1900) in Old Town Alexandria, offer English-style (owner lives in the house) B&B accommodations under the aegis of Mr. E. J. Mansmann, **Princely Bed & Breakfast Ltd.,** 819 Prince Street, Alexandria, VA 22314 (tel. 703/683-2159). Best time to call for reservations is Monday through Friday between 10am and 6pm. Rooms are nicely furnished, some with antiques and fireplaces, and cost $75 to $80, plus tax, per room per night. There's a $10 surcharge on those rates if you stay only 1 night.

The **Bed & Breakfast League/Sweet Dreams & Toast,** P.O. Box 9490, Washington, DC 20016 (tel. 202/363-7767), has several reasonably priced accommodations in Alexandria. Hosts are encouraged (though not required) to offer such niceties as fresh-baked muffins for breakfast. The accommodations are all screened, and guest reports are given serious consideration. Rates range from $30 to $60 single,

$45 to $70 double. There's a booking fee of $10, and a 2-night minimum stay is required.

WHERE TO DINE

In addition to its historic attractions, Alexandria has many fine restaurants, with fare ranging from haute cuisine to traditional southern cooking.

EXPENSIVE

LA BERGERIE, 218 N. Lee St. Tel. 703/683-1007.
   Cuisine: FRENCH. **Reservations:** Required.
$ Prices: Appetizers $6.50–$10; entrees $19–$24. AE, CB, DC, DISC, MC, V.
   Open: Lunch Mon–Sat 11:30am–2:30pm; dinner Mon–Sat 6–10pm.
Alexandria's fanciest restaurant features Basque specialties in a fittingly provincial setting with crystal chandeliers and oil paintings of the Pyrenées countryside on exposed brick walls. Plush royal-blue and sienna leather furnishings and white-linened tables, each adorned with a pink rose in a silver vase, add an elegant note. Exquisite desserts and a large floral arrangement grace an antique dresser up front, and there are many hanging and potted plants. Lunch fare includes hors d'oeuvres of pâté, escargots, and salmon terrine with green peppercorns; main courses of chicken in white wine and filet of fresh sole sautéed with apples. Dinner entrees include salmon en croûte, swordfish with ginger and scallions, or pheasant. Fresh raspberry soufflé is a delicious finish.

TWO-NINETEEN, 219 King St. Tel. 703/549-1141.
   Cuisine: AMERICAN/CREOLE. **Reservations:** Suggested, especially for dinner in the formal dining rooms.
$ Prices: Appetizers $5.95–$8.95; entrees $14.95–$23.95. AE, DC, DISC, MC, V.
   Open: Lunch Mon–Sat 11:30am–5pm; dinner Sun–Thurs 5–10:30pm, Fri–Sat 5pm–midnight; brunch Sun 10am–5pm.
Two-Nineteen is comprised of three formal Victorian-like dining rooms and a basement rathskellar, the Bayou Room. Crystal chandeliers, rose velvet upholstery, and a floral-patterned carpet highlight the elegant dining rooms. New Orleans cuisine is featured. Begin with oysters Bienville (baked in cream sauce with shrimp and crab) or crabmeat royale (with artichoke bottoms and hollandaise sauce). Seafood entrees include blackened gulf fish with blue crab claws, poisson en papillote, and seafood-stuffed rainbow trout. Other specialties are filet mignon and breast of duck served in a sauce of grapes and sweet sausage with New Orleans "dirty" rice.
   In the Bayou Room you'll find many of the same items featured upstairs, plus sandwiches and salads. The setting is highly atmospheric, with stone and brick walls, oak beams, a leaded-glass and oak bar, and a ceiling that's plastered with a collection of business cards from all over the country.

MODERATE

BILBO BAGGINS, 208 Queen St. Tel. 703/683-0300.
   Cuisine: AMERICAN. **Reservations:** Suggested, especially for dinner on weekends.
$ Prices: Appetizers $4.50–$7.95; entrees $13.95–$17.95. AE, CB, DC, MC, V.
   Open: Lunch daily 11:30am–2:30pm; dinner daily 5:30–10:30pm.
Named for a character in Tolkien's *The Hobbit,* this charming two-story restaurant offers fresh homemade fare. The downstairs area has rustic wide-plank floors,

wood-paneled walls, oak tables, and a brick oven centerpiece. Upstairs there's another dining room with stained-glass windows and seating on old church pews. It adjoins a skylit wine bar with windows overlooking Queen Street treetops. Candlelit at night, it becomes an even cozier setting. The eclectic menu changes daily to reflect seasonal specialties, but lunch entrees ($5.95 to $7.95) usually include quiche Lorraine, tortellini pesto, and spinach/bacon/mushroom salad. At dinner, we've enjoyed entrees like salmon topped with crabmeat and red and black caviar and lamb chops brushed with Dijon mustard and sautéed in breadcrumbs. An extensive wine list is available (32 boutique wines are offered by the glass), as are all bar drinks and excellent homemade desserts like steamed dark-chocolate bread pudding topped with sliced bananas.

CHART HOUSE, 1 Cameron St. Tel. 703/684-5080.

Cuisine: AMERICAN. **Reservations:** Advised.

$ **Prices:** Appetizers $3.95–$6.25; entrees $14.45–$21.95; Sun brunch $16.95. AE, CB, DC, DISC, MC, V.

Open: Dinner Mon–Thurs 5–10:15pm, Fri 5–11pm, Sat 4–11pm, Sun 4–10pm; brunch Sun 10am–2pm.

The Chart House, on Alexandria's waterfront, enjoys a unique perch on the dock, giving diners a view of the Potomac. Under a soaring cathedral ceiling, the interior is decidedly tropical, sparked by brilliant hues of green, turquoise, pink, and purple, with rattan furniture, potted palms, and a copper-covered salad bar. Straightforward American fare includes steaks, prime rib, and seafood, supplemented by daily specials. All entrees come with freshly baked squaw and sourdough breads and unlimited salad-bar selections. For dessert, try the house specialty—mud pie, Kona coffee ice cream in a Oreo cookie crust, topped with fudge, whipped cream, and diced almonds.

GADSBY'S TAVERN, 138 N. Royal St., at Cameron St. Tel. 703/548-1288.

Cuisine: AMERICAN. **Reservations:** Advised.

$ **Prices:** Appetizers $2.95–$6.25; entrees $13.50–$21.50; Publick Table fixed-price dinner $25. CB, DC, DISC, MC, V.

Open: Lunch Mon–Sat 11:30am–3pm; dinner Mon–Sat 5:30–10pm; brunch Sun 11am–3pm. Publick Table, Sun–Mon at 8pm (some Sun at 5:30pm).

In the spirit of history, pass through the portals where Washington reviewed his troops for the last time and eat at the famous Gadsby's Tavern, where the period furnishings, wood-plank floors, fireplace, and gaslight-style lamps re-create an authentic Colonial atmosphere. You'll dine off the same kind of pewter and china plates our ancestors used, and waiters and waitresses are appropriately costumed. The coachyard serves as an outdoor dining area. All the fare is homemade, including the Sally Lunn bread baked daily. Lunch (entrees $6.50 to $8.50) might consist of an appetizer of shrimp and clams in puff pastry, chicken roasted on an open fire served with fried potatoes, and a dessert of buttermilk pie. In winter, warm yourself with drinks like hot buttered rum and Martha's Remedy—coffee, cocoa, and brandy. At dinner, entrees usually include roast turkey, crabcakes, stuffed flounder, and a colonial game pie.

A special offering at Gadsby's is the "Publick Table," a bountiful 18th-century feast consisting of a savory first course, two entrees, two seasonal vegetables, English trifle, coffee or tea, and a choice of port or madeira. This is more than just a meal—it's a full evening, complete with period entertainment, singing, and toasts.

GERANIO, 722 King St. Tel. 703/548-0088.

Cuisine: ITALIAN. **Reservations:** Recommended on weekends.

$ **Prices:** Appetizers $4.95–$5.75; entrees $10.25–$14.25. AE, DC, MC, V.

Open: Lunch Mon–Fri 11:30am–2:30pm; dinner Mon–Sat 6–10:30pm, Sun 5:30–9:30pm.

⭐ Romantic country Italian atmosphere is the keynote of Geranio, with its pretty tile floors, hanging plants, hand-decorated plates, Italian paintings on white walls, and inviting fireplace. Pink-clothed tables are set with nosegays of fresh flowers, and soft lighting emanates from brass candelabras. Lunches are extremely reasonable, especially the pastas, which are just $5.95 and come with soup of the day or salad. In the evening, begin with a selection from the antipasti table. Dinner entrees include large grilled prawns in butter, garlic, and parsley; fresh tuna steak with capers; and chicken in green-olive and mushroom sauce. The dessert list offers many temptations—a luscious tartufo, fresh raspberries, and mud pie, among them.

LE REFUGE, 127 N. Washington St. Tel. 703/548-4661.

Cuisine: FRENCH. **Reservations:** Recommended, especially at dinner.

$ **Prices:** Appetizers $2.50–$4.50; entrees $13.95–$16.50; early-bird dinner $15.95. AE, CB, DC, MC, V.

Open: Lunch Mon–Sat 11:30am–2:30pm; dinner Mon–Sat 5:30–10pm (early-bird dinner 5:30–7pm).

⭐ There's a model of the Eiffel Tower in the bowfronted window of this charming little restaurant to guide you to one of the best-kept dining secrets in Alexandria. The intimate setting is typically French—stucco walls adorned with wine labels and provincial ceramics, bentwood chairs, black leather ⓢ banquettes, and tables covered with beige-and-brown napery. The three-course early-bird dinner is a great buy: It includes soup or salad; fresh catch of the day, leg of lamb, or calf's liver; and crème brûlée or peach Melba for dessert. At lunch there's usually a fresh quiche, and, sometimes, bouillabaisse. There's an excellent veal in cream-brandy-mushroom sauce on the regular dinner menu, as well as fresh seafood, chicken, and beef selections.

THE WAREHOUSE, 214 King St. Tel. 703/683-6868.

Cuisine: AMERICAN. **Reservations:** Recommended.

$ **Prices:** Appetizers $4.95–$6.95; entrees $12.95–$19.95. AE, DC, MC, V.

Open: Mon–Thurs 11am–10:30pm, Fri–Sat 11am–11pm, Sun 5–9:30pm.

⭐ The Warehouse is popular with locals, possibly because one wall of this cheerful spot is covered with pastel caricatures of Alexandria leaders. The other walls are a deep green, forming a clubby background for prints of Old Town. Green leather upholstered bentwood chairs, and deep-green cloths set with white china and adorned with fresh flowers further enhance the cozy ambience. At lunch, try the Light Horse Harry Lee, an all-lump-crabcake sandwich served with your choice of fries, cole slaw, or potato salad. Lunch entrees—seafood, poultry, salads—range from $7.50 to $12.95. At dinner, a good beginning is blue crab claws with mustard sauce. Follow with New Orleans blackened fish or spicy pecan crusted chicken. Desserts are all recommendable, particularly Mae's pecan pie, with ice cream.

INEXPENSIVE

FISH MARKET, 105 King St., at Union St. Tel. 703/836-5676.

Cuisine: SEAFOOD.

$ **Prices:** Appetizers $1.95–$4.75; entrees $11.95–$14.50. AE, MC, V.

Open: Sun–Thurs 11:15am–1am, Fri–Sat 11:15am–2am (kitchen closes at midnight).

⭐ So popular is the Fish Market that its original seven dining rooms were not ample to contain potential patrons, so it expanded to include the building next door. The original corner location is an over-200-year-old warehouse, with terra-cotta tile floors, exposed brick and stucco walls adorned with nautical antiques, copper pots suspended over a fireplace, copper-topped bars, and saloon doors. The newer Sunquest Room is bright and sunny, with light streaming in through floor-to-ceiling windows; its white walls are graced with musical instruments. At lunch you might have a crabcake sandwich, seafood stew, or a platter of fried oysters. The same menu is available at dinner, when platters cost $2 more. There's live entertainment—ragtime piano and sing-along every night in the downstairs piano bar, the upstairs Main Dining Room, and the Sunquest Room.

EAST WIND, 809 King St. Tel. 703/836-1515.
Cuisine: VIETNAMESE. **Reservations:** Suggested.
$ Prices: Appetizers $4.95–$5.50; entrees $9.50–$14.95 AE, CB, DC, MC, V.
Open: Lunch Mon–Fri 11:30am–2:30pm; dinner Mon–Thurs 6–10pm, Fri–Sat 5:30–10:30pm, Sun 5:30–9:30pm.

The decor of this Vietnamese restaurant is very appealing: Sienna stucco and knotty-pine-paneled walls are adorned with works of talented Vietnamese artist Minh Nguyen. There are planters of greenery, a lovely floral arrangement on each table, and a large floral display up front. An East Wind lunch might begin with an appetizer of cha gio (delicate Vietnamese eggrolls) or a salad of shredded chicken and vegetables mixed with fish sauce. One of our favorite entrees is bo dun—beef tenderloin strips marinated in wine, honey, and spices, rolled in fresh onions, and broiled on bamboo skewers. Also excellent is grilled lemon chicken or charcoal-broiled shrimp and scallops served on rice vermicelli.

BUDGET

BREAD AND CHOCOLATE, 611 King St. Tel. 703/548-0992.
Cuisine: CONTINENTAL.
$ Prices: Breakfast $3.20–$5.45; lunch or dinner less than $8. MC, V.
Open: Mon–Sat 7am–7pm, Sun 8am–5pm.

Modeled after a Swiss *konditerei,* this cheerful place has a counter up front displaying an array of fresh-baked breads, croissants, napoleons, chocolate truffle cakes, Grand Marnier cakes, Bavarian fruit tarts, and other goodies. The interior features folk-art prints on white walls lit by gallery lights. At breakfast you can get a café mocha and an almond croissant or opt for a 3-minute egg with a selection of cheeses and a basket of bread. The rest of the day, entrees like quiche Lorraine, baker's salad (like a chef salad), and a fresh fruit plate with brie are served with fresh breads.

DELI ON THE STRAND, 211 The Strand. Tel. 703/548-7222.
Cuisine: AMERICAN.
$ Prices: Sandwiches $1.95–$4.50. AE, MC, V.
Open: Mon–Thurs 8am–8pm, Fri–Sat 8am–9pm, Sun 8am–7pm.

Buy the fixings for a picnic at the Deli on the Strand. They bake bread on the premises, so the aroma is divine, and you can get reasonably priced cold-cut sandwiches, as well as croissants, muffins, and, on weekends, bagels. Also available are luscious home-made salads, cheeses, beer, and wine. There are a few picnic tables outside.

HARD TIMES CAFE, 1404 King St. Tel. 703/683-5340.
Cuisine: AMERICAN.
$ Prices: Entrees $3.95–$5.25. MC, V.
Open: Mon–Thurs 11am–10pm, Fri–Sat 11am–11pm, Sun 4–10pm.

Like its Arlington counterpart, this authentically Texas-style chili parlor features award-winning "bowls of red." At lunch or dinner you can get a big bowl of Texas, Cincinnati, or vegetarian chili with or without beans and including a big hunk of cornbread. Available extras are cheese (parmesan or Cheddar), chopped onions, and side dishes of steak fries cooked with the skins and fried onion rings. For dessert there's pecan-walnut or apple crumb pie. The ambience is Old Southwest, with roomy oak booths, country music on the jukebox, and a laid-back young staff in jeans and T-shirts.

SHOPPING

Old Town has hundreds of charming boutiques, antique stores, and gift shops selling everything from souvenir T-shirts to 18th-century reproductions. Plan to spend a fair amount of time browsing in between visits to historic sites. A guide to antiques stores is available at the Visitor Center. Here are some suggestions to get you started.

ON KING STREET

THE TINY DWELLING, 1510 King St. Tel. 703/548-1223.
   This charming shop is filled with dollhouses, furnishings, and accessories. There are little framed paintings, wallpapers, floor tiles, rugs, tiny electrical supplies, beautiful porcelain sinks and tubs, and more.

ANGIE'S DOLL BOUTIQUE, 1114 King St. Tel. 703/683-2807.
   New and antique dolls of all races and nationalities are featured, along with handcrafted dolls, modern collectibles, clothing, and clothing patterns.

THE WINTERTHUR MUSEUM STORE, 207 King St. Tel. 703/684-6092.
   Most appropriately located in a restored 1810 brick town house, the store is named for the magnificent country estate of horticulturist Henry Francis du Pont, which is now a renowned museum of American decorative arts in Delaware. This first off-site venture of the museum is a delightful browse, including the back garden, which features all sorts of garden plants and ornaments. You'll come across fine reproductions from the Winterthur collections, including lamps, prints, ceramics, brassware, jewelry, garden furniture, and statuary.

SMALL MALL, 118 King St. Tel. 703/683-3555.
   This is a little warren of shops (about 11 of them), the most intriguing of which is Serendipity, featuring traditional American craft items (much stenciling equipment), porcelain dolls, folk art, and suchlike.

ON CAMERON STREET

JOHN DAVY TOYS, 301 Cameron St. Tel. 703/683-0079.
   John Davy Toys has a lovely selection of dolls, books, games, building things, and puppets.

GRANNY'S PLACE and GRANNY'S PLACE TWO, 303 and 309 Cameron St. Tel. 703/549-0119.
   These adjoining stores specialize in imported and domestic children's clothing (up to size 14 for boys and girls) and wooden toys. Many excellent gifts for toddlers here.

LA CUISINE, 323 Cameron St. Tel. 703/836-4435.
   A delight for those who can pore endlessly over copperware, cookbooks, terrines, and cooking implements.

GOSSYPIA, 325 Cameron St. Tel. 703/836-6969.
   Herein, an exquisite line of Mexican and South American wedding dresses, Guatemalan and Mexican masks, and beautiful clothing and jewelry from India, Central America, and Thailand.

ON SOUTH UNION STREET

THE CHRISTMAS ATTIC, 125 S. Union St. Tel. 703/548-2829.
   Christmas decorations and gifts are sold year round, as well as accoutrements of other holidays in their proper months.

CARRIAGE HOUSE, 215 S. Union St.

This very pleasant mall contains about six shops. Do check out **Rocky Road to Kansas** (tel. 703/683-0116) where more than 100 traditional, new, and antique quilts are on display along with country accessories. Also notable is the aromatic **Olde Town Coffee, Tea & Spice** (tel. 703/683-0856), which in addition to about 40 kinds of coffee and 60 kinds of tea has gourmet imports like German cornichons, Swiss vegetable pâté, and cordial balls with various liqueurs in the center.

ON NORTH LEE STREET

CRILLEY WAREHOUSE MALL, 218 N. Lee St.

Another minimall, Crilley houses about eight shops on two levels in a turn-of-the-century bakery. In later years the building served as a storehouse, hence the name. Among the most interesting of its shops are **Monday's Child** (tel. 703/548-3505) featuring gorgeous clothing for children and **Slightly Laced** (tel. 703/836-2666) for French brassieres, satin remarqué loungewear, hand-embroidered petticoats from Madeira, and other lovely underthings.

ON PRINCE STREET

OLDE TOWNE GEMSTONES, 6 Prince St. Tel. 703/836-1377.

Some of the fossils you can buy here are 500-million-year-old specimens. There's also a wide-ranging collection of minerals, gemstones, petrified wood, and objets d'art and jewelry made from them. Banded-agate clocks are a big item.

EVENING ENTERTAINMENT

King Street restaurants are the center of Alexandria's nightlife. Especially noteworthy are **Two-Nineteen,** 219 King Street (tel. 703/549-1141), which features live jazz every night in the Basin Street Lounge; **Murphy's,** 713 King Street (tel. 703/548-1717), where live bands lead Irish and Welsh sing-alongs nightly; and **Henry Africa,** 607 King Street (tel. 703/549-4010), featuring dancing and jazz Tuesday through Sunday evenings. For bluegrass, country, and folk, head out to **Birchmere,** 3901 Mount Vernon Avenue (tel. 703/549-5919), a showcase for nationally known stars.

3. HUNT COUNTRY

Leesburg: 35 miles NW of Washington, 115 miles NW of Richmond;
Middleburg: 45 miles W of Washington, 95 miles NW of Richmond

GETTING THERE   By Car   Leesburg: From the Capital Beltway, I-495, take Route 7W to Leesburg. **Middleburg:** From I-495, follow Route 50W into town. Route 15S from Leesburg intersects with Route 50W just east of Middleburg.

ESSENTIALS   For information about Hunt Country, contact the **Loudoun County Information Office,** 108-D South Street SE, Leesburg, VA 22075 (tel. 703/777-0519, or toll free 800/752-6118). The **tourist office** is in Market Station, a renovated complex of shops and restaurants. There's also an **information center** in Middleburg, in the Pink House, Madison Street, Middleburg, VA 22117 (tel. 703/687-8888).

The colonial tradition of foxhunting continues today in Virginia's Hunt Country, a lush green landscape studded with expansive horse farms, elegant plantations, picturesque villages, historic country inns, and fine restaurants.

LEESBURG

WHAT TO SEE & DO

Leesburg is a good base for exploring Hunt Country. Its architecture ranges from pre-Revolutionary to late 19th century. The present brick **Court House,** 10 North King Street, built in 1894, is a mix of Roman Revival and classical elements. The **Loudoun Museum,** 16 West Loudoun Street (tel. 703/777-7427), open Monday through Saturday from 10am to 5pm and on Sunday from 1 to 5pm, is a small regional museum housing memorabilia about the county from pioneer days; be sure to pick up a walking-tour brochure that will guide you around Leesburg's quaint streets. The little circle of stone markers in **Ball's Bluff Cemetery** and the adjacent **Civil War battlefield** are located at the edge of the Potomac River in northeast Leesburg.

Not far from town are two historic plantations. **Oatlands,** Route 15 (tel. 703/777-3174), is an 1803 Greek Revival mansion with a Corinthian portico and beautiful gardens. About 6 miles south of Leesburg, it's open April 1 to December 26, Monday through Saturday from 10am to 5pm and on Sunday from 1 to 5pm; admission is $5 for adults, $4 for seniors and children (under 12 free). On the 1,200-acre estate of **Morven Park** (tel. 703/777-2414) are the Museum of Hounds and Hunting and the Carriage Museum, and there are lovely nature trails to explore. To reach Morven Park, take Route 7 west 1 mile from Leesburg, then turn right onto Morven Park Road. The estate is open Memorial Day to Labor Day, Tuesday through Saturday from 10am to 5pm and on Sunday from 1 to 5pm; in May and October, on weekends only. Admission is $4 for adults, $3.75 for seniors, and $2 for children.

Nearby Attractions

WATERFORD VILLAGE, Tel. 703/882-3018, or toll free 800/752-6118.
The enchanting hamlet of Waterford, with numerous 18th- and 19th-century buildings, is a National Historic Landmark. Surrounded by a lush landscape of 1,420 acres, its vistas of farmland and pasture unfold behind barns and churches. You'll feel as though you've entered an English country scene painted by Constable. A Quaker from Pennsylvania, Amos Janney, built a mill here in the 1740s. Other Quakers followed, and by 1840 most of the buildings now on Main Street and Second Street were in place. In 1870 the railroad bypassed Waterford; and because the pace of change slowed, much of the town was preserved.
Open: Daily 24 hours.
Admission: Free. **Directions:** From Leesburg, take Route 7 west, turn right onto Route 9, then follow Route 662 (right turn) into Waterford. This is one of the most scenic drives in the area.

HARPERS FERRY NATIONAL HISTORIC PARK, Harpers Ferry, W.Va. Tel. 304/535-6298.
The site of John Brown's raid is a fascinating excursion. It seems ironic that this beautiful spot, at the confluence of the broad Shenandoah and Potomac rivers, was the scene of the awful events that presaged the war. Brown, born in Torrington, Conn., in 1800, was an ardent foe of slavery. He dedicated his life to its destruction after his friend, abolitionist editor Elijah Lovejoy, was murdered by a mob in 1837. After the Dred Scott decision—wherein the Supreme Court decreed that slaves were property, and Congress could not deprive slave owners of their property—Brown led a raid into Missouri and freed 11 slaves. He then came to Harpers Ferry, to raid its arsenal for weapons he planned to use to free more slaves. Brown arrived on July 3, 1859, and gathered his forces in a nearby farmhouse. On October 16 he and his men moved to take possession of the arsenal. On October 17 at 11pm, 90 U.S. Marines, under the command of Col. Robert E. Lee, entered the arsenal and demanded the raiders' surrender. The next morning, Col. J. E. B. Stuart

HUNT COUNTRY

0 — 12 mi / 19.2 km
N

ACCOMMODATIONS:
- Laurel Brigade Inn **1**
- Little River Inn **2**
- Norris House Inn **3**
- Red Fox Inn & Mosby's Tavern **4**
- Windsor House **5**

DINING:
- Black Walnut ◆1
- Coach Stop Restaurant ◆2
- The Green Tree ◆3
- Tuscarora Mill ◆4
- Upper Crust Bakery ◆5

ATTRACTIONS:
- Ball's Bluff Cemetery **1**
- Harpers Ferry National Historical Park **2**
- Meredyth Vineyard **3**
- Morven Park **4**
- Oatlands **5**
- Piedmont Vineyards **6**
- Waterford Village **8**

twice delivered surrender demands to Brown. A storming party of 12 marines then smashed the door and captured Brown and the surviving raiders. Brown was tried for treason and hanged in Charles Town on December 2.

Today the National Park Service owns and operates the **Harpers Ferry Historic Area,** where many original buildings are open, including a restored dry-goods store, blacksmith shop, and armorer's house. The **Visitors Center** and parking lot are half a mile away. You can hop a free shuttle bus to the Historic Area, where the **John Brown Museum** vividly recounts the story of the raid with photographs, documents, and a slide show.

Admission: $5 per car.

Open: Daily 8am–6pm. **Closed:** Christmas Day. **Directions:** From Leesburg, it's about 12 miles to Harpers Ferry. Take Route 7 west, turning right at Route 9. Take another right at Route 671. Turn left at the intersection of Route 340, and go west to Harpers Ferry.

SULLY PLANTATION, Chantilly. Tel. 703/437-1794.

Sully Plantation, a two-story clapboard farmhouse, was built in 1793 by Richard Bland Lee (brother of Light Horse Harry Lee and a member of the Virginia Assembly) for his wife, Elizabeth Collins. The original plantation was situated on more than 3,000 acres and consisted of a main house, dairy, smokehouse, kitchen building, and slave quarters.

Today the house is furnished with antiques of the Federal period and looks much as it would have during the 1795–1842 era. Mahogany furniture, Wilton carpets, and imported silver approximate the style in which the Lees lived. Living-history programs further re-create the era.

Admission: $3 adults, $1 seniors and children under 16.

Open: Mid-Mar to Dec, Wed–Mon 11am–5pm; Jan to mid-Mar, Sat–Sun 11am–4pm. **Closed:** New Year's, Thanksgiving, and Christmas days. **Directions:** Sully is on Route 28, three-quarters of a mile north of Route 50, 9 miles south of Route 7.

WHERE TO STAY

Moderate

NORRIS HOUSE INN, 108 Loudoun St., Leesburg, VA 22075. Tel. 703/777-1806. 5 rms (none with bath), 2 suites (both with bath).

$ Rates (including breakfast): $70–$112 single or double. No credit cards.

A charming 2½-story red-brick 1806 home, Norris House was renovated in the Eastlake style in the Victorian era. Its facade is bedecked with black shutters and a white-columned entrance porch, the whole capped by three pedimented dormer windows. The common rooms include two parlors: one with a rose-colored Sheraton sofa, green-painted woodwork and window trim, and an oak fireplace; the other a formal dining room where a full breakfast is served. The breakfast might feature fresh fruit or juice, quiche, home-baked muffins, and coffee or tea. Bedroom furnishings are an exquisite mix of antiques. All share baths and have light attractive color schemes, pretty quilts, fireplaces, stenciled fireplace surrounds, four-poster beds (some with lace canopies), rockers, wicker pieces, and framed botanical prints on the walls.

Inexpensive

LAUREL BRIGADE INN, 20 W. Market St., Leesburg, VA 22075. Tel. 703/777-1010. 6 rms (all with bath). A/C

$ Rates: $30 single; $50–$75 double. No credit cards. **Closed:** Jan 2–Feb 13.

To secure a room at this very popular inn, reserve at least 4 to 6 weeks in advance for weekends, a week to 10 days otherwise. The history of this two-story Federal period charmer goes back to 1766, when town records show that a tavern operator named

John Miller became the owner of an "ordinary" on this lot. (An "ordinary" was the colonial equivalent of a British pub.) In 1817 the hotel was purchased by Eleanor and Henry Peers, and it became the Peers Hotel. The hotel's kitchen was so highly regarded that it was chosen to prepare the food for the collation on the courthouse green when Lafayette visited Leesburg in 1825. In 1946 the building became the Laurel Brigade Inn, named for the Civil War brigade led by local Col. Elijah V. White. Rooms today are pleasantly furnished with wing chairs, chenille spreads, and hooked rugs, and some have fireplaces. Although there are no phones in the bedrooms, a pay phone is in the lobby. Rooms facing the back overlook a lovely garden stretching back to a gazebo that's been the setting for weddings.

Dining/Entertainment: The Laurel Brigade Restaurant is open for lunch and dinner. At lunch the price of the entree ($8.75 to $9.75) brings you a full meal: appetizer, an entree (perhaps chicken pot pie, crabcakes, or grilled pork chop with spiced apple), vegetable and hot rolls, a dessert such as apple dumpling with hard sauce, and coffee or tea. Or you can order an à la carte soup, sandwich, or salad at lunch. Dinner is fixed price ($13.50 to $19), featuring entrees like crab imperial, baked scallops, and strip steak.

WHERE TO DINE

Moderate

THE GREEN TREE, 15 S. King St., Leesburg. Tel. 703/777-7246.
   Cuisine: AMERICAN. **Reservations:** Recommended, especially for dinner on weekends.
$ **Prices:** Appetizers $3.25–$7.95; entrees $9.25–$19.95. AE, CB, DC, MC, V.
   Open: Lunch Mon–Sat 11:30am–3pm; dinner daily 5–9:30pm; brunch Sun 11:30am–3:30pm.

Not only is the decor Colonial at this downtown restaurant, but most of the dishes are made from faithfully reproduced 18th-century recipes gathered from the Library of Congress and the National Archives. Recipes for green herb soup, Sally Lunn bread, roast prime rib with Yorkshire pudding, and rum and black-walnut pie are among the stellar results of this research. Both dining rooms have wide-plank floors, harvest dining tables, ladderback chairs, brass chandeliers, working fireplaces, and walls hung with hunting prints. Servers are in period dress as well. A full dinner could start with cabbage pie or a sampling platter of smoked-sausage pie, seafood, mushroom canapes, pâté with rusks, and English beer cheese. Among the entrees are rabbit fricassee, crab, roast chicken, and broiled brook trout. For dessert—hot bread pudding with rum sauce. There's a small wine list.

TUSCARORA MILL, 203 Harrison St., Market Station, Leesburg. Tel. 703/771-9300.
   Cuisine: AMERICAN. **Reservations:** Recommended, especially at dinner.
$ **Prices:** Appetizers $3.95–$8.50; entrees $15.50–$19.95. AE, MC, V.
   Open: Lunch daily 11:30am–2:30pm; dinner daily 5:30–9:30pm; café daily 2:30–5:30pm.

Housed in a renovated turn-of-the-century mill, this simpatico restaurant has a casual ambience—a combination of light jazz music and a decor utilizing flourishing plants suspended from wood-beamed high ceilings, skylights, pretty paisley tablecloths, big bouquets of flowers, and black wrought-iron street lamps. It's one of the six historic buildings renovated in 1985 to make up Market Station. Red metal exterior siding, grain bins, old belts and pulleys, and a grain scale evoke the mill's past. Local businesspeople and visiting Washingtonians fill the tables at lunch, both in the cozy Café at the front of the restaurant, and the sunny, spacious back room. Delicious luncheon fare ($7 to $10) includes a grilled marinated swordfish sandwich on a kaiser roll with fries, beef stew, and sautéed shrimp, scallops, and salmon over fettuccine.

Begin dinner with lobster and crab with three caviars and dill in light pastry, duck pâté with pistachios and green peppercorns, or baked oysters with spinach. Follow with an entree of smoked tuna, stir-fried chicken breast with Oriental vegetables, or grilled salmon with mushrooms, hearts of palm, hazelnuts, and radicchio served with fried spinach. A la carte vegetables such as braised endive and baked tomatoes with olive oil and garlic are tempting extras. The house special dessert is chocolate soufflé.

MIDDLEBURG

Middleburg likes to call itself the unofficial capital of the Hunt Country. Home to those interested in horses and their breeding, this historic hamlet, founded in 1731, is included on the National Register of Historic Villages. Note the small Gothic Revival **Emmanuel Episcopal Church** (1842), at Liberty Street; it was the first example of mid-19th-century architecture in the village.

Adding to the area's interest are a number of wineries. Just 5 minutes south of Middleburg is the **Meredyth Vineyard,** on Route 628 (tel. 703/687-6277). A beautiful setting in the Bull Run Mountains distinguishes the 56 acres of this farm winery. There are tours daily from 10am to 5pm (except New Year's, Thanksgiving, and Christmas days). There's a picnic area (see Black Walnut and Upper Crust food shops described below for picnic fare) and gift shop. **Piedmont Vineyards,** on Route 626 about 3 miles south of town (tel. 703/687-5528), was formerly a dairy farm; its barn now houses a winery, tasting room, and gift shop. Tours are given daily from 10am to 4pm (open major Monday holidays).

NEARBY ATTRACTIONS

MANASSAS NATIONAL BATTLEFIELD PARK, 6511 Sudley Rd. (Rte. 234), Manassas. Tel. 703/754-7107.

The first massive clash of the Civil War took place here on July 21, 1861. A well-equipped, but poorly trained Union army of 35,000 under Gen. Irvin McDowell had marched from Washington, where cheering crowds expected them to return victorious within several days. Most of the men were 90-day volunteers, who had little knowledge of what war would mean. Their goal was Richmond, and to meet the oncoming army, Gen. P. G. T. Beauregard deployed his Confederate troops along a stream known as Bull Run to the north and west of the important railroad junction of Manassas. The 10 hours of heavy fighting on the first day stunned soldiers on both sides, and the violence and destruction they encountered shattered their hopes that the war would end quickly. McDowell's plan was to feign an attack at the Stone Bridge over Bull Run, but really advance his forces around the Confederate left. However, his inexperienced troops moved too slowly. Confederate Col. Nathan Evans, commanding at the Stone Bridge, realized the ploy and rushed forces to meet McDowell's lead unit. The fighting culminated on Henry Hill, where newly arrived Southern troops put McDowell's tired and discouraged army to flight. The defeat became a rout, but the Confederates were too disorganized to follow the Union troops, which historians later argued could have resulted in an even more decisive victory, perhaps even ending the war, for the South.

Union and Confederate armies met again on the fields of Manassas in August 1862. The Second Battle of Manassas secured Gen. Robert E. Lee's place in history as his 55,000 men soundly defeated the Union army under Gen. John Pope.

The two battles are commemorated at the 5,000-acre battlefield park. Start your tour here at the visitors center, where a museum, a 13-minute slide show, and a battle map program tell the story of the battle. There are a number of self-guided walking tours that highlight Henry Hill, Stone Bridge, and the other critical areas of the First Manassas battlefield. A 12-mile driving tour covers the sites of Second Manassas, which raged over a much larger area.

Admission: $1 adults, free for seniors over 62 and children under 16.

Open: Summer, daily 8:30am–6pm; winter, daily 8:30am–5pm. **Directions:** From Middleburg (about 11 miles), take Route 50 east, turn right onto Route 15 south, turn left at Route 234, and continue southeast to Manassas.

WHERE TO STAY

RED FOX INN & MOSBY'S TAVERN, 2 E. Washington St. (P.O. Box 385), Middleburg, VA 22117. Tel. 703/687-6301, or toll free 800/223-1728. Fax 703/687-3338. 19 rms and suites (all with bath). A/C TV TEL

$ Rates (including continental breakfast): $125–$225 single or double. AE, DC, MC, V.

The historic Red Fox Inn in the center of Middleburg maintains the romantic charm of early Virginia in its original 1728 stone structure. Later additions are the Stray Fox Inn building, so called because a misfired cannon ball struck its foundation in the Civil War, and the McConnell House Inn building. In the Red Fox are three rooms and three suites, all with wide-plank floors and 18th-century furnishings; several have working fireplaces. Rooms in the Stray Fox and McConnell also preserve a traditional character with hand-stenciled floors and walls, canopy beds, hooked rugs, and original fireplace mantels. Continental breakfast is served in the rooms, and terry bathrobes, bedside sweets, fresh flowers, and a morning Washington newspaper are extra amenities.

Dining/Entertainment: The Red Fox Inn restaurant occupies the first floor of the inn. It features a Hunt Country ambience—low beamed ceilings, pewter dishes, and equestrian prints lining the walls. The seasonal menu runs the gamut from pastas (such as angel hair with smoked salmon, smoked scallops, green onion, dill, and shiitake mushrooms) to dinner entrees ($16.50 to $19.50) like chicken breast stuffed with boursin cheese. Mosby's Tavern serves Mexican lunch/brunch and dinner.

WINDSOR HOUSE, 2 W. Washington St., Middleburg, VA 22117. Tel. 703/687-6800. 2 rms (without bath), 2 suites (with bath). A/C

$ Rates (including continental breakfast): $115–$225 single or double. MC, V.

Innkeeper Jacqueline Watson has transformed this 1824 building into an exquisite country inn. All the rooms are furnished with authentic period pieces collected over the years. The three-room Blue Suite has a luxurious bedroom, with a queen-size canopy bed that is made up with fine, imported white-on-white linens, a fainting couch, lady's writing desk, marble-top dresser, and working fireplace. Its cozy sitting room has a blue-and-white love seat and a spinning wheel, and its large bathroom features thick white towels on a warming rack, terry bathrobes, potpourri, and fine soaps and lotion. The Gold Suite is equally luxurious. Two cozy bedrooms, on the third floor, include the Rose Room, with a spindle bed, needlepoint sofa, and white wicker rocker; the other is furnished in white and pale-green wicker. Bedside sweets and a decanter of sherry are nice touches.

Dining/Entertainment: The three cozy dining rooms here, all with fireplaces, maintain a high standard of contemporary American and French cuisine at lunch and dinner. Among the entrees ($15 to $23) are such creative specialties as roast duck leg baked in puff pastry with spinach and wild mushrooms, served with sautéed duck breast in lingonberry sauce; angel-hair pasta with baby shrimp and parmesan cheese; and roast pheasant with mushroom sauce.

Nearby Accommodations

LITTLE RIVER INN, Rte. 50 (P.O. Box 116), Aldie, VA 22001. Tel. 703/327-6742. 5 rms (2 with bath), 2 cottages (with bath). A/C **Directions:** Aldie is on Route 50, about 5 miles east of Middleburg.

$ Rates (including breakfast): $80–$125; $210 for a house. MC, V.

The peaceful setting of this country inn is so appealing that it's almost worth coming to Aldie just to stay here. Farm animals, a small garden, and a patio are behind the main house, an early 19th-century farmhouse. The living room has polished, wide-plank floors; in front of the fireplace are two antique wing chairs and a sofa, all upholstered in Colonial print fabrics. Fresh flowers, a basket of magazines, and a few decorative pieces of china add warmth to the setting. Accommodations range from one room to a cottage of your own. The main house has five bedrooms, all charmingly furnished with antique pieces and pretty quilts; one has a working fireplace. Three small houses are also on the property, one a log cabin with a working stone fireplace; another, the Patent House, a small late 1700s domicile, also with a working fireplace. And Hill House (ca. 1870) sits on 2 acres of landscaped gardens and can be rented in its entirety, or the two bedrooms may be rented separately. Breakfast includes such home-baked goodies as poppyseed muffins and giant popovers filled with cooked apples, raisins, and cinnamon sauce.

WHERE TO DINE

In addition to the following recommendation, the Red Fox Inn and Windsor Inn (see "Where to Stay," above) have fine restaurants.

COACH STOP RESTAURANT, 4 E. Washington St., Middleburg. Tel. 703/687-5515.
   Cuisine: AMERICAN.
$ **Prices:** Appetizers $2.25–$7.50; entrees $10.50–$19.50. AE, CB, DC, MC, V.
   Open: Mon–Sat 7am–9pm, Sun 8am–9pm.
Locals flock here for good, old-fashioned American fare—everything from a delicious breakfast of Virginia country ham and eggs or creamed chipped beef to a dinner of honey-dipped fried chicken. Seating is at the counter, tables, and booths set with hunting-themed place mats and green napkins. Ceiling fans keep the breezes moving as you tuck into a hearty meal. Lunchtime sandwiches, including turkey, bacon, and avocado or a grilled Reuben, are served with french fries or pasta salad. Dinner entrees—comfort foods like roast turkey with stuffing and gravy or pork chops—are served with two vegetables.

FOR PICNICS

Before you set out on a day's excursion in Hunt Country, you may want to buy the fixings for a gourmet picnic at the **Black Walnut,** 20 East Washington Street (tel. 703/687-6833), or the **Upper Crust Bakery,** 2 North Pendleton Street (tel. 703/687-5666).

CHAPTER 5

ALONG THE POTOMAC

1. MOUNT VERNON
**2. WOODLAWN
   PLANTATION**
**3. OTHER POTOMAC
   ATTRACTIONS**

Though the riverside plantations described below date from colonial rather than Civil War times, they are the vast white-columned mansions with shady tree-lined drives you've always imagined. It's easy to picture Scarlett saying "fiddle-dee-dee" to Rhett Butler on the spacious lawns of Mount Vernon or Gunston Hall. These are the homes of the men who shaped our government and its institutions. To visit them is an education in early American thought, politics, sociology, art, architecture, fashion, and the decorative arts.

1. MOUNT VERNON

In 1784 George Washington wrote the Marquis de Lafayette, "I am become a private citizen on the banks of the Potomac, and under the shadow of my own Vine and my own Fig-tree, free from the bustle of a camp and the busy scenes of public life. . . . I am not only retired from all public employments, but I am retiring within myself; and shall be able to view the solitary walk, and tread the paths of private life with heartfelt satisfaction. . . ."

Alas, Washington's announcement of retirement to his beloved ancestral plantation home was premature. In 1787 he once again heeded the call to duty, presiding over the Constitutional Convention in Philadelphia. In 1789 he became the first President of the United States, and managed to visit Mount Vernon only once or twice a year during his 8-year term. It wasn't until 1797, 2 years before his death, that Washington was finally able to devote himself fully to the "tranquil enjoyments" of Mount Vernon.

The home and final resting place of George and Martha Washington has been one of America's most-visited shrines since the mid-19th century. For more than 100 years there's been an ongoing effort to locate and return the estate's scattered contents and memorabilia, thus enhancing its authentic appearance circa 1799.

GETTING THERE

There are several ways to get to Mount Vernon. From Arlington or Washington, D.C., you can take the **Tourmobile,** daily, April to October, at $16 for adults and $8 for children 3 to 11. Call 202/554-7950 for details.

By car it's a pleasant drive 14 miles south of Alexandria via the George Washington Parkway/Mount Vernon Memorial Highway.

You can also take either the Blue or Yellow Washington **Metro** line to Huntington and there catch the 11P bus to the entrance gate to Mount Vernon. Call 703/637-2437 for departure times.

TOURING THE ESTATE

A visit to Mount Vernon provides a unique glimpse into 18th-century plantation life. Washington's original estate contained five independent farms on which more than 200 slaves toiled. It was Washington's custom when in residence to ride daily about these farms, directing operations and planning for the future. These outlying farms no longer exist (Washington's will, which also freed his slaves, divided the land), but you will see the mansion and surrounding grounds—a New World version of an English country gentleman's estate.

There's no formal tour of Mount Vernon, but attendants stationed throughout the house and grounds provide explanatory commentary. The house itself—an outstanding example of Georgian architecture—is constructed of beveled pine painted to look like stone. You'll enter by way of the "large dining room" which contains the original chairs, Hepplewhite mahogany sideboards, and paintings. Step outside and enjoy the view that prompted Washington to declare, "No estate in United America is more pleasantly situated than this."

In the central hall (the social center of the house in Washington's day) hangs a key to the Bastille that Lafayette presented to Washington in 1790 via messenger Thomas Paine. Four adjoining rooms can be seen from the passage. The "little parlor" contains the English harpsichord of Martha Washington's granddaughter, Nelly Custis. In the "west parlor" you'll see Martha's china tea service laid out on the table. In the "small dining room," the sweetmeat course set up on the original mahogany dining table is based on a description of an actual Mount Vernon dinner in 1799. And the "downstairs bedroom," was used to accommodate the many overnight guests Washington mentions in his diary.

Continuing upstairs, you'll view five additional bedchambers, including the "Lafayette Room" named for its most distinguished occupant, and George and Martha's bedroom, the room in which Washington died.

Downstairs again, Washington's study contains its original globe, desk, and dressing table. It was from this room that Washington managed his estate and penned numerous letters of historic import.

The kitchen is in a separate building, one of several outbuildings, or "dependencies," on view. A museum on the property contains many interesting exhibits and memorabilia.

Allow at least 2 hours to tour the entire house and grounds. A detailed map is provided at the entrance. Best time to visit Mount Vernon is off-season, when the crowds are sparser. If you must visit in spring or summer, avoid weekends and holidays or resign yourself to very long lines. On Washington's Birthday, by the way (the federal holiday, not the actual date), admission is free and a wreath-laying ceremony is held at his tomb. Admission is $6 for adults, $5.50 for senior citizens, $3 for children 6 to 11 years old, free for under-6s. The house and grounds are open to the public from March 1 to October 31, daily from 9am to 5pm; till 4pm the rest of the year.

WHERE TO DINE

There are several dining options. At the entrance is a **snack bar** serving light fare, open daily from 9:30am to 5:30pm; there are picnic tables outside.

If you pack your own picnic, consider driving about a mile north on the George Washington Memorial Parkway to **Riverside Park,** where picnic tables overlook the Potomac.

MOUNT VERNON INN, Mount Vernon, Va. Tel. 703/780-0011.
   Cuisine: AMERICAN. **Reservations:** Suggested at dinner.
$ **Prices:** Appetizers $3.50–$5; entrees $12–$24; prix-fixe dinner $14. AE, MC, V.
   Open: Lunch Mon–Sat 11am–3:30pm, Sun 11:30am–4pm; dinner Mon–Sat
   5–9pm.

The Mount Vernon Inn, to the right of the snack bar at the entrance to the plantation, is a quaintly charming colonial-style restaurant complete with period furnishings and working fireplaces. At lunch, be sure to begin with an order of homemade peanut-and-chestnut soup. Entrees range from colonial pye (a crock of meat or fowl and garden vegetables with a puffed pastry top; $5.75) to a 20th-century fried-chicken-breast sandwich and fries ($5.75). There's a full bar, and premium wines are offered by the glass. At dinner, tablecloths, candlelight, and more expensive entrees make this a much plusher choice. There is, however, a fixed-price dinner option that includes soup or salad, entree, homemade breads, and dessert. Such a dinner might consist of broccoli-Cheddar soup, tenderloin medallions, and Bavarian parfait.

2. WOODLAWN PLANTATION

Continue your plantation sightseeing at Woodlawn (tel. 703/780-4000), just 3 miles west of Mount Vernon on Route 1.

   Originally a 2,000-acre part of the Mount Vernon estate (today some 130 acres remain), Woodlawn was a wedding gift from George Washington to his adopted daughter (and Martha's actual granddaughter), the beautiful Eleanor "Nelly" Parke Custis, and his nephew, Maj. Lawrence Lewis. The Lewises married in 1799 and moved into the house—designed by William Thornton, first architect of the Capitol—in 1802. They furnished it primarily with pieces from Mount Vernon and had trees cut away to afford views of that estate and the Potomac.

   Under the auspices of the National Trust for Historic Preservation, the restored mansion and its elegant formal gardens reflect many periods of history. Post-Lewis occupants included antislavery Quaker and Baptist settlers from the North (1846–89); New York City playwright Paul Kester (1901–05), and Elizabeth Sharpe of Pennsylvania (1905–25), who commissioned noted architect Waddy Wood to restore the house to a semblance of its original appearance. Finally, Sen. Oscar Underwood of Alabama and his wife, Bertha, retired here in 1924. The Underwood family occupied the house through 1948, retaining Waddy Wood to continue its restoration.

TOURING THE ESTATE

Allow at least an hour to see the house and grounds.

   Like Mount Vernon, Woodlawn has a regal "Lafayette Bedroom" named for its most famous guest. You'll also see additional bedchambers, two dining rooms, and the music room (where a recording of Nelly's music is played).

   The grounds, with nature trails designed by the National Audubon Society, are representative of many periods in the estate's history, and the gardens include the largest collection on the East Coast of 19th-century species of roses.

   Also on the premises are two other houses: **Grand View,** a house built about 100 yards from the mansion in 1858, and Frank Lloyd Wright's **Pope-Leighey House,** designed in 1940 for the Loren Pope family of Falls Church. In the path of highway construction, Pope-Leighey was rescued from demolition and brought to the Woodlawn grounds in 1964. The house, built of cypress, brick, and glass, was created as a prototype of well-designed architectural space for middle-income people. "The house of moderate cost," said Wright in 1938, "is not only America's major architectural problem but the problem most difficult for her major architects. . . ." In

1946 the house was purchased by a Mr. and Mrs. Robert A. Leighey, hence the double name. After living in the house for 17 years, the Leigheys donated to the National Trust both the house and the money to dismantle and move it.

Woodlawn and the Pope-Leighey House are open daily from 9:30am to 4:30pm. Thirty-minute tours of Woodlawn are given on the half hour. Grand View is not open to the public. All are closed New Year's, Thanksgiving, and Christmas days. Admission is $5 for adults, $3 for students and seniors (under 5, free), but a reduced-price combination ticket to both attractions is available. Admission may be higher during special events.

3. OTHER POTOMAC ATTRACTIONS

THE GRIST MILL

Mount Vernon (the part of it that later became Woodlawn) contained a grist mill that neighboring farmers used for grinding corn and wheat. In 1932 the Virginia Conservation Commission purchased part of the property known as Dogue Run Farm on which the mill and other buildings had been located. The site was excavated, and part of the original water wheel, the bearings for the wheel, part of the trundlehead, complete wheel buckets, and other articles were found.

Three miles west of Mount Vernon on Route 235, what is now called George Washington's Grist Mill Historic State Park is open Memorial Day through Labor Day, daily from 9am to 5pm. Admission is $2 for adults, $1 for children 7 to 12 (under 7, free). Guided tours are given throughout the day. For further information, call 703/780-3383.

POHICK CHURCH

Travel farther south along Route 1 for about 4½ miles and you'll come to the pre-Revolutionary Pohick Church, 9301 Richmond Highway (tel. 703/339-6572), built in the 1770s from plans drawn up by George Washington. The interior was designed by George Mason, owner of Gunston Hall (see below), with box pews like those prevalent in England at the time. During the Civil War, Union troops stabled their horses in the church and stripped the interior. The east wall was used for target practice. Today the church is restored to its original appearance and has an active Episcopal congregation. It's open daily from 9am to 4:30pm. No admission is charged.

GUNSTON HALL

Yet another 18th-century plantation awaits exploration if you continue south on Route 1 to Route 242, also known as Gunston Road. It's the magnificent estate (originally 5,000 acres; 550 remain) of George Mason (1725–92), a statesman and political thinker who, while shunning public office, played an important behind-the-scenes role in founding our nation. Jefferson called him "the wisest man of his generation." Mason drafted the Virginia Declaration of Rights, model for the Bill of Rights and for constitutions of subsequent emerging democracies throughout the world. The most famous sentence of the Declaration of Independence is based on Mason's statement, "That all men are by nature equally free and independent and have certain inherent rights . . . namely, the enjoyment of life and liberty, with the means of acquiring and possessing property, and pursuing and obtaining happiness and safety. . . ." A little editing, and *voilà!* A staunch believer in human rights, Mason refused to sign the Constitution (which he helped write) because it didn't abolish slavery or, initially, contain a Bill of Rights.

At the reception center a 15-minute film introduces visitors to the estate. En route to the house you'll pass a small museum of Mason family memorabilia. And inside the house a guide is on hand to answer questions.

A highlight is the Palladian Room, the chef d'oeuvre of Gunston Hall's brilliant young creator, an indentured English craftsman in his early 20s named William Buckland who worked here from 1755 to 1759. The room's intricately carved woodwork was inspired by the 16th-century Italian architect Andrea Palladio. Also worth noting is a room with chinoiserie interior, the latest London rage in the mid-18th century. In Mason's library and study is the writing table on which he penned the Virginia Declaration of Rights. Balls were held in the center hallway, with musicians on the balcony providing guitar, flute, and harpsichord tunes for minuets, reels, and country dances. And the upstairs bedrooms, domain of the nine young Masons and an English governess, evoke the lively atmosphere of games and laughter that must surely have existed in this house.

After touring the house, proceed to the outbuildings—a kitchen, smokehouse, dairy, schoolhouse, well, and laundry. Hog Island sheep graze in pastures adjacent to the lawn. The formal gardens focus on the 12-foot-high English boxwood allée planted by Mason more than 200 years ago and contain only plants found in colonial days. A nature trail leads down the Potomac past the deer park and woodland area. Also on the premises is the family graveyard where George and Ann Mason are buried.

Gunston Hall is open daily from 9:30am to 5pm (except New Year's, Thanksgiving, and Christmas days) for self-guided tours. Admission is $4 for adults, $2.50 for seniors, $1 for children 6 through 15 (under 6, free). For details, call 703/550-9220.

POHICK BAY REGIONAL PARK

Close to Gunston Hall, also on Route 242, is a 1,000-acre park focusing on water-oriented recreations, occupying a spectacular bayside setting on the historic 100,000-acre Mason Neck peninsula. It offers the largest swimming pool on the East Coast, boat access to the Potomac (sailboat and paddleboat rentals are available), 200 campsites available on a first-come, first-served basis, a 4-mile bridle path, scenic nature trails, an 18-hole golf course and pro shop, miniature golf, and sheltered picnic areas with grills. It's the perfect place to refresh yourself after a morning spent traipsing around old plantations.

The park is open daily all year from 8am to dark; the pool, from Memorial Day to Labor Day. Admission is $4 per car. Use of the pool is $2.75 for children 2 to 11 and senior citizens, $3.25 for adults. For further details, call 703/339-6100.

CHAPTER 6

FREDERICKSBURG & THE NORTHERN NECK

1. FREDERICKSBURG
- **WALKING TOUR: OLD TOWN FREDERICKSBURG**

2. THE NORTHERN NECK

The tranquil southern town of Fredericksburg came into being in 1728 as a frontier settlement of 50 acres on the banks of the Rappahannock River. Like other early Virginia towns it is steeped in American history, with a heritage spanning 3 centuries of colonial, Revolutionary, and Civil War events. George Washington, James Monroe, Thomas Jefferson, and George Mason are among the great names who once walked Fredericksburg's cobblestoned streets. And during the Civil War, military heroes such as Stonewall Jackson fought here. Remarkably, Fredericksburg survived, though the scars of war are still visible, a 40-block area of the town has been designated a National Register Historic District.

Both George Washington and Robert E. Lee were born on the bucolic Northern Neck, a peninsula set apart by the broad Potomac on one side and the winding Rappahannock River on the other. Toward the Chesapeake Bay, there are resorts and remote fishing villages like tiny Reedville, built up in the Victorian era. Large and small creeks crisscross the neck, and bald eagles, blue heron, flocks of waterfowl, and an occasional wild turkey inhabit the unspoiled marshland.

1. FREDERICKSBURG

50 miles S of Washington, D.C.; 45 miles S of Alexandria;
50 miles N of Richmond

GETTING THERE   By Train   Amtrak (tel. toll free 800/USA-RAIL) serves Fredericksburg with several trains daily from Washington, D.C., and New York City.

By Bus   Fredericksburg is also accessible by **Greyhound/Trailways,** 1400 Jefferson Davis Boulevard (tel. 703/373-2013).

By Car   Fredericksburg is about an hour's drive from Washington, D.C.; a little less from Alexandria. Go south on I-95 to Exit 45A, Route 3 East, which becomes William Street and takes you to the heart of town.

ESSENTIALS   The **telephone area code** is 703. The **Fredericksburg Visitor Center** is at 706 Caroline Street (tel. 703/373-1776, or toll free 800/678-4748).

Though George Washington always called Alexandria his hometown, he spent his formative years in the Fredericksburg area at Ferry Farm (that's where he supposedly chopped down the cherry tree with his little hatchet). His mother later lived in a house he bought her on Charles Street, and she is buried on the former Kenmore estate, home of his sister, Betty Washington Lewis.

The town was a hotbed of revolutionary zeal in the 1770s. Troops drilled on the courthouse green on Princess Anne Street, and it was in Fredericksburg that Thomas Jefferson, George Mason, and other founding fathers met in 1777 to draft what later became the Virginia Statute of Religious Freedoms, the basis for the First Amendment guaranteeing separation of church and state. James Monroe began his law career in Fredericksburg in 1786.

During the Civil War, its strategic location—equidistant from two rival capitals, Richmond and Washington—made Fredericksburg a fierce battlefield, scene of one of the war's bloodiest conflicts. Clara Barton nursed wounded Federal soldiers in the still-extant Presbyterian church. Cannonballs embedded in the walls of some prominent buildings, and the 17,000 Civil War soldiers buried in the town's cemeteries, are grim reminders of that era.

WHAT TO SEE & DO

Make your first stop in town the **Fredericksburg Visitor Center** at 706 Caroline Street (tel. 703/373-1776, or toll free 800/678-4748), itself housed in a historic 1824 house. Here you can see a 12-minute slide presentation on Fredericksburg's colonial history, pick up maps and brochures, obtain a pass for free parking anywhere in the city (including the lot across the street), and purchase a **Hospitality Pass** ticket for seven main attractions. This block ticket costs $16, a saving of 25% over individual admissions, and includes the Hugh Mercer Apothecary, the Rising Sun Tavern, the James Monroe Museum, the Mary Washington House, Belmont, the Fredericksburg Area Museum, and Kenmore. Children 13 and under are admitted free when accompanied by an adult. The ticket can also be purchased at any of these attractions. The center is open Memorial Day to Labor Day, daily from 9am to 7pm; the rest of the year, 9am to 5pm (except New Year's and Christmas days).

Note: The seven block-ticket attractions listed below are closed January 1, Thanksgiving, and December 24, 25, and 31. All these attractions, except Belmont, are within walking distance of the Visitor Center (see the Walking Tour of Old Town later in this chapter).

THE BLOCK-TICKET ATTRACTIONS

KENMORE, 1201 Washington Ave., between Lewis and Fauquier Sts. Tel. 703/373-3381.

This mid-18th-century Georgian mansion was built for Betty Washington (George's sister) by her husband, Fielding Lewis, one of the wealthiest planters in Fredericksburg. The original 861-acre plantation produced tobacco, grains, and flax. In addition to George Washington (who involved himself considerably in the building, decoration, and furnishings of the estate), Kenmore's illustrious guests included Lafayette, Rochambeau, John Paul Jones, Patrick Henry, and Thomas Jefferson. During the Revolution, Lewis financed a gun factory and built vessels for the Virginia navy. As a result of his large expenditures in the cause of patriotism, he eventually had to sell Kenmore to liquidate his debts. He died soon after the victory at Yorktown.

Today the house is meticulously restored to its Colonial appearance. The original exquisitely molded plaster ceilings and cornices are its most outstanding features. Most of the floors and all the woodwork and paneling are also original, and the authentic 18th-century English and American furnishings contain several Lewis family pieces.

A very interesting **tour** winds up in the kitchen, where spiced tea and delicious gingerbread (Mary Washington's recipe, the same she served to Lafayette in 1784) is served—a lovely treat. After touring the house, take a walk through the famous boxwood gardens, restored and maintained according to the original plans by the Garden Club of Virginia. A gift shop is also on the premises.

Admission (without block ticket): $5 adults, $2.50 children (under 6, free).
Open: House tours, Mar–Nov, daily 9am–5pm; Dec–Feb daily 10am–4pm.

MARY WASHINGTON HOUSE, 1200 Charles St. at Lewis St. Tel. 703/373-1569.

George Washington purchased this house for his mother, Mary Ball Washington, in 1772. She was then 64 years old and had been living at nearby Ferry Farm since 1739. Lafayette visited during the Revolution to pay respects to the mother of the greatest living American. And Washington came in 1789 to receive her blessing before going to New York for his inauguration as President. He did not see her again; she died later that year.

Thirty-minute **tours** are given by hostesses in Colonial garb throughout the day.
Admission (without block ticket): $3 adults, 75¢ children.
Open: Mar–Nov, daily 9am–5pm; Dec–Feb, daily 10am–4pm.

JAMES MONROE MUSEUM AND MEMORIAL LIBRARY, 908 Charles St., between William and George Sts. Tel. 703/889-4559.

This low brick building commemorates Monroe's life and times. He came to Fredericksburg in 1786 to practice law, and went on to hold a number of high public offices—senator; minister to France, England, and Spain; governor of Virginia; secretary of state; secretary of war; and fifth President of the United States. His shingle hangs outside, and within, all of the furnishings are from the Monroes' White House years or their retirement home.

In a cozy office much like one Monroe might have used, you can peruse correspondence from Thomas Jefferson (a letter partially in code), James Madison, George Washington, Lafayette, and Benjamin Franklin. Here, too, is the gun and canteen Monroe used in the American Revolution. Other than Washington, he was the only president actually to fight in the war for independence and he shared the grim winter at Valley Forge.

In the museum, cases are filled with china and silver the Monroes used in the White House. Also on display are a Rembrandt Peale portrait of Monroe, the outfits the Monroes wore at the court of Napoleon, silhouettes of the Monroes by Charles Willson Peale, her teensy wedding slippers, his dueling pistols, and other memorabilia. The library of some 10,000 books is a reconstruction of Monroe's own personal collection.

Thirty-minute **tours** given throughout the day are enhanced by recorded information in each room.
Admission (without block ticket): $2.50 adults, 50¢ children.
Open: Daily 9am–5pm.

THE RISING SUN TAVERN, 1306 Caroline St. Tel. 703/371-1494.

At the Rising Sun Tavern, you'll be shown around by a tavern wench—an indentured servant sentenced to 7 years for stealing a loaf of bread in England. "My only hope," she confides, "is that a wealthy farmer might buy me from the tavern keeper for a wife."

The Rising Sun was originally a residence, built in 1760 by Charles Washington, George's youngest brother, but it served as a tavern for some 50 years, beginning in the early 1780s. The building is preserved, not reconstructed, though the 17th- and 18th-century furnishings are not all originals.

The 30-minute **tour** provides many insights into colonial life. The Rising Sun was a proper high-class tavern—not for riffraff like tinkers and razor grinders. Men were required to take off their boots and spurs in bed, and only five were allowed per bed! (People slept sitting up across the bed rather than lengthwise.) Not exactly the Holiday Inn.

In the Great Room the gentry congregated over madeira and cards, while ladies were consigned to the Retiring Room where they would spend the entire day gossiping, doing needlework, and reading the Bible (novel reading was verboten). Their meals were served here, and they didn't even leave to use the women's room; there was none, just a chamber pot. At bedtime (5:30pm) the hostess would show them to their rooms by candlelight.

Meanwhile the menfolk were having a rollicking good time in the Taproom over multicourse meals and numerous tankards of ale. (The tavernkeeper's son will serve you wassail—a delicious spiced drink—here during the tour.)

You'll see the bedrooms, including a room where Lafayette once stayed among other rooms. In the downstairs hall the tavern's original license is displayed, along with a standing desk designed by Thomas Jefferson.

Admission (without the block ticket): $3 adults, 75¢ children.

Open: Mar–Nov, daily 9am–5pm; Dec–Feb, daily 10am–4pm.

HUGH MERCER APOTHECARY SHOP, 1020 Caroline St. at Amelia St. Tel. 703/373-3362.

You've only to visit this colonial apothecary to realize the ghastliness of getting sick in the 18th century. Dr. Hugh Mercer practiced medicine and operated the shop from 1761 to 1776 before giving his life as a Revolutionary War brigadier-general at the Battle of Princeton. (General George S. Patton was his great-great-great-grandson.) Mercer was a much-admired patriot and scholar—a close friend of George Washington—but I can't help feeling, though he suffered a violent death, that Mercer gave as good as he got.

For openers, the waiting room at this little shop of horrors doubled as an operating room, since those waiting for treatment often had to hold down the wretch under the knife. Opium, the only known anesthesia, was too expensive and too difficult to obtain. On display are Mercer's various instruments of torture—bleeding devices, a heated cup for removing boils and carbuncles, a knife to cut out cataracts, an ominous-looking tooth key (dental needs were also seen to here), and a saw (hence the early name "sawbones" for doctors). You could also get your wig powdered here.

Downstairs in the apothecary are the drugs commonly dispensed in the 18th century, such as snake root (to make you sweat), senna (for a laxative), and ipecac (to make you vomit). Come in with a simple case of the flu and, after being bled with leeches, you'd be administered all three!

A fascinating **tour** is given by a hostess in Colonial dress.

Admission (without block ticket): $3 adults, 75¢ children.

Open: Mar–Nov, daily 9am–5pm; Dec–Feb, daily 10am–4pm.

BELMONT, Va. 1001, just off Rte. 17. Tel. 703/373-3634.

Situated on 27 hillside acres overlooking the falls of the Rappahannock River, Belmont began as an 18th-century farmhouse (the central six rooms of the house date to the 1790s) and was enlarged to a 22-room estate by a later owner. The house is furnished with the art treasures, family heirlooms, and European antiques of famed American artist Gari Melchers, who lived here from 1916 until his death in 1932. His wife, Corinne, gave Belmont to the Commonwealth of Virginia in 1955. In addition to Melchers's own works, there are many wonderful paintings in the house—a watercolor sketch by Jan Brueghel, 19th-century paintings by Morisot, and works by Rodin. **Tours** (about an hour long) are given throughout the day.

Admission (without block ticket): $3 adults, $1 children 6–18, free for children under 6.

Open: Apr–Sept, Mon–Sat 10am–5pm, Sun 1–5pm; Oct–Mar, Mon–Sat 10am–4pm, Sun 1–4pm. **Directions:** From the Visitors Center, take Route 17N across the river, turn left at the traffic light in Falmouth, and go a quarter mile up the hill; turn left on Va. 1001 to Belmont.

FREDERICKSBURG AREA MUSEUM AND CULTURAL CENTER, 907 Princess Anne St., at William St. Tel. 703/371-5668.

The Fredericksburg Area Museum and Cultural Center occupies the 1816 Town Hall located in Market Square. Market Square (in existence since 1733) was, for over a century, the center of trade and commerce in Fredericksburg, while Town Hall served as the city's social and legal center. Lafayette was entertained at Town Hall in 1824 with lavish parties and balls, and the building continued in its original function through 1982. Now it is restored both for its own historical importance and to serve as a museum of regional history.

The first level is a changing exhibit area for displays relating to regional and cultural history. The second floor houses permanent exhibits on Native American settlements and pre-English explorers (the earliest years); natural history; colonial settlement; the Revolution and Federal Fredericksburg, including architectural and decorative aspects of the period; the antebellum period (1825–61), focusing on the development of canals, early industry, railroads, and the cholera epidemic of 1833; the Civil War and its aftermath, graphically depicting the reality of the war as experienced by the local citizenry; Fredericksburg's evolution from town to city (1890–1920); and, finally, 20th-century Fredericksburg. Exhibits are enhanced by audiovisual presentations, crafts demonstrations, and symposiums. On the third floor, the hall's 19th-century Council Chamber is another area used for changing exhibits.

Admission (without block ticket): $3 adults, $1 students, free for children under 6.

Open: Mar–Nov Mon–Sat 9am–5pm, Sun 1–5pm; Dec–Feb, Mon–Sat 10am–4pm, Sun 1–4pm.

OTHER TOP ATTRACTIONS

MASONIC LODGE NO. 4, Princess Anne and Hanover Sts. Tel. 703/373-5885.

Not only is this the mother lodge of the father of our country, it's also one of the oldest Masonic lodges in America, established, it is believed, around 1735. Though the original building was down the street, Masons have been meeting at this address since 1812. On display are all kinds of Masonic paraphernalia and memorabilia, among them the Masonic punchbowl used to serve Lafayette, a Gilbert Stuart portrait of Washington in its original gilt Federalist frame, and the 1668 Bible on which Washington took his Masonic obligation (oath). **Tours** are given throughout the day.

Admission: $2 adults, $1 college students, 50¢ children under 13.

Open: Mon–Sat 9am–4pm, Sun 1–4pm.

CHATHAM, 120 Chatham Lane. Tel. 703/373-4461.

This pre-Revolutionary mansion built between 1768 and 1771 by wealthy planter William Fitzhugh has figured prominently in American history. Fitzhugh was a fourth-generation American who supported the Revolution both politically and financially. In the 18th century Chatham was a center of southern hospitality, often visited by George Washington.

During the Civil War the house, then belonging to J. Horace Lacy, served as headquarters for Federal commanders and as a Union field hospital. Lincoln visited the house twice, and Clara Barton and Walt Whitman nursed the wounded here. Exhibits on the premises tell about the families who've owned Chatham and detail the role the estate played during the war. Plaques on the grounds identify battle landmarks, and in summer there's a "living-history" program.

Five rooms and the grounds can be viewed on a self-guided tour, with National Park Service employees on hand to answer questions. A picnic area is on the premises.

Admission: Free.

Open: Daily 9am–5pm. **Directions:** Take Route 3 (William Street) east across the river and follow the signs.

THE OLD STONE WAREHOUSE, 923 Sophia St. at William St.
Originally used to store tobacco, this warehouse is Fredericksburg's oldest building. Built before 1760 of sandstone blocks and massive wooden beams, its walls were 18 to 25 inches thick to provide ample protection for the valuable contents housed within. (In colonial times a tobacco warehouse was like a bank, and tobacco a viable form of currency.)

From 1900 to 1936 the building was used as a salted-herring factory; it then stood vacant for the next 45 years. Today it contains a museum of colonial and Civil War artifacts, some of which were found on the premises. The collection is a fascinating jumble of crocks, bottles, Spanish silver, clay pipes, buckles, medicinal vials, buttons, weapons, and more.

Admission: Free.
Open: Sun 1–4pm.

MORE ATTRACTIONS

ST. GEORGE'S EPISCOPAL CHURCH, Princess Anne St., between George and William Sts. Tel. 703/373-4133.
Martha Washington's father and John Paul Jones's brother are buried in the graveyard of this church, and members of the first parish congregation included Mary Washington and Revolutionary War generals Hugh Mercer and George Weedon. The original church on this site was built in 1732, the current Romanesque structure in 1849. During the Battle of Fredericksburg the church was hit at least 25 times, and in 1863 it was used by General Lee's troops for religious revival meetings. In 1864, when wounded Union soldiers filled every available building in town, it served as a hospital. Do note the three signed Tiffany windows.

Admission: Free.
Open: Mon–Sat 9am–5pm (unless a wedding is taking place Sat), Sun services at 8 and 11am.

THE PRESBYTERIAN CHURCH, George and Princess Anne Sts. Tel. 703/373-7057.
This Presbyterian church dates to the early 1800s, though the present Greek Revival building was completed in 1855—just in time to be shelled during the Civil War, and, like St. George's, to serve as a hospital where Clara Barton nursed Union wounded. Cannonballs in the front left pillar and scars on the walls of the loft and belfry remain to this day. The present church bell replaced one that was given to the Confederacy to be melted down for making cannons.

Admission: Free.
Open: Mon–Sat 9am–3pm, Sun service at 11am.

THE COURTHOUSE, Princess Anne and George Sts.
Those of you interested in architecture should be sure to look at the Gothic Revival Courthouse, built in 1853. Its architect was James Renwick, who also designed New York's St. Patrick's Cathedral and, in Washington, D.C., the original Smithsonian "Castle" and Renwick Gallery. Exhibits in the lobby include originals of Mary Ball Washington's will and George Washington's address to the city council in 1784.

Admission: Free.
Open: Mon–Fri 9am–4pm.

Washington Avenue

Washington Avenue, just above Kenmore, is the site of several notable monuments. A brochure detailing its historic buildings is available at the Visitor Center. Mary Washington is buried at **Meditation Rock,** a spot where she often came to pray and meditate; there's a monument in her honor. Just across the way is the **Thomas**

Jefferson Religious Freedom Monument, commemorating Jefferson's Fredericksburg meeting with George Mason, Edmond Pendleton, George Wythe, and Thomas Ludwell Lee in 1777 to draft the Virginia Statute of Religious Freedom. The **Hugh Mercer Monument,** off Fauquier Street, honors the doctor and Civil War general.

TOURING CIVIL WAR BATTLEFIELDS

Fredericksburg has never forgotten its Civil War victories and defeats. In **Fredericksburg and Spotsylvania National Military Park** you can take a self-guided auto tour of 16 important sites relating to four major battles.

Starting point is the **Fredericksburg Battlefield Visitor Center,** 1013 Lafayette Boulevard, at Sunken Road (tel. 703/373-6122), where you can get detailed tour brochures and rent 2½-hour-long auto-tour tapes ($2.75 per battlefield for cassette player and tape). We definitely recommend the tapes; they enhance the experience. The center offers a 12-minute slide-show orientation and related exhibits. Inquire here, too, about "living-history" programs in the park. Open daily from 9am to 5pm, with extended hours in summer determined annually.

The Battle of Fredericksburg took place December 11–15, 1862, when the Union army, commanded by Gen. Ambrose E. Burnside, attempted to occupy the town with a strength of 110,000 men and push on toward Richmond. However, the Northern army took a drubbing at the hands of Lee's smaller (75,000 men) but better-situated force. You can stand on the hill from which Lee directed the victorious Confederate defense, see the remains of fortifications, and visit sites like the Upper Pontoon Crossing, where the Union army crossed the Rappahannock by means of boat bridges called "pontoons." The Georgian mansion, Chatham (details above), is on the auto-tour tape; during the war it became frontline headquarters for Union generals.

The first leg takes you as far as Chancellorsville (about 10 miles), site of another important battle. Stop at the **Chancellorsville Visitor Center** (tel. 703/786-2880) to see another 12-minute audiovisual orientation and related exhibits. Once again an auto-tour tape is available.

The Battle of Chancellorsville was fought May 1–4, 1863. Union commander Gen. Joseph Hooker led about 80,000 men in a flanking maneuver up the north side of the Rappahannock, leaving another 25,000 in Fredericksburg to hold Lee in position. General T. J. "Stonewall" Jackson moved toward Chancellorsville, and General Hooker retreated under Jackson's pressure. Although this battle, too, resulted in a Confederate victory, it was a costly one in which Jackson was accidentally shot by his own men. The house in which he died (22 miles from Chancellorsville) is still standing, and a recording and signs on the grounds tell of Jackson's final days. Other sites on the tour include the bivouac where Lee and Jackson met for the last time on the night of May 1 and planned the Battle of Chancellorsville; Catharine Furnace, a Confederate munitions factory and scene of a sharp engagement; and Hazel Grove, the battlefield's most important military position. You might also want to make a stop at Old Salem Church, 6 miles east of Chancellorsville, around which battle swirled on May 3–4, 1863, in conjunction with the Chancellorsville Campaign.

From Chancellorsville, enthusiasts can continue farther to the Wilderness and Spotsylvania Battlefields, while the battle-weary return to Fredericksburg.

The battlefield outing makes a pleasant family excursion. Even if Civil War sites don't excite you, the drive is scenic, and there's lots of walking through woods and meadows.

Information If you'd like to do a little advance planning, write to the Superintendent, Fredericksburg and Spotsylvania National Military Park, 210 Chatham Lane, Fredericksburg, VA 22404, for information.

WALKING TOUR — Old Town Fredericksburg

Start: Visitors Center, 706 Caroline Street.
Finish: Fredericksburg Area Museum and Cultural Center, 907 Princess Anne Street, near Prince William Street.
Time: Allow approximately 2½ hours, not including museum, shopping, or refueling stops.
Best Times: Any sunny day in late spring, when azalea, rhododendron, and dogwood trees are in bloom.
Worst Times: August, when the heat and humidity soar.

A stroll through picturesque Old Town reveals the best of Fredericksburg—fine examples from every period of American architecture (including pre-Revolutionary and Georgian structures), interesting museums, and charming boutiques.

Begin at the:

1. **Visitors Center,** where you can buy a block ticket to the top seven attractions. As you leave the Visitors Center, turn left and walk up Caroline Street, a shopper's paradise, with quaint shops on either side and spilling down the side streets. Turn right at Hanover Street, and left at Sophia to the:

2. **Old Stone Warehouse,** to your right on the riverbank. Across William Street, almost hidden in the shrubbery, is the:

3. **Leaselands Historic Marker,** HERE FREDERICKSBURG BEGAN, THE LEASE LAND JOHN BUCKNER AND THOMAS ROYSTON FIRST SETTLED MAY 2, 1671. Cross Sophia for a:

REFUELING STOP The **4. Virginia Deli,** 101 William Street, features down-home hickory-smoked and pit-cooked barbecue. Yum!

Continue on Sophia Street to Amelia. Turn left to Caroline Street. Across the street is the:

5. **Hugh Mercer Apothecary Shop,** a small clapboard Colonial house with green shutters where Washington often stopped to visit his friend, Hugh Mercer. Walk up Caroline to Fauquier Street, and turn left to see the tiny:

6. **Kitchen Dependency** (it's a private house now, no visitors please), a typical pre-Revolutionary structure apart from the main house, where food was cooked in a colonial household. Continue walking up Caroline Street, and you'll come to the:

7. **Rising Sun Tavern** on your left. Costumed guides take you around this old clapboard building where Charles Washington, George's brother, once lived. Continue on Caroline to Pitt Street, and walk up the hill to Washington Avenue where:

8. **Meditation Rock** marks the site where Mary Washington often came to pray for her son during the dark days of the Revolutionary War. At her request she is buried here. The nearby:

9. **Religious Liberty Monument** commemorates the Statute of Religious Freedom, authored by a committee of Virginians, including Thomas Jefferson, in Fredericksburg on January 13, 1777. This statute was the basis for the U.S. Constitution's guarantee of religious freedom. Turn left from Pitt and walk down Washington Street to the:

10. **Statue of Hugh Mercer,** who died in battle at Princeton in 1777, which dominates the avenue near Fauquier Street, where you'll come to the low brick wall setting off the magnificent house and gardens of:

11. **Kenmore,** estate of George's sister, Betty Washington Lewis and her husband,

Fielding. Turn left at Lewis Street and continue to Charles Street where, to your left, you'll find the:

12. **Mary Washington House,** where Washington's mother lived from 1772 to 1789. The boxwood in her back garden is reputed to be the very shrubbery she laid out. From the cottage, turn right and go down Charles Street to the corner of William, where the:

13. **Slave Auction Block,** a simple stone slab set on the sidewalk, is a mute reminder of the sad days when slaves were auctioned from this spot. Cross William Street and, to your right, is the:

14. **James Monroe Museum and Memorial Library.** A bronze plaque on the back of the building, facing the garden, spells out the famous Monroe Doctrine, which sought to keep the U.S. free of foreign entanglements. The Masonic Cemetery is behind the library. Turn left on George Street, and you'll see the:

15. **Presbyterian church** where Clara Barton nursed wounded Union troops during the Civil War. Turn right and cross Princess Anne Street to the:

16. **Court House,** and on the same block, the:

17. **Masonic Lodge.** Backtrack to George Street to:

18. **St. George's Church and Graveyard.** John Paul Jones's brother is buried here, as are many of Fredericksburg's founders. A step further up Princess Anne Street is the:

19. **Fredericksburg Area Museum and Cultural Center.** Its entrance is around the corner on William Street. Don't forget to visit their gift shop, where you'll find toys, games, books, and lots of memorabilia to browse through.

WHERE TO STAY

On the outskirts of Fredericksburg you'll find plenty of chain motels. In town are three very special inns whose charm and warmth can only enhance the journey-into-history experience.

IN-TOWN ACCOMMODATIONS

Expensive

KENMORE INN, 1200 Princess Anne St., Fredericksburg, VA 22401. Tel. 703/371-7622. Fax 703/371-5480. 14 rms, including 1 suite (all with bath). A/C TEL

$ Rates (including continental breakfast): $68.75–$89.75 single; $78.75–$99.75 double. Extra person $10. Packages available. AE, MC, V. **Parking:** Street parking with free card from Visitors Center.

An elegant white pediment supported by fluted columns and a front porch with wicker chairs welcome you to this late 1700s mansion right in Old Town. The property was originally owned by George Washington's brother-in-law, Fielding Lewis.

Crystal chandeliers, Oriental rugs, polished Georgian side tables, and an enormous gold-framed mirror enhance the foyer. A sweeping staircase leads to the guest rooms—a handsome assortment of both cozy and spacious accommodations furnished with a mix of antiques, many of them in Regency style. Expect to find four-poster beds with pretty coverlets and lacy canopies, coordinating-color draperies framing louver-shuttered windows, antique chests, and walls hung with botanic prints and engravings. The house has eight working fireplaces, four in the bedrooms.

Dining/Entertainment: The Kenmore has a fine dining room, cozy lounge with TV, and a downstairs Pub. In the morning a continental breakfast, including both juice and fresh fruit, home-baked muffins and croissants, tea and coffee, is served in the elegant dining room. In the evening the softly candlelit restaurant provides an

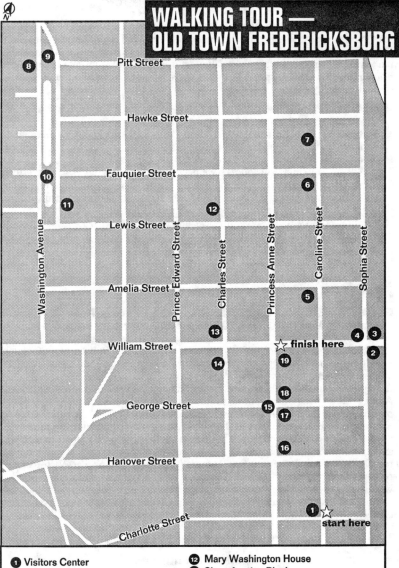

WALKING TOUR — OLD TOWN FREDERICKSBURG

N

Pitt Street

Hawke Street

Fauquier Street

Lewis Street

Amelia Street

William Street ☆ finish here

George Street

Hanover Street

Charlotte Street

start here ☆

Washington Avenue

Prince Edward Street

Charles Street

Princess Anne Street

Caroline Street

Sophia Street

1. Visitors Center
2. Old Stone Warehouse
3. Leaselands Historic Marker
4. Virginia Deli
5. Hugh Mercer Apothecary Shop
6. Kitchen Dependency
7. Rising Sun Tavern
8. Meditation Rock
9. Religious Liberty Monument
10. Statue of Hugh Mercer
11. Kenmore
12. Mary Washington House
13. Slave Auction Block
14. James Monroe Museum and Memorial Library
15. Presbyterian church
16. Court House
17. Masonic Lodge
18. St. George's Church and Graveyard
19. Fredericksburg Area Museum and Cultural Center

elegant period setting with two fireplaces. Entrees ($15 to $25) might include veal scallops sautéed with Virginia bourbon, shallots, and wild mushrooms; lamb Wellington; or chicken breast with julienne Virginia ham in a creamy wine sauce. The inn serves lunch and afternoon tea Tuesday through Saturday; on Sunday there's brunch from 11:30am to 2pm. The Pub, a convivial spot, offers live music Wednesday through Saturday nights.

RICHARD JOHNSTON INN, 711 Caroline St., Fredericksburg, VA 22401. Tel. 703/899-7606. 9 rms, 2 suites (all with bath). A/C
$ Rates (including continental breakfast): $55–$85 double; $120 suite. Extra person $10. Children under 12 stay free in parents' room. AE, MC, V. **Parking:** Free.

Two 18th-century brick rowhouses have been joined to form this elegantly restored inn directly across the street from the Visitors Center. The downstairs sitting rooms and dining room, where continental breakfast is served, are invitingly furnished, and there's a TV in the back parlor. Second-floor guest rooms are furnished with country charm: braided rugs, rockers, oak dressers, and four-poster beds. Some have working fireplaces. Third-floor dormer rooms are cozy, with low ceilings. One of the most popular accommodations is the very private ground-floor suite, entered from the rear courtyard; its living-room area has polished brick floors, a huge fireplace, and decorative copper pots on the wall.

Moderate

FREDERICKSBURG COLONIAL INN, 1707 Princess Anne St., Fredericksburg, VA 22401. Tel. 703/371-5666. 30 rms, 10 suites (all with bath). A/C TV
$ Rates (including complimentary coffee and doughnuts): $45 single; $60 double; $70 two-room family unit for four. Additional person $5. Children 6 and under stay free in parents' room. AE, MC, V. **Parking:** Free.

A stay here can only enhance the Fredericksburg journey-into-history experience. Among other things, it happens to be a hub for Civil War buffs, and people participating in local Civil War reenactments often drop by; don't be surprised to see musket-toting Blues and Grays in the lobby. And in the Conference Room there's a display of Civil War weaponry and Confederate dollars. The rooms are furnished with antiques (owner Alton Echols, Jr., is an avid collector). Perhaps you'll draw a marble-top walnut dresser, rag rug, canopied bed, bowl and pitcher, Victorian sofa, or a bed that belonged to George Mason's son. The lobby is comfortably furnished with wicker rocking chairs, magazines and books are provided, and there's a player piano. One final plus: a laundry room where guests can use washers and dryers free of charge.

NEARBY ACCOMMODATIONS

Moderate/Budget

DUNNING MILLS INN, 2305C Jefferson Davis Hwy. (Rte. 1 Bypass), Fredericksburg, VA 22401. Tel. 703/373-1256. 44 suites. A/C TV TEL
$ Rates: $55 single; $60 double. Special rates for longer stays. Extra person $5. AE, DC, MC, V. **Parking:** Free.

All-suite hotels like the Dunning Mills Inn, 2½ miles north of I-95 at Exit 44, deliver a lot of convenience and comfort at affordable prices. At this two-story establishment, grounds are tastefully landscaped and all accommodations have either balconies or patios. The decor here is contemporary, done up in pale blue-gray, peach, and blue tones. Comfortable living-room areas have pull-out couches and desks with computer modem hookups, and kitchens are fully equipped. Guests can

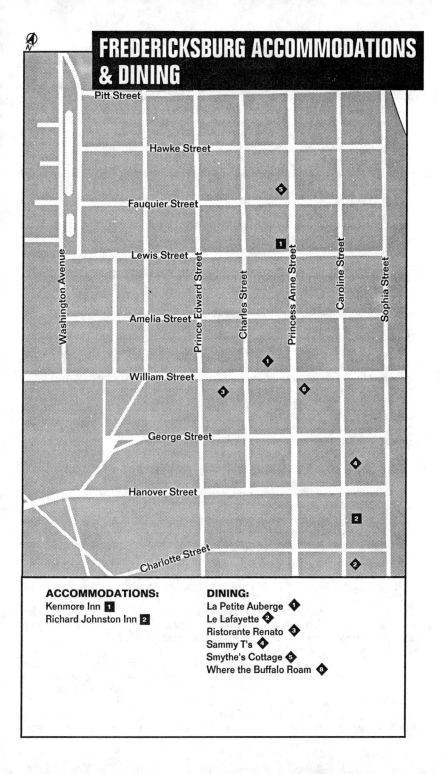

FREDERICKSBURG ACCOMMODATIONS & DINING

Pitt Street
Hawke Street
Fauquier Street
Lewis Street
Amelia Street
William Street
George Street
Hanover Street
Charlotte Street

Washington Avenue
Prince Edward Street
Charles Street
Princess Anne Street
Caroline Street
Sophia Street

ACCOMMODATIONS:
Kenmore Inn **1**
Richard Johnston Inn **2**

DINING:
La Petite Auberge ◆**1**
Le Lafayette ◆**2**
Ristorante Renato ◆**3**
Sammy T's ◆**4**
Smythe's Cottage ◆**5**
Where the Buffalo Roam ◆**8**

use an on-site laundry. Barbecue grills are on hand for summer cookouts, and there's an outdoor pool.

ECONO LODGE, I-95 and Rte. 3W, Fredericksburg, VA 22404. Tel. 703/786-8374, or toll free 800/446-6900. 96 rms (all with bath). A/C TV TEL **Directions:** Take I-95 Exit 45B to Route 3.

$ Rates: $27–$30 single; $39 double. Extra person $4. Children under 18 stay free in parents' room. Seventh night free if you stay for six. AE, DISC, MC, V. **Parking:** Free.

Here you have your standard modern American motel room with all the expected amenities.

If this Econo Lodge is filled, or you'd like a motel with a swimming pool, there's another Econo Lodge (this one with 175 rooms) a few miles south just above the intersection of I-95 and U.S. 1 (tel. 703/898-5440, or toll free 800/446-6900). Rates here are just a tad higher, especially in summer, I suppose because of the pool and a Scotty's Pancake House on the premises.

HAMPTON INN, 2310 William St., at I-95, Fredericksburg, VA 22401. Tel. 703/371-0330, or toll free 800/HAMPTON. 166 rms (all with bath). A/C TV TEL

$ Rates (including continental breakfast and local calls): $40 single; $44–$49 double. AE, CB, DC, DISC, MC, V. **Parking:** Free.

The Hampton Inn is part of an affordable-accommodations chain operated by Holiday Inn. Its hotels have no on-premises restaurants or lounges, but are located near such facilities. In this case Shoney's (see below) is just across the street, and seafood, Mexican, and Chinese restaurants are very close by. The inn's rooms are nicely decorated in forest green/sienna/ecru color schemes and furnished with attractive oak pieces. On-premises facilities include a nice-sized outdoor pool and a washer/dryer for guest use.

Under the same ownership are two nearby hostelries offering similar facilities and rates. So if the Hampton Inn is fully booked, ask to be placed at one of these.

WHERE TO DINE

EXPENSIVE

LA PETITE AUBERGE, 311 William St., between Princess Anne and Charles Sts. Tel. 703/371-2727.
Cuisine: FRENCH. **Reservations:** Recommended, especially at dinner.

$ Prices: Appetizers $1.95–$6.50; entrees $12.50–$19.95; early-bird dinner $9.95. AE, CB, DC, MC, V.

Open: Lunch Mon–Fri 11:30am–2:30pm; dinner Mon–Sat 5:30–10pm (early-bird dinner Mon–Thurs 5:30–7pm).

The delightful La Petite Auberge was designed to look like a garden, an effect enhanced by white latticework and garden furnishings. Unpainted brick walls are hung with copper pots and cheerful oil paintings, and candlelit tables are adorned with fresh flowers. A cozy lounge adjoins.

The menu changes daily. On a recent dinnertime visit, appetizers included baked brie amandine, smoked Virginia trout with red-pepper jelly, and escargots with garlic butter. Among entree choices were fresh Norwegian salmon poached with hollandaise, blackened mahi mahi with bananas and spring onions, and baked duckling with black-cherry sauce. For dessert, opt for the Myers' rum cake. The early-bird dinner here is an attractive offering—soup, salad, a choice of seven entrees from the regular dinner menu, and homemade ice cream.

LE LAFAYETTE, 623 Caroline St. Tel. 703/373-6895.
Cuisine: FRENCH. **Reservations:** Recommended.
$ **Prices:** Appetizers $3.95–$7.50; entrees $12.95–$21. AE, CB, DC, MC, V.
Open: Lunch Mon–Sat 11:30am–3pm; dinner daily 5–10:30; brunch Sun 11:30am–3pm.

★ Owners Pierre and Edith Muyard have restored a Georgian-style private home, once called The Chimneys, to create an elegant restaurant named for the famed French marquis. The interior retains much of its period character, with original wide-plank flooring, paneling, and dining-room fireplaces. Tables are set with white cloths, gleaming china, and silver. During the day, sunlight pours in through the many-paned windows; at night, lamps on each table glow in crystal holders.

Traditional French cuisine dominates the menu, but you'll also note many nouvelle innovations. Dinner might start out with onion soup gratiné, a mixed grill of vegetables, or a salmon mousse. Specialties among the entrees include salmon en croûte, bourbon-marinated beef tenderloin with bleu-cheese butter, and rack of lamb. There is an extensive wine list with both French and domestic offerings. Desserts vary, but usually include a delectable chocolate mousse.

SMYTHE'S COTTAGE, 303 Fauquier St., at Princess Anne St. Tel. 703/373-1645.
Cuisine: TRADITIONAL SOUTHERN. **Reservations:** Suggested on weekends.
$ **Prices:** Appetizers $1.50–$4.95; entrees $9.95–$15.95. DISC, MC, V.
Open: Mon and Wed–Sat 11am–9pm, Sun noon–9pm.

At Smythe's Cottage you can dine on traditional Virginia fare on the site of a blacksmith's stable once operated by George Washington's brother. The current building, dating from 1840, was once a blacksmith's stable. The original owner hailed from an old Virginia family, hence the photograph of General Grant upside down next to a photo of her great-great-grandfather who was hanged by the Union army in the Civil War. The low-ceilinged interior is extremely cozy with Colonial-style furnishings, old oil portraits and family memorabilia on the walls, white-curtained multipaned windows, and oak tables (candlelit at night) adorned with Federalist blue napkins wound in the drinking glasses. In summer there's al fresco dining in a flower-bordered garden. The innlike ambience is enhanced by a menu featuring dinner items like peanut soup, a hearty beef stew in ginger sauce, and delicious chicken pot pie. The latter entrees are served with a basket of oven-fresh bread, soup or salad, and vegetable. Homemade desserts include hot cherry or apple turnovers. Lunch here is very reasonable.

SOPHIA STREET STATION, 503 Sophia St. Tel. 703/371-3355.
Cuisine: AMERICAN. **Reservations:** Recommended for the River Room, especially on weekends.
$ **Prices:** Appetizers $2.25–$5.95; entrees $8.95–$14.95; brunch Sun $11.95, $5.95 for children under 12. AE, MC, V.
Open: Daily 10am–10pm, with extended hours in summer.

The Sophia Street Station, on the Rappahannock River, can offer a festive evening's entertainment with music in the clubby front room, or a more sedate ambience in the formal River Room, which has a terrace overlooking the river. Appetizers and snacks range from shrimp cocktail and Buffalo chicken wings to a giant nacho platter. Main dishes—like New York strip steak, filet mignon wrapped with bacon and topped with béarnaise sauce, or shrimp and scallops over linguine—are served with vegetable, baked potato or rice, and soup or house salad. At lunch there are croissant sandwiches and burgers, including a blackened one with Cajun spices. The lavish Sunday brunch buffet features omelets and crêpes made to order, salads, hot roast beef, curried chicken, and much more.

WHERE THE BUFFALO ROAM, 216 William St. Tel. 703/373-BUFF.
 Cuisine: SOUTHWESTERN.
$ **Prices:** Appetizers $2.50–$5; entrees $8.50–$15. AE, MC, V.
 Open: Mon–Tues 11am–9pm, Wed–Sat 11am–2am, Sun noon–8pm.
Whether you go for cocktail-hour drinks and delicious crab nachos or a full meal, you'll be glad you stopped in this casual storefront eatery. It's decorated in low-key desert tones, with blond-wood furniture and pastel-hued prints of western landscapes. Everything is made from scratch here. Owner/chef David Haynes personally oversees the kitchen, down to the buffalo burgers and steaks, made from, yes, buffalo meat, supplied by a buffalo ranch in northern Virginia. Other choices here include blackened prime rib béarnaise, mesquite-smoked pork barbecue, and sautéed catfish. The Upstairs Club offers live music, ranging from country to blues to rock 'n roll, Wednesday through Saturday night from 10pm.

BUDGET

SAMMY T'S, 801 Caroline St., at Hanover St. Tel. 703/371-2008.
 Cuisine: AMERICAN.
$ **Prices:** Appetizers $1.40–$2.50; entrees $4.75–$7. DISC, MC, V.
 Open: Mon–Sat 11am–midnight, Sun 11am–9pm.
Sammy T's is a simpatico eatery offering a tasteful setting, good music, and a vaguely health-food orientation. It has a western feel, with large overhead fans suspended from a high pressed-tin ceiling, roomy knotty-pine booths, a long oak bar, and painted barnwood walls adorned with framed art posters. Everything here is made from scratch. You might begin your meal with one of the hearty homemade soups, perhaps a Brunswick stew of chicken, tomatoes, potatoes, okra, lima beans, and corn. Entree selections include vegetarian lasagne; a baked potato stuffed with mushrooms, tomatoes, walnuts, sunflower seeds, three cheeses, and sprouts, topped with sour cream and served with soup; and a cook's special salad. Among the beverage choices are more than 50 international beers, a French house wine, and gourmet teas and coffees. For dessert, try fresh-baked creamy cheesecake with graham-cracker crust.

SHONEY'S FAMILY RESTAURANT, 2203 William St. Tel. 703/371-5400.
 Cuisine: TRADITIONAL SOUTHERN. **Directions:** Follow William Street toward the junction of I-95 and Route 3.
$ **Prices:** All-you-can-eat breakfast buffet Mon–Fri $4, Sat–Sun and hols $5; children under 12 pay $2. AE, MC, V.
 Open: Mon–Thurs 6am–11pm, Fri–Sat (in summer) 6am–midnight.
Though generally we avoid restaurant chains, you can't beat Shoney's for breakfast. At all its 80 locations, this southern chain offers an all-you-can-eat buffet of eggs, bacon, home-fries, sausage, French toast, sautéed apples, pancakes, grits, fresh-baked biscuits, country gravy, blueberry muffins, fruit, grated Cheddar cheese, sliced tomatoes, strawberry shortcake, and coffee. Shoney's has a comfortable coffee-shop atmosphere with seating in roomy leather booths and a large glass-enclosed café area under a striped awning.

2. THE NORTHERN NECK

Washington Birthplace (at land's end of peninsula): 38 miles SE of
Fredericksburg; Irvington (at bay end): 125 miles SE of Fredericksburg

GETTING THERE   By Car   From Fredericksburg, take Route 3 East, which goes down the length of the peninsula.

ESSENTIALS   A long, narrow strip of land, the Northern Neck is bounded by the Potomac and Rappahannock rivers and Chesapeake Bay.

For information, contact the **Northern Neck Travel Council,** P.O. Drawer H, Callao, VA 22345 (tel. 804/529-7400).

The picturesque Northern Neck is a blend of venerable colonial history and saltwater vitality. The Popes Creek Plantation, site of George Washington's birthplace, and Stratford Hall, ancestral home of the Lee family, are both on the Potomac riverfront. Nearby, the Ingleside Plantation Vineyards offer tours and tastings.

At the mouth of the Rappahannock is Windmill Point, one of Virginia's best-known marine resorts, and in the riverfront town of Irvington is the Tides Inn, one of the premier resorts in the country. Not far from the inn stands Christ Church, which has been described as the most perfect example of Colonial church architecture remaining in the U.S.

WHAT TO SEE & DO

INGLESIDE PLANTATION WINERY, Oak Grove. Tel. 804/224-8687.

The rich soil and mild climate of the Northern Neck provide ideal grape-growing conditions for this 2,500-acre plantation winery. In addition to winery tours, tastings, and a gift shop selling wine-related items, Ingleside has a small exhibit area displaying colonial wine bottles, Chesapeake waterfowl carvings, and Native American artifacts.

Admission: No charge for small groups; 15 or more, $1.50 per person.

Open: Mon–Sat 10am–5pm, Sun noon–5pm. **Closed:** Major hols. **Directions:** Traveling east from Fredericksburg on Route 3, turn right in Oak Grove on Route 638 and continue about 2½ miles south.

GEORGE WASHINGTON BIRTHPLACE NATIONAL MONUMENT, R.R. #1, Washington's Birthplace, Va. Tel. 804/224-1732.

A quiet country road leads off Route 3 to the Visitors Center of this charming re-creation of Washington's first home. Encompassing some 500 acres along Pope's Creek, actually a tributary of the Potomac, the parklike farm is a living-history display, complete with costumed guides and crafts demonstrations.

On this site, his father's tobacco farm, George Washington was born on February 22, 1732. He lived here until he was 3½, when the family moved to the Mount Vernon estate. The land was first settled by Washington's great-grandfather, John, in the mid-17th century. The original farmhouse burned down in 1779 and was never rebuilt. The re-created building we see today is called the Memorial House. There are no historic records detailing what the house looked like, so this memorial, operated by the National Park Service, is a representation of a typical farmhouse of Washington's childhood, with antique furnishings appropriate to the period.

At the Visitor Center, a 14-minute film called *A Childhood Place,* evokes life at the plantation. There is an uphill climb of some 300 yards to the historic area; transportation is provided for those unable to walk that distance. In the historic area are the birthplace site, a herb garden, a separate building housing the plantation's kitchen (cooking demonstrations are often in progress here), and a weaving room. Graves of some Washington family members, including George's father, are in a small burial ground on the property.

Tours are offered throughout the day. Children will enjoy particularly the small-scale farm, with horses, chickens, and cows. A picnic area is available but no refreshments, except for soda and vending-machine snacks, are sold at the park.

Admission: $1; free for seniors over age 61 and children under 17.

Open: Daily 9am–5pm. **Closed:** New Year's and Christmas days. **Directions:** Going east on Route 3, turn left onto Route 204.

STRATFORD HALL PLANTATION, Stratford. Tel. 804/493-8038.

★ This is one of the great houses of the South, magnificently set on 1,600 acres above the Potomac, renowned not only for its distinctive architectural style but for the illustrious family who lived there.

Thomas Lee (1690–1750), a planter who later served as governor of the Virginia colony, built Stratford in the late 1730s. Five of his sons played major roles in the forming of the new nation, most notably Richard Henry Lee, who made the motion for independence in the Continental Congress in 1776. He and Francis Lightfoot Lee were the only brothers to sign the Declaration of Independence. General Henry Lee, a cousin, married into this family. He was a hero of the Revolution, a friend of George Washington, and father of the most famous Lee child born at Stratford—Robert E. Lee.

The H-shaped manor house, its four dependencies, coach house, and stables have been brilliantly restored. On approaching the imposing two-story-high stone entrance staircase, a costumed guide will point out one of the mansion's most striking features—the brick chimney groupings that flank the roofline.

The paneled Great Hall, one of the finest rooms to have survived from colonial times, runs the depth of the house and has an inverted tray ceiling. On the same floor are bedrooms and a nursery, where you can see Robert E. Lee's crib. The fireplace in the nursery is trimmed with sculpted angels' heads.

Tours conclude in the winter kitchen and estate offices, with ginger cookies and cider. Thus fortified, you can then stroll the meadows and gardens of this 1,600-acre estate, still operated as a working farm.

Also on the estate is a rustic log-cabin-style public dining room (open April to November 1), with a screened-in terrace; it offers light snacks and a plantation lunch with fried chicken, crab cakes, or ham for $7.75.

Admission: $5 adults, $4 seniors, $2.50 children under 18, free for children under 6.

Open: Daily 9am–5pm. **Closed:** Christmas Day. **Directions:** Drive east from Fredericksburg on Route 3 and turn left onto Route 214.

FISHERMAN'S MUSEUM, Reedville.

The small village of Reedville on Cockrell's Creek, an inlet of Chesapeake Bay, provides a living image of the past with its Victorian mansions and seafaring atmosphere. The Fisherman's Museum, in the 1875 William Walker House, commemorates the town's leading industry, based on a small, toothless fish, the menhaden, which is of little use for human consumption, but extremely valuable for its by-products: meal, oil, and protein supplements used in animal feeds. Captain Elijah Reed, who came to this area from Maine in 1874, built a menhaden factory, a steamboat wharf, and home (still standing).

Admission: By donation.

Open: Fri–Sun 1–5pm. **Directions:** From Route 3 east, take Route 360 north to northern tip of the peninsula.

HISTORIC CHRIST CHURCH, Irvington. Tel. 804/438-6855.

★ Elegant in its simplicity and virtually unchanged since it was completed in 1732, Christ Church, listed on the National Register of Historic Places, was the gift of one man, Robert "King" Carter. Carter offered to finance the building of the church if his parents' graves remained in the chancel. In the chancel today are interred the bodies of John Carter, four of his five wives, and two infant children. Robert Carter's tomb is on the church grounds. Among the descendants of the Carters are eight governors of Virginia, two Presidents of the United States (the two Harrisons), Gen. Robert E. Lee, and Edward D. White, a Chief Justice of the U.S. Supreme Court.

The building is cruciform in shape, its brick facade laid in a pleasing Flemish bond pattern, with a three-color design that saves the expanse of brick from monotony.

Inside, the three-decker pulpit is in excellent condition, and all 26 original pews remain. No structural changes have ever been made. The building has no artificial heat or light, and is now used for services only during the summer.

Admission: Free.

Open: Church, daily 9am–5pm. Carter Reception Center, Apr–Thanksgiving, Mon–Fri 10am–4pm, Sat 1–5pm, Sun 2–5pm. **Closed:** Christmas Day. **Directions:** On Route 646, off Route 3 about 2 miles north of Irvington.

WHERE TO STAY

EXPENSIVE

THE TIDES INN, Irvington, VA 22480. Tel. 804/438-5000, or toll free 800/TIDES-INN. 110 rms (all with bath). A/C TV TEL **Directions:** From Route 3, take Route 200N, 2 miles to Irvington; the inn is at the head of King Carter Drive.

$ Rates (including three meals daily): $137–$218 single; $120–$143 per person double. Family rate for two rooms $398 per couple (no charge for children under age 10, $40 for children 10–16, $60 over 16). Golf packages available. AE, MC, V. **Parking:** Free. **Closed:** Early Jan to mid-Mar.

Rated one of America's top 20 resorts by Condé Nast's *Traveler* magazine, The Tides has maintained a tradition of gracious service under the auspices of the Stephens family since 1947. The sprawling resort complex consists of several low-rise buildings encircling a nicely landscaped entrance. Guests can choose accommodations in the Main Building, where the dining room and gift shop are located; or the Windsor or Lancaster House, where the rooms are more spacious and have dressing rooms, living areas, and, in some cases, balconies overlooking Carter's Creek.

Across Carter's Creek, a more casual, 60-room resort, the Tides Lodge (tel. 804/438-6000, or toll free 800/446-5660) is also owned by the Stephens family.

Dining/Entertainment: Menus feature seafood items like soft-shell crabs and fried-oyster sandwiches, along with prime ribs of beef and pork tenderloin. The wine list is reasonable; it includes Virginia, California, and French vintages.

Facilities: Yacht cruises; unlimited tennis, sailboats, paddleboats, canoes, bicycles, and croquet; heated pool; three golf courses with discounted rates for guests—the 6,950-yard Golden Eagle Course, the Executive Nine, and the 5,600-yard Tartan Course at the lodge.

MODERATE

THE INN AT MONTROSS, Courthouse Sq. (P.O. Box 908), Montross, VA 22520. Tel. 804/493-9097. 6 rms (all with bath). A/C TV TEL

$ Rates (including continental breakfast): Sun–Thurs $65–$75 double, Fri–Sat $115–$125. DISC, MC, V. **Parking:** Free.

The Montross Inn, about half a block north of Route 3, is a convenient place to stop while you're touring the Northern Neck. Hosts Michael and Eileen Longman have restored the 1790 building and offer 20th-century comfort in a homey setting that includes at least four cats and a dog or two. Guest rooms are tastefully furnished with original antiques and good-quality reproductions, including handsome four-poster canopied beds. The inn's history goes back to 1683, when one John Minor was granted permission to keep an "ordinary" (tavern) on this site. Thomas Lee, builder of Stratford Hall, was a frequent visitor.

Dining/Entertainment: In Colonial-style dining rooms, lunch features oyster stew and shepherd's pie among other hot entrees, as well as salads and sandwiches. Dinner entrees ($15 to $18) might include crab cakes, chicken breast en croûte with shiitake mushrooms, and pork medallions in Calvados-cream sauce. For dessert there's chocolate Bavarian cake. A downstairs tavern, John Minor's Ordinary, serves lighter fare and an extensive selection of imported beers.

WINDMILL POINT MARINE RESORT, Windmill Point, VA 22578. Tel. 804/435-1166, or toll free 800/552-3743 in Virginia. 65 rms. A/C TV TEL **Directions:** From Route 3 in Whitestone, take Route 695 for 7 miles to Windmill Point.

$ Rates: $69–$79 single or double landside rooms; $89 single or double waterfront rooms; $129 suite. Children under 16 stay free in parents' room. MC, V. **Parking:** Free.

This modern beachfront resort complex, fronted by an impressively landscaped entranceway, commands superb views of Chesapeake Bay. The balconied rooms, offering panoramic marine vistas, are attractively decorated in soft contemporary blue and rose color schemes, furnished with light wood pieces, and fitted out with all the modern amenities. There are slips for 150 yachts.

Dining/Entertainment: The Dockside Hearth lounge and restaurant overlooks the pool and beachfront. All three meals are served in season.

Facilities: Golf, tennis, marina, fishing.

BUDGET

CEDAR GROVE BED & BREAKFAST INN, Fleeton Rd. Rte. 1, Box 2535, Reedville, VA 22539. Tel. 804/453-3915. 3 rms (1 with bath). **Directions:** From Reedville, follow Fleeton Road (Route 657) approximately 3 miles, to Cedar Grove.

$ Rates (including full breakfast): $60–$75 double. No credit cards. **Parking:** Free.

Surrounded by farm fields, Cedar Grove is a stately 1913 Colonial Revival house that looks out over Chesapeake Bay and the lighthouse at the mouth of the Great Wicomico River. Arctic swans spend the winter here in the coves and marshes of the bay, and ospreys nest on nearby Big Fleet's Pond. In this tranquil setting, hosts Susan and Bob Tipton run an appealing B&B, with three spacious guest rooms decorated with white wicker and Victorian pieces. One room has a private balcony. Downstairs, the formal parlor features Oriental rugs and Victorian Eastlake furnishings. The sun room is a pleasant spot to read or watch TV. Outdoors are a tennis court and croquet, and bicycles are available for touring the area. Less active types can kick back in a hammock or the rocking chairs on the porch.

WHERE TO DINE

Besides the restaurants in the above hotels, the following is noteworthy:

THE RIVER CAFE, Rte. 695, White Stone. Tel. 804/435-0113.
   Cuisine: AMERICAN/SEAFOOD. **Directions:** Follow Route 695 from its junction with Route 3 in White Stone for about 3 miles.

$ Prices: Appetizers $4.95; entrees $9.50–$18.95. MC, V.
   Open: Dinner only, Tues–Sat 5–10:30pm.

At this popular local hangout Jim and Mary McDaniel serve excellent homemade fare, especially seafood, in a casual setting. Walls are adorned with nautical prints, maps, and a Chesapeake Bay landscape mural. There are glass-top white tablecloths on the cozy tables, and seating is in sturdy captain's chairs. Mrs. McDaniel creates many of the recipes herself, and if it's on the menu, we strongly recommend her well-seasoned carrot soup.

A favorite entree here is the fried crab cake platter, which comes with rice pilaf or stuffed potato, vegetable, green salad, and fresh bread. Other dinner choices are seafood shish kebab with lobster, shrimp, scallops, green peppers, red onions, mushroom, and tomato, all charcoal-grilled; salmon with creamy basil sauce; and homemade pasta with white clam sauce. If you want lighter fare, sandwiches such as soft-shell crab, served with french fries and cole slaw, are a modest $6.95.

CHAPTER 7
THE PIEDMONT

1. CHARLOTTESVILLE
2. LYNCHBURG

With the serene blue horizon of the Blue Ridge Mountains to the west, the rolling hills of the Piedmont, watered by the James River, reveal a scenic pastoral landscape. No wonder Peter Jefferson, coming here to survey the land, decided to settle, and amassed hundreds of acres. His son, America's third president, inherited not only his father's property but an abiding attachment to the land where he, too, spent much of his life.

Today Charlottesville is a lively university town, filled with visitors drawn by the monuments to Thomas Jefferson's genius. Historic Lynchburg, on the James River, has interesting sights of its own, including the tiny village of Appomattox Court House.

1. CHARLOTTESVILLE

72 miles W of Richmond, 120 miles SW of Washington, D.C.

GETTING THERE · By Plane USAir flies to Charlottesville-Albemarle Airport, 201 Bowen Loop (tel. 804/973-8341), and has several flights daily to and from Washington, D.C., and Richmond.

By Train Amtrak, offering daily service to points north and south, has its station at 810 West Main Street (tel. 804/296-4559, or toll free 800/872-7245).

By Bus The Greyhound/Trailways Bus Terminal is at 310 West Main Street (tel. 804/295-5131).

By Car Charlottesville is easy to reach from all directions; it is immediately accessible by both U.S. 29 and I-64, which connect directly with I-81 and I-95.

ESSENTIALS Orientation Charlottesville has not one but two downtowns: the **"Corner" neighborhood,** encompassing West Main and adjoining streets across from the University of Virginia, and the **historic downtown,** centered around a pedestrian mall and the old Court House.

Charlottesville Transit Service (tel. 804/296-RIDE) provides bus service Monday through Saturday from 6:30am to 6:30pm throughout the city and surrounding Albemarle County.

Information The **Charlottesville/Albermarle Information Center** is in the Thomas Jefferson Visitor Center on Route 20, just off I-64 (tel. 804/977-1783).

In the foothills of the Blue Ridge Mountains, Charlottesville is "Mr. Jefferson's Country." One of America's most passionate believers in freedom and human rights, Thomas Jefferson was born 4 miles east of Charlottesville. Here he built his famous mountaintop home, Monticello; selected the site for and helped plan Ash Lawn–Highland, home of James Monroe; designed his "academical village," the still-extant

University of Virginia; and died on July 4, 1826, at home—"All my wishes end where I hope my days will end . . . at Monticello."

Established in 1762 as the county seat for Albemarle, the town originally consisted of 50 acres centered on Court Square, its Court House complete with a jail, whipping post, pillory, and stocks to keep fractious citizens in line. In the early days the Court House doubled as a church, with rotating services for different denominations; Jefferson called it the "Common Temple." It also served as a marketplace. Elections were held in Court Square followed by raucous political celebrations. The taverns across the street were well patronized. Today the historic square is a quiet place, and the action centers on a very up-to-date pedestrian mall of shops and restaurants adjacent to it.

Jefferson and Monroe were not Charlottesville's only famous early citizens. James Madison also lived close by. The trio were instrumental in developing the emerging nation. Jefferson, our first great democrat, advocated freedom of religion, public education, and the abolition of slavery, and wrote the Declaration of Independence. Madison was involved in the development of our Constitution and Bill of Rights. And Monroe, one of the two American Presidents to actually fight in the Revolution, not only contributed to the expansion of the country's boundaries by negotiating the Louisiana Purchase, but established the nation's fundamental foreign policy via his Monroe Doctrine, warning European rulers that this hemisphere was off-limits.

Though today's Charlottesville is a cosmopolitan center, it is still sufficiently unchanged and pastoral for visitors to imagine themselves back in colonial times when Jefferson would ride 2 miles on horseback to visit his friend, Monroe.

WHAT TO SEE & DO

Make your first stop in town the **Charlottesville/Albemarle Information Center,** housed in the Thomas Jefferson Visitor Center (tel. 804/977-1783), on Route 20 just off I-64. The center provides maps and literature about local and state attractions, makes hotel/motel reservations, and answers any questions. In addition to welcoming visitors, the center houses a marvelous permanent exhibit called "Thomas Jefferson at Monticello." After viewing the exhibition, purchase the **Presidents' Pass,** a discount block ticket combining admission to Monticello, Michie Tavern, and Ash Lawn–Highland. The cost is $16, a savings of about $2. Don't buy it for children under 12—they pay less at each attraction. The center is open March through October, daily from 9am to 5:30pm; the rest of the year, to 5pm.

If you'd like to receive information before you arrive, write to the **Charlottesville/Albemarle Visitors Bureau,** P.O. Box 161, Charlottesville, VA 22902.

BLOCK-TICKET ATTRACTIONS

MONTICELLO, Off Rte. 53. Tel. 804/295-8181 or 295-2657.

 The phrase "Renaissance man" might have been coined to describe Thomas Jefferson. Perhaps our most important founding father, he was also a lawyer, architect, scientist, musician, writer, educator, and horticulturist. Monticello

---

IMPRESSIONS

Both the natural beauty of the surrounding countryside and the man-made beauty of Charlottesville combine to weave a tapestry of American history which few other towns or cities can boast.
—JOHN F. KENNEDY, CHARLOTTESVILLE, 1962

N

CHARLOTTESVILLE

↑ Courtyard by Marriott

Hampton Inn

Comfort Inn

Route 654

250 Bypass

Barracks Rd.

English Inn

20

Rugby Ave.

Massie Rd.

Econo Lodge South

Emmet St.

Preston Ave.

McIntire Rd.

Park St.

Locust Ave.

250

Ivy Rd.

Grady Ave.

Bear's Head Inn

250

University of Virginia

High St.
Market St.

The Mall

E. Market St.

McCormick Rd.

W. Main St.

Water St.

South St.

Virginia Discovery Museum

29 Bypass

Park Ave.

Jefferson Park Ave.

Amtrak Station

Bus Terminal

Monticello Ave.

To Interstate 95 & Richmond (70 miles) →

Cherry Ave.

Elliott Ave.

Avon St.

Fontaine Ave.

5th St. Ext.

64

Historic Michie Tavern

29

Harris Rd.

Charlotte/Abemarle Information Center

Route 53

Monticello

To Lynchburg (62 miles) ↙

64

Old Lynchburg Rd.

Holiday Inn

Route 742

i

20

To Scottsville ↓

To Ash Lawn (Rte 795) ↓

LYNCHBURG

501

Boonsboro Rd.

Rivermont Ave.

Point of Honor

Cabell St.

ALT 29

Boonsboro Shopping Center

Link Rd.

Langhorne Rd.

Pest House Medical Museum

Hollins Mill Rd.

Mansion Inn

Main St.

29

Colony Rd.

Cranehill Dr.

Old City Cemetery

Federal St.

501

Old Forest Rd.

Lynchburg Fine Arts Center

Memorial Ave.

5th St.

Park Ave.

12th St.

Florida Ave.

Visitors Information Center

i

501

221

Lakeside Dr.

Kemper St.

Anne Spencer House

501

Campbell Ave.

460

Thomas Rd.

ALT 29

29

Mayflower Dr.

460

501

501

Graves Mill Rd.

Fort Ave.

Wards Rd.

Candlers

Mountain Rd.

460

Poplar Forest

ALT 460

Wards Ferry Rd.

Leesville Rd.

Timberlake Rd.

Wards

501

Information ①

(pronounced "Mon-ti-*chel*-lo"), the home he built over a 40-year period (1769–1809), is considered an architectural masterpiece, and was the first Virginia plantation to sit atop a mountain (great houses were usually by rivers). Rejecting the Georgian architecture that characterized his time, Jefferson opted instead for the 16th-century Italian style of Andrea Palladio. Later, during his 5-year term as minister to France, he was influenced by the homes of noblemen at the court of Louis XVI, and on his return to the U.S. in 1789, he enlarged his home, incorporating features of the Parisian buildings he so admired.

Today the house is restored as closely as possible to its appearance during Jefferson's retirement years. Nearly all its furniture and other household objects were owned by Jefferson or his family. The garden has been extended to its original 1,000-foot length, and the Mulberry Row dependencies—a joinery, smokehouse, dairy, nailery, blacksmith shop, weaver's cottage, slave and servants' quarters—have been excavated.

In Jefferson's day the Entrance Hall was a museum (the antlers displayed here were brought back from Lewis and Clark's famed expedition). This room also contains one of his inventions, a 7-day calendar clock, which still works. Just off the Entrance Hall is Jefferson's high-ceilinged bedroom, where he died at the age of 83. Opposite the bedroom is Jefferson's library, which contained more than 6,000 books, later sold to the government as the nucleus of the Library of Congress. In the study, one of his telescopes (he was also an amateur astronomer) sits in the south window. The adjacent "South Square Room," used as a sitting room, displays a portrait of Jefferson's oldest daughter, Martha, painted by Thomas Sully in 1836 when she was 64. Martha inherited the home along with sizable debts, and within 5 years sold it for a mere $7,000. The Parlor, a semi-octagonal room with a Jefferson-designed parquet cherry floor, was the scene of marriages, christenings, and family musicales (Jefferson played the violin; his wife, Martha, the harpsichord). Many of the furnishings here were Paris purchases, and the walls are hung with many of the finest paintings from Jefferson's collection.

The Parlor opens into the Dining Room, where the family would assemble for the evening meal at 3:30pm. Jefferson kept books by the table, so he could read while waiting for the family to join him. The busts of Benjamin Franklin, John Paul Jones, George Washington, John Adams, and Lafayette in the connecting Tea Room are copies of Houdon originals that once graced this room. Across the passage is the octagonal Madison Room, its wallpaper of the lattice-and-treillage pattern Jefferson saw and admired in Paris. An unusual feature for the 18th century was a built-in closet, though even Jefferson didn't think of hangers.

Under the house and terraces you'll see the "dependencies," including the kitchen, wine cellar, smokehouse, and stables. There's also an orchard with about 30 varieties of fruit, a vineyard, a vegetable garden, and a beautiful landscape garden with ornamental trees and flower beds. Mulberry Row was named for the mulberries Jefferson planted there. At the end of the south terrace is the "Honeymoon Cottage," to which Jefferson brought his bride in 1772. Crisscrossing the grounds are farm roads, roundabouts, serpentine walks, and wooded pathways. Jefferson's grave is in the family burial ground (still in use), inscribed according to his instructions with his own words "and not a word more": HERE WAS BURIED THOMAS JEFFERSON/ AUTHOR OF THE DECLARATION OF AMERICAN INDEPENDENCE/ OF THE STATUTE OF VIRGINIA FOR RELIGIOUS FREEDOM/ AND FATHER OF THE UNIVERSITY OF VIRGINIA.

After visiting the graveyard, you can take a shuttle bus back to the visitor parking lot or walk through the woods via a delightful path.

It's best to avoid weekends when the tourist traffic is heaviest, and during summer, the first tour (at 8am) is advised. There is a lovely wooded picnic area with tables and grills on the premises, and in summer, lunch fare can be purchased.

Admission: $7 adults, $6 seniors, $3 children 6–11.

Open: 25-minute guided tours offered Mar–Oct, daily 8am–5pm; Nov–Feb, daily 9am–4:30pm. **Directions:** From the Visitors Center on Route 20, go south to Route 53 and turn left; Monticello's entrance is about 2 miles farther.

HISTORIC MICHIE TAVERN, Rte 53. Tel. 804/977-1234.

Unless you're picnicking at Monticello, plan your visit to Michie Tavern (pronounced "Mickey") to coincide with lunchtime. In the "Ordinary," a converted log cabin with original hand-hewn walls and beamed ceilings, hot meals are still served to weary travelers for reasonable pence. An all-you-can-eat buffet of southern fare is priced at under $10 for adults, half price for children ages 6 to 11 (under 6, free). You'll dine off pewter plates at rustic oak tavern tables, and in winter there's a blazing fire. The meal is served daily from 11:30am to 3pm.

In 1746 Scotsman John Michie (known as "Scotch John") purchased 1,152 acres of land from Patrick Henry's father, and in 1784 Michie's son, William, built this historic tavern on a well-traveled stagecoach route. In addition to running the inn, the Michies also farmed the land, did some blacksmithing, and ran a general store, and their descendants owned the property through 1910.

In 1927, the tavern was moved to its present location, but was otherwise unchanged from William's time. Today it contains an excellent collection of pre-Revolutionary War furniture and artifacts. In the Ladies' Parlor you'll see 18th-century women's boots and a skirt hoop. The Ballroom was the social center of the whole countryside, where fiddlers played tunes like "Lumps of Pudding," and lively Virginia reels were danced. Items like a cheese press, curd breaker, and corn shucker can be seen in the Keeping Hall.

Behind the tavern are reproductions of the "dependencies"—an old log kitchen; a "necessary" (note the corncobs, not exactly squeezably soft); the dairy, which in Michie's time would have been filled with crocks of butter, milk, cream, eggs, and cheeses; the smokehouse, where deer, rabbit, and other game would have been cured; the ice house; and the root cellar, in which apples, corn, and wheat would have been stored.

The general store was re-created, along with an excellent crafts shop; the Virginia Wine Museum is also on the premises. Behind the store is a grist mill that has operated continuously since 1797.

Admission: $5.50 adults, $2.50 children 6–11, under 6 free.

Open: Self-guided tour with recorded narratives, daily 9am–5pm. **Closed:** New Year's and Christmas days. **Directions:** From the Visitors Center on Route 20, go south to Route 53 and turn left; Michie Tavern is about 1 mile farther.

ASH LAWN–HIGHLAND, Rte. 795. Tel. 804/293-9539.

James Monroe played a sizable role in early American history. He fought in the Revolution and was wounded in Trenton, recovered, and went on to hold more offices than any other president, including several foreign ministries. Monroe's close friendship with Thomas Jefferson brought him to Charlottesville, where Jefferson wished to create "a society to our taste." In 1793 he purchased 1,000 acres adjacent to Monticello and built an estate he called Highland, perhaps because of his Scottish ancestry. (The name Ash Lawn dates to 1838.)

Before Monroe had a chance to settle in, Washington named him minister to France and sent him off to Europe for 4 years. During his absence, Jefferson sent gardeners over to start orchards, and the Madisons also made agricultural contributions. By the time Monroe returned from France and moved into Highland in 1799 with his wife, Elizabeth, he was already in financial difficulties, and his "cabin castle" developed along more modest lines than originally intended. When he retired in 1825 his debts totaled $75,000, and he was forced to sell the beloved farm where he had hoped to spend his last days.

Since 1975 Ash Lawn-Highland and 550 surrounding acres have been under the auspices of the College of William and Mary (Monroe's alma mater), and restoration/excavation/historical research has been an ongoing process. On a

40-minute house **tour** you'll see some of the estate's original furnishings and artifacts, and learn a great deal about our fifth president. Many special events (concerts, festivals) take place here, and there are crafts demonstrations as well. Horses and cattle graze in the fields, and about two dozen peacocks roam the boxwood gardens.

Five of the original rooms remain today, along with the basement kitchen, the overseer's cottage (Monroe owned about 30 slaves), restored slave quarters, and the old smokehouse. A later owner, John Massey, built the two-story addition to the main house in 1884. On the grounds are a gift shop and picnic tables.

Admission: $6 adults, $2 children 6–11, under 6 free.

Open: Mar–Oct, daily 9am–6pm; Nov–Feb, daily 10am–5pm. **Directions:** Follow the directions to Monticello. Ash Lawn is 2½ miles past Monticello on Route 795.

MORE ATTRACTIONS

In-Town Attractions

UNIVERSITY OF VIRGINIA, University Ave. Tel. 804/924-7969.

Jefferson's "academical village," the University of Virginia is graced with spacious lawns, serpentine-walled gardens, colonnaded pavilions, and a classical rotunda inspired by the Pantheon in Rome. Jefferson regarded its creation (all the more remarkable when you consider that it was begun in his 73rd year) as one of his three greatest achievements.

He was in every sense the father of this institution. He conceived it, wrote the charter, raised money for its construction, drew the plans, selected the site, laid the cornerstone in 1817, supervised construction, served as the first rector, selected the faculty, and created the curriculum. His good friends, Monroe and Madison, sat with him on the first board, and Madison succeeded him as rector, serving for 8 years.

Focal point of the university and starting point for **tours** is the Rotunda (at Rugby Road). Some 600 feet of tree-dotted lawn extends from the south portico of the Rotunda to what is now Cabell Hall, a building designed at the turn of the century by Stanford White. On either side of the lawn are pavilions designed and still used for faculty housing, each of a different architectural style "to serve as specimens for the Architectural lecturer." Behind each pavilion is a large garden, originally practical (faculty members grew vegetables and kept livestock), but today maintained as decorative landscaping. Behind the gardens are the original student dormitories, used—and greatly coveted—by students today; though centrally heated, they still have working fireplaces. The room Edgar Allan Poe occupied when he was a student here is furnished as it would have been in 1826 and is open to visitors.

Paralleling the lawn, and its buildings to the rear along either side, are more rows of student rooms called the Ranges. Equally spaced within each of the Ranges are "hotels," originally used to accommodate student dining. Each hotel was to represent a different country where the students would have to eat the food and speak the language of that particular country. This was a wonderful idea on Jefferson's part but lasted only a short while as everyone wanted to eat French but no one wanted to eat German.

Lest you think colleges were serene havens of learning in Jefferson's day, it may interest you to know that the first year of the University of Virginia's existence (1825) was marked by student rioting and a consequent faculty resignation.

The Rotunda is today restored as Jefferson designed it. On the tour you'll see the oval chemistry room; the Rotunda bell, originally hung on the south portico and used to wake students at dawn (no wonder they rioted); classrooms; the library; and the magnificent colonnaded Dome Room. The Alexander Galt statue of Jefferson on the second floor (originally the main entry level) is said to be an excellent likeness; there's another statue of him, by Sir Moses Ezekiel, on the esplanade north of the Rotunda. While exploring the grounds and gardens, do note the lovely chapel built in 1890.

Open: 45-minute tours given daily at 10 and 11am, and 2, 3, and 4pm. **Closed:** 2 weeks around Christmas.

ALBEMARLE COUNTY COURT HOUSE, 501 E. Jefferson St.

The center of village activity in colonial days, today the Court House in the historic downtown area has a facade and portico dating from the Civil War. There's no tour here, but you can take a glance at Jefferson's will in the County Office Building. Pick up a brochure called "A Guide to Historic Downtown Charlottesville" for a walking tour detailing this and other historic downtown sights.

Admission: Free.
Open: Mon–Fri 9am–5pm.

THE MALL, Main St. between 2nd St. W. and 6th St. E. Tel. 804/295-7973 for mall events.

Stroll into the 20th century along a charming pedestrian brick mall extending for about eight blocks on downtown Main Street. You can park free for 2 hours with merchant validation in the lot at 505 East Market Street or on any of the lots along Water Street. In addition to shops and restaurants, the mall has a movie theater that charges only $1.50 for tickets. It's enhanced by fountains, benches under shade trees, and big pots of flowers.

MCGUFFEY ART CENTER, 201 Second St. NW, between Market and Jefferson Sts. Tel. 804/295-7973.

At the center, located just a few blocks off the Mall, local artists and craftspeople have studio exhibits and sell their creations. The **Second Street Gallery,** showing contemporary art from all over the U.S., is also located here.

Admission: Free.
Open: Tues–Sat 10am–5pm, Sun 1–5pm.

VIRGINIA DISCOVERY MUSEUM, East End of downtown Mall. Tel. 804/293-5528.

The Virginia Discovery Museum is a place of enchantment, offering numerous hands-on exhibits and programs for young people. Here kids can dress up as firefighters, soldiers, police, and other grownups. The Colonial Log House, an authentic structure that once stood on a site in New Bedford, Virginia, is outfitted with the simple furnishings appropriate to an early 19th-century life-style. A series of fascinating exhibits deals with the senses, and the Fun and Games exhibit has a wonderful array of games, including bowling and giant checkers. An arts and crafts studio, a Garden of Smells, and a changing series of traveling exhibits round out the fun.

Admission: $3 adults, $2 seniors and children 1–13.
Open: Tues–Sat 10am–5pm, Sun 1–5pm.

Nearby Attractions

MONTPELIER, Rte. 20, Montpelier Station. Tel. 703/672-2728 or 672-2206.

The home of James Madison, Montpelier was opened to the public in 1987 after decades as a private residence belonging to the du Pont family. However, from 1723 to 1844, the 2,700-acre estate overlooking the Blue Ridge Mountains was home to three generations of the Madison family.

Born in 1751, James Madison rose to prominence early in life. At the 1776 Constitutional Convention in Williamsburg, he made sure that the guarantee of religious freedom was included in the Virginia Declaration of Rights. Later, as a member of the federal Constitutional Convention, he worked for passage of the Bill of Rights and for the creation of the executive departments, efforts that earned him the title "Father of the Constitution." After four terms in Congress (1789–97), Madison retired to his father's modest two-story, red-brick Georgian residence, and with advice from his good friend Jefferson, began expanding its proportions. In 1801, Madison became secretary of state under Jefferson and in 1809 succeeded Jefferson as President, leading the fledgling nation during the War of 1812. After his term, Madison returned to his Montpelier plantation. Like Jefferson, he pioneered agricultural improvements and struggled with the moral dilemma posed by slavery. He proposed a plan for gradual emancipation and the transportation of freed slaves to Liberia; however, for economic reasons he was never able to free his own slaves. Madison's final years, once again like Jefferson's, were much taken up with the University of Virginia where he served as rector.

The estate changed hands many times between 1844 and 1901, when it was purchased by William du Pont, Sr. He enlarged the mansion and added barns, staff houses, a saw mill, blacksmith shop, train station, dairy, and greenhouses. His wife created a 2½-acre formal garden. And when daughter Marion du Pont Scott inherited the property she had a steeplechase course built on it and initiated the Montpelier Hunt Races, which are still held here every November. The National Trust acquired the property following her death in 1984.

To date, little has been done to restore the sparsely furnished 55-room house. While it still makes for an interesting tour, keep in mind that this is no Monticello. Years of research into architecture and social history will be necessary before Montpelier takes its place alongside similar Virginia restorations.

Admission (including 10-minute slide show, bus tour of grounds, and house tour): $6 adults, $5 seniors, $1 children 6–11, free for children under 6.

Open: Tours given daily every 30 min 10am–4pm. **Directions:** Take Route 29N to Route 33E at Ruckersville. At Barboursville, turn left onto Route 20N. Montpelier is 25 miles north of Charlottesville.

OAKENCROFT VINEYARD, Barracks Rd. Tel. 804/296-4188.

There have been vineyards here since the 18th century, and Jefferson hoped to someday produce quality wines in Virginia. Today his dream is a reality, and many area wineries offer tours and tastings. A case in point is Oakencroft Vineyard, set on 17 acres of rolling farmland on a bucolic country road. A pretty red barn houses the tasting room, and there are rustic tables for al fresco lunching (bring your own picnic). A self-guided tour takes about 20 minutes.

For a list of other Charlottesville-area wineries, pick up a brochure at the Visitors Center.

Admission: Free.

Open: Apr–Dec, daily 11am–5pm; Jan–Mar, by appointment. **Directions:** Drive 3½ miles west of Va. 29 on Barracks Road.

WHERE TO STAY

In addition to the establishments recommended below, bed-and-breakfast accommodations in elegant homes and private estate cottages are handled by **Guesthouses Reservation Service, Inc.,** P.O. Box 5737, Charlottesville, VA 22905 (tel. 804/979-7264). You can write for a brochure, but reservations must be made by phone. Rates range from $48 and up for singles, $56 and up for doubles, and credit cards can be used only for deposits. The office is open Monday through Friday from noon to 5pm.

EXPENSIVE

BOAR'S HEAD INN & SPORTS CLUB, 200 Ednam Dr., Charlottesville,

VA 22901. Tel. 804/296-2181, or toll free 800/476-1988. Fax 804/971-5733. 175 rms and suites. A/C TV TEL **Directions:** Drive about 2 miles west of downtown Charlottesville on Route 250.

$ Rates: $95–$175 single or double; $160–$208 suite. Extra person $10. Weekend and other packages available. AE, CB, DC, MC, V. **Parking:** Free.

⭐ Named for the traditional symbol of hospitality in Shakespeare's England, the Boar's Head is a first-class combination of rural charm and sophisticated facilities. The focal point of the resort is a reconstructed historic grist mill that was dismantled and brought here in the early 1960s. The Tavern, Garden Room, and Old Mill dining room, and some guest rooms are in this section. Adjoining low-rise wings are more modern in feel, though furnishings throughout are Colonial reproductions.

Room decor varies. One attractive room has bright cabbage-rose print bedspreads and draperies, a dark-mahogany highboy with polished brass trim, Windsor chairs, and pretty botanical and hunt prints. Some rooms offer lake views; some have working fireplaces. All suites have one bedroom and one sitting room, with either kitchenette or wet bar; six have fireplaces. Many business travelers stay in the special concierge-staffed section of the inn, where amenities include a bathrobe, hairdryer, computer hookup, and complimentary morning newspaper.

Dining/Entertainment: Open for all three meals, the Old Mill Room offers candlelight dining in a historic setting of beamed ceilings, multipaned windows, and random-width plank floors. The dinner menu features entrees like roast goose Shenandoah, medallions of venison, and pan-seared swordfish ranging from $14.95 to $19.95. At lunch, you might dine on chicken and dumplings or hunter's chili with beef, venison, goose, and boar. The downstairs Tavern is a convivial spot with a glowing fire in winter. It offers lighter fare as well as full-course meals, and has live entertainment on weekends. In the separate Sport Club building are two additional dining rooms.

Services: Room service, turndown.

Facilities: Tennis, squash, platform tennis, fishing, hot-air balloon flights, jogging trail, health club, three swimming pools (including an Olympic-size pool in the Sports Club building), adjacent 18-hole golf course, gift shop.

MODERATE

COURTYARD BY MARRIOTT, 638 Hillsdale Dr., Charlottesville, VA 22901. Tel. 804/973-7100, or toll free 800/321-2211. 150 rms, 12 suites. A/C TV TEL **Directions:** Hillsdale Drive abuts the Fashion Square mall; take Route 29 north of downtown.

$ Rates: $62 single; $72 double, $62 Fri–Sat for up to four in a room. Children under 18 stay free in parents' room. Extra person $10. AE, CB, DC, DISC, MC, V. **Parking:** Free.

The Courtyard is set on a hill well off the highway, on several acres of attractively landscaped grounds. Its peach-colored 2½-story building houses nicely decorated rooms in soft mauves, pinks, and muted blues. Every bedroom has a walk-in closet, working desk, and couch (some are convertible). Interior rooms open onto the courtyard—a spacious grass-and-stone patio area with lounge chairs, umbrella tables, and a white latticed gazebo. Exterior rooms have tiny enclosed terraces.

Dining/Entertainment: The hotel's restaurant serves all three meals at moderate prices. The lounge, open daily from 4 to 11pm, has a working fireplace and overlooks the courtyard.

Services: Room service.

Facilities: Games room, pool, exercise room, Jacuzzi, coin-op laundry.

ENGLISH INN OF CHARLOTTESVILLE, 2000 Morton Dr., Charlottes-

ville, VA 22901. Tel. 804/971-9900, or toll free 800/338-9900. Fax 804/977-8008. 88 rms. A/C TV TEL **Directions:** Follow Route 29 north to the Route 250 Bypass.

$ Rates (including continental breakfast): $68–$75 single; $75–$82 double. Children under 12 stay free in parents' room. Extra person $7. AE, CB, DC, MC, V. **Parking:** Free.

Ⓢ A traditionally English Tudor-style building is the setting for this hospitable inn. You'll feel as though you're in the staid precincts of an English club when you enter the comfortable wood-paneled lobby, its floors strewn with Oriental rugs. Step down into the Conservatory, where cozy seating areas with wing chairs and small tables in front of an oversize fireplace make a perfect setting for the continental breakfast served daily. Rooms are variously decorated, many in Queen Anne–style reproduction pieces; others are more contemporary looking. Rose-colored floral-print spreads, matching draperies, and plush wall-to-wall rose carpets make a pleasing foil to polished wood furnishings. All rooms have a clock radio, remote-control color TV, and Water-Pik shower massage.

Dining/Entertainment: The Piccadilly Pub continues the English theme, with its tavern atmosphere. It offers light fare, full meals, and Sunday brunch.

Facilities: Pool, exercise room, sauna.

HOLIDAY INN MONTICELLO, 1200 Fifth St., Charlottesville, VA 22901. Tel. 804/977-5100, or toll free 800/HOLIDAY. Fax 804/293-5228. 131 rms. A/C TV TEL **Directions:** Take Exit 23 from I-64 and drive north (you will be on Fifth Street) over the highway; the hotel is on the right.

$ Rates: $50 single; $68 double. Children under 18 stay free in parents' room. Extra person $8. AE, CB, DC, DISC, MC, V. **Parking:** Free.

This pleasant Holiday Inn offers an easy-going atmosphere, a hospitable staff, and spacious accommodations decorated in beige and teal. A sixth-floor suite has a full kitchen and separate bedroom and living room. All king rooms are equipped with hairdryers, and some have good-size desks. A large outdoor pool is open seasonally. The on-premises restaurant serves reasonably priced American fare at breakfast, lunch, and dinner.

BUDGET

COMFORT INN, 1807 Emmet St. (Va. 29), Charlottesville, VA 22901. Tel. 804/293-6188, or toll free 800/228-5150. 64 rms. A/C TV TEL

$ Rates: $42–$49 single; $48–$58 double. Extra person $6; rollaway bed $6. Children under 18 stay free in parents' room. AE, DC, DISC, MC, V. **Parking:** Free.

Public areas in this four-story property north of downtown are exceptionally tasteful for a budget establishment. Complimentary breakfast of juice, coffee, and danish is available daily in the comfortably furnished lobby. Guest rooms are decorated in either blue-and-rose or ivory-and-rose color scheme and equipped with the standard amenities. There's an outdoor pool and sundeck; restaurants and a coin-op laundry are close by.

ECONO LODGE SOUTH, 400 Emmet St. (Va. 29), Charlottesville, VA 22903. Tel. 804/296-2104, or toll free 800/446-6900. 60 rms. A/C TV TEL

$ Rates: $36–$39 single; $40–$46 double. Children under 18 stay free in parents' room. Extra person $5. AE, CB, DC, DISC, MC, V. **Parking:** Free.

There are two Econo Lodges in Charlottesville; this one is north of downtown adjacent to the University of Virginia. Rooms are decorated in a handsome light-brown and navy-blue color scheme with attractive oak furnishings. This Econo offers all the modern amenities, plus a good-size swimming pool.

The other is the 48-room Econo Lodge North at 2014 Holiday Drive (off Va. 29),

Charlottesville, VA 22901 (tel. 804/295-3185, or toll free 800/446-6900). There's no pool, but rooms are cheerful. Rates are about $1 to $2 less across the board.

HAMPTON INN, 2035 India Rd., Charlottesville, VA 22906. Tel. 804/ 978-6777, or toll free 800/HAMPTON. 123 rms. A/C TV TEL **Directions:** Next to Seminole Square shopping center at India Road; take Va. 29 north of downtown.

$ Rates (including continental breakfast): $45–$47 single; $55–$57 double. Extra person free. AE, DC, DISC, MC, V. **Parking:** Free.

This well-run hotel has handsomely decorated rooms with oak furnishings and walls hung with Gauguin and Cézanne prints. All rooms have pull-out sofas, clock radios, and, in many cases, desks and/or armchairs with hassocks. Facilities include a nice-sized outdoor pool and sundeck.

NEARBY ACCOMMODATIONS

A Lovely Country Inn

SILVER THATCH INN, 3001 Hollymead Dr., Charlottesville, VA 22901. Tel. 804/978-4686. 7 rms (all with bath). A/C **Directions:** Hollymead Drive is just off Va. 29 (right turn), about 8 miles north of town.

$ Rates (including continental breakfast): $105–$125 double. Extra person $20. MC, V. **Parking:** Free.

Occupying a rambling white clapboard house, a section of which dates back to Revolutionary days, this charming hostelry is located on a quiet back road and set in a pretty country garden. Attractively decorated with authentic 18th-century pieces, the original part of the building now serves as a cozy common room, where inn guests are invited for afternoon refreshments. The 1812 center part of the house is now one of the dining rooms. Guest rooms are lovely, with down comforters on canopied four-poster beds, antique pine dressers, carved walnut and mahogany armoires, and exquisite quilts. Several rooms have working fireplaces. Hosts Joe and Mickey Geller are on hand to help make arrangements for nearby activities—trail rides, jogging, tennis, swimming, golf, fishing, and biking. Complimentary airport transportation is another plus. Telephones and TVs are available in the common areas.

Dining/Entertainment: Dinner is served in the candlelit dining rooms open to the public (inn guests should be sure to reserve a table in advance as they may find the restaurant all booked when they arrive). Nightly specials ($14 to $23) might include Thai shrimp and cucumber curry, Cornish hens Jamaican, or fresh-caught salmon in sorrel sauce. European and domestic wines are featured.

A Mountain Getaway

WINTERGREEN RESORT, Wintergreen, VA 22958. Tel. 804/325-2200, or toll free 800/325-2200. 1,300 accommodations. A/C TV TEL **Directions:** Take I-64 west to Exit 20 and follow Route 250 west; turn left onto Route 6 east and continue to Route 151 south to Route 664; then turn right and Wintergreen is 4½ miles farther on Route 664. It's about 35 miles from Charlottesville.

$ Rates: $95 nightly, $68 per night for a week stay, studio, double occupancy. Weekend and longer packages available. AE, MC, V.

A mountain resort with 6,700 of its 11,000 acres dedicated to the remaining undisturbed forestland, Wintergreen offers year-round vacation activities in a magnificent Blue Ridge Mountain setting. The resort's focal point is the tastefully lodgelike Inn, which has a huge grist-mill wheel occupying the two-story registration area.

Most accommodations are in small enclaves scattered throughout the property, but there are also two- to seven-bedroom homes, one- to four-bedroom condos, and studios and lodge rooms. Since the homes and condos are privately owned, furnishings are highly individual, ranging from country quaint to sleek and sophisticated settings of cutting-edge design. Condos are appointed with modern kitchen facilities, living areas, a bathroom for each bedroom, and balconies or patios (the mountain views are superb); most have working fireplaces.

Dining/Entertainment: Wintergreen has six full-service restaurants. The Copper Mine Restaurant and Lounge, at the Inn, offers noteworthy American cuisine in a relaxed casual setting. The Garden Terrace Restaurant in the sports center features casual dining, plus a kids-eat-free special Wednesday through Friday and Sunday evenings, 5:30 to 6:30pm. The Grist Mill in the Inn lobby is a coffee shop serving light meals. The Rodes Farm Inn has country, family-style meals. The Verandah specializes in Virginia regional items. And Trillium House offers fine dining in a charming country inn.

Facilities: Skiing (five lifts), hiking, nature programs, horseback riding, golf, tennis, indoor and outdoor swimming pools, lake swimming and boating, children's center, health club, hair salon, shops, grocery store.

WHERE TO DINE

In addition to the establishments listed below, the Old Mill Room in the Boar's Head Inn and the Silver Thatch Inn offer (see "Where to Stay," above) exceptional quality dining.

MODERATE/EXPENSIVE

C&O RESTAURANT, 515 E. Water St. Tel. 804/971-7044.
Cuisine: FRENCH. **Reservations:** Required.
$ Prices: Appetizers $5.50–$8; entrees $18–$27. AE, DC, DISC, MC, V.
Open: Downstairs, lunch Mon–Fri 11:30am–3pm; dinner daily 5:30–10:30pm. Upstairs, dinner only, seatings Mon–Sat at 6:30 and 9:30pm.

An unprepossessing brick front, complete with faded Pepsi sign, might make you think twice, but don't be deterred. This fine restaurant, located a block off the Mall, has received kudos from major critics. Raved a *Food & Wine* reviewer: "I can assure you that not since Jefferson was serving imported vegetables and the first ice cream at Monticello has there been more innovative cooking in these parts. . . ." And should you need further reassurance, the entrance, warmed by a wood-burning fireplace, is most welcoming.

Upstairs is a very elegant restaurant where menus change daily. Appetizer choices might include mussel soup or shrimp remoulade. Possible entrees: fresh tuna filet provençal, scallops with fennel, or filet of beef stuffed with roast shallot duxelles and topped with foie gras and morel butter. In the French style, salad and cheese are offered following the main course. Desserts are simple but perfectly executed versions of favorites like Linzer torte, lemon tart, and a layered hazelnut-and-chocolate genoise with espresso-butter-cream filling.

Downstairs, in the rustic bar area, lunch choices might include homemade spinach-and-egg fettuccine with fresh mussels and cream sauce or calf's liver with mustard-cream sauce; entrees like crab cakes and spicy ribeye steak are dinnertime favorites downstairs. The setting is a mix of exposed brick and rough-hewn barnwood, subdued lighting, and walls hung with an array of prints and photos. A bit of charm is added by white-clothed tables adorned with pretty flower arrangements. Premium wines by the glass are available upstairs or down.

LE SNAIL, 320 W. Main St. Tel. 804/295-4456.
Cuisine: FRENCH. **Reservations:** Advised.
$ Prices: Appetizers $4.75–$6.95; entrees $15.50–$22.50; Fixed-price dinner Mon–Thurs $16.95. AE, CB, DC, DISC, MC, V.
Open: Dinner only, Mon–Sat 6–10pm.

★ A marquee with a snail logo will guide you to this elegant restaurant. It occupies the first floor of a two-story 1880s residence; living quarters upstairs belong to chef Ferdinand Bazin and his wife, Judy. As you enter the foyer you'll note the stained-glass door (another snail pattern) and a collection of snail figurines which bring a note of whimsy to the dining areas. Note the pretty stencilwork on the walls in the back room—chef Bazin's own handiwork. Appetizers range from baby shrimp in creamy Grand Marnier sauce to snails in garlic butter topped with pastry crust. Main courses the night we visited included baked filet of flounder stuffed with smoked salmon mousse, pork loin medallions in curry sauce, and duck breast in a delicate raspberry-and-cassis sauce. The best deal is the fixed-price dinner, which includes a choice of soup or appetizers like shrimp in ravigote sauce, salad, a choice of several entrees, dessert (perhaps crème caramel), and coffee.

MODERATE

EASTERN STANDARD, downtown Mall, west end. Tel. 804/295-8668.
   Cuisine: AMERICAN. **Reservations:** Suggested, especially for dinner upstairs.
$ **Prices:** Appetizers $5.50–$6.25 upstairs, $3.50–$5 downstairs; entrees $13.95–$19.95 upstairs, $4.95–$10.25 downstairs. MC, V.
   Open: Upstairs, dinner only, Mon–Sat 6–11pm; downstairs, dinner only, daily 6–11pm.

Eastern Standard is paradoxically the last building on the western end of the Mall. Its airy and elegant contemporary decor is lovely. The downstairs dining room has pale-peach walls hung with the work of regional artists, tables lit by small shaded lamps, and a cream-colored, pressed-tin ceiling. The upstairs dining rooms have bare oak floors, Japanese prints on peach walls, and big arched windows overlooking the Mall. There's also a delightful graveled patio out back enclosed by a white fence.

Menus change frequently, but appetizers might include stacked crêpes layered with smoked salmon, tomato, red onion, herb cheese, and spinach; broiled clams and mussels with garlic butter and breadcrumbs; and sea scallops with chicory, strawberries, and raspberry vinaigrette. There are usually eight or so entree choices, perhaps boned Cornish game hen braised with mushrooms, pearl onions, and bacon; osso bucco; and baby rack of lamb with rosemary butter. Desserts, made on the premises, include such delectables as chocolate and Cointreau pot de crème and raspberry cheesecake. Dinner downstairs features similar selections, with additional lower-priced options like crab cakes and shrimp with black-bean sauce.

INEXPENSIVE

THE HARDWARE STORE, 316 E. Main St. (downtown Mall). Tel. 804/977-1518.
   Cuisine: AMERICAN.
$ **Prices:** Sandwiches, salads, soups, main courses, soda fountain $1.75–$10.75. MC, V.
   Open: Mon 11am–5pm, Tues–Thurs 11am–9pm, Fri–Sat 11am–10pm.

Old rolling ladders; stacks of oak drawers that once held screws, nuts and bolts; and vintage advertising signs—all display the old-time origins of this high-energy spot. A long, narrow space with an upstairs gallery, it provides comfortable seating in spacious leather-upholstered booths. Specialties include quiches and crêpes, tortilla basket salads, hamburgers, baked potatoes with great toppings, platters of fried fish, and barbecued ribs. There are soda-fountain treats, and pastries and cakes run the gamut from dense double-chocolate truffle cake to southern pecan pie. The Hardware Store has a fully stocked bar.

MILLER'S, 109 W. Main St. Tel. 804/971-8511.
   Cuisine: AMERICAN.

$ Prices: Appetizers $1.25–$4; entrees $5.50–$8.95; sandwiches $3.50–$4.50. MC, V.

Open: Lunch Mon–Fri 11:30am–2pm; dinner Mon–Thurs 5:30–9pm, Fri–Sat 5:30–10:30pm; light fare Fri–Sat 10:30pm–midnight.

Miller's is a converted old-time pharmacy with the original white-tile floor, pressed-tin ceiling, mahogany soda fountain as a back bar, and cherry woodwork and shelving. Walls display historic photos of old Charlottesville drugstores. Out front on the Mall, tree-shaded tables are enclosed by planters with flowers. Roast beef and turkey, roasted and carved on the premises and served on homemade French bread, are available at lunch and dinner. Dinner entrees might include jambalaya, chicken teriyaki, vegetable stir-fry, and fettuccine marinara. Desserts are homemade. Wine, beer, and mixed drinks are served till 2am. There's nighttime entertainment—jazz, classical, pop, folk, or blues—and on weekends there's a nominal cover charge after 9:30pm.

THE VIRGINIAN, 1521 W. Main St. Tel. 804/293-2606.
Cuisine: AMERICAN.
$ Prices: Appetizers $3.50–$4.25; entrees $6.95–$9.95. AE, MC, V.
Open: Mon–Fri 9am–2am, Sat–Sun 10am–2am.

A congenial student hangout across the street from the university, this simpatico spot has roomy oak booths and an always well-populated bar. Good jazz or rock is played at a low-decibel level, pine-paneled walls are hung with a changing exhibit of works by local photographers, and shaded wall sconces provide subdued lighting. All the fare is homemade, including yummy fresh-baked breads, and portions are large enough to satisfy the most voracious of students. At lunch or dinner you can't go wrong with a heaping bowl of linguine marinara with fresh mushrooms and mozzarella. Fresh seafood is featured at dinner in entrees like blue fish in lime sauce with almond-studded green beans and sautéed potatoes. Oven-fresh desserts change daily; the chocolate pecan pie is scrumptious.

BREAKFAST & LIGHT FOOD

THE COFFEE EXCHANGE, 120 E. Main St. Tel. 804/295-0975.
Cuisine: AMERICAN.
$ Prices: Sandwiches $4.25–$5.25; weekend champagne brunch $6.50.
Open: Mon–Thurs 8:30am–5:30pm, Fri–Sat 8:30am–9pm, Sun 10am–9pm.

This small eatery on the Mall is a pristinely charming setting in which to enjoy fresh-ground morning coffee and fresh-from-the-oven croissants. They come in many varieties—plain, almond-strawberry, raspberry-cheese, cinnamon, blueberry, and chocolate—and there are also muffins and sticky buns. Later in the day, try the Exchange for sandwiches (like chicken salad, turkey and Swiss, and roast beef—all made from meats cooked on the premises), a cold pasta-primavera salad, or a stuffed baked potato. The bakery goodies are excellent, and the aroma of fresh-baked breads and roast coffee is ambrosial. With its delicate shell-pink walls and tablecloths, a high Wedgwood-blue ceiling, art posters, and shelves of coffee makers and mugs lining the walls, this is the perfect place for afternoon tea or cappuccino with white-chocolate cheesecake or homemade cookies.

2. LYNCHBURG

66 miles S of Charlottesville, 112 miles W of Richmond

GETTING THERE   By Plane   The Lynchburg Regional Airport, Va. 29 south and Airport Road (tel. 804/847-1632), has direct service via USAir and United to Baltimore, Washington, D.C. (Dulles), and Pittsburgh.

By Train   At the Amtrak station, Kemper Street and Park Avenue (tel. toll free 800/872-7245), there is daily service to New York City and New Orleans.

By Bus   Frequent bus service is available at the Greyhound/Trailways Terminal, Wildflower Drive at Odd Fellows Drive (tel. 804/846-6614).

By Car   From Charlottesville, the shortest route is Va. 29 south. From Richmond, follow Route 360 west to Route 460, which goes directly to Lynchburg.

ESSENTIALS   The **telephone area code** is 804. The **Lynchburg Visitors Information Center,** 216 12th Street, at the corner of Church Street (P.O. Box 60), Lynchburg, VA 24505 (tel. 804/847-1811), is open daily from 9am to 5pm, and provides maps, brochures, and self-guided walking tours of historic districts. For information about guided tours, contact **City-Scape Tours Ltd.,** P.O. Box 3424, Lynchburg, VA 24503 (tel. 804/384-8337).

The City of Seven Hills, Lynchburg is on the James River. A large white granite rock on the riverbank at Ninth Street marks the place where John Lynch, the Quaker son of an Irish immigrant, began operating a ferry across the river in 1757. In the late 18th and 19th centuries, as the tobacco business boomed, the small town grew into an important shipping point.

Today the Lynchburg area offers visitors a look at Jefferson's country home, Poplar Forest, and Red Hill, the plantation where Patrick Henry spent his last years. For Civil War buffs, the principal attraction is nearby Appomattox Court House, where Gen. Robert E. Lee surrendered to Union troops, ending the Civil War.

WHAT TO SEE & DO

Start your tour in downtown Lynchburg at **Monument Terrace,** an imposing 139-step staircase built as a memorial to soldiers of all America's wars. From Church Street, at the base of the staircase, where there is a statue of a World War I doughboy, you can see the imposing Greek Revival facade of the **Old Court House,** on Court Street between 8th Street and 10th Street (tel. 804/847-1459), open daily from 1 to 4pm; admission is $1 for adults and 50¢ for students (children free when accompanied by an adult). Built in 1855, this outstanding example of civic architecture now houses artifacts and displays tracing the city's history. **Point of Honor,** 112 Cabell Street (tel. 804/847-1459), was built around 1815 for Dr. George Cabell, Sr., whose most famous patient was Patrick Henry. Aside from its historic and architectural interest (the house has an unusual octagonal bay facade), Point of Honor is a showcase of decorative arts of the period. The gardens, grounds, and auxiliary buildings have also been restored. Open daily from 1 to 4pm; admission is $1 for adults and 50¢ for students (children free when accompanied by an adult).

A designated historic landmark, the home and garden cottage of Harlem Renaissance poet **Anne Spencer,** 1313 Pierce Street (tel. 804/846-0517), is open by appointment, $2 suggested donation. The red-shingled house, built by Edward Spencer for his family in 1903, was her home until her death in 1975. The **Pest House Medical Museum** is a tiny building where Lynchburg residents suffering from such contagious diseases as smallpox and measles were quarantined in the 1800s. The Pest House is in the **Old City Cemetery,** Fourth Street and Taylor Street (tel. 804/847-1811), in the Confederate soldiers' section. The Visitor Center has a free guide to the cemetery.

NEARBY ATTRACTIONS

POPLAR FOREST, Forest, Va. Tel. 804/525-1806.

At Thomas Jefferson's "other home," you can see the restoration of a National Historic Landmark as it happens. Opened to the public in 1985, octagonal Poplar Forest is now undergoing archeological and architectural research, and visitors are able to see relics from the buildings and grounds as they are brought to light and exhibited. At one time the seat of a 4,819-acre plantation, and the source of much of Jefferson's income, Poplar Forest was designed by him to utilize light and air flow to the maximum in as economical a space as possible. In 1806, while he was President, Jefferson himself assisted the masons in laying the foundation for the dwelling; today it is considered one of his most creative and original designs.

Admission: $5 adults, $1 children.

Open: Apr–Oct, Wed–Sun 10am–4pm (last tour begins at 3:45pm). Closed Nov–Mar. **Directions:** The main entrance is on Route 661, 1 mile from Route 221 and about 6 miles southwest of town.

APPOMATTOX COURT HOUSE NATIONAL HISTORIC PARK, Appomattox Court House. Tel. 804/352-8987.

Here, in the parlor of Wilmer McLean's farmhouse, on April 9, 1865, Robert E. Lee's surrender of the Army of Northern Virginia to Ulysses S. Grant signaled the end of a bitter conflict. Today the 20 or so houses, stores, courthouse, and tavern that comprised the little village called Appomattox Court House have been restored, and visitors can walk the country lanes in the rural stillness where these events took place. At the Visitors Center, pick up a map of the park. Upstairs, slide presentations and museum exhibits include fascinating excerpts from the diaries and letters of Civil War soldiers.

Buildings open to the public include McLean's farmhouse, Clover Hill Tavern, Meeks' Store, the Woodson Law Office, the Court House (totally reconstructed), jail, the Kelly House, and the Mariah Wright House. Surrender Triangle, where the Confederates lay down their arms and rolled up their battle flags, is outside the Kelly House.

There are picnic tables at the entrance, where visitors must park; no cars are allowed in the village.

Admission: $2 ages 16–62, free for those under 16 and over 62.

Open: Daily 8:30am–5pm. **Directions:** The park is on Route 24, about 4 miles north of Route 460 and about 22 miles east of Lynchburg.

RED HILL, PATRICK HENRY NATIONAL MEMORIAL, Brookneal. Tel. 804/376-2044.

The fiery orator's last home, Red Hill is a modest frame farmhouse with several dependencies, including the overseer's cottage that Patrick Henry used as a law office. Henry retired to Red Hill in 1794 after serving five terms as governor of Virginia. Failing health forced him to refuse numerous posts, including Chief Justice of the Supreme Court, secretary of state, and minister to Spain and France. When he died here on June 6, 1799, he was buried in the family graveyard.

The main house, destroyed by fire in 1919, has been authentically reconstructed on the original foundation. The law office is an original structure; the carriage house and other small buildings were added to represent the plantation as it was in Henry's time.

Admission: $3 adults, $2 seniors, $1 students.

Open: Apr–Oct, daily 9am–5pm; Nov–Mar, daily 9am–4pm. **Closed:** New Year's, Thanksgiving, and Christmas days. **Directions:** From Lynchburg, take Route 501 south to Brookneal, then Route 40 east and follow the brown RED HILL signs. Red Hill is 35 miles from Lynchburg.

BOOKER T. WASHINGTON NATIONAL MONUMENT, Hardy. Tel. 703/721-2094.

Although Booker T. Washington called his boyhood home a plantation, the

Burroughs farm was small, 207 acres, with never more than 10 slaves. Washington's mother was the cook, and the cabin where he was born was also the plantation kitchen. He and his brother and sister slept on a dirt floor and there was no glass on the window openings; in his autobiography *Up from Slavery,* he recalls the winter cold.

At this memorial to one of America's great black leaders, visitors can conjure up the setting of Washington's childhood in reconstructed farm buildings and demonstrations of farm life in pre–Civil War Virginia. Begin at the Visitors Center, which offers a slide show and a map with a self-guided plantation tour and nature walks that wind through the original Burroughs property.

The Washingtons left the Burroughs farm when Booker was 9, in 1865. Overcoming the obstacles of poverty and prejudice, he determinedly sought an education and actually walked most of the 400 miles from his new home in West Virginia to a then-new secondary school, Hampton Institute. He worked his way through school and achieved national prominence as an educator, founder of Tuskegee Institute in Alabama, author, and advisor to Presidents. In 1957, a century after he was born, this national monument was established to honor his life and work.

Admission: $1 ages 17–61, $3 families.

Open: Daily 8:30am–5pm. **Directions:** From Lynchburg, take Route 460 west to Route 122 south.

WHERE TO STAY

MANSION INN, 405 Madison St., Lynchburg, VA 24504. Tel. 804/528-5400, or toll free 800/352-1199. 5 rms (all with bath). A/C TV TEL

$ Rates (including full breakfast): $79–$89 double. MC, V. **Parking:** Free.

This two-story Spanish Georgian mansion, set behind a cast-iron fence in downtown Lynchburg between Fourth Street and Fifth Street, fits right in with the other Victorian mansions on Quality Row in the Garland Hill Historic District. A massive, two-story, six-columned portico heralds the entrance, but guests actually drive up past the carriage house to the porte-cochère side entrance. The front door opens to a 50-foot great hall, with soaring ceilings and polished cherrywood columns and wainscoting.

Guest rooms, with remote-control color TVs and clock radios, are extremely spacious and beautifully furnished in a variety of stunning decors. The Gilliam Room is Victorian, with a mahogany four-poster bed, a rose-print comforter edged in lace, and a dresser strewn with turn-of-the-century bibelots. The country French room has a Laura Ashley look, with a bleached wood four-poster and armoire. And the Nantucket Room is nautical in feel, with blue-and-white print fabrics, and bamboo and wicker pieces. You'll find a morning newspaper at your door, and on an antique dresser in the upstairs hall, a fresh-brewed pot of coffee and pitcher of juice is set out to tide over early risers until breakfast. Nightly turndown is another amenity. A full breakfast, served in the formal dining room, might consist of fresh fruit cup and juice, bacon, scrambled eggs (with cheese, chives, and watercress), crumpets, and coffee and tea.

WHERE TO DINE

When you set out from Lynchburg to see area sights, it's a good idea to take along a picnic lunch. In addition to the box lunches prepared by the **Farm Basket** (see below), you can shop for picnic fare in the **Lynchburg Community Market,** at Bateau Landing, Main Street and 12th Street (tel. 804/847-1499), open Monday through Friday from 8am to 2pm and on Saturday from 6am to 2pm.

EMIL'S CAFE & ROTISSERIE, Boonsboro Shopping Center, Rte. 501. Tel. 804/384-3311.

Cuisine: AMERICAN. **Reservations:** Recommended for the Rotisserie. **Directions:** The shopping center is about 3 miles north of downtown on Route 501.

$ Prices: Café, appetizers $4.25–$7.50; entrees $7.95–$14.95. Rotisserie, appetizers $3.95–$8.50; entrees $11.95–$19.50. AE, DC, DISC, MC, V.

Open: Mon–Sat 10am–10pm.

Run with loving care by the Gabathuler family (husband Emil is the chef), these two restaurants—an unpretentious café and elegant Rotisserie—have a common entrance foyer and offer excellent preparations in different price ranges.

The more casual café has a greenhouse look with many hanging plants; seating is in Windsor chairs, at bare wood tables. Salads, sandwiches, and hot entrees are available for lunch (try crabmeat imperial on an English muffin or seafood au gratin). For dinner, you could start with a homemade soup—lentil and bacon or French onion. Entrees might include pork scaloppine with mushroom crème fraîche sauce or beef kebabs béarnaise. Desserts such as soufflé glacé Grand Marnier are extraordinary for such an inexpensive place.

The Rotisserie is a formal dining room with Victorian etched-glass dividers, brass chandeliers, and seating in comfortable armchairs. Appetizers like angel-hair pasta with crème fraîche and shrimp, baked Brie, and oysters stuffed with crabmeat are followed by entrees like oven-baked quail stuffed with apple and served with grapes and zinfandel sauce or beef Stroganoff in sour-cream-and-burgundy sauce, served with tiny dumplings. There are rich desserts—baked Alaska among them.

THE FARM BASKET, 2008 Langhorne Rd. Tel. 804/528-1107.

Cuisine: AMERICAN.

$ Prices: Box lunch $5; sandwiches $2.50–$4.75. MC, V.

Open: Lunch counter, Mon–Sat 10am–3pm; shops, Mon–Sat 10am–5pm.

A charming little complex of shops backing onto a tiny stream, the Farm Basket specializes in freshly made box lunches you can eat in the shop or on the back deck, or take away. The menu changes daily, but the box lunch always includes a choice of sandwich, salad, dessert, and drink—for example, sandwich choices of chicken-salad roll, ham hoe cake, and beef biscuit; salads like tomato aspic or three bean; and, for dessert, lemon bread with cream cheese or an apple-dapple cake. Fresh fruit and yogurt, barbecued sandwiches with cole slaw, and smoked turkey croissant are à la carte options.

CHAPTER 8

THE SHENANDOAH VALLEY & THE VIRGINIA HIGHLANDS

Native Americans called the 200-mile-long valley "Shenandoah," meaning Daughter of the Stars. Today a national park with the same name provides spectacular landscapes and protects the beauty and peace of the Blue Ridge Mountains east of the valley. Along the ridge of those mountains, and paralleling the valley, the scenic 107-mile-long Skyline Drive runs the full length of Shenandoah National Park and connects directly with the Blue Ridge Parkway, which continues south to North Carolina.

The history of the Shenandoah Valley begins some 100 years after the settlement of Jamestown, as pioneer settlers from the Tidewater moved west to explore the wilderness. Scottish-Irish emigrants from the northern colonies were also attracted to the rich farming country of the valley. George Washington was sent west by Lord Fairfax to survey the valley, and there are reminders of his visit in Natural Bridge, where he carved his initials. All the way down the valley in Winchester, Washington's office during the French and Indian Wars is preserved. (The Shenandoah River flows from south to north, and so "down the valley" means going north.)

The Shenandoah Valley and its residents played a major role in the Civil War: Stonewall Jackson left his home and work at Lexington's Virginia Military Institute to become one of the leading figures of the Confederacy; major valley engagements included the legendary battle at New Market when a corps of VMI cadets fought heroically; and both Jackson and Lee are buried in Lexington. Woodrow Wilson was born in Staunton in 1856, and a museum adjoining his restored birthplace pays tribute to his peace-loving ideals.

Visit the Shenandoah Valley to discover its picturesque and historic cities and towns; to hike the Appalachian Trail; to enjoy the sights, colors, and sounds of the

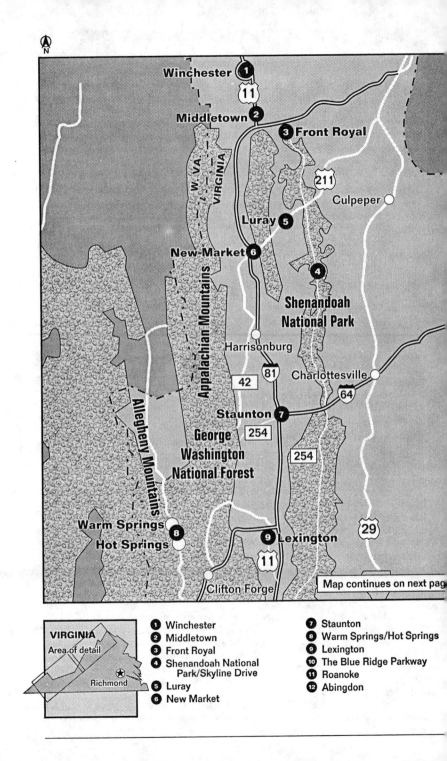

Map continues on next page

VIRGINIA Area of detail			

Richmond ★

1 Winchester
2 Middletown
3 Front Royal
4 Shenandoah National Park/Skyline Drive
5 Luray
6 New Market

7 Staunton
8 Warm Springs/Hot Springs
9 Lexington
10 The Blue Ridge Parkway
11 Roanoke
12 Abingdon

THE SHENANDOAH VALLEY & THE VIRGINIA HIGHLANDS

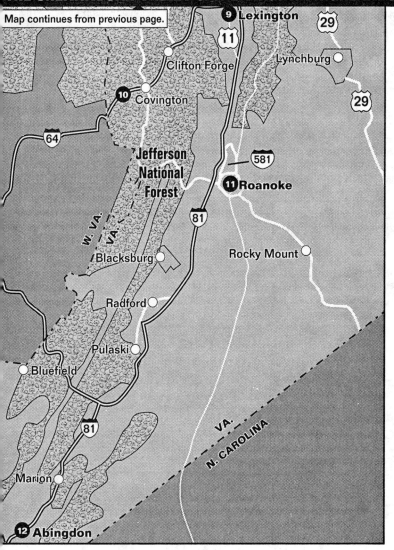

Map continues from previous page.

9 Lexington

11

29

Clifton Forge

Lynchburg

10 Covington

29

64

Jefferson
National
Forest

581

11 Roanoke

81

W. VA.

VA.

Blacksburg

Rocky Mount

Radford

Pulaski

Bluefield

81

VA.

N. CAROLINA

Marion

12 Abingdon

changing seasons; to marvel at the subterranean landscapes of stalagmites and stalactites in one of its many caverns; to rough it at a mountain camp or enjoy the luxury of a great resort.

SEEING THE SHENANDOAH VALLEY
GETTING THERE

While there are regional airports in Roanoke (see below) and Charlottesville (see Section 1 in Chapter 7), the nearest large airport is Dulles Airport, near Washington, D.C. Charlottesville is served by Amtrak, but you'll need a car to visit western Virginia.

Three very different routes parallel the valley. Driving at least part, if not all, of your trip on the Skyline Drive and Blue Ridge Parkway is a must. Since the 45-m.p.h. speed limit is strictly enforced on them, you may also want to use I-81, which passes through very beautiful country and has been designated one of America's top 10 most scenic interstates. The oldest road, Route 11, is like a trip back in time about 50 years, with its old-fashioned gas pumps, small motels, shops, and restaurants.

Mountain roads are open year round, but snow and ice can close the Skyline Drive in midwinter, and in fall, foliage traffic is heavy.

INFORMATION

For information about attractions, accommodations, restaurants, and services, contact the **Shenandoah Valley Travel Assn.,** P.O. Box 1040, New Market, VA 22844 (tel. 703/740-3132).

1. WINCHESTER

76 miles W of Washington, D.C.; 189 miles NW of Richmond

GETTING THERE   By Car   Winchester is easily accessible from north or south via I-81 or Route 11, and from east or west via Route 50.

ESSENTIALS   The **telephone area code** is 703. The **Visitors Center,** 1360 South Pleasant Valley Road, Winchester, VA 22604 (tel. 703/662-4135), is open daily from 9am to 5pm; closed major holidays. From I-81, take Exit 80 to Pleasant Valley Road.

Winchester, once the site of a Shawnee Indian campground, was settled by Pennsylvania Quakers in 1732. During the Civil War, thanks to its strategic site at the head of the Shenandoah Valley, Winchester changed hands 72 times!

WHAT TO SEE & DO

Begin your tour at the Visitors Center, where you can see an 18-minute film about Winchester and Frederick County, and purchase a discounted **block ticket** to the three major historic attractions. Price of the ticket is $7.50 for adults, $6.50 for seniors, and $4 for children 6 to 12, under 6 free.

ABRAM'S DELIGHT, 1340 S. Pleasant Valley Rd. Tel. 703/662-7384.
Adjoining the Visitor's Center is a native limestone residence built in 1754 by Quaker Isaac Hollingsworth on a pretty site beside a lake. The house is fully restored and furnished with simple 18th-century pieces appropriate to Isaac's time.
Admission: (without the block ticket) $3.50 adults, $3 seniors, $1.75 children.
Open: Apr to Nov, daily 9am–5pm. **Closed:** Dec to Mar.

STONEWALL JACKSON'S HEADQUARTERS, 415 N. Braddock St. Tel. 703/667-3242.

This Victorian cottage, used by Stonewall Jackson in the winter of 1861–62, is filled with maps, photos, and memorabilia, making it a must for Civil War buffs.

Admission: (without block ticket) $3.50 adults, $3 seniors, $1.75 children.
Open: Apr to Nov, daily 9am–5pm. **Closed:** Dec to Mar.

WASHINGTON'S OFFICE MUSEUM, 32 W. Cork St. Tel. 703/662-4412.

On the short seven block walk here, you can't miss the elaborately designed Handley Library, at the corner of Braddock Street and Piccadilly Street, adorned with a full panoply of Classic Revival statues and columns, topped off with a dome. Across the street from the library is the white-columned Elks building; in 1864–65 it was the headquarters of Union Gen. Philip Sheridan (see Section 2, "Middletown," below). Washington's office is a very small log cabin museum with relics of the French and Indian and later wars.

Admission: (without block ticket) $3.50 adults, $3 seniors, $1.75 children.
Open: Apr to Nov, daily 9am–5pm. **Closed:** Dec to Mar.

2. MIDDLETOWN

13 miles S of Winchester, 174 miles NW of Richmond, 76 miles W of Washington, D.C.

GETTING THERE **By Car** From I-81, take Exit 77 west to Route 11 into Middletown.

ESSENTIALS The **telephone area code** is 703. The **Winchester–Frederick County Visitors Center,** 1360 South Pleasant Road, Winchester, VA 22601 (tel. 703/662-4135), has in-depth information. Open daily from 9am to 5pm; closed major holidays.

Middletown's historic sights will interest history and architecture buffs, while its Wayside Theatre will entertain theater enthusiasts and nearby Route 11's shops will distract antiques seekers on their way into town.

WHAT TO SEE & DO

BELLE GROVE PLANTATION, Middletown. Tel. 703/869-2028.

One of the finest homes in the Shenandoah Valley, this beautiful stone mansion was built in the late 1700s by Maj. Isaac Hite, whose grandfather, Joist Hite, first settled in the valley in 1732. Now owned by the National Trust, it is at once a working farm, a restored 18th-century plantation house, and a center for the study and sale of traditional rural crafts.

Thomas Jefferson was actively involved in Belle Grove's design. James Madison, Jefferson's close friend and brother-in-law of Isaac Hite, wrote Jefferson for advice on the plan of the house. The Palladian-style front windows and columns are just one example of Jefferson's influence. The interior is furnished with period antiques.

During the Civil War the house suffered considerable damage in the Battle of Cedar Creek. Union Gen. Philip Sheridan's army, which occupied the plantation, was attacked by Confederate forces led by Gen. Jubal Early. The battle took place on October 19, 1864, and resulted in a decisive defeat for the Confederates. But Sheridan's troops swept through the valley, laying waste the rich farmlands that were the breadbasket of the Confederacy.

Below the front portico is the entrance to the crafts center and gift shop, featuring an outstanding selection of locally made quilts, pillows, small rugs, and other handworked items.

Admission: $3 adults, $2.50 seniors, $1.50 children 6–16, under 6 free.
Directions: From Middletown, follow Route 11 south 1 mile.
Open: Mid-Mar to mid-Nov, Mon–Sat 10am–4pm (last tour at 3:30pm), Sun 1–5pm (last tour at 4:30pm). **Closed:** Mid-Nov to mid-Mar.

WHERE TO STAY & DINE

IN TOWN

WAYSIDE INN, 7783 Main St., Middletown, VA 22645. Tel. 703/869-1797. Fax 703/869-6038. 22 rms and suites (all with bath). A/C TV TEL
Directions: From I-81, take Exit 77 to Route 11 (Main Street).
$ Rates: $70–$125 single or double. Weekend and other packages available. AE, DC, MC, V. **Parking:** Free.

This rambling white roadside inn dates to 1797, when it first offered bed and board to Shenandoah Valley travelers. Some 20 years later, when the Valley Pike, now Route 11, was hacked out of the wilderness, it became a stagecoach stop, and it has continued to be an inn ever since. In the 1960s a Washington financier and antiques collector restored it, and today rooms are beautifully decorated with an assortment of 18th- and 19th-century pieces. Each room's decor reflects a period style, from Colonial to elaborate Victorian Renaissance Revival; expect to find canopied beds, armoires, highboys, writing desks, antique clocks, and stenciled or papered walls adorned with fine prints and oil paintings. One of the suites has a Napoleonic theme, with exquisite gilt-trimmed Empire furnishings and a red sofa.

Dining/Entertainment: Regional American cuisine is served in seven antique-filled dining rooms. Dinner entrees ($12.95 to $19.25) include whole stuffed valley trout, roast duckling, and smothered chicken in white wine. Breakfast and lunch are also available; cocktails are served in the Coachyard Lounge.

NEARBY

HOTEL STRASBURG, 201 Holliday St., Strasburg, VA 22657. Tel. 703/465-9191. Fax 703/465-4788. 19 rms, 6 suites (all with bath). A/C TV TEL
Directions: From I-81, take Exit 75 and go south on Route 11 1½ miles to the first traffic light; turn right one block, left at the light (Holliday Street). It's 5 miles south of Middletown.
$ Rates: $69–$79 single or double. Weekend and other packages available. AE, CB, DC, MC, V. **Parking:** Street parking.

Strasburg likes to call itself the Antiques Capital of Virginia, and, fittingly, this restored Victorian hotel is furnished with an impressive collection of period pieces. The hotel's owner, proprietor of the Wayside Inn in Middletown (see above), also owns the Strasburg Emporium (see "Shopping," below); all the furnishings here are supplied by the Emporium, and every piece of it is for sale. Hence, decor changes constantly. Some rooms have Jacuzzis.

Dining/Entertainment: The hotel dining room is open for all three meals. Dinner entrees ($9.95 to $16.95) might include shrimp and scallop cassoulet, chicken breast with walnuts and bacon in cream sauce, or Bavarian pork chops with onions, apples, and sauerkraut. A first-floor pub offers occasional live entertainment.

SHOPPING

After perusing the shops along Route 11, antiques lovers will want to continue their hunt in nearby Strasburg, including a stop at the **Strasburg Emporium,** 100 North

Massanutten Street (tel. 703/465-3713), an enormous antiques warehouse that's open daily from 10am to 5pm.

EVENING ENTERTAINMENT

WAYSIDE THEATRE, Main St. Tel. 703/869-1776.

In 1991 the Wayside celebrated its 30th anniversary season with six fine productions by contemporary dramatists, including Tennessee Williams, Alan Ayckbourn, and Arthur Miller. Peter Boyle, Susan Sarandon, Jill Eikenberry, and Donna McKechnie began their careers at the Wayside. The Curtain Call Café offers posttheater light fare and a chance for audience members to mingle with the performers.

Admission: Single show prices $11.75 Wed and Sat matinee, $12.75 Mon–Fri and Sun night, $15.75 Sat night; $10.75 seniors and students (except Sat night). Subscriptions for six-play season offer 25% discount.

Open: End of May to mid-Oct, Wed–Sun. **Closed:** mid-Oct to late May. **Directions:** On Route 11, near the Wayside Inn (see above).

3. FRONT ROYAL

13 miles SE of Strasburg, 174 miles NW of Richmond,
89 miles W of Washington, D.C.

GETTING THERE   By Car From I-66, take Exit 2, Routes 340-522 south; it's just 5 minutes to town. Front Royal is also easily reached from I-81; take Route 66 east, then continue as detailed above.

ESSENTIALS The **telephone area code** is 703. For travel information, contact the **Front Royal Chamber of Commerce,** 414 Main Street (P.O. Box 568), Front Royal, VA 22630 (tel. 703/635-3185).

Gateway to the Shenandoah National Park and the Skyline Drive, Front Royal offers some fine accommodations and dining choices, including a nationally famous inn and restaurant in Virginia's Washington, nearby.

WHAT TO SEE & DO

There are many caverns beneath the Blue Ridge Mountains, but the first one you'll encounter coming from the north is **Skyline Caverns,** a mile north of the entrance to the Shenandoah National Park on Route 340 (tel. 703/635-4545, or toll free 800/635-4599). The caverns are open June 15 to Labor Day, daily from 9am to 6pm; March 15 to June 14 and Labor Day to November 14, Monday through Friday from 9am to 5pm, and on Saturday and Sunday from 9am to 6pm; November 15 to March 14, daily 9am to 4pm. The temperature in the caverns is a cool 54° year round, so take a sweater even in summer. Skyline boasts unique rock formations called anthodites, delicate white spikes that spread in all directions, including upward, from their position on the cave ceiling. Their growth rate is only about 1 inch every 7,000 years. A sophisticated lighting system dramatically enhances such formations as the Capitol Dome, Rainbow Trail, and Painted Desert. A miniature train covering about a half mile is a popular attraction for kids.

The **Front Royal Canoe Co.,** P.O. Box 473, Front Royal, VA 22630 (tel. 703/635-5440), offers canoe, tube, and flat-bottom-boat rentals on the Shenandoah River daily March 15 through November 15. They range from white-water adventures to fishing excursions. Call or write for reservations and prices.

NEARBY ACTIVITIES

In addition to the outdoor attractions in Shenandoah National Park (see Section 4, below), **Marriott Ranches,** Route 1, Hume, VA 22639 (tel. 703/364-2627), offers instruction at varied levels of horseback riding. The 5,000-acre ranches also offer daily guided trail rides, both hour-long and overnight, into the Blue Ridge Mountains. Horse shows, rodeos, and competitive endurance trials are among the special events sponsored here. Whether you plan to ride or just want to see the ranch, it's an interesting excursion.

WHERE TO STAY

IN TOWN

CHESTER HOUSE INN, 43 Chester St., Front Royal, VA 22630. Tel. 703/635-3937. 6 rms and suites (2 with bath). A/C.

$ Rates (including continental breakfast): $55–$80 double. AE, MC, V. **Parking:** On-site lot.

A stately 1905 Georgian Revival mansion set on 2 pretty acres of gardens, Bill and Ann Wilsons' B&B is a friendly place, attractively furnished with a mix of antiques and reproductions. The premier accommodation is the Royal Oak Suite, a spacious, high-ceilinged bedroom with fireplace, separate sitting room, and private bath; it overlooks formal boxwood gardens. Another charmer is the Blue Ridge Room, which has a curly maple bed with an old coal stove. The fireplaces downstairs have marble mantels and there is exquisite dentil molding in the living room. There is a dining room and TV parlor, as well as terraced gardens adorned with a fountain, statuary, and brick walks.

WHERE TO DINE

PALACE CAFE, 300 E. Main St. Tel. 703/636-3123.
Cuisine: AMERICAN.
$ Prices: Sandwiches $1.95–$4.25; entrees $3.75–$4.25. AE, MC, V.
Open: Mon–Wed 7am–5pm, Thurs–Sat 7am–9pm.

Locals flock to this no-frills spot, where Formica-top tables make a utilitarian setting for the excellent food made from scratch. Homemade soups, such as split pea or vegetable, might be followed by scrumptious chicken filet with mashed potatoes, gravy, green beans, cole slaw, and homemade bread. The chili is hot and spicy, and there are deli sandwiches, salads, and ice-cream desserts. Great brownies and cinnamon buns, too.

NEARBY ACCOMMODATIONS

Very Expensive

INN AT LITTLE WASHINGTON, Middle and Main Sts. (P.O. Box 300), Washington, VA 22747. Tel. 703/675-3800. Fax 703/675-3100. 8 rms, 2 suites (all with bath). A/C TEL

$ Rates (including continental breakfast): $240–$380 doubles, suites $410–$490. MC, V. **Parking:** Free.

⭐ The list of accolades for this extraordinary restaurant and elegant country inn includes glowing notices in *The New York Times, Washington Post,* and *San Francisco Chronicle.* The Inn at Little Washington is simply splendid. Located on Business Route 211 in the sleepy village of Washington, Virginia (population 158), it was opened as a restaurant in 1978 by owners Patrick O'Connell, who is the chef, and Reinhardt Lynch, who serves as maître d'hôtel.

Rooms are magnificently furnished according to the design of an English decorator; her original sketches are framed and hang in the inn's upstairs hallways. The two bilevel suites have loft bedrooms, balconies overlooking the courtyard garden, and bathrooms with Jacuzzi tubs. Terry robes, thick towels, hairdryers, and elegant toiletries comprise the sumptuous bath facilities. Antiques and Oriental rugs add warmth to the English country-house print fabrics lavishly decorating the sofas, armchairs, and windows. Extravagantly canopied beds, hand-painted ceiling borders, and faux-bois woodwork adorn the rooms.

Dining/Entertainment: The 65-seat restaurant pays homage to French cuisine but relies on regional products—trout, Chesapeake Bay seafood, nearby dairies for cheese, wild ducks—for culinary inspiration. Patrick O'Connell changes the menu constantly for his fabulous $68 fixed-price dinners, which might begin with a timbale of Virginia lump crabmeat and spinach mousse. Typical entree selections are veal Shenandoah with local cider, apples, and apple brandy; barbecued grilled boneless rack of lamb in a pecan crust with shoestring sweet potatoes; and Canadian salmon baked in strudel leaves with mushroom duxelles. Desserts include warm custard bread pudding with Jack Daniels sauce and swans of white-chocolate mousse in passion fruit purée. Reservations for Saturday and Sunday evening must be made 3 weeks in advance, 2 weeks in advance for Friday. Other evenings, reservations are suggested.

Moderate

CALEDONIA FARM, Rte. 1, Box 2080, Flint Hill, VA 22627. Tel. 703/ 675-3693. 2 rms, 1 guesthouse suite. A/C. **Directions:** From Front Royal, take Route 522 south to Flint Hill and turn right onto Route 628; look for a sign indicating a right turn to the farm about 1 mile past the intersection.

$ Rates (including full breakfast): $70–$85 single or double with shared bath; $100 suite, double occupancy. Late reservations may be secured with MC or V, but payment accepted only by personal check, traveler's check, or cash.

This 1812 Federal-style stone farmhouse, in the beautiful foothills of the Blue Ridge, comprises not only a delightful B&B but a 52-acre working cattle farm. Scenic old barns, livestock and domestic animals, and open pastureland make for a pastoral setting. Flint Hill is just 4 miles from the Inn at Little Washington (see above), and oftentimes guests make dinner reservations there and stay in Caledonia Farm's less pricey but very comfortable accommodations.

Owner Phil Irwin is an exceptionally thoughtful host, serving late-afternoon refreshments to arriving guests. Smoking is not permitted indoors. The common rooms are furnished with country charm, and two guest rooms upstairs are equally pretty. In the spacious Captain John's Room, a double bed is beautifully made up with flowered sheets and a color-coordinated quilt, a twin bed has a white chenille spread, and a blue velvet wing chair, Oriental rugs, and a working fireplace add to the cozy decor. All accommodations offer working fireplaces, as well as clock radios and bathrobes. A breezeway connects the main house with the romantically private 2½-room guesthouse. TV is available on request, and there's a credit-card pay phone. The full breakfasts are a treat; eggs Benedict or another main dish is preceded by fresh fruit and juice, and accompanied by warm pastries or breads, and tea or coffee.

4. SHENANDOAH NATIONAL PARK & THE SKYLINE DRIVE

A haven for plants, wildlife, and people, Shenandoah National Park encompasses over 190,000 acres of mountains, forests, waterfalls, and rock formations. From overlooks along the Skyline Drive, one of America's most scenic routes, you can see many of the wonders of the park, including the peaks of the Blue Ridge Mountains, which especially in summer have a distinctly bluish cast. The drive provides access to the major hiking trails, attractions, and visitor facilities in the park.

First settled by Europeans in 1716, the Blue Ridge lowlands had become farm country by 1800, and, as farmland became scarce, settlements spread into the mountains. Mountain farmers cleared land, hunted wildlife, and grazed sheep and cattle. By the 20th century the thin mountain soil was wearing out, forests were depleted, and game animals were dying out. The population was steadily declining by 1926, when plans for establishment of a national park got under way. President Franklin D. Roosevelt's innovative Civilian Conservation Corps built the recreational facilities, and, in 1939, the Skyline Drive was completed. Today over two-fifths of the park is considered wilderness, with more than 100 species of trees. Animals like deer, bear, bobcat, and turkey have returned, and sightings of smaller animals are frequent. In spring the green of leafing trees moves up the ridge at the rate of about 100 feet a day. Wildflowers begin to bloom in April; by late May the azaleas are brilliant, and the dogwood is putting on a show. Nesting birds abound. The park attracts the most visitors between October 10 and 25, when fall foliage peaks. In winter, when the trees are bare, you'll find the clearest views across the distant mountains.

GETTING THERE

The northern park entrance is near the junction of I-81 and I-66, 1 mile south of Front Royal, 90 miles west of Washington, D.C., and 170 miles northwest of Richmond. The Skyline Drive runs the 105.4-mile length of Shenandoah National Park. The park's southern entrance is at Rockfish Gap, near the junction of Route 250 and I-64, 18 miles east of Staunton (see Section 7, below) and 90 miles west of Richmond.

INFORMATION

Headquarters of Shenandoah National Park, located about 31½ miles from the northern entrance, is 4 miles west of Thornton Gap and 4 miles east of Luray on Route 211. For full information, write Superintendent, Shenandoah National Park, Luray, VA 22835 (tel. 703/999-2266).

If you want to find out about hiking on the Appalachian Trail, write or call **Appalachian Trail Conference,** P.O. Box 807, Harpers Ferry, WV 25425-0807 (tel. 304/535-6331).

There are two park visitors centers that provide information, interpretive exhibits, films, slide shows, and nature walks. The **Dickey Ridge Visitors Center** (milepost 4.6) is open April to November. **Byrd Visitors Center** (milepost 51) at Big Meadows is open daily from early March through December, and on an intermittent schedule in January and February.

WHAT TO SEE & DO

To help visitors find facilities and services, concrete mile markers have been placed on the right-hand side of the Skyline Drive heading south; they are numbered from north to south. We've used the same system below to identify locations in the park.

SCENIC OVERLOOKS

Among the most interesting of the 75 designated overlooks along the drive are the **Shenandoah Valley Overlook** (milepost 2.8), with views west to the Signal Knob of Massanutten Mountain across the south fork of the river; **Range View Overlook** (milepost 17.1), elevation 2,800 feet, providing fine views of the central section of the park, looking south; and **Stony Man Overlook** (milepost 38.6) offering panoramas of Stony Man Cliffs, the valley, and the Alleghenies.

HIKING

Hiking trails, totaling more than 500 miles, vary in length from short walks to a 95-mile segment of the Appalachian Trail. Five backcountry shelters for day use offer only a table, fireplace, pit toilet, and water. The **Potomac Appalachian Trail Club,** 118 Park St. SE, Vienna, VA 22180, maintains five fully enclosed cabins that can accommodate up to 12 people. Seven huts for Appalachian Trail hikers are within the park. The fee for these is $1 per night. On weeknights cabins cost $4 per person, on weekends $14. For either accommodation, reserve in advance.

WHERE TO STAY & DINE

ARA Virginia Sky-Line Co., P.O. Box 727, Luray, VA 22835 (tel. 703/999-2211, or toll free 800/999-4714), is the park concessioner, operating food, lodging, and other services for park visitors. Reservations, especially for the peak fall season, should be made well in advance. Nearby accommodations outside the park are described above (see Section 3 on Front Royal) and below (see Sections 5 and 7 on Luray and Staunton). Along the drive are picnic areas with tables, fireplaces, water fountains, and toilet facilities.

SKYLAND LODGE, milepost 41.8. Tel. 703/999-2211, or toll free 800/999-4714. 186 rms, including 23 cabins and 5 suites (all with bath).

$ Rates: Apr–Sept, $63–$73 double; $88–$117 suite; $34–$66 cabin. Extra person $5. Rates are $3 higher, across the board, in Oct; $10–$15 lower Nov–Dec. Weekend and other packages available. MC, V. **Closed:** Jan–Mar.

Skyland was built by naturalist George Freeman Pollock in 1894 as a summer retreat atop the highest point on the drive. Encompassing 52 acres, the resort offers rustic wood-paneled cabins as well as modern motel-type accommodations with wonderful views. Some of the buildings are dark-brown clapboard, others fieldstone, and all nestle among the trees. The central building has a lobby with a huge stone fireplace, TV (also in some, but not all, rooms), and comfortable seating areas.

Dining/Entertainment: Complete breakfast, lunch, and dinner menus are offered at reasonable prices. Dinner entrees ($5.60 to $11.90) include vegetarian lasagne, steak, roast turkey, and pan-fried rainbow trout. There's a fully stocked taproom.

BIG MEADOWS LODGE, milepost 51.2. Tel. 703/999-2221, or toll free 800/999-4714. 102 rms (all with bath).

$ Rates: $39–$61 double in main lodge, $62–$69 in motel; $79–$88 suite; $55–$59 cabin rooms. Extra person $5. MC, V. **Parking:** Free. **Closed:** Late Oct to early May.

Accommodations at Big Meadows comprise 21 rooms in the main lodge, 81 in rustic cabins, and multi-unit lodges with modern suites. The area is a major recreational center; many hiking trails start here, and this is also the site of the Byrd Visitor Center. The resort is built on a large grassy meadow and families of deer often come to graze in the early-morning hours. A grocery store is nearby.

Dining/Entertainment: The dining room features traditional dishes of the area like fried chicken, mountain trout, and country ham. Blackberry-ice-cream pie with blackberry syrup is a dessert specialty. Wine, beer, and cocktails are available. During the season live entertainment keeps the Taproom busy.

CAMPGROUNDS

Going from north to south, there are campgrounds at **Mathews Arm** (tent and trailer sites, sewage-disposal station), milepost 22.2; **Big Meadows** (tent and trailer sites, showers, laundry, ice, firewood, summer campfire program), milepost 51.2;

Lewis Mountain (tent and trailer sites, cabins, campfire programs), milepost 57.5; and **Loft Mountain** (tent and trailer sites, sewage disposal, store, gift shop, nature trail, laundry), milepost 79.5.

All campgrounds except Big Meadows offer overnight camping on a first-come, first-served basis. Reservations are required at Big Meadows from the end of May to the end of October; they can be made via your local Ticketron outlet or by calling 900/370-5566. Further information about camping can be obtained from the park concessioner, ARA Virginia Sky-Line Co. (see above).

---

5. LURAY

6 miles W of Shenandoah National Park; 91 miles SW of Washington, D.C.; 135 miles NW of Richmond

GETTING THERE By Car From Shenandoah National Park, take Route 211 west. From I-81, follow Route 211 east. Route 340 is also a major north-south thoroughfare.

ESSENTIALS Contact the **Page County Chamber of Commerce**, 46 East Main Street, Luray, VA 22835 (tel. 703/743-3915).

The most popular caverns in the East draw thousands of tourists to Luray, seat of Page County. Lush farmland surrounds the town, which also serves as the central gateway to Shenandoah National Park.

WHAT TO SEE & DO

LURAY CAVERNS, Rte. 211, Luray. Tel. 703/743-6551.

The formation of these caverns, an extensive series of limestone caves and streams in the bowels of the Shenandoah Valley, began over 400 million years ago as water from the earth's surface penetrated the limestone rock through cracks made during the shifting of the earth's crust. As water filled the openings, it dissolved more rock, thus enlarging the spaces. The process continued to shape rooms and passageways and eventually hollowed out a labyrinth of underground chambers. Stalactites, formed when water drips from the ceiling, and stalagmites, formed from the ground up, met and formed columns. In an active cave such as Luray, stalactites and stalagmites "grow" 1 cubic inch every 120 years.

In addition to the monumental columns in rooms more than 140 feet high, the caverns are noted for the beautiful cascades of natural colors found on interior walls. This U.S. Registered Natural Landmark also combines the works of man and nature into an unusual organ with a sound system directly connected to stalactites. Music is produced when the stalactites are electronically tapped by rubber-tipped plungers controlled by an organist.

Admission: $9 adults, $8 seniors, $4.50 children 7–13, under 7 free.

Open: June 15–Labor Day, daily 9am–7pm; Mar 15–June 14 and the day after Labor Day to Nov 14, daily 9am–6pm; Nov 15–Mar 14, Mon–Fri 9am–4pm, Sat–Sun 9am–5pm. Conducted tours follow a system of brick and concrete walkways and take about 1 hour.

WHERE TO STAY & DINE NEARBY

JORDAN HOLLOW FARM INN, Rte. 2, Stanley, VA 22851. Tel. 703/
778-2209 or 778-2285. 21 rms (all with bath). A/C TEL **Directions:** From Luray, take Route 340S 6 miles to Stanley; turn left onto Route 689 and then right onto Route 626.

$ Rates: $65 single; $75–$125 double. Extra person over 16 $10. CB, DC, DISC, MC, V. **Parking:** Free.

On the eastern edge of the Shenandoah Valley, this country horse farm/inn is a secluded getaway where owners Jetze and Marley Beers have created a wonderfully homey atmosphere. The farm and inn buildings form a charming enclave of small structures. Arbor View, for example, is a vine-covered lodge surrounded by a sun deck, offering porch sitters glorious mountain or meadow views; it has 16 rooms furnished with 19th-century oak pieces, white ruffled curtains, lace-trimmed coverlets on the beds, and Tiffany-style lamps. And Mare Meadow Lodge, a rough-hewn log building, offers rustic rooms with white cedar pieces.

Dining/Entertainment: Dining is in the Colonial farmhouse in cozy wood-paneled rooms. Dinner entrees ($12.95 to $19.95) such as sautéed quail on a bed of wild rice, rainbow trout amandine with crab stuffing, and pasta primavera, are served with soup, salad, two vegetables, and fresh-baked bread. The Watering Trough has live entertainment on weekends.

Facilities: Trail rides, children's pony rides, volleyball, Ping-Pong, cross-country skiing.

6. NEW MARKET

Even if your knowledge of the Civil War doesn't extend to distinguishing the troops in gray from the troops in blue, you'll be fascinated by the exposition of the Civil War in the Hall of Valor Museum in **New Market Battlefield Historical Park,** New Market (tel. 703/740-3101). To reach the museum from I-81, Exit 67, take Route 211W, then an immediate right onto Route 305 (George Collins Parkway); the battlefield park is 1¾ miles away, at the end of the road. From Luray, follow Route 211W, as above.

The park commemorates the corps of Virginia Military Institute schoolboys, who, with an outnumbered force of Confederate soldiers, withstood the attack of Union Maj. Gen. Franz Sigal on May 15, 1864. At the Visitors Center you can see two films, one about the battle, the other about Stonewall Jackson's Shenandoah campaign. The final Confederate assault on the Union line is covered in a self-guided 1-mile walking tour of the grassy field. In the center of the line of battle was the Bushong farmhouse, today a museum of 19th-century valley life.

The park is open daily from 9am to 5pm; admission is $4 for adults, $3.50 for seniors, $1.50 for children ages 7 to 15, under 7 free, and includes the battlefield, Hall of Valor Museum, and Bushong Farm.

Three miles south of New Market Battlefield on Route 11 is **Endless Caverns** (tel. 703/740-3993 or toll free 800/544-CAVE), its awesome natural beauty is enhanced by the dramatic use of day-glo lighting to display spectacular rooms, each boasting a variety of stalactites, stalagmites, giant columns, and limestone pendants orchestrated into brilliant displays of nature's work. Endless Caverns maintains a year-round temperature of 56°.

Tours are given March 15 to June 14, daily from 9am to 5pm; June 15 to Labor Day, daily from 9am to 7pm; the day after Labor Day to November 14, daily from 9am to 5pm; and November 15 to March 14, daily from 9am to 4pm. Admission is $8 for adults, $4.50 for children ages 3 to 12, under 3 free.

7. STAUNTON

42 miles S of New Market; 142 miles SW of Washington, D.C.; 92 miles NW of Richmond

GETTING THERE By Plane The nearest regional airport is in Charlottesville (see above).

By Train Amtrak trains serve Staunton's station at 1 Middlebrook Avenue (tel. toll free 800/872-7245).

By Bus The Greyhound/Trailways terminal is a half block from the train station, on South New Street.

By Car Staunton is near the junctions of I-64 and I-81 and Routes 11 and 250.

ESSENTIALS Contact the **Staunton–Augusta County Travel Information Center,** 1303 Richmond Avenue (I-81, Exit 57), Staunton, VA 24404 (tel. 703/885-8504), open daily from 9am to 5pm.

Settled well before the Revolution, Staunton (pronounced "*Stan*-ton") was a major stop for pioneers on the way west and is now noted mainly as the birthplace of Woodrow Wilson, our 28th President. The town's 19th-century downtown buildings have been refurbished and restored, making it a pleasant place to stop in the Shenandoah Valley.

WHAT TO SEE & DO

MUSEUM OF AMERICAN FRONTIER CULTURE, Rte. 250. Tel. 703/332-7850.

In light of its history as a major stopping point for pioneers, Staunton seems like a logical location for this museum. Located west of I-81 near Exit 57, a short walk from the Visitor Center Complex, the museum consists of four 18th-century working farmsteads, where trained staff members in period costumes plant fields, tend livestock, and do domestic chores.

Admission: $5 adults, $4.50 seniors, $2.50 children 6–12, under 6 free.
Open: Mid-Mar–Nov, daily 9am–5pm; Dec–mid-March, daily 10am–4pm.

WOODROW WILSON BIRTHPLACE, 24 N. Coalter St. Tel. 703/885-0897.

This handsome Greek Revival building, built in 1846 by a Presbyterian congregation as a manse for their ministers, stands next to an excellent museum detailing Wilson's life. As a minister, Wilson's father had to move often, and so the family left here when the future president was only 2. The house is furnished with many family items, including the crib Wilson slept in and the chair in which his mother rocked him. The galleries of the museum next door trace Wilson's Scottish-Irish roots, his academic career as a professor and president at Princeton University, and, of course, his eight presidential years (1913–21). America's entry into World War I and Wilson's unsuccessful efforts to convince the U.S. Senate to participate in the League of Nations are also explored. Don't overlook the beautiful garden or the carriage house that shelters Wilson's presidential limousine, a shiny Pierce-Arrow.

Admission: $5 adults, $4.50 seniors, $1 children 6–12, under 6 free.
Open: Memorial Day–Labor Day, daily 9am–6pm; rest of year, daily 9am–5pm.

WHERE TO STAY

ASHTON COUNTRY HOUSE BED & BREAKFAST, 1205 Middlebrook Rd., Staunton, VA 24401. Tel. 703/885-7819. 5 rms (all with bath). **Directions:** From the train station, follow Middlebrook Road 1 mile.

$ Rates (including full breakfast): $60–$75 double. Extra person $10. No credit cards. **Parking:** Free.

⑤ On the outskirts of Staunton, Ashton Country House is in a totally rural setting with 20 acres of pasture fronting a quiet country road. A shaded driveway leads past the spacious front lawn to the columned entrance of a Greek Revival brick house. Here, owners Sheila Kennedy and Stanley Polanski have kept period character intact while adding modern amenities. Charming country furnishings include sleigh beds, a faux-wood-grain antique bedroom suite, washstands, brass lamps, and lace curtains; pretty color schemes feature pinks and greens. One of the owners is a musician, so piano music sometimes accompanies afternoon tea and scones. A full breakfast includes fresh fruit compote, a hot egg dish with sausage or bacon, and homemade breakfast pastries.

BELLE GRAE INN, 515 W. Frederick St., Staunton, VA 24401. Tel. 703/886-5151. 17 rms, including suites and a small cottage (13 with bath). A/C **$ Rates** (including continental breakfast): $55–$90 double; $90–$150 suite. Packages available. AE, DC, MC, V. **Parking:** Free.

★ This beautifully restored 1873 Victorian house, with white gingerbread trim and an Italianate wraparound front porch, sits well back from the street atop a sloping lawn. It houses eight guest rooms. Additional accommodations are in adjoining 19th-century houses. Rooms throughout are furnished in period antiques and reproductions, with wicker pieces, Oriental rugs, and canopied four-poster, sleigh, and brass beds. Some rooms have fireplaces, and many have phones and TVs. There are also sets in the Bistro bar and the main-house sitting room.

Dining/Entertainment: All meals are served in the Bistro or an adjoining dining room in the main house. Dinner entrees ($10 to $16) include crab cakes, chicken piccata, and baked swordfish.

WHERE TO DINE

23 BEVERLEY, 23 E. Beverley St. Tel. 703/885-5053.
   Cuisine: AMERICAN.
   $ Prices: Appetizers $4.95–$6.95; entrees $7.95–$17.50. AE, MC, V.
   Open: Dinner Tues–Sat 5:30–9:30pm; brunch Sun noon–3pm.

With a sophisticated regional menu featuring local produce and meats, Keith Van Yahres and Rick Small have won so much acclaim that they expanded their restaurant into the next-door storefront. The original restaurant now serves as a bar. The new quarters feature a sleek art deco black-and-gray decor, punctuated by beautiful floral arrangements. Dinner might begin with scalloped oysters with mushrooms and wild-boar ham, sautéed sweetbreads with roasted garlic and preserved lemon, or steamed shrimp dumplings with black-bean and blood-orange sauces. Possible entrees include rack of lamb with hazelnuts, tangelos, and creamed leeks; breast of duck on warm greens with cracklings and warm potato salad; and braised rabbit with mushroom, asparagus, and parmesan risotto. Desserts are delicious; try strawberry ice cream in a flour tortilla shell with white-chocolate sauce or steamed chocolate pudding with coconut custard and bananas. Wines, both domestic and imported, are reasonably priced.

THE DEPOT GRILLE, 42 Middlebrook Ave. at Staunton Station. Tel. 703/885-7332.
   Cuisine: AMERICAN.
   $ Prices: Appetizers $1.95–$5.95; entrees $6.95–$13.95. AE, MC, V.
   Open: Daily 11am–midnight.

This popular steak-and-seafood house has a festive atmosphere, highlighted by a long Victorian bar and railroad memorabilia. Seating is in spacious wood-paneled booths or Windsor chairs at small wooden tables. A seasoned crabcake sandwich, with french fries or cole slaw, is $4.95; a mesquite-grilled chicken-breast sandwich, $5.50.

Black Angus sirloin for two makes a hearty dinner, and comes with salad, fresh bread, potato, and vegetable. A children's menu offers a choice of four entrees, each just $2.

A PICNIC STOP EN ROUTE

A good place to stop for a picnic lunch midway between Staunton and Lexington is the picturesque **Cyrus McCormick Farm** (tel. 703/377-2255). From I-81, Exit 54 is well marked to the village of Steele's Tavern and the McCormick birthplace. In a lovely rural setting, it contains a small blacksmith shop and other log cabins in which exhibits include a model of McCormick's invention, the first reaper. Open daily from 8am to 5pm; no admission fee.

8. WARM SPRINGS/HOT SPRINGS

Hot Springs: 220 miles SW of Washington, D.C.; 160 miles W of Richmond
Warm Springs: 5 miles N of Hot Springs

GETTING THERE   By Plane   Nearest regular air service is provided by USAir (tel. toll free 800/428-4322) to Roanoke Regional Airport; Woodrum Livery Service (tel. 703/345-7710) offers connecting transportation.

By Train   The nearest Amtrak station is on Ridgeway Street, in Clifton Forge, Va. (tel. toll free 800/872-7245).

By Bus   Covington, Va., 20 miles south of Hot Springs, is served by Greyhound/Trailways; the terminal is at the corner of Chestnut Street and Highland Street (tel. 703/962-5022).

By Car   Route 220 runs north and south through Hot Springs and Warm Springs, with easy access to I-64 in Covington and I-81.
   Note: Take the 42-mile drive at least one way between Lexington and Warm Springs on Route 39, a lovely scenic byway that follows the Maury River through Goshen Pass.

ESSENTIALS   Contact the **Bath County Chamber of Commerce,** Hot Springs, VA 24445 (tel. 703/839-5098, or toll free 800/628-8092).

Thermal springs, at temperatures ranging from 77° to 106°F, rise throughout the mountains and valleys of Bath County. Most famous are the **Warm Springs pools,** opened in 1761 and still utilizing its 19th-century bathhouses. The crystal-clear waters of these natural rock pools circulate gently and offer a wonderfully relaxing experience. Open mid-April through October, Monday through Saturday from 10:30am to 5pm and on Sunday from 1 to 5pm. Closed November to mid-April. Charge is $6 per 1-hour session.

WHERE TO STAY & DINE

HOT SPRINGS

This tiny village spreads out from the Homestead resort along Main Street, where you'll find a country grocery store, an interesting crafts outlet called the Bacova Guild Showroom (tel. 703/839-2105), and Sam Snead's Tavern (see below).

THE HOMESTEAD, Hot Springs, VA 24445. Tel. 703/839-5500, or toll free 800/336-5771, 800/542-5734 in Virginia. Fax 703/839-3056. 521 rms and suites. A/C MINIBAR TV TEL **Directions:** The main entrance is off Route 220.
$ Rates (Modified American Plan, including breakfast and dinner): Winter, $150–

$180 single; $120–$145 per person double; $70–$90 parlor suite. Summer, $245–$325 single; $157.50–$197.50 per person double; $80–$90 parlor suite. European Plan (no meals), deduct $50 per person per day. Children 12 and under stay free in parents' room; children 13 and over pay $75. Weekend and other packages available. AE, MC, V. **Parking:** Free.

★ This country spa's prodigious reputation, going back to the 18th century, rests on outstanding service and cuisine, myriad recreational activities, and lovely rooms. Over the years the Homestead has been host to presidents (Jefferson, Wilson, Hoover, F.D.R., Truman, Eisenhower, Carter, and Reagan) and the social elite (the Henry Fords, John D. Rockefeller, the Vanderbilts, Lord and Lady Astor).

Built of red Kentucky brick with white limestone trim, the hotel's main building is capped by a clock tower. Guests enter via the magnificent Great Hall, where 16 Corinthian columns line the bright floral carpet that runs 211 feet. Two fireplaces, comfortable wing chairs, Chippendale-reproduction tables with reading lamps, and deep sofas create a warm atmosphere. Afternoon tea is served here daily to the light classical background music of the piano.

Guests have a variety of accommodations in the old section of the hotel, the new South Wing, and the Tower. Rooms are elegantly residential in feel, with pastel floral-print quilted spreads and matching draperies and Chippendale-reproduction brass-trimmed furnishings. Gilt-framed prints, China jar or brass lamps, and comfortable seating areas add to the charm. Most rooms offer spectacular mountain views. And 75 suites, including duplexes in the newer section, have special features such as working fireplaces, private bars, sun porches, two remote-control TVs, and two phones.

Dining/Entertainment: In the Homestead's pink-walled, white-pilastered main dining room, an orchestra plays during six-course dinners. The adjoining Commonwealth Room, also very spacious, is adorned with murals of such Virginia landmarks as Mount Vernon and Monticello. Tables throughout are elegantly appointed, and under the supervision of European-trained chefs, the cuisine features regional favorites like fresh rainbow trout, grilled lamb chops, and roast beef with Armagnac sauce. Cocktails, hors d'oeuvres, and after-dinner espresso are served in The View. Bountiful country breakfasts here, too. In summer there's also dining in the Sun Room, the Grille, and Café Albert. Evening entertainment includes live music, dancing, and free movies. Sam Snead's Tavern, an inviting pub serving standard American fare, also operated by the Homestead, is across Main Street from the hotel.

Services: Room service, turndown, concierge, travel agency, children's programs.

Facilities: Spa with full health club facilities, indoor and outdoor pools, archery, bowling, fishing, three golf courses, hiking trails, horseback riding, ice skating on an Olympic-size rink, lawn bowling and croquet, billiards, skeet and trap, downhill and cross-country skiing mid-December to March, warm springs pools, 19 tennis courts, horseshoes, volleyball, video game room, board games, numerous shops, florist, hair salon.

WARM SPRINGS

A charming little community with many historic homes, Warm Springs centers around its natural pools, described above.

INN AT GRIST MILL SQUARE, Rte. 645, Warm Springs, VA 24484. Tel. 703/839-2231. 14 rms and suites (all with bath). TV TEL **Directions:** From Route 220N, turn left onto Route 619 and left again onto Route 645.

$ Rates (including continental breakfast): $70 single; $90 double. Extra person $10. With breakfast and dinner, $93 single; $141 double; extra person $32.50, $15 for children under 10. MC, V. **Parking:** Free.

Five restored 19th-century buildings, including an old mill, comprise this unique hostelry. It includes the Blacksmith Shop, which houses the country store; the Hardware Store, with six guest units; and the Steel House, with four accommodations. The Miller's House has the Oat, Barley, Rye, and Wheat rooms. Furnishings are charming period pieces, with comfortable upholstered chairs, brass chandeliers, pretty quilts on four-poster beds, marble-top side tables, and working fireplaces, the total effect is warm and homey. Breakfast is served in your room in a picnic basket.

Dining/Entertainment: The rustic Waterwheel Restaurant and Simon Kenton Pub are cozy spots in the old mill building. The restaurant features notably good American cuisine, with entrees like grilled trout, pork Calvados, and filet of salmon with béarnaise sauce for $15.25 to $19.75. In the wine cellar, the wines are displayed among the gears of the waterwheel. The Waterwheel also serves Sunday brunch.

Facilities: Outdoor pool, three tennis courts, sauna, country store. The Homestead's sports and recreation facilities are 5 miles away.

9. LEXINGTON

36 miles S of Staunton; 180 miles SW of Washington, D.C.;
138 miles NW of Richmond

GETTING THERE   By Car   Lexington is easily accessible to I-81, via Route 60. Route 11 also goes directly into town.

ESSENTIALS   The **telephone area code** is 703. The **Visitor Bureau,** 102 East Washington Street, Lexington, VA 24450 (tel. 703/463-3777), is a block from Main Street. Be sure to see the engrossing slide show about Lexington history here.

A lively college-town atmosphere, a beautifully restored downtown, and interesting historic associations involving Robert E. Lee and Stonewall Jackson make Lexington a must for anyone touring the Shenandoah Valley. Fine old homes line tree-shaded streets, among them the house where Stonewall Jackson lived when he taught at Virginia Military Institute. Lexington is a fine base for exploring the central valley.

WHAT TO SEE & DO

LEE CHAPEL AND MUSEUM, Washington and Lee University. Tel. 703/463-8768.

This magnificent Victorian-Gothic brick and native limestone chapel, today used for concerts and other events, was built in 1867 at the request of General Lee. A white marble sculpture of Lee by Edward Valentine portrays the general recumbent. Lee's remains are in a crypt below the chapel along with other family members. His office was in the lower level of the building, and it is now part of the chapel museum, preserved just as he left it on September 20, 1870. His beloved horse, Traveller, is buried in a plot outside the office. Among the museum's most important possessions are Charles Willson Peale's portrait of George Washington wearing the uniform of a colonel in the British Army and the painting of General Lee in Confederate uniform by Theodore Pine. The two portraits hang in the chapel auditorium.

Washington and Lee has one of the oldest and most beautiful campuses in the country. The oldest of the red-brick buildings, Washington Hall, built in 1824, is topped by a masterpiece of American folk art, an 1840 carved-wood statue of George Washington. The massive trees dotting the campus are believed to have been planted by Lee.

Admission: Free.

IMPRESSIONS

Gentlemen . . . I trust you will do your duty.
—GENERAL BRECKINRIDGE, BATTLE OF NEW MARKET, MAY 15, 1864

I look back upon that orchard as the most awful spot on the battlefield.
—CADET JOHN C. HOWARD, BATTLE OF NEW MARKET, MAY 15, 1984

Open: Mid-Oct to mid-Apr Mon–Sat 9am–4pm; mid-Apr to mid-Oct, Mon–Sat 9am–5pm, Sun 2–5pm. **Directions:** Washington and Lee University borders Washington Street and Letcher Avenue. The chapel is closest to Washington Street.

VIRGINIA MILITARY INSTITUTE MUSEUM, Jackson Memorial Hall, VMI Campus. Tel. 703/464-7232.

The VMI Museum displays uniforms, weapons, and memorabilia from cadets who attended the college and fought in numerous wars. Of special note: the VMI coatee or tunic that belonged to Gen. George S. Patton, Jr., VMI 1907; Stonewall Jackson's uniform coat worn at VMI and the bullet-pierced raincoat he was wearing at the Battle of Chancellorsville; and, thanks to taxidermy, Jackson's war horse, Little Sorrel.

An all-male school, VMI, sometimes called the West Point of the South, opened in 1839 on the site of a state arsenal, just east of the campus of Washington and Lee. The most dramatic episode in the school's history took place during the Civil War at the Battle of New Market on May 15, 1864. In a desperate move to halt the advancing Union troops of Gen. Franz Sigal, Confederate Gen. John Breckenridge sent 257 teenaged VMI cadets to war. The boys marched in the rain for 4 days to reach the front line. They charged the enemy, won the day, and returned home victorious, losing only 10 cadets with 47 wounded. Grant, hearing of the battle, exclaimed, "The South is robbing the cradle and the grave." A month later, Union Gen. David Hunter got even, bombarding Lexington and burning down VMI. Fifty years later Congress appropriated $100,000 in partial payment of the damage.

To commemorate the cadets killed at New Market, every year on May 15 a parade is held in their honor. Each of the boys' names is called, and a current cadet responds, "Died on the field of honor, sir."
Admission: Free.
Open: Mon–Sat 9am–5pm, Sun 2–5pm.

GEORGE C. MARSHALL MUSEUM, VMI Campus. Tel. 703/463-7103.

Looking more like a mausoleum than a museum, this white box of a building houses the archives and research library of General of the Army George C. Marshall. A 1901 graduate of VMI, Marshall had an illustrious career including service in France in 1917, when he was aide-de-camp to General Pershing. In World War II he was army chief of staff, then secretary of state and secretary of defense under President Truman. Best remembered for his European Recovery Program (the Marshall Plan) to foster the economic recovery of Europe, Marshall proposed: "It is logical that the United States should do whatever it is able to do to assist in the return of normal economic health in the world. . . . Our policy is directed not against any country or doctrine but against hunger, poverty, desperation and chaos." For his role in promoting peace, he became the first career soldier to be awarded the Nobel Peace Prize.
Admission: Free.
Open: Mon–Sat 9am–5pm, Sun 2–5pm.

STONEWALL JACKSON HOUSE, 8 E. Washington St. Tel. 703/463-2552.

Major Thomas Jonathan Jackson came to Lexington in 1851 to take a post as

IMPRESSIONS

Let us cross the river and rest under the shade of the trees.
—STONEWALL JACKSON'S LAST WORDS, MAY 10, 1863

teacher of natural philosophy (physics) and artillery tactics at Virginia Military Institute. A rigid teacher, his philosophy class was not popular, but his artillery class and discussions of military tactics and strategy were said to be lively and interesting. The cannons he used to train hundreds of cadets now stand guard in front of the cadet barracks on the VMI campus.

In 1858, Jackson purchased this house, five blocks from VMI, which has been restored with many of his personal possessions. He lived here until he went off to Richmond to answer General Lee's summons in 1861. Two years later his body was returned to Lexington for burial.

Photographs, text, and a slide show tell the story of the Jacksons' stay here. Upstairs, much of their furniture is placed as it was. The upright desk at which Jackson stood to prepare his lessons is among the original pieces, and the razor he used each morning rests on the bureau in the bedroom. Appropriate period furnishings duplicate the items on the inventory of Jackson's estate made shortly after his death at Chancellorsville in 1863. The Jacksons put in three wood-burning stoves, a modern improvement over fireplaces for the Victorian era.

Jackson was buried nearby in the Presbyterian church cemetery on South Main Street. **Admission:** $3.50 adults, $2 children ages 6–12, free for children under 6.

Open: Mon–Sat 9am–5pm, Sun 1–5pm. Guided tours begin on the hour and half hour (last tour at 4:30pm). **Closed:** Major hols.

VIRGINIA HORSE CENTER, Lexington. Tel. 703/463-7060.

Sprawling across nearly 400 acres just outside Lexington, the Virginia Horse Center offers horse shows, educational seminars, and sales of fine horses. Annual events include an Arabian Horse Show, Miniature Horse Classic, and qualifying competitions for the Pan American Games. Also on the schedule are drill-team exhibitions, English and Western riding demonstrations, equine art and photography shows, wagon rides, fox-hunting demonstrations, and tack and equipment displays. For a full program of events, contact the center at P.O. Box 1051, Lexington, VA 24450.

Admission: $2 adults, $1 children under 12; no charge to 4-H Club members.

Open: Mar–Sept; future plans call for year-round events. **Directions:** The center is near the intersection of I-64 and I-81. Take I-64 west to Exit 13, turn right onto Route 11 north for a tenth of a mile, turn left onto Route 39 west, and continue about 1 mile to the center.

NEARBY ATTRACTIONS

NATURAL BRIDGE, Natural Bridge, Va. Tel. 703/291-2121, or toll free 800/336-5727, 800/533-1410 in Virginia.

A hugely impressive limestone formation, the Natural Bridge is owned by a private corporation and has become the focus of a small one-industry enclave; a department-store-size souvenir shop adjoins the ticket window.

Thomas Jefferson called this bridge of limestone "the most sublime of nature's works . . . so beautiful an arch, so elevated, so light and springing, as it were, up to heaven." The bridge was part of a 157-acre estate Jefferson acquired in 1774 from King George III. It was included in the survey of western Virginia carried out by

George Washington, who carved his initials into the face of the stone. This geological oddity rises 215 feet above Cedar Creek; its span is 90 feet long and spreads at its widest to 150 feet. It is believed that the Monocan Indian tribes used the bridge as a passageway and fortress; it was worshipped by them as "the bridge of God." Today it is also the bridge of man, as Route 11 passes over it.

A 45-minute sound-and-light show called *The Drama of Creation* is conducted nightly beneath the bridge. Across the parking lot from the upper bridge entrance is the Natural Bridge Wax Museum. A restaurant and lodging facilities are on the premises.

Admission: Combined ticket for two of the three attractions (Natural Bridge, Wax Museum, and nearby caverns): $12 adult, $7 children ages 6–15. Individual admissions to each attraction: $7 adult, $3.50 children.

Open: Bridge daily, 7am–dusk; drama presented after dark. **Directions:** The bridge is 12 miles south of Lexington; from I-81, take Exit 49 or 50.

SHOPPING

Lexington's charming 19th-century downtown offers many interesting shops. **Artists in Cahoots,** 1 Washington Street (tel. 703/464-1147), a cooperative venture run by local artists and craftspeople, features an outstanding selection of crafts—hand-painted silk scarves, porcelain jewelry, hand-woven baskets, watercolors of Virginia flowers, hand-blown glass, pottery, Shaker-design furniture, and hand-forged sterling-silver jewelry. Dolores Bausum's **Quilters of Virginia,** 22 West Washington Street (tel. 703/464-3023), displays museum-quality hand-stitched American quilts, pillows, and wall hangings. And **Virginia Born & Bred,** 16 West Washington Street (tel. 703/463-1832), has made-in-Virginia gifts.

EVENING ENTERTAINMENT

The ruins of an old limestone kiln provide the backdrop for the open-air **Theater at Lime Kiln,** Borden Road off Route 60W (tel. 703/463-3074), which presents musicals, plays, and concerts from Memorial Day to Labor Day at 8pm. Typical productions have ranged from a Civil War epic called *Stonewall Country,* based on Jackson's life, to Shakespeare, Appalachian folktales, even a South African dance troupe. Tickets to plays and musicals are $12; and concerts run $10 to $14; seniors pay $1 less, and children under 10 are half price.

To reach the theater from downtown Lexington, take Route 11S and turn right onto Route 60W.

WHERE TO STAY

HISTORIC COUNTRY INNS

Historic Country Inns, 11 North Main Street, Lexington, VA 24450 (tel. 703/463-2044), owns the three hostelries described below. Reservations should be made through Historic Country Inns.

ALEXANDER-WITHEROW HOUSE and MCCAMPBELL INN, entered from Washington St. off N. Main St. Tel. 703/463-2044. 14 rms, 8 suites (all with bath). A/C TV TEL

$ Rates (including continental breakfast): $70–$95 double. MC, V. **Parking:** Lot behind the McCampbell Inn.

The Alexander-Witherow House is a lovely late Georgian town house built in 1789 as a family residence over a store. The ground floor is occupied by Artists in Cahoots (see "Shopping," in "What to See and Do," above); the inn occupies the upper floors.

Accommodations include homey suites with separate living rooms and small kitchens. Furnishings offer traditional comfort, with wing chairs, four-poster beds, and hooked rugs on wide-board floors.

The McCampbell Inn, across the street, houses the main office for Historic Country Inns and is where guests at both hostelries eat breakfast. Begun in 1809, with later additions in 1816 and 1857, it occupies a rambling building, with rooms facing both Main Street and the quieter back courtyard. Furnishings are a pleasant mix of antiques and reproductions.

MAPLE HALL, on Rte. 11. Tel. 703/463-6693. 29 rms and suites (all with bath). A/C TV **Directions:** Take Route 11 7 miles north of town near Exit 53 of I-81.

$ Rates: $70–$95 double; $115 guesthouse. MC, V. **Parking:** Free.

This handsome red-brick, white-columned 1850 plantation house offers a restful country setting. Old boxwood surrounds the inn, which consists of a main house, a restored Guest House, and a Pond House. You'll feel as though you're a guest on a southern plantation in these spacious quarters. Rooms are individually furnished, many with antiques, Oriental rugs, and massive Victorian pieces; 10 rooms have working fireplaces. The Guest House has a living room, kitchen, and three bedrooms with baths. The Pond House, added in 1990, contains four suites and two minisuites. Guests relax on the shaded patio, on porches with rocking chairs, and on back verandas overlooking the fishing pond and nearby hills. A pool, tennis court, and 3-mile hiking trail are on site.

Dining/Entertainment: Elegant dining in pretty gardenlike surroundings attracts a good following to the Maple Hall restaurant, open daily for dinner. Regional southern entrees like grilled quail, chicken breast with Virginia ham topped with cheese sauce, and filet mignon wrapped in bacon and served with béarnaise sauce, range from $14.50 to $19.50.

A BED-AND-BREAKFAST

LLEWELLYN LODGE, 603 S. Main St., Lexington, VA 24450. Tel. 703/463-3235. 6 rms (all with bath). A/C

$ Rates (including full breakfast): $55–$70 double. AE, MC, V. **Parking:** On-site lot.

S A 50-year-old brick Colonial-style house, the Llewellyn Lodge is within easy walking distance of all of Lexington's historic sites. On the first floor are a cozy sitting room with a working fireplace and a TV room. Guest rooms are decorated in exceptionally pretty color schemes. One has a cool and lovely look with white wicker furniture and green-ivy patterned fabrics and wallpaper, another a separate sitting area with TV; all rooms have ceiling fans.

WHERE TO DINE

MODERATE

WILLSON-WALKER HOUSE, 30 N. Main St. Tel. 703/463-3020.
Cuisine: AMERICAN. **Reservations:** Required at dinner.

$ Prices: Appetizers $3.25–$6; entrees $11–$16.25; sunset special $10 adults, $5 children under 10. AE, MC, V.

Open: Lunch Tues–Sat 11:30am–2:30pm; dinner Tues–Sat 5:30–9pm.

Occupying the first floor of an 1820 Greek Revival home, this distinctive restaurant, furnished in period antiques, offers first-rate regional cuisine in pretty peach-and-green surroundings. The building has verandas behind massive two-story white columns on both the first and second floors. At dinner, start with aromatic duck salad with mushrooms or Stilton and Cheddar cheese phyllo triangles with port wine and walnuts. Medallions of venison with cherries, apples and currants is one of the chef's special creations, or you might try a Virginia favorite, crab cakes with mustard-cream sauce. The fixed-price Sunset Dinner, served from 5:30 to 6:30pm, includes salad, a choice of three entrees, vegetable, potato or rice, and beverage. At lunch there are sandwiches in the $5 range, including an excellent beefburger with bleu or Cheddar cheese—also pasta dishes, crêpes, soups, and salads.

INEXPENSIVE

HARBS', 19 W. Washington St. Tel. 703/464-1900.
  Cuisine: CONTINENTAL.
$ **Prices:** Sandwiches $2.25–$4.50; entrees $6.95–$11.95. No credit cards.
  Open: Daily 8am–midnight.
Good mornings begin at Harbs', with oversize blueberry, cranberry-orange, banana-walnut, honey-bran, apple-raisin, pumpkin, or cream-cheese-swirl muffins and a steaming cup of coffee. A favorite of local students, who come in to play pool in the back room, Harbs' has a French bistro look, with black and white tile floors, small café tables, and a magazine rack providing reading matter for customers. The menu features muffins, croissants and bagels, hero and pita sandwiches, salads, and pasta dishes. Beer is on tap.

THE PALMS, 101 W. Nelson St. Tel. 703/463-7911.
  Cuisine: AMERICAN.
$ **Prices:** Entrees $7.25–$13.50. CB, DC, MC, V.
  Open: Mon–Fri 11:30am–1am, Sat noon–1am, Sun noon–10pm.
With neon palms in its storefront window, this plant-filled eatery offers a simpatico faux-tropical setting for hearty meals. Deli sandwiches run the gamut from roast beef to smoked turkey. Mexican specialties, like tacos, burritos, and tostadas, spice up the proceedings. Dinner entrees, served with salad, vegetable, and garlic bread, include choices like fettuccine Alfredo, shish kebab, and lamb chops. At lunch or dinner, Palms Platters, served with steak fries and cole slaw, are good values and could include deep-fried flounder stuffed with crabmeat ($7.95) or a barbecued-pork sandwich ($5.95). The Palms has a full bar.

10. THE BLUE RIDGE PARKWAY

The 470-mile scenic highway that links the Shenandoah National Park in Virginia with the Great Smokies National Park in North Carolina begins at the terminus of the Skyline Drive in Rockfish Gap. This motor route winds through the southern Appalachian Mountains, offering magnificent vistas. The natural beauty of the mountain forests, wildlife, and wildflowers, combined with the pioneer history of the area, make this a fascinating route.

GETTING THERE

The parkway entrance is at Route 250, 140 miles southwest of Washington, D.C., 97 miles west of Richmond, and 4 miles west of Waynesboro, at the junction of the Skyline Drive. I-64 leads from Charlottesville to the east and Staunton to the west.

INFORMATION

Contact the **National Park Service,** U.S. Dept. of the Interior, 200 BB&T Building, Asheville, NC 28801 (tel. 704/259-0701).

WHAT TO SEE & DO

Milepost markers, similar to those on the Skyline Drive, are on the right-hand side of the parkway heading south.

There are several visitor centers along the parkway, including one at **Rockfish Gap,** at milepost 0. **Humpback Rocks Visitor Center,** at milepost 5.8, has picnic tables, rest rooms, and a self-guiding trail to a reconstructed mountain homestead. **James River and Kanawha Canal Visitors Center,** milepost 63.8, has a footbridge that crosses the river to the restored canal locks and exhibits. **Peaks of Otter,** milepost 84, is the site of a historic farm, self-guided walking trails, and rest rooms. **Rocky Knob,** milepost 169, has some 15 miles of hiking trails, including the Rock Castle Gorge National Recreational Trail, a comfort station, and picnic area. **Mabry Mill,** milepost 176, a picturesque vignette of a mill and its giant wheel on a little stream, is probably the most visited spot along the parkway. Displays of pioneer life, including crafts demonstrations, are featured, and the restored mill still grinds flour. A restaurant, open May through October, adjoins.

Over 200 **scenic overlooks** line the parkway. Notable are the ones at Greenstone, milepost 8.8; the highest point on the parkway in Virginia, Apple Orchard Mountain, milepost 76.5; Roanoke Valley, milepost 129.6; and Pine Spur, milepost 144.8.

There are also many **hiking trails,** including the Appalachian Trail, which follows the parkway from milepost 0 to about milepost 103.

WHERE TO STAY & DINE

PEAKS OF OTTER LODGE, milepost 86 (P.O. Box 489), Bedford, VA 24523. Tel. 703/586-1081, or toll free 800/542-5927 in Virginia. 59 rms, 3 suites (all with bath). A/C

$ Rates: $45 single; $65 double; $75–$85 suite. Extra person $4. Children under 16 stay free in parents' room. MC, V. **Parking:** Free.

At Peaks of Otter, everything is in harmony with nature—from the lakeside mountain setting to the rustic room decor of natural rough-grained wood with slate-top furnishings and a color scheme of subtle gray and blue tones. The main lodge building has a restaurant, a crafts and gift shop, and a games and TV room with a view of the lake. Accommodations are in motellike attached units on a grassy slope overlooking the lake. Split-rail fences and small footbridges add to the picturesque beauty of this serene valley. Each room has a private balcony or terrace to maximize the splendid view, but only suites have TVs and phones. These accommodations are highly popular, especially in the fall; reservations are accepted beginning October 1 for the *following* year. Winter and early spring are not overly crowded, but for the good-weather months, reservations should be made 4 to 6 weeks ahead.

Dining/Entertainment: The lodge's dining room is low key and pleasant, with a cathedral ceiling, hanging plants, and windows on the lake. Reasonably priced American fare is served at all three meals. Regional specialties include fried whole rainbow trout, Virginia ham croquettes, and southern fried chicken. A fixed-price $12.50 dinner, offered nightly, includes salad bar, entree, vegetable, and dessert. There is a full bar.

Facilities: Hiking trails, fishing in season.

CAMPGROUNDS

Campgrounds are at **Otter Creek,** milepost 56, open year round; **Peaks of Otter,** milepost 86; **Roanoke Mountain,** milepost 120.4, and **Rocky Knob,** milepost 167. Housekeeping cabins are available at Rocky Knob; to make reservations, write

Rocky Knob Cabins, Meadows of Dan, VA 24120 (tel. 703/593-3503). Campgrounds are open from about May 1 to early November, depending on weather conditions. Drinking water and rest rooms are provided, shower and laundry facilities are not. There are tent and trailer sites, but none has utility connections. Charge per night for each site is $8; the daily permit is valid only at the campground where it is purchased and until noon the following day. Golden Age and Golden Access Passport holders are entitled to a 50% discount.

11. ROANOKE

189 miles SW of Richmond, 232 miles SW of Washington, D.C.

GETTING THERE   By Plane   The **Roanoke Regional Airport** is 5½ miles northwest of downtown. USAir is the major carrier.

By Train   There is an Amtrak Thruway Bus Connection daily between Roanoke and the station on Ridgeway Street in Clifton Forge, Va. (45 miles away). For information, call toll free 800/872-7245.

By Bus   The **Greyhound/Trailways** terminal in Roanoke is at 26 Salem Avenue (tel. 703/345-7345).

By Car   From I-81, take I-581 into the heart of Roanoke.

ESSENTIALS   The **telephone area code** is 703. Contact the **Roanoke Convention and Visitors Bureau,** 114 Market Street, Marketplace Center, 2nd Floor, Roanoke, VA 24011 (tel. 703/342-6025).

Roanoke Valley, Virginia's largest metropolitan area west of Richmond, likes to call itself the capital of the Blue Ridge. Colonial explorers discovered the Roanoke Valley in the 17th century, and several small settlements were established here, including Big Lick, which later became the city of Roanoke. It was a thriving rail center in the 1880s, but the city's economy was shaken with the railroad's decline. Milestones in its recovery were construction of the Civic Center, a convention and cultural complex, and the restoration of Market Square. Roanoke's attractions have a special appeal for children; families should plan to spend at least a full day exploring the sights detailed below.

WHAT TO SEE & DO

Roanoke citizens know they're home when they can see the red neon **"Star on the Mountain,"** erected in 1949. It stands 88½ feet tall, and uses 2,000 feet of neon tubing. It's visible from many parts of the city, but to see it up close, and for a panoramic view of the city, take Walnut Avenue to the Mill Mountain Parkway Spur Road. While you're at the viewpoint, you may want to take the kids to nearby **Mill Mountain Zoological Park** (tel. 703/343-3241). Open daily from 10am to 4:30pm (till 6pm in summer), it is a 3-acre home to 40 animal species. Kids can pet goats, sheep, and rabbits. Admission is $2.75 for adults, $1.75 for children ages 3 to 12, free for children under 3.

The **Roanoke Historic City Market Square** is a lively spot. Its **Farmers Market** is open daily, with colorful sidewalk stands displaying plants, flowers, fresh fruits and vegetables, dairy and eggs, and farm-cured meats. In the landmark **Central Market Building** is a food court offering the downtown lunch crowd an international menu.

Three separately owned and operated museums and a theater share the precincts of **Center in the Square,** 1 Market Square (tel. 703/342-5700), a five-story converted warehouse. Children will be fascinated by the high-tech exhibits at the **Science Museum of Western Virginia and Hopkins Planetarium,** on Levels 1, 4, and 5 (tel. 703/342-5710). "Hands-on" is the buzz word here. Open Tuesday through Saturday from 10am to 5pm and on Sunday from 1 to 5pm, admission is $4 for adults, $2.50 for seniors and students 5 to 17 years old; under 5 free. The **Roanoke Valley History Museum,** on Level 3 (tel. 703/342-5770), houses documents, tools, costumes, and weapons that tell the story of Roanoke from pioneer days to the 1990s. Open Tuesday through Saturday from 10am to 5pm and on Sunday from 1 to 5pm; admission is $2 for adults, $1 for seniors and children ages 6 to 12, under 6 free. The **Roanoke Museum of Fine Arts,** on Levels 1 and 2 (tel. 703/342-5760), displays ancient and contemporary works, from tribal African to contemporary American. Open Monday through Saturday from 10am to 5pm and on Sunday from 1 to 5pm; admission is free. The **Mill Mountain Theater** offers children's productions, lunchtime readings, and year-round matinee and evening performances; call the box office at 703/342-5740 to find out what's on. A recent season featured *Evita, A Christmas Carol, A Midsummer Night's Dream, The Boys Next Door,* and *Me and My Girl.* Tickets are $8.50 to $9.50 for the intimate Theater B, $11 and $16 for the Main Stage. Seniors, students, and children receive a $2 discount.

As a crossroads city, Roanoke is an appropriate home for the **Virginia Museum of Transportation,** 303 Norfolk Avenue (tel. 703/342-5670), located downtown in a restored freight station. Kids will have a ball climbing aboard a caboose, strolling through a railway post office car, and seeing the classic steam giants up close. Open Monday through Saturday from 10am to 5pm and on Sunday from noon to 5pm; admission is $3 for adults, $2.50 for seniors, $2 for students 13 to 18, $1.75 for children 3 to 12, under 3 free.

WHERE TO STAY

EXPENSIVE

ROANOKE AIRPORT MARRIOTT, 2801 Hershberger Rd. NW, Roanoke, VA 24017. Tel. 703/563-9300, or toll free 800/228-9290. 320 rms. A/C TV TEL **Directions:** From I-581 south, take Exit 3W, Hershberger Road; make a right U-turn at the first light; the hotel is on the left.

$ Rates: $95–$118 single; $95–$128 double. Extra person $10. Children under 18 stay free in parents' room. Weekend packages; special discounts may apply. AE, CB, DC, DISC, MC, V. **Parking:** Free.

This eight-story Marriott is built like a Mediterranean villa, utilizing decorative objects from Italy, France, and Spain in the spacious lobby, where brick walls, Oriental rugs, and a huge fireplace provide a warm atmosphere. A new addition blends in well with the original building and includes a concierge level offering upgraded amenities and a private lounge. Rooms are conventionally decorated with dark-wood brass-trimmed traditional pieces, pretty mauve-print quilted spreads, and matching draperies.

Dining/Entertainment: Remington's is the Marriott's fine-dining spot, with beamed ceilings, stucco walls, French provincial armchairs, and pink napery on the tables. Entrees such as saltimboca, filet mignon, and swordfish steak range from $17.95 to $21.95. Lily's, an inviting room with skylights and high ceilings, is open for all meals. Whispers is the lobby bar; Charades, the entertainment lounge.

Services: 24-hour room service, courtesy airport shuttle.

Facilities: Indoor and outdoor pools, fitness center, sauna, Jacuzzi, two lighted tennis courts, gift shop.

MODERATE

PATRICK HENRY HOTEL, 617 S. Jefferson St., Roanoke, VA 24011. Tel. 703/345-8811, or toll free 800/833-4567. Fax 703/342-9908. A/C TV TEL
$ Rates: $79 single; $89 double. AE, CB, DC, MC, V. **Parking:** Hotel guests can use the public lot across the street at no charge.

A downtown Roanoke landmark since 1925, the hotel recently underwent a major renovation and has been restored to its original grandeur. A marble staircase leads into the magnificent two-story lobby with massive windows and polished marble floors. A brilliant gold bas-relief frieze embellishes ceilings and walls. Chandeliers, antique lamps, Oriental rugs, and period furnishings make the lobby a charming place. And guest rooms are spacious, many with Chippendale-style sofas and four-poster beds, lavish window treatments, and beautiful wallpapers; all have kitchenettes.

Dining/Entertainment: The British Tradition Pub and restaurant is open for all meals. A carvery featuring a fresh roast daily is a house specialty.

Services: Complimentary airport shuttle, laundry, turndown on request.

Facilities: Nearby health-club facilities, barbershop, hair salon.

BUDGET

HOLIDAY INN AIRPORT, 6626 Thirlane Rd., Roanoke, VA 24019. Tel. 703/366-8861, or toll free 800/HOLIDAY. 162 rms. A/C TV TEL **Directions:** From I-581S, take Exit 2S onto Peters Creek Road South and turn right at Thirlane Road.
$ Rates: $55–$72 single; $65–$73 double. Children under 18 stay free in parents' room. AE, DC, DISC, MC, V. **Parking:** Free.

This is a well-run property, with accommodations in a two-story typical motel U-shaped configuration around an outdoor pool. The rooms are a good size, with pink-and-red-striped bedspreads, matching draperies, wall-to-wall carpeting, and warm oak furnishings. The Fox Hunt restaurant, off the lobby, offers American fare, a salad bar, and a variety of reasonably priced buffets. There's dancing in the Foxes Den Lounge and a wide-screen TV for sports fans. Free airport transport is a plus.

A LOVELY MOUNTAIN RESORT

MOUNTAIN LAKE, Mountain Lake, VA 24136. Tel. 703/626-7121, or toll free 800/346-3334. Fax 703/626-7172. 100 rms, including 16 cabins. TEL **Directions:** From I-81 south, take Exit 37, Route 460 west; turn right onto Route 700 and it's 7 miles to Mountain Lake.
$ Rates (including breakfast and dinner): Main hotel, $100–$110 single; Cottages, $80–$100 single; Main hotel, $160; Chestnut Lodge $175. Children 12 and older in parents' room are charged $35 per day; ages 5–12, $20; 4 and under, free. AE, DC, DISC, MC, V.

If you saw the movie *Dirty Dancing* you're already familiar with this rustic mountaintop resort. Surrounded by a 2,600-acre wildlife conservancy, its rough-cut-stone stately lodge is the main building, with clusters of small white clapboard summer cottages nearby. The lobby has stone walls, thick rugs over a terra-cotta-tile floor, and comfortable seating in front of a massive fireplace. Complimentary tea and coffee are always kept hot on the sideboard. And a stone archway separates the lobby from the adjoining bar and lounge, where complimentary wine and cheese are served every afternoon.

The popular parlor suites have Jacuzzis and fireplaces, and some rooms offer full lake views. Decor has a warm, traditional look, with dark-wood Chippendale-reproduction furnishings, flame-stitch patterned fabric on sofas and chairs, and pale-green or burgundy color schemes predominating. Cottages are more simply furnished, although guests here have porches with rockers. Chestnut Lodge, the most recent addition, is a three-story gray clapboard building set on the side of a hill. Rooms here are decorated in country style, with fireplaces and private balconies.

Dining/Entertainment: The spacious stone-walled dining room has large windows providing panoramic lake views; at night it's a romantic setting. A recent dinner here began with an appetizer of sautéed mushrooms in burgundy sauce, followed by swordfish in sour cream–dill sauce, and chocolate mousse for dessert. There's also a snack bar in the Recreation Barn.

Facilities: Health club with sauna and weight room; clothing/souvenir/sporting goods shops; summer program for children; Recreation Barn for Ping-Pong, billiards, and evening entertainment; hiking trails; cross-country skiing; sleigh rides; tennis; boathouse with canoes and rowboats; fishing.

WHERE TO DINE

MACADO'S, 120 Church St. Tel. 703/342-7231.
  Cuisine: AMERICAN.
$ Prices: Sandwiches $2.95–$4.95; entrees $4.95–$6.95. MC, V.
  Open: Daily 11:30am–1am.

The whole family will enjoy this lively spot, part of a successful Virginia chain. The decor is eclectic—old Coke ads, beer signs, an elk head, and other odds and ends on the walls; a small airplane is suspended in midair, and there are many hanging plants. Seating, on several levels, is divided by brass rails into intimate areas. The menu offers sandwiches, salads, soups, and hot entrees. Pita pizzas and baked potatoes topped with cheese sauces are other options. Ice-cream sodas, sundaes, apple cobbler, and pecan pie are among the desserts. There's a full bar.

12. ABINGDON

133 miles SW of Roanoke; 437 miles SW of Washington, D.C.;
315 miles SW of Richmond

GETTING THERE   By Car   From I-81, take Route 58East directly into town.

ESSENTIALS   The **telephone area code** is 703. Contact the **Visitors & Convention Bureau,** 208 West Main Street, Abingdon, VA 24210 (tel. 703/676-2282).

Abingdon, tucked away in the fertile hills of southwest Virginia, makes a convenient base for a driving tour eastward to Mount Rogers National Recreation Area, and west to the Appalachians and Big Stone Gap. Daniel Boone led his family through Abingdon in 1773 on his way west. A marker on Route 58 near the I-81 intersection marks his passage. The small farming community, called Wolf Hill by Boone, got its present name in 1778.

WHAT TO SEE & DO

Even though there's not a lot to see and do here, Abingdon's picturesque beauty is hard to resist as you stroll on tree-shaded **Main Street.**

Mountain arts and crafts are for sale in the **Cave House Crafts Shop,** 279 East Main Street (tel. 628-7721), a cooperative housed in an 1858 Victorian landmark home.

A short drive on Route 58 east will bring you to the **Mount Rogers National Recreation Area** (tel. 703/783-5196), 154,000 acres of woodlands. The scenic

Virginia Creeper trail, which goes through the park, follows an old railroad bed the 34 miles from Abingdon to Whitetop, passing some of the most beautiful scenery in southwest Virginia. Galax, home of the famous **Fiddler Festival** in August (call 703/236-6355 for information), is 45 miles farther east on Route 58.

Going west from Abingdon, Route 58 will bring you past the Route 614 turnoff to the Carter Family Museum and Music Center (see "Evening Entertainment," below), where old-time country and bluegrass shows take place every Saturday night. Route 23, which continues Route 58 past Weber City, leads to **National Tunnel State Park,** where you'll get good views of the 10-story-high natural phenomenon. Route 23 then climbs through **Jefferson National Forest** into the Appalachian mining town of **Big Stone Gap,** home of John Fox, author of *Trail of the Lonesome Pine.* The sentimental drama is reenacted every July and August on Thursday, Friday, and Saturday night in the outdoor **June Tolliver Playhouse** in Big Stone Gap (tel. 703/523-2060). Tickets are $6 for adults, $5 for seniors, and $4 for children. The 1888 **John Fox, Jr., house** is filled with family furnishings and mementoes. It is open Tuesday through Saturday from 2 to 5pm and on Sunday from 2 to 6pm; admission is $3 for adults and $1 for children. The **Southwest Virginia Museum,** West First Street and Wood Avenue (tel. 703/523-1322), currently undergoing renovation in its late Victorian quarters, will display artifacts of the history and culture of the area.

WHERE TO STAY

MODERATE/EXPENSIVE

MARTHA WASHINGTON INN, 150 W. Main St., Abingdon, VA 24210. Tel. 703/628-3161, or toll free 800/533-1014 in Virginia. 61 rms and suites. A/C TV TEL

$ Rates: $75–$125 single or double; $145–$375 suite. Children staying in parents' room are charged $7. **Parking:** Free.

The stately Greek Revival portico of the Martha Washington Inn creates a formal facade for this 2½-story red-brick hotel. White wicker rocking chairs give the front porch the look of an old-time resort. The lobby and adjoining parlor—setting for daily afternoon tea—are elegantly decorated, with original marble fireplaces and crystal chandeliers. There are regular and deluxe rooms, the latter more lavishly appointed, with rich fabrics and fine antiques. Suites have museum-quality furnishings. One, decorated in red silk with lavish gold-leaf trim, has a working fireplace.

Dining/Entertainment: First Lady's Table features steak, chicken, and veal entrees for $14.95 to $19.95. The Pub is a cozy cocktail spot, and there's a lounge for entertainment and dancing.

Services: Room service (7am to 11pm), turndown, shoeshine, concierge.

INEXPENSIVE

VICTORIA AND ALBERT INN, 224 Oak Hill St., Abingdon, VA 24210. Tel. 703/676-2797. 4 rms (none with bath). A/C TV TEL

$ Rates (including full breakfast): $65–$75 single or double. MC, V. **Parking:** Street parking.

Two blocks from Main Street, a white picket fence sets off this turn-of-the-century white clapboard B&B, wherein interior decor is superb, thanks to the talent (and antiques store) of owners Lesley and Frank Hubbard. Lesley grew up on the Isle of Wight in England, and she has tried to duplicate her grandmother's cozy Yorkshire home here. The guest rooms have gas-log fireplaces and each room is uniquely decorated with sumptuous fabrics and wicker and carved-wood furniture. Thoughtful touches include clock radios and bathrobes. There is a sideboard in the second-floor hallway set up with snacks and drinks. A full breakfast might consist of fresh fruit, yogurt, homemade croissant stuffed with ham and cheese, muffins, tea, and coffee.

A COUNTRY B&B

FOX HILL INN, Rte. 2, Troutdale, VA 24378. Tel. 703/677-3313, or toll free 800/874-3313. 6 rms (all with bath). TV TEL **Directions:** From Abingdon, take Route 58E to Konnarock, then Route 603 to Troutdale (about 35 miles). From I-81, take the Marion exit, then Route 16S (20 miles).

$ Rates (including full breakfast): $65 double. Children stay free in parents' room. MC, V.

On a secluded hilltop amid 70 acres of fields and woods, this comfortable country home offers a big living room with a fireplace, a dining room and terrace with great mountain views, and a roomy country kitchen. A basement game room has Ping-Pong and board games. Guest rooms are furnished in simple country style. This is also a working farm, where cattle and sheep graze the meadows, and children can get a real feel for farm life. Canoe trips on the New River, horseback riding, and camping trips can be arranged.

WHERE TO DINE

MODERATE

THE TAVERN, 222 E. Main St. Tel. 703/628-1118.
 Cuisine: CONTINENTAL. **Reservations:** Suggested.
$ Prices: Appetizers $4.95–$5.95; entrees $14.95–$19.95. MC, V.
 Open: Lunch Mon–Sat 11:30am–2:30pm; dinner Mon–Sat 5:30pm–closing.
Built in 1779, the Tavern, originally an overnight inn for stagecoach travelers, is the oldest building in Abingdon. Exposed brick and stone walls, log beams, and hand-forged locks and hinges make for an appropriately rustic setting. Tables are set with pretty blue Bennington pottery and pink napkins. There are three upstairs dining rooms and a terrace overlooking a herb garden. The dinner menu starts off with appetizers like mixed game liver pâté, shrimp remoulade, and smoked salmon. Entrees include rack of lamb, Cornish hen, and Cajun scampi. Desserts are made fresh daily. An extensive wine list features imported and domestic vintages. At lunch, there are sandwiches, salads, and soups; a hearty whole-wheat hoagie stuffed with imported hard salami and ham, sauerkraut, and melted Cheddar is $4.95.

INEXPENSIVE

STARVING ARTIST CAFE, 134 Wall St., Depot Sq. Tel. 703/628-8445.
 Cuisine: AMERICAN. **Reservations:** Not accepted.
$ Prices: Appetizers $2.25–$5.95; entrees $12.95–$15.95. AE, MC, V.
 Open: Lunch Mon 11am–2pm, Tues–Sat 11am–3pm; dinner Tues–Sat 5–9pm.
The Starving Artist is the hot place to eat in Abingdon. Its small dining room is usually full, so arrive off-hours or prepare for a wait. It's worth it. Walls are decorated with works by regional artists, and ceiling fans keep the air moving. In summer there's outdoor dining on the patio. The food is of the finest quality. Appetizers of sautéed escargots, fried mozzarella with tomato-basil sauce, and French onion soup are among the choices. Entrees might include Cajun shrimp, lemon chicken, and baked orange roughy (a New Zealand fish) with béarnaise sauce. Fresh-baked desserts are excellent. At lunch, the menu bestows artists' names on the sandwiches; an Andy Warhol is the most POP burger in town, a Jackson Pollock has roast beef "dripping" with Monterey jack cheese, and so on.

EVENING ENTERTAINMENT

BARTER THEATER, at the corner of W. Main and College Sts. Tel. 703/628-3991, or toll free 800/368-3240.

⭐ The famous Barter Theater was founded during the Great Depression—when going to the theater was not a priority. Robert Porterfield, an enterprising young Virginia-born actor, sought his fortune on the New York stage, but his career came to a halt when the company he was touring with went broke. Facing unemployment, he had the brilliant idea of returning home to farm country with a troupe of actors who would barter their theatrical talents for surplus produce. Finding 22 out-of-work actors in New York in the grim summer of 1933 was easy, and Porterfield brought his eager company to Abingdon.

Barter's first presentation was John Golden's *After Tomorrow,* in 1933, for which he charged an admission of 40¢ or the equivalent in produce. The first season wound up with a profit of $4.30, and all the actors ate. Playwrights who contributed to the theater—Noel Coward, Thornton Wilder, Robert Sherwood, and Maxwell Anderson, among them—were paid with a token Virginia ham. Although most theatergoers pay money for their tickets today, the official policy still permits barter for admission (with prior notice). It is now the State Theatre of Virginia and America's longest-running professional repertory theater.

Recent productions, performed by an Actor's Equity company, have included *Arsenic and Old Lace, Steel Magnolias, Deathtrap,* and *The Diary of Anne Frank.* The theater's impressive alumni include Frank Lovejoy, Hume Cronyn, Patricia Neal, Fritz Weaver, Ernest Borgnine, Gregory Peck, and Ned Beatty. The season runs from April through December.

Prices: Fri–Sat evenings $11, Tues–Thurs and Sun evenings and all matinees $9; students under 25 half price, except Fri–Sat evenings.

CARTER FAMILY FOLD MUSIC SHOWS, Carter Family Museum and Music Center, Maces Spring, Va. Tel. 703/386-9480.

Every Saturday night throughout the year the Carter Family Music Center keeps alive the spirit of traditional mountain music by presenting the best regional country/bluegrass performers. Set among the hills in Maces Spring, the auditorium occupies a huge shed. Electronic equipment is banned. There's a small dance floor in front of the stage for hoe-down tunes, and local residents are adept at traditional dance styles like buck dancing and clogging. The first weekend in August, an annual festival draws many music groups, local artisans who sell crafts, and clog-dance performers. The museum is open on Saturday from 5 to 7pm, before the show.

To reach Maces Spring from Abingdon, take Route 58 west to Hiltons (about 17 miles) and turn right onto Route 614E for 3 miles to the Fold.

Prices: Music show tickets, $3.50 adults, $1 children ages 6–12, free for under 6.

INTRODUCING RICHMOND

Richmond has been the capital of Virginia since 1780 when it supplanted the more militarily vulnerable Williamsburg. But its history dates from 1609 when John Smith sailed up the James River looking for a short route to the Pacific. It was the site of the first Thanksgiving in 1619, though the settlers were not much later besieged by Indian attacks; a 1622 massacre resulted in death by tomahawk of a third of the population. It was in Richmond's St. John's Church that Patrick Henry concluded his address to the second Virginia Convention with the stirring words "Give me liberty or give me death." The traitorous Benedict Arnold led British troops down what is now Main Street in 1781 and set fire to many buildings, including tobacco warehouses, in those days the equivalent of banks. Cornwallis briefly occupied the town; Lafayette came to the rescue.

All this colonial history notwithstanding, Richmond is more famous for its role in the Civil War. For 4 years the capital of the Confederacy, it was surrounded by battling troops while hospitals overflowed with the wounded and converted tobacco warehouses filled with Union prisoners. Here Jefferson Davis presided over the Confederate Congress and Robert E. Lee accepted command of Virginia's armed forces.

Richmond visitors can explore nearby battlefield sites and peruse war-related exhibits and artifacts at the Museum of the Confederacy and the Valentine Museum. Imposing statues of Civil War heroes line Monument Avenue, and at Hollywood Cemetery monuments, stones, and epitaphs mark the graves of Davis, Stuart, and 18,000 Confederate soldiers.

1. ORIENTATION

ARRIVING

BY PLANE

Richmond International Airport, Airport Drive off I-64 and Williamsburg Road (tel. 804/226-3056), locally known as Byrd Field, is just 10 minutes east of downtown.

There's no bus service from the airport into Richmond. **Groome Transporta-**

tion (tel. 804/222-7222, or toll free 800/552-7911 in Virginia) offers service into town; for one person the cost is $11.25, $16 for two people, $19.75 for three people, and $5.75 each for four or more. **Virginia Limousine, Inc.** (tel. 804/358-3600), also provides service.

BY TRAIN

Amtrak trains pull into the station at 7519 Staples Mill Road (tel. 800/872-7245). About a dozen trains stop daily from Washington, D.C., and points north and from Raleigh, N.C., and points south. From the train station there's no direct public transportation downtown, so you're probably best off taking a taxi.

BY BUS

Greyhound/Trailways offers regularly scheduled service to Richmond; the terminal is at 2910 North Boulevard (tel. 804/353-8903).

BY CAR

Two major interstate highways intersect in Richmond—**I-64,** traveling east-west, and **I-95,** traveling north-south. **U.S. 1** (north-south) is another major artery. Here are a few approximate driving distances in miles to Richmond: from Atlanta, 511; from Boston, 535; from Columbus, Ohio, 440; from Miami, 950; from New York, 340; from Philadelphia, 235; from Washington, D.C., 100.

TOURIST INFORMATION

For orientation and information, make your first stop the **Metro Richmond Visitors Center,** 1710 Robin Hood Road, Boulevard Exit 14 from I-95/64 (tel. 804/358-5511). They provide brochures, maps, a 10-minute video orientation, tour information, and assistance with dining and lodging. The office is open daily from 9am to 5pm, with extended hours in summer. There's a small picnic/playground area just outside.

CITY LAYOUT

Foushee Street divides the city east and west, while **Main Street** divides it north and south. **Broad Street** is the major east-west thoroughfare, and it's one of the few downtown streets with two-way traffic.

NEIGHBORHOODS IN BRIEF

Metropolitan Richmond grew from east to west, along the banks of the James River. As you explore the neighborhoods described below (moving roughly from east to west) you'll get a good sense of Richmond's history.

Church Hill   On the east side of downtown, Church Hill is a largely residential neighborhood with many 19th-century Greek Revival houses; St. John's Church is the outstanding landmark of the area. It borders:

Shockoe Bottom   Shockoe Bottom is currently undergoing restoration as shops and restaurants move into this once-industrial section. The Edgar Allan Poe House, 17th Street Farmers Market, and old Main Street are in the area.

Shockoe Slip   This area, between 10th Street and 14th Street, between Main Street and Canal Street, is an area of restaurants, nightspots, and trendy shops housed in renovated warehouses near the James River. Cobblestone streets and old-fashioned street lamps provide historic ambience. Although this was the city's original site, established as a trading post by William Byrd in the 1670s, the area was reduced to rubble in 1865 and rebuilt as a manufacturing center after the war. Today it is a Historic Area in the heart of downtown Richmond.

Downtown   North of Shockoe Slip, downtown includes government buildings in and near Capitol Square, the historic homes and museums of the Court End area, and the shops at Sixth Street Marketplace. It is the financial and business center of Richmond.

Jackson Ward   Jackson Ward is a downtown National Historic District and home to many famous black Richmonders, including Maggie Walker and Bill "Bojangles" Robinson.

The Fan   Just west of downtown, the Fan is named for the shape of the streets bordered by West Broad and Boulevard, West Main and Belvedere. It includes Virginia Commonwealth University and many turn-of-the-century town houses, now occupied by homes, restaurants, and galleries. Monument Avenue's most scenic blocks, with its famous statues, are in the Fan.

Carytown   Just west of the Boulevard, Carytown has been called Richmond's answer to Georgetown. Cafés, restaurants, boutiques, and the restored Byrd Theatre, an old movie palace, bring Saturday-afternoon crowds to stroll the tree-lined streets.

2. GETTING AROUND

BY PUBLIC TRANSPORTATION

The Greater Richmond Transit Company (tel. 704/358-GRTC) operates the **public bus** system. Fare is 75¢. Service on most routes begins at 5am and ends at midnight. GRTC also operates **trackless trolley cars** in the downtown area which are free to the public. There are two routes: Broad Street to Shockoe Slip (operates Monday through Friday from 11am to 3pm) and Sixth Street Marketplace to Riverfront (Monday through Friday from 11am to 5pm and on Saturday from 10am to 6pm; after 5pm Monday through Friday the trolley route expands to Shockoe Bottom).

Also on weekends, the **Culture Link Trolley** travels on a continuous loop, linking major cultural and historic sites from 10am to 5pm on Saturday and noon to 5pm on Sunday. The trolley can be boarded at any attraction along the route, and at GRTC bus stops displaying the Culture Trolley signs; tickets are $5, $2.50 for ages 5 to 12 (under 5, free).

BY TAXI

All cab companies in the area have the following rates: $1.50 for the first one-fifth mile, 30¢ for each additional one-fifth mile, 30¢ for each minute of delay after the trip

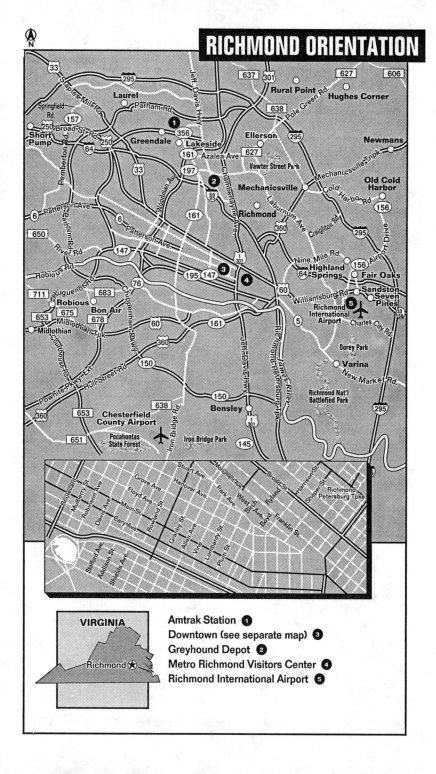

RICHMOND ORIENTATION

VIRGINIA
Richmond ★

Amtrak Station **1**
Downtown (see separate map) **3**
Greyhound Depot **2**
Metro Richmond Visitors Center **4**
Richmond International Airport **5**

has begun, and 30¢ for each additional passenger; a 50¢ surcharge may be added between 9pm and 6am; children under 6 ride free if accompanied by an adult. Call **Yellow Cab Co.** (tel. 804/355-4321) or **Veterans Cab Assn.** (tel. 804/329-1414).

BY CAR

Richmond is fairly easy to navigate by car, although streets tend to run one way. Right turns may be made on a red light after you've come to a full stop; left turns from a one-way street onto another one-way street may also be made at red lights after a full stop.

CAR RENTALS

All the major car-rental companies are represented here: At the airport are **Thrifty** (tel. 804/222-7022, or toll free 800/367-2277), **Avis** (tel. 804/222-7416, or toll free 800/331-1212), and **Hertz** (tel. 804/222-7228, or toll free 800/654-3131).

BY BICYCLE

The **Richmond Area Bicycling Association** (tel. 804/346-0242) has maps outlining area bike tours, available at **Two Wheel Travel,** 2934 West Cary Street (tel. 804/359-2453), and **Rowlett's,** Broad Street at Staple Mill Road (tel. 804/353-4489).

 RICHMOND

Area Code   The telephone area code for Richmond is 804.

Baby-sitters   Ask at your hotel.

Camera/Film   The **Richmond Camera Shop,** 217 East Grace Street (tel. 804/648-5895), is a convenient downtown store and repair center.

Car Rental   See Section 2, "Getting Around," above.

Climate   See Section 2, "When to Go," in Chapter 2.

Crime   See "Safety," below.

Dentist   The **Dental Referral Service** (tel. 804/649-0230) operates a professional referral service for general dental care.

Doctor   The **Greater Richmond Physician Referral Service** (tel. 804/330-4000) and the **Medical College of Virginia Associated Physicians** (tel. toll free 800/762-6161) have trained personnel to help choose a physician.

Drugstore   A chain, **People's Drug Stores,** open 24 hours, has many locations, including one at 2730 West Broad Street (tel. 804/359-2497).

Emergencies   Call **911** for the police or an ambulance, or to report a fire.

Eyeglasses   Two offices of **Lenscrafters,** one at the Shops at Willow Lawn, 5000 W. Broad St. (tel. 804/288-8938), the other at Cloverleaf Mall, 7201 Midlothian Tpke. (tel. 804/745-0173), offer 1-hour service.

Hairdressers/Barbers   You'll find **The Hair Cuttery,** a local chain, happy to cut the whole family's hair, with branches at almost every shopping center in or near Richmond. There's a shop at the Shops at Willow Lawn, 5000 W. Broad St. (tel. 804/288-9644).

Hospitals   The **Medical College of Virginia Hospital,** 401 North 12th Street (tel. 804/786-9000), is in downtown Richmond, and **Chippenham Medical**

Center, 7101 Jahnke Road (tel. 804/320-3911), is in southwest Richmond; both offer full emergency-room services.

Libraries   The **main library,** 1101 East Franklin Street (tel. 804/780-4774), is open Monday through Friday from 9am to 9pm and on Saturday from 9am to 1pm. Virginia's **State Library,** at 12th Street and Broad Street (tel. 804/786-8929), is a fine resource for books, historic documents, and maps.

Liquor Laws   In Virginia many grocery and convenience stores sell beer and wine, but only state-controlled Alcoholic Beverage Control (ABC) stores are permitted to sell other kinds of liquor. The drinking age is 21.

Lost Property   To report a lost or found item on the bus or trolley, call 804/358-4782. The airport has a lost-and-found department, as does each airline.

Luggage Storage/Lockers   You'll find them at the train station, 7519 Staples Mill Road.

Newspapers/Magazines   The city's daily newspaper is the *Richmond Times-Dispatch*. There are several local weeklies: *Style Weekly* is a guide to cultural and entertainment activities distributed around town free on Tuesday; the Visitors Center usually has copies. *Night Moves* is a free bimonthly tabloid covering music and entertainment. *Richmond Surroundings,* sold at newsstands, is a bimonthly city magazine; its annual newcomers guide is an excellent reference.

Police   See "Emergencies," above.

Post Office   The main post office, 1801 Brook Road (tel. 804/775-6292), is open Monday through Friday from 8:30am to 5pm and on Saturday from 8:30am to noon.

Religious Services   There are over 700 places of worship in the metropolitan area, representing congregations of the Christian, Jewish, Islamic, and Ba'hai faiths; they're listed in the *Yellow Pages* under "Churches," by denominations.

Safety   Richmond is a safe city, but downtown does become deserted after 9pm. In Shockoe Slip the late-night restaurants and bars keep the area lively until around midnight. In any city, even in the most heavily touristed areas, it's wise to stay alert and be aware of your surroundings, whatever the time of day.

Taxes   Virginia state sales tax is 4½%; hotels add on to that a room tax of 5%.

Taxis   See Section 2, "Getting Around," above.

Television   Local affiliates of national networks are WTVR-6 (CBS), WXEX-8 (ABC), WWBT-12 (NBC), and WRLH-35 (Fox). Two channels, WCVE-23 and WCVW-57, feature educational programming during the day and PBS telecasts at night.

Transit Information   See Section 2, "Getting Around," above.

Useful Telephone Numbers   Poison Center (tel. 804/786-9123), time and temperature (tel. 804/844-3711), Travelers Aid Society (tel. 804/648-1767), weather (tel. 804/268-1212).

3. ACCOMMODATIONS

Many Richmond hotels are clustered downtown, and during the week cater primarily to business travelers. Weekends, vacationers can enjoy hotels at discount prices. If you have a car, stay at one of the hotels a few miles from downtown at more reasonable rates with no parking fees.

FROMMER'S COOL FOR KIDS: HOTELS

Holiday Inn Koger Center *(see page 154)* With a pool and a lovely wooded park next door, this Holiday Inn offers lots of space to run around and play. It's also near Chesterfield Mall shopping and movies.

Jefferson Sheraton *(see page 150)* Even if you don't stay here, bring the kids in to see the awe-inspiring, grand proportions of the palatial lobby, the alligator sculptures, and the magnificent stained-glass domes. It's the stuff that dreams are made on.

Omni *(see page 150)* Older kids will enjoy being able to walk across the street and explore the Shockoe Slip shops on their own. There is also a heated indoor/outdoor pool to keep younger ones amused.

Radisson *(see page 152)* It welcomes kids and has a great indoor pool that overlooks the James River.

DOWNTOWN HOTELS
EXPENSIVE

BERKELEY HOTEL, 1200 E. Cary St., Richmond, VA 23219. Tel. 804/780-1300. Fax 804/343-1885. 55 rms. A/C TV TEL **Bus:** 51, 53, 62, or 63.

$ Rates: $90–$105 single; $105–$125 double. Extra person $10. Weekend and other packages available. AE, CB, DC, DISC, MC, V. **Parking:** Complimentary valet parking.

At this elegant little Shockoe Slip hostelry, a handsome red-brick facade provides access to a seemingly old-world interior. Opened in 1988, the hotel creates the illusion that it was built hundreds of years ago. Rooms are very residential in feel, luxuriously appointed, with fine period-reproduction furnishings, floral-print bedspreads and draperies, and walls hung with botanical prints; some have Jacuzzis.

Dining/Entertainment: Berkeley's restaurant, an upscale dining room open for all three meals, features continental favorites—steak au poivre, shrimp scampi, linguine Alfredo, and veal chardonnay—at prices ranging from $10.75 to $17.25. Nightingale's Lounge adjoins.

Services: Concierge.

Facilities: Pool and health club nearby.

COMMONWEALTH PARK SUITES HOTEL, Ninth and Bank Sts. (P.O. Box 455), Richmond, VA 23203. Tel. 804/343-7300, or toll free 800/343-7300. Fax 804/343-1025. 49 suites. A/C MINIBAR TV TEL **Bus:** 22, 72, or 73.

$ Rates: $120–$195 single; $130–$215 double. Weekend and other packages available. AE, DC, MC, V. **Parking:** Valet parking $9.75.

Quiet elegance is the keynote at this small luxury hotel which has hosted Britain's former prime minister, Margaret Thatcher, and various entertainment stars over the years. Built in 1912, the white limestone and brick 11-story building is within walking distance of all downtown restaurants and attractions.

The one- and two-bedroom suites are tastefully decorated with 18th-century mahogany reproduction pieces. Spacious living rooms, which can be completely closed off for privacy, have museum-quality prints, sofas and easy chairs upholstered in soft pastel colors, and wall-to-wall carpeting covered with Oriental area rugs.

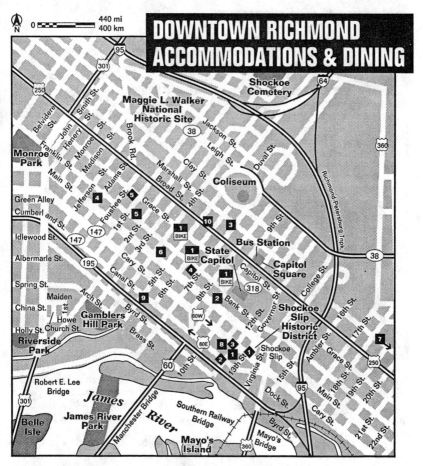

440 mi
400 km

Shockoe
Cemetery

Maggie L. Walker
National
Historic Site

Monroe
Park

Coliseum

Green Alley

Cumberland St.

Idlewood St.

Albermarle St.

Spring St.

Maiden

China St.

Holly St.

Riverside
Park

Gamblers
Hill Park

State
Capitol

Bus Station

Capitol
Square

Shockoe
Slip
Historic
District

Shockoe
Slip

Robert E. Lee
Bridge

James

James River
Park

Belle
Isle

River

Manchester Bridge

Southern Railway
Bridge

Mayo's
Island

Mayo's
Bridge

VIRGINIA

RICHMOND

ACCOMMODATIONS:
Berkeley **1**
Commonwealth Park **2**
Days Inn Downtown **3**
Jefferson Sheraton **4**
Linden Row **5**
Massad House **6**
Mr. Patrick Henry's Inn **7**
Omni **8**
Radisson **9**
Richmond Marriott **10**

DINING:
Morton's Tea Room ◆**5**
Peking Pavilion ◆**1**
Sam Miller's Warehouse ◆**3**
Tobacco Company ◆**2**
Travellers ◆**4**

Bedrooms contain four-poster beds with Colonial print spreads and closets that lock. Luxurious extras in the marble baths include oversize tubs, hairdryers, and bathrobes.

Dining/Entertainment: The garden-motif Maxine's Restaurant is open for breakfast and lunch. The candlelit Assembly, a more formal venue decorated in shades of burgundy and pink, with seating in Victorian-style chairs and rose-colored banquettes, serves dinner only. Entrees ($15.95 to $25) include rack of lamb, beef tenderloin with oyster cream, crab cakes, and roast duck. And there's piano music Thursday through Saturday night in Memories Lounge.

Services: 24-hour room service; shoe shine; complimentary limousine in downtown area, concierge.

Facilities: 24-hour exercise room, sauna.

JEFFERSON SHERATON, Franklin and Adams Sts., Richmond, VA 23220. Tel. 804/788-8000, or toll free 800/325-3535. Fax 804/344-5162. 274 rms. A/C MINIBAR TV TEL **Bus:** 13, 15, or 16.

$ Rates: $120–$130 single; $135–$140 double. Extra person $10. Children under 17 stay free in parents' room. Weekend and other packages available. AE, CB, DC, MC, V. **Parking:** Free self-parking in lot across the street.

A stunning Beaux Arts landmark, the Jefferson was opened in 1895 by Maj. Lewis Ginter, among Richmond's wealthiest citizens, who wanted his city to have one of the finest hotels in America. He hired the architectural firm of Carrere & Hastings, who had designed the monumental New York Public Library and the Frick Mansion on Fifth Avenue. Although the hotel suffered two major fires, and was closed in 1980, it reopened in 1986, restored to all its former glory. Its magnificent limestone-and-brick facade is adorned with Renaissance-style balconies, arched porticos, and an Italian clock tower. The majestic lobby has two levels. Two-story, faux-marble columns, embellished with gold-leaf trim, encircle the Rotunda, or lower lobby. Acres of Oriental area rugs define the central seating area, furnished with elegant tufted-leather sofas amid potted palms. The marble Grand Staircase, magnificently wide and red carpeted, leads to the upper lobby, the Palm Court, which is under a beautiful, domed stained-glass skylight, 9 of its 12 panes are original Tiffany glass.

Rooms are furnished with custom-made 18th-century-reproduction pieces, in varying color schemes. All contain three telephones, clock radio, and an in-house channel on the cable TV. Hundreds of notables have stayed here, including Presidents (Harrison, McKinley, Wilson, Coolidge, and both Roosevelts), Charles Lindbergh, Henry Ford, Charlie Chaplin, even Elvis Presley. And Scott and Zelda Fitzgerald held glamorous parties here.

Dining/Entertainment: Sunday brunch in the Rotunda is a bountiful all-you-can-eat feast in opulent surroundings. The Terrace Ice Cream Parlor and T.J.'s restaurant, bar, and oyster bar are just off the Rotunda. Off the Palm Court there's elegant dining at Lemaire's (named for Thomas Jefferson's maître d'), a warren of seven handsome rooms, one featuring a library. Breakfast, lunch, and dinner are served here, the last featuring regional entrees ($15.95 to $17.95) such as hickory-smoked rabbit, peanut-roasted pork loin, and grilled scallops.

Services: 24-hour room service, concierge; shuttle to theaters and Shockoe Slip can be arranged.

Facilities: Gift shop; health-club facilities at the Y across the street.

OMNI HOTEL, 100 S. 12th St., Richmond, VA 23219. Tel. 804/344-7000, or toll free 800/THE-OMNI. 363 rms, 12 suites. A/C MINIBAR TV TEL **Bus:** 62 or 63.

$ Rates: $69–$120 single; $69–$130 double. Extra person $15. Children under 12 stay free in parents' room. Weekend and other packages available. AE, CB, DC, DISC, MC, V. **Parking:** $10 Mon–Fri, $2.50 Sat–Sun.

One of Richmond's top hotels, the Omni is a luxury-class downtown property in the James Center office towers, close to the Richmond Convention Center and Shockoe Slip attractions. It boasts a handsome pink marble lobby, with green velvet-upholstered chairs and sofas around a working fireplace. Rooms are decorated in soft pastels, and some have spectacular views of the nearby James River. Club-floor rooms offer access to a private lounge, where a complimentary continental breakfast and afternoon refreshments are served.

Dining/Entertainment: Gallego Restaurant and Winebar features classic American fare in an upscale setting with dark-wood paneling, gold-leaf-framed oil paintings, oversize booths, and well-appointed tables. Café Gallego, a New Wave Italian restaurant, features pastas and pizzas. And a gourmet take-out deli shares the café space.

Services: Room service (7am to midnight), concierge.

Facilities: Capital Club, with indoor/outdoor pool, sun deck, squash and racquetball courts, and Nautilus equipment, is on the premises, available to Omni guests for $10 per day fee. James Center shops adjoin the hotel lobby.

RICHMOND MARRIOTT, 500 E. Broad St., Richmond, VA 23219. Tel. 804/643-3400, or toll free 800/228-3400. 401 rms, 10 suites. A/C TV TEL **Bus:** 1, 2, or 3.

$ Rates: $120 single; $135 double; suites $200–$500. Weekend and other packages available. AE, DC, DISC, MC, V. **Parking:** Free.

Ideally located for convention goers, the Marriott is connected via a skywalk to the Richmond Convention Center. Exceptionally spacious accommodations, in lovely dusty-rose/pink-beige color schemes, are handsomely furnished with dark-wood pieces and comfortable armchairs. Many offer panoramic city views.

Dining/Entertainment: The Court Plaza Café serves breakfast, lunch, and dinner in a cheerful atmosphere. The intimate Chardonnay offers gourmet cuisine and elegant ambience. And Triplett's, the lobby lounge and cocktail bar, provides live music and dancing on weekends. Sporting events are aired on the big TV in Triplett's.

Services: Concierge, free newspaper.

Facilities: Health club, indoor pool, adjacent to Sixth Street Marketplace shops.

MODERATE

LINDEN ROW, 101 N. First St., Richmond, VA 23219. Tel. 804/783-7000, or toll free 800/533-INNS. Fax 804/648-7504. 73 rms, 7 suites (all with bath). A/C TV TEL **Bus:** 15 or 16.

$ Rates (including continental breakfast): $59–$99 single or double; $99–$119 suite. Extra person $10. Children under 18 stay free in parents' room. AE, CB, DC, MC, V. **Parking:** Complimentary valet parking.

A row of seven 140-year-old Greek Revival town houses comprise this charming property. Not only have the facades have remained intact; original interior features such as fireplaces, marble mantels, and crystal chandeliers still grace the inn. The buildings are linked in the back by a terraced gallery that runs the length of the row.

Furnishings in the spacious main-house rooms are a harmonious mix of late Empire and early-Victorian pieces, with beautiful wallpapers, damask draperies, flower-patterned carpets, and marble-top dressers. Remote-control TV and Caswell-Massey toiletries are welcome extras. Back rooms overlook a brick-walled garden and patio, and the garden dependencies (small, separate buildings) of the original town houses have been restored and offer accommodations with private entrances. These rooms have a country look, with wicker pieces, chenille spreads, and ruffled curtains. Guests have access to two handsomely furnished parlors, with leather couches and working fireplaces. An inviting collation of cheese, crackers, and drinks in the early evening and hot beverages after dinner are laid on, buffet style, in one of these sitting rooms.

Dining/Entertainment: Off the garden patio is the inn's main dining room, a cozy, low-ceilinged precinct with whitewashed-brick walls. The buffet-style continental breakfast is served here. Luncheon fare—salads, fruit and yogurt, and sandwiches—is reasonably priced and nicely presented. Continental cuisine with a southern accent is offered in the evening, with entrees ($11 to $18) running the gamut from veal parmigiana to crab cakes and swordfish (blackened, grilled, broiled, or lemon peppered).

Services: Concierge, free daily newspaper, limo service, room service (7 to 9am and 5:30 to 10pm).

Facilities: Use of YMCA Fitness Center free to guests; fax and copy service (minimal charge).

RADISSON HOTEL, 555 E. Canal St., Richmond, VA 23219. Tel. 804/ 788-0900, or toll free 800/333-3333. 300 rms. AC MINIBAR TV TEL **Bus:** 32, 70, or 71.

$ Rates: $49–$70 single; $59–$89 double. Extra person $10. AE, DC, DISC, MC, V. **Parking:** Free.

You can't mistake the Radisson for any other building in town—it's a starkly modern, triangular high-rise with reflecting glass windows. The 16-story hotel has a friendly, accommodating staff and comfortable rooms decorated in restful tones of mauve and teal. Mirrored sliding closet doors reflect the clean, simple look of the rooms, which boast such nice touches as Edward Hopper prints on the walls. Most rooms offer stunning city views.

Dining/Entertainment: The 555 Canal Club is a pleasant lounge. The Pavilion, a casual eatery, serves a buffet breakfast daily from 6:30am; it's also open for lunch and dinner.

Services: Room service (6:30am to 10:30pm).

Facilities: Indoor pool overlooking the James River, health club, sauna, Jacuzzi, Nautilus equipment, gift shop.

BUDGET

DAYS INN DOWNTOWN, 612 E. Marshall St., Richmond, VA 23219. Tel. 804/649-2378, or toll free 800/325-2525. 140 rms. A/C TV TEL **Bus:** 1, 2, or 3.

$ Rates: $39–$56 single; $45–$65 double. Extra person $6. Children under 18 stay free in parents' room. AE, DC, DISC, MC, V. **Parking:** Free.

Adjacent to the Sixth Street Marketplace (see Section 1, "Attractions," in Chapter 10) and within easy walking distance of many of Richmond's major sights, this convenient property also boasts an indoor pool and on-premises restaurant. Lobby and bedrooms are comfortably furnished and decorated in burgundy and blue. Some rooms are balconied around a catwalk overlooking the Coliseum.

MASSAD HOUSE HOTEL, 11 N. Fourth St., Richmond, VA 23219. Tel. 804/648-2893. 64 rms (all with bath). A/C TV TEL **Bus:** 51, 70, or 71.

$ Rates: $34 single; $44 double; $55 suite (sleeps four). Extra person $5. MC, V. **Parking:** Free.

Centrally located between Main Street and East Franklin Street, the Massad House is a four-story Tudor-style brick building that looks as if it belongs in an English village. Inside it's homey and immaculate, from the cheerful lobby to the freshly painted hallways hung with prints, to the comfortable rooms. The latter have Colonial-style maple furnishings, along with some modern pieces, and white stucco walls hung with paintings. An inexpensive restaurant is right next door, and a Budget Rent-A-Car agency is on the premises. Reserve far in advance.

BED-AND-BREAKFAST

Carefully chosen bed-and-breakfast accommodations are offered by **Bensonhouse of Richmond,** 2036 Monument Avenue, Richmond, VA 23220 (tel. 804/648-7560). Administrator Lyn Benson has 18 listings, all within 10 minutes of major attractions. All her hosts are knowledgeable about the city. Rates range from $50 and up for a single, from $60 for a double, continental breakfast included. Many hosts even prepare a full breakfast. At the lower end of the scale you're generally sharing a bath. The choices range from an 1870 Victorian home to a stunning 1914 Italian Renaissance-style residence on historic Monument Avenue. Reserve far in advance.

CHURCH HILL

MODERATE/EXPENSIVE

MR. PATRICK HENRY'S INN, 2300-02 E. Broad St., Richmond, VA 23223. Tel. 804/644-1322. 2 rms, 3 suites (all with bath). A/C TV TEL **Bus:** 41 or 51.

$ **Rates** (including full breakfast for two): $85–$95 double; $115–$135 suite. AE, DC, DISC, MC, V.

One block west of historic St. John's Church, Mr. Patrick Henry's Inn is in Richmond's oldest neighborhood, Church Hill. Innkeepers James and Lynn News began renovating the two Greek Revival town houses in 1986 and have produced a charming inn on a tree-lined, residential street. The first two floors are given over to a tavern and restaurant whose cuisine has received critical acclaim in both local and regional periodicals. James is the talented chef. All accommodations have working fireplaces, suites offer kitchenettes as well, and one has a private balcony overlooking the garden. Furnishings are a mix of antiques and reproductions, featuring four-poster beds, wing chairs, and pretty ruffled curtains.

Dining/Entertainment: On the basement level, the tavern, with low beamed ceilings and whitewashed brick walls, serves up light fare. Upstairs, the Colonial-style dining room, with oak chairs and crystal candle lamps on the tables, offers New American cuisine dinners (entrees $18 to $25). A typical dinner here: sea scallops with corn pancakes garnished with red caviar and sour-cream sauce, followed by salmon en croûte and a dessert of flourless chocolate cake with homemade crème caramel ice cream.

RICHMOND WEST

About 5 miles from downtown, these two West Broad Street properties are near I-64, allowing you to zip into downtown Richmond in about 10 to 15 minutes by car.

MODERATE

COURTYARD BY MARRIOTT, 6400 W. Broad St., Richmond, VA 23229. Tel. 804/282-1881, or toll free 800/321-2211. 145 rms. A/C TV TEL **Directions:** From I-64 west, take Exit 38B (Broad Street South); the hotel is half a mile from I-64 on the left.

$ **Rates:** $56–$78 single; $56–$92 double. Children under 18 stay free in parents' room. AE, CB, DC, DISC, MC, V. **Parking:** Free.

This motor inn offers a friendly, residential environment, with an atrium lobby overlooking a nicely landscaped courtyard and pool. Some first-floor rooms face the courtyard and have sliding glass doors; others, on upper floors, have private balconies. Furnishings are contemporary in style, with floral-patterned, quilted spreads, color-coordinated draperies and carpets, abstract prints on the walls, and ginger-jar lamps.

Dining/Entertainment: A pleasant lobby restaurant, overlooking a garden, serves breakfast, lunch, and dinner daily. Prices are reasonable. A comfortable lounge adjoins.

Facilities: Pool, coin-op laundry, sauna, Jacuzzi, exercise room with Universal equipment.

BUDGET

ECONO LODGE, 8008 W. Broad St., Richmond, VA 23229. Tel. 804/ 346-0000, or toll free 800/446-6900. 194 rms (all with bath). A/C TV TEL **Directions:** From I-64W, take Exit 37B (Parham Road) and turn right onto Broad Street; the Econo Lodge is half a mile on the left.

$ Rates (including continental breakfast): $32–$40 single; $36–$54 double. Extra person or rollaway bed $5. Children under 18 stay free in parents' room. AE, DC, MC, V. **Parking:** Free.

Nicely decorated motel rooms offering all the expected amenities plus an AM/FM clock radio, a pool, and a sun deck, There's no on-premises restaurant, but Piccadilly Cafeteria and Bennigan's adjoin.

RICHMOND SOUTH

MODERATE

HOLIDAY INN KOGER CENTER SOUTH, 1021 Koger Center Blvd., Richmond, VA 23235. Tel. 804/379-3800, or toll free 800/HOLIDAY. Fax 804/379-2763. 200 rms. A/C TV TEL **Directions:** From I-95S, take I-195 to Powhite Parkway, then Route 60W; Koger Center Boulevard is to the right, just past Johnston-Willis Hospital.

$ Rates: $70–$80 single; $77–$87 double. Children under 18 stay free in parents' room. Weekend and other packages available. AE, DC, DISC, MC, V. **Parking:** Free.

This Holiday Inn has a six-story atrium lobby filled with shrubs and greenery and a raised lounge area in the center where the soothing sounds of a waterfall serve as a backdrop for quiet conversation. Rooms are large and well appointed, decorated in tones of plum, pink, and gray. Each contains a desk, clock radio, and remote-control TV.

Dining/Entertainment: The Court Café features breakfast and lunch buffets daily and à la carte dinners nightly. There's DJ music in Visions Lounge, and dancing in Chesterfields on weekends.

Services: Room service (6am to 10pm), airport shuttle on request.

Facilities: Outdoor pool and sun deck; exceptionally well-equipped Robius Fitness Center next door ($7 daily fee for Holiday Inn guests); Huguenot Park with jogging trails, playground, tennis courts abuts Koger Center; full business/meeting facilities; gift shop, coin-op laundry on second floor.

RICHMOND EAST

BUDGET

MOTEL 6, 5704 Williamsburg Rd. (Rte. 60), Sandston, VA 23150. Tel. 804/222-7600. 121 rms (all with bath). A/C TV TEL **Directions:** Drive 7 miles east of downtown on Route 60.

$ Rates: $24.95 single; additional adults $6 each. Children under 18 stay free in parents' room. AE, DC, DISC, MC, V. **Parking:** Free.

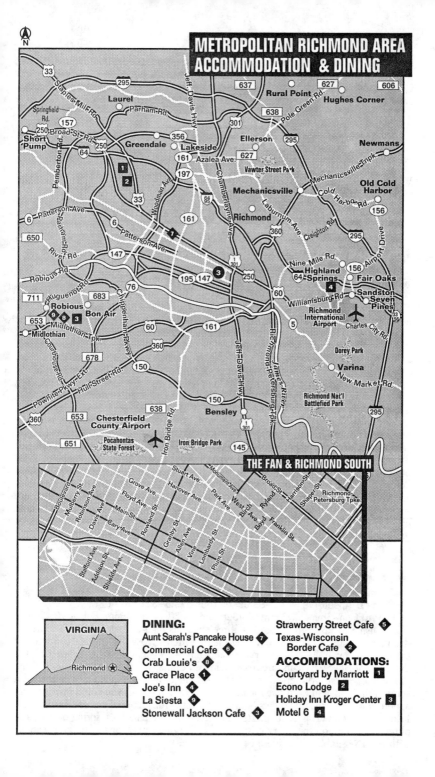

Just across the road from the Richmond airport, this budget accommodation is not far from downtown, but also convenient for day trips to the James River plantations and Colonial Williamsburg (39 miles). Standard rooms are neat and clean. There's a swimming pool on the premises, and many restaurants are close by.

4. DINING

While most Richmond hotels are in the downtown / Shockoe Slip area, there are good restaurants in other neighborhoods as well, especially the Fan.

DOWNTOWN / SHOCKOE SLIP
EXPENSIVE

TRAVELLER'S RESTAURANT, 707 E. Franklin St. Tel. 804/644-1040.
  Cuisine: AMERICAN. **Reservations:** Recommended. **Bus:** 32 or 34.
  $ Prices: Appetizers $4.95–$10.95; entrees $14.95–$39.95. AE, MC, V.
  Open: Lunch Mon–Fri 11:30am–2:30pm; dinner Mon–Sat 5:30–10pm.
The building that houses the Traveller's Restaurant (named for Gen. Robert E. Lee's horse) is the small brick house that Lee returned to after surrendering to Grant at Appomattox. The restaurant maintains the equine theme with a handsome painting of three famous Virginia horses—Traveller, Secretariat, and Sir Archie. Its Victorian ambience is quietly elegant, with soft lighting from antique sconces and chandeliers casting a warm glow on flocked wallpaper and pink tablecloths. The basement of the old Lee house has a solid mahogany bar complete with a brass footrest, an oil painting of General Lee, and a Mathew Brady photograph of Lee in full uniform. A brick patio is open for good weather dining.
   The menu highlights corn-fed prime beef, and Traveller's can compete with the best steakhouses in the country. Your dinner might begin with lobster bisque, crabmeat-stuffed mushrooms, or sautéed oysters (in season). Spinach salad with hot bacon dressing is also excellent. Beef entrees include New York strip steak (12 or 18 ounces), prime ribs, filet mignon with sauce béarnaise, and a thick and juicy 2-pound Porterhouse. All entrees come with baked potato, steak fries, or rice pilaf. Vegetables are available à la carte. Seafood and chicken dishes are also options. Desserts are sumptuous and sizable. Rum-walnut bread pudding is a house specialty, as is Key lime pie. The wine list features domestic and imported vintages, including some Grand Cru designations.

MODERATE

PEKING PAVILION, 1302 E. Cary St. Tel. 804/649-8888.
  Cuisine: CHINESE. **Bus:** 51, 52, or 63.
  $ Prices: Appetizers $1.20–$8.95; entrees $7.25–$21.95. AE, MC, V.
  Open: Sun–Thurs 11:30am–9:45pm, Fri 11:30am–10:45pm, Sat 5–10:45pm.
This plush Shockoe Slip choice has three spacious high-ceilinged dining rooms, all decorated in cream and pale pink, set off by flattering rosy lighting and a burgundy carpet. The exquisite wood carvings and tapestries on the walls, as well as the dragon-motif-backed chairs, are from mainland China. Yet, for all its elegance, Peking Pavilion offers surprisingly inexpensive combination lunch platters—entree with soup, spring roll, and fried rice for $5.25 to $6.95. For dinner you could start with an appetizer of pan-fried dumplings or fantail shrimp. House special entrees lead off with Peking duck with crispy skin and tender meat, Chinese pancakes, spring onions, and plum sauce. Or you might try crispy beef with orange peel, or shrimp and scallops with fresh vegetables in Chinese barbecue sauce.

SAM MILLER'S WAREHOUSE, 1210 E. Cary St. Tel. 804/643-1301.
    Cuisine: AMERICAN. **Reservations:** Suggested, especially for dinner on weekends. **Bus:** 51, 52, or 63.
$ Prices: Appetizers $4.95–$7.75; entrees $8.95–$22.50. AE, DC, MC, V.
    Open: Lunch daily 11am–5pm; dinner daily 5–11pm; brunch Sun 11am–5pm; entertainment till 2am.

Entered via a casual bar and dining area with red leather banquettes and bare wood tables, Sam Miller's main dining rooms are one flight up a majestic staircase. Here, seating is in cozy booths, and small dark-green tole lamps on the tables keep lighting romantically low. At lunch, terrific sandwiches include beef or pork barbecue with cole slaw, crab cakes, and a juicy 5-ounce hamburger. Chespeake Bay seafood and prime rib are dinner-menu highlights. A heaping platter of steamed mussels with garlic butter is an excellent way to start off dinner. Among the seafood entrees, all served with vegetable du jour and wild rice or baked potato, are fresh broiled swordfish with béarnaise sauce, shrimp stuffed with crab imperial, and an enormous seafood platter piled high with scallops, oysters, clams, shrimp, fresh fish, and crab cake. For dessert, there's carrot cake with cream cheese and walnut icing, Kahlúa cheese cake, and walnut/chocolate-chip pie.

THE TOBACCO COMPANY, 1201 E. Cary St. Tel. 804/782-9555.
    Cuisine: AMERICAN. **Reservations:** Recommended. **Bus:** 51, 52, or 63.
$ Prices: Appetizers $3.95–$7.95; entrees $13.95–$21.95. AE, DC, MC, V.
    Open: Lunch Mon–Sat 11:30am–2:30pm; dinner Mon–Fri 5:30–10:30pm, Sat 5pm–midnight, Sun 5:30–10pm; brunch Sun 10:30am–2pm.

The Tobacco Company, housed in a former tobacco warehouse, evokes the Victorian era in a sunny, three-story, plant-filled atrium setting. An exposed antique elevator carries guests from the first-floor cocktail lounge to the two dining floors above. Nostalgic touches abound—brass chandeliers, a cigar-store Indian, even an old ticket booth that is now the hostess desk. Tiffany-style lamps cast a glow on the various seating areas, which are handsomely sectioned off by white porch-style banister railings. Exposed brick walls are festooned with antique collector's items.

Contemporary American cuisine is featured. Lunch specialties ($3.95 to $9.95) could be as light as a vegetarian stir-fry, as hearty as chicken chimichangas (tortilla stuffed with chicken, chiles, and Jack cheese, with guacamole, salsa, sour cream, and black-bean cakes). Also on tap: omelets, salads, sandwiches, and burgers. At dinner you might begin with shrimp and Virginia ham with papaya or an innovative pairing of tortellini and escargots. Salmon filet is served with capers, mushrooms, and lemon butter, accompanied by polenta and fresh asparagus. Grilled rainbow trout is smothered in Cajun butter, then served with fried grits, red beans, and sautéed Swiss chard. Desserts range from deep-dish apple pie topped with ice cream to English trifle. Sunday-brunch entrees, served with a pastry basket and choice of juice, include palascintas (stuffed crêpes), seafood fettuccine, and quiche of the day. Most nights there's live music on the first floor and dancing in the Club downstairs.

BUDGET

MORTON'S TEA ROOM, 2 E. Franklin St., at Foushee St. Tel. 804/648-7062.
    Cuisine: AMERICAN. **Reservations:** Recommended for large groups. **Bus:** 13, 15, or 16.
$ Prices: Entrees (including appetizer and beverage) $4.50–$7.50 at lunch, $12.95–$15.75 at dinner. No credit cards.
    Open: Lunch Mon–Fri 11:30am–2:15pm; dinner Mon–Fri 5–7:30pm.

Morton's Tea Room occupies four parlor-level rooms of a historic mid-1880s brick house. There's real lavender-and-old-lace charm in the decor: parquet floors, high ceilings, white wainscoting beneath red-flocked or gold silk shantung wall coverings, rich brocade draperies, and a fireplace in every room. There are daily specials such as a fried-oyster sandwich on a roll, served with two vegetables (collard greens, candied yams, and fried apples, among others). Or consider sausage cakes or fried Virginia ham, both served with buttered apples and a vegetable. Finish up with moist and sweet peach or apple cobbler with vanilla or rum-raisin ice cream.

THE FAN

BUDGET

COMMERCIAL CAFE, 111 N. Robinson St., between Floyd and Grove Aves. Tel. 804/643-RIBS.
  Cuisine: AMERICAN. **Bus:** 3 or 4.
$ **Prices:** Entrees $5.50–$13.95 at lunch or dinner. MC, V.
  Open: Lunch Tues–Fri 11:30am–2:30pm; dinner Mon–Fri 5–11pm; Sat–Sun 11:30am–11pm.

The Commercial Café is hip and simpatico—a place for good atmosphere, good food, and good music. The setting: fans, lush hanging plants, and globe lights with rattan shades suspended from a pressed-tin ceiling; red-and-white checkered tablecloths, gallery lights over the bar, and barnwood walls hung with news clippings of major events like "Nixon Resigns." Dinah Shore included the café's recipes in her cookbook, *Gourmet* magazine has published them, and the ribs here have merited much national attention in cook-off circles. Hickory-smoked meats from "plump, pampered, peanut-fed hogs" are the house specialty: Try a smoked-pork barbecue or western beef sandwich served with cole slaw and delicious fresh-cut fried potatoes or barbecued beans. Omelets, barbecued chicken, burgers, and salads are also offered, as is chocolate cheesecake for dessert.

GRACE PLACE, 826 W. Grace St., between Schaeffer and Laurel Sts. Tel. 804/353-3680.
  Cuisine: VEGETARIAN. **Bus:** 15 or 16.
$ **Prices:** Entrees $4–$7 at lunch, $6.50–$8 at dinner. No credit cards.
  Open: Lunch Tues–Sat 11:30am–3pm; dinner Tues–Sat 5:30–9pm.

This delightful vegetarian restaurant occupies the second floor of a classic Victorian home. It has pine plank floors, white and unpainted brick walls hung with paintings by local artists, a fireplace, pots of geraniums in lace-curtained windows, and flower-bedecked oak tables. Low-key, low-decibel recorded background music (classical or folk) helps set the tone; occasionally there's even a guitarist on hand. You can also dine al fresco on the outdoor patio under shade trees. Throughout the day you can order big salads and sandwiches such as falafel, avocado melt, and pizza in a pita. Evening specials include pastas, burritos, and other substantial items. Wine, beer, and coffee are available. Purists have a wide selection of herbal teas and specialty drinks like organic carrot juice and smoothies—icy fruit-and-yogurt shakes. Home-made desserts range from sugarless (apple crisp) to sinful (cheesecake).

JOE'S INN, 205 N. Shields Ave., between Grove and Hanover Sts. Tel. 804/355-2282.
  Cuisine: ITALIAN. **Reservations:** Not accepted. **Bus:** 3 or 4.
$ **Prices:** Appetizers $1.65–$5.50; entrees $3.95–$8.50. AE, MC, V.
  Open: Daily 9am–2am.

This casual neighborhood hangout serves terrific Italian fare (Greek accented) at reasonable prices. House specialties include steaks (club, sirloin tip), veal parmigiana, seafood, pizzas, and pasta. Soups, salads, omelets, and sandwiches are also options.

Stop by for a mouth-watering stack of hotcakes or French toast at breakfast. The house specialty here is spaghetti, prepared in a number of interesting ways. Portions are gargantuan, so two can easily share a order of spaghetti à la Joe, which arrives steaming hot en casserole, bubbling with a layer of baked provolone between the pasta and heaps of rich meat sauce. Joe's Greek version combines feta cheese with the provolone. The bar area has sleek mahogany booths and ornate brass-trimmed ceiling fans.

STONEWALL JACKSON CAFE & EMPORIUM, 1520 W. Main St., at Lombardy St. Tel. 804/359-6324.
   Cuisine: AMERICAN. **Reservations:** Not accepted. **Bus:** 13.
$ **Prices:** Appetizers $4.25–$5.50; entrees $3.75–$9.95. MC, V.
   Open: Daily 11:30am–2am (kitchen closes at midnight).
A favorite college hangout for University of Richmond students, Stonewall Jackson's Café is housed in the basement of a massive turn-of-the-century school building. Inside, the ambience is cheerful and lively, with rock-and-roll memorabilia and many hanging plants. There are several dining rooms, a bar, a small dance floor, and a patio. A confetti sprinkling of colors on the black Formica tables gives the restaurant an artsy look. A specialty here is pasta pie—a pizza-pie shell topped with a pasta dish, say linguine and shrimp or pasta primavera. Nachos here are as good as nachos get—piled high with chili, cheese, sour cream, lettuce, tomatoes, and jalapeños. A superb house specialty is the chicken chimichanga—an enormous tortilla filled with seasoned chicken and vegetables and topped with guacamole, sour cream, and salsa. And there's delicious homemade lasagne, cannelloni, and manicotti. New York cheesecake and Barricini ice cream are dessert specialties. Live music—everything from rock to jazz to blues—six nights.

STRAWBERRY STREET CAFE, 421 N. Strawberry St., between Park and Stuart Aves. Tel. 804/353-6860.
   Cuisine: AMERICAN. **Reservations:** Only needed for large groups. **Bus:** 15 or 16.
$ **Prices:** Appetizers $2.50–$5.95; entrees $5.95–$11.95. MC, V.
   Open: Lunch Tues–Fri 11:30am–2:30pm; dinner Tues–Thurs and Sun 5–11pm, Fri–Sat 5pm–midnight; brunch Sat 11am–5pm, Sun 10am–5pm.
The Strawberry Café is decorated in turn-of-the-century style, with a beautiful oak bar, Casablanca fan chandeliers, and a plant-filled café-curtained window. Flower-bedecked tables (candlelit at night) add a cheerful note. Lunch or dinner, you can help yourself to unlimited offerings from a bountiful salad bar—just $2.95 with any entree, pasta dish, sandwich, or quiche. At lunch you might get a broccoli and Cheddar quiche or a 6-ounce burger. At dinner, entrees like blackened Cajun chicken or fried gulf shrimp include your choice of two of the following: baked potato, fries, rice, cole slaw, fresh vegetable, or fruit. There's strawberry shortcake for dessert. A good selection of premium wines are available by the glass or bottle.

TEXAS-WISCONSIN BORDER CAFE, 1501 W. Main St., at Plum St. Tel. 804/355-2907.
   Cuisine: AMERICAN. **Bus:** 13.
$ **Prices:** Appetizers $2.25–$5.95; entrees $3.50–$8. MC, V.
   Open: Daily 11am–2am.
The Texas-Wisconsin Border Café is exactly what its name evokes: a rustic/western/hip eatery offering the kind of cookoff-winning chili—and chili-parlor ambience—seldom found outside the Lone Star State. The setting: a longhorn steer horn over the door, fans suspended from a dark-green pressed-tin ceiling, and pine-wainscoted cream walls hung with boar and elk heads, photos of everyone from Pancho Villa to LBJ (showing his scar), and works of local artists. The music is mellow rock, blues, or country. Sporting events are aired on the TV over the bar—a bar that serves 15 types of

bottled beers plus 4 on tap. The food is all fresh and homemade, highlighting from Texas: widow-maker chili; a baked potato filled with fajitas and drenched in chili con queso; and red beans and rice. From Wisconsin there's a quarter-pound Milwaukee hot dog topped with melted Swiss and sauerkraut; Welsh rarebit (what could be more Wisconsin than a dish made with Cheddar cheese and beer); and potato pancakes. In addition, you can order terrific salads, omelets served with thick slabs of Texas toast and homemade fries, and sandwiches. Homemade desserts like cheesecake and rich chocolate cake round things (and people) out.

RICHMOND SOUTH
MODERATE

CRAB LOUIE'S SEAFOOD TAVERN, in the Sycamore Shopping Center, Midlothian Turnpike. Tel. 804/275-CRAB.
    Cuisine: SEAFOOD. **Reservations:** Accepted for dinner. **Directions:** The restaurant is on Route 60W, about 4 miles west of the intersection of Route 60 and Powhite Parkway (about 7 miles from downtown).
$ Prices: Appetizers $2.50–$5.95; entrees $10.95–$14.95. AE, MC, V.
    Open: Mon–Thurs 11:30am–10pm, Fri–Sat 11:30am–11pm; Sun 11:30am–9pm.

Many of the shops in this center are housed in charming, white frame cottages, so it all looks more like a small town than a modern mall. Crab Louie's building is an authentic landmark, built in 1745. The interior evokes a country tavern in a warren of dining rooms, with working fireplaces, duck decoys, brass-and-china chandeliers. Seating is in comfortable wing chairs or spacious wooden booths. Before you've placed your order, a friendly server brings a snack of three relishes—sauerkraut, corn, and kidney bean—along with a wonderful assortment of homemade breads.

If it's on the menu, start off with Louisiana barbecued shrimp sautéed in garlic and Cajun spices and served over tarragon rice; another winner is bacon-wrapped scallops. Chowders are highly recommended, especially the rich she-crab soup with jumbo crabmeat in a sherry-cream base. Fresh-fish dinners include orange roughy broiled with almonds, blackened mahi mahi, and grilled yellowfin tuna. Nonseafood offerings range from pecan chicken Kiev to a 7-ounce filet mignon béarnaise. For dessert there's ultra-rich triple-chocolate cheesecake.

BUDGET

LA SIESTA, 9900 Midlothian Turnpike. Tel. 804/272-7333.
    Cuisine: MEXICAN. **Directions:** On Route 60, about 2 miles west of the Powhite Parkway intersection.
$ Prices: Appetizers $3.75–$4.95; entrees $5.95–$9.95. AE, MC, V.
    Open: Lunch Tues–Fri 11:30am–2:30pm; dinner daily 4–10pm.

Authentic Mexican specialties lure crowds to this rambling adobe structure. It's a huge place, with many intimate dining spaces, so when you're seated, it feels cozy. Brilliantly colored folk-art objects, a huge mural, and terra-cotta-tile floors, create a festive Mexican atmosphere. Get the fiesta started with a margarita or a nonalcoholic nada colada. Nachos are a tasty accompaniment to your drinks.

Main dishes from the grill include zacatecana (grilled boneless pork in two soft flour tortillas covered with a mild red salsa and melted cheese), chicken quesadillas, and carne tampiqueña—beef, peppers, and onions served with a cheese enchilada and homemade guacamole. Vegetarian dishes such as stuffed chiles and cheese enchiladas are also an option. Entrees are served with Mexican rice and refried beans. Typical Mexican desserts include fried ice cream (rolled in cookie crumbs and topped with either honey and cinnamon or chocolate), flan, and cookies sprinkled with sugar and cinnamon.

RICHMOND WEST

BUDGET

AUNT SARAH'S PANCAKE HOUSE, 4205 W. Broad St., between Antrim St. and Sauer Ave. Tel. 804/358-8812.
  Cuisine: AMERICAN. **Bus:** 6.
$ **Prices:** Entrees $3.50–$5; children's entrees $2.75.
  Open: Daily 24 hours.

Whenever you start your dining day, do it at Aunt Sarah's Pancake House, with an old-fashioned buttermilk stack and a choice of syrups. The pancakes come in all varieties—banana nut, stoneground buckwheat, blueberry, apple, southern pecan—and there are corncakes, waffles, and Irish potato pancakes as well. Aunt Sarah's is a good place for inexpensive family lunches and dinners, too. You might try a Chesapeake Bay crabcake sandwich with french fries, a half-pound burger with cole slaw and fries, or three big pieces of honey-dipped chicken with pancakes or fries. A spaghetti-and-meatball platter with milk or soda is one of several meals for children under 10. For everyone there's apple pie à la mode for dessert.

SPECIALTY DINING

PICNIC FARE

One of the best places to get it is **Coppola's Delicatessen,** 2900 West Cary Street (tel. 804/359-NYNY). Owner Joe Coppola is an Italian guy from Brooklyn and he says of his store, "It's not *like* New York, it *is* New York." The aromatic clutter of cheeses, sausages, olives, pickles, and things marinated evokes Little Italy, and Joe enhances the setting by playing Italian music. Behind-the-counter temptations include pasta salads, antipasti, stromboli (sesame bread stuffed with thinly sliced salami, ham, pepperoni, cheeses, and sweet peppers), cannolis, even sfogiatelle (a yummy pastry) from Brooklyn. Prices are low; this is a down-to-earth deli, not a pretentious gourmet emporium, though Joe's fare is as good as any of the latter offer. Joe has some tables inside and a few out on the street.

CHAPTER 10

WHAT TO SEE & DO IN RICHMOND

1. ATTRACTIONS
- DID YOU KNOW . . . ?
- WALKING TOUR— COURT END
2. SPORTS & RECREATION
3. SAVVY SHOPPING
4. EVENING ENTERTAINMENT
5. EASY EXCURSIONS FROM RICHMOND

A visit to Richmond will enhance your understanding of the Civil War era in the same way that Colonial Williamsburg, Fredericksburg, Alexandria, and Charlottesville shed light on America's earliest days.

Note: The James River plantations (see Section 5, "Easy Excursions," below) are about midway between Richmond and Williamsburg. Consider visiting them en route in either direction.

1. ATTRACTIONS

For an overall view of the city, start at the observation deck of City Hall, at Ninth Street and Broad Street for a (free) panoramic view of Richmond and the James. Several of the top attractions are nearby, and you can buy a **Court End block ticket** to them for $9 for adults, $8.50 for seniors, $4 for children 7 to 12, under 7 free. These attractions are: the John Marshall House, the Valentine Museum, and the Museum and White House of the Confederacy. The **Three Century House Tour block ticket,** for the Valentine Museum, Wilton House, and Agecroft Hall, costs $7 for adults, $6.50 for seniors, $3.50 for children 7 and over; free for children under 7. See below for full descriptions of these houses. An additional benefit is a $1 discount on the **Court End block ticket.**

SUGGESTED ITINERARIES

IF YOU HAVE 1 DAY

Day 1: Spend the morning exploring the Court End area, visiting the State Capitol first. Walk to the Museum and White House of the Confederacy, and the Valentine Museum. Stop in at the John Marshall House, then proceed to Church Hill to look at St. John's Church. Return downtown in the late afternoon, passing the Edgar Allan Poe house, Farmer's Market, and old City Hall, to Shockoe Slip for strolling, shopping, and dinner.

IF YOU HAVE 2 DAYS

Day 1: As outlined above.

DID YOU KNOW . . . ?

- Richmond is the only major metropolitan area in the country that has white-water rafting trips in the heart of the city.
- In 1972 Richmond suffered a devastating natural disaster when the James River, swollen with the rainstorms of Hurricane Agnes, rushed down the city streets, causing damage in excess of $350 million.
- The oldest lawmaking body in the western hemisphere is the General Assembly of Virginia, which has convened in Richmond since 1788.
- The Houdon statue of George Washington in the Rotunda of the State Capitol is the only one ever made of the first President from life.

Day 2: Go to Richmond National Battlefield Park in the morning. Return to downtown to visit the Maggie Walker House in the Jackson Ward neighborhood, then lunch at Sixth Street Marketplace. In the afternoon, visit Monument Avenue, viewing the grand boulevard and its statuary. Spend the rest of the afternoon at the Virginia Museum of Art. Dinner in the Fan.

IF YOU HAVE 3 DAYS

Days 1 and 2: As outlined above.

Day 3: Visit the Science Museum of Virginia in the morning, then head out to one of the historic mansions in the West End—Maymont is a good choice if you have kids, the surrounding park with its zoo, carriage house, and playing fields will let them run off steam. Agecroft Hall and Wilton are also out this way, as is Hollywood Cemetery.

IF YOU HAVE 5 DAYS OR MORE

Days 1–3: As outlined above.

Day 4: Drive to Scotchtown, Patrick Henry's country home, and have lunch in Ashland. Spend the rest of the day at King's Dominion amusement park. Spend the evening at King's Dominion as well, or go to Hanover for dinner theater at the Barkesdale.

Day 5: To venture farther afield, consider Petersburg or the James River Plantations.

THE TOP ATTRACTIONS

VIRGINIA STATE CAPITOL, Ninth and Grace Sts. Tel. 804/358-4901.

The first of many public buildings in the New World created in the Classical Revival style of architecture, and the second-oldest working capitol in the U.S. (in continuous use since 1788), the Virginia State Capitol was designed by Thomas Jefferson. Jefferson was minister to France when he was commissioned to work on the Capitol, and greatly admired the Maison Carrée, a Roman temple built in Nîmes during the 1st century A.D. The Capitol is closely patterned after it. The colonnaded wings on either side were added between 1904 and 1906.

The central portion of the Capitol is the magnificent Rotunda, its domed skylight ceiling ornamented in Renaissance style. The room's dramatic focal point is Houdon's

---

IMPRESSIONS

Broad-streeted Richmond . . . The trees in the streets are old trees used to living with people, Family trees that remember your grandfather's name.
—STEPHEN VINCENT BENET, *JOHN BROWN'S BODY*

life-size statue of George Washington, said to be a perfect likeness. "That is the man, himself," said Lafayette. "I can almost realize he is going to move." A Carrara marble bust of Lafayette by Houdon also graces the Rotunda, as do busts of the seven other Virginia-born presidents (Jefferson, Madison, Monroe, William Henry Harrison, Tyler, Taylor, and Wilson).

Resembling an open courtyard, the old Hall of the House of Delegates where the Virginia House of Delegates met from 1788 to 1906 is now a museum. Here, in 1807, Aaron Burr was tried for treason (and acquitted) by John Marshall while Washington Irving took notes. The room was also a meeting place of the Confederate Congress when Richmond was the capital of the Confederacy.

In the former Senate chamber, now used for occasional committee meetings, Stonewall Jackson's body lay in state after his death in 1863.

Free 30-minute **tours** are given throughout the day. After the tour, explore the **Capitol grounds.** To the east is the **Executive Mansion,** official residence of governors of Virginia since 1813. Another historic building is the old **Bell Tower,** built in 1824, often the scene of lunch-hour entertainment in summer. The Bell Tower building, by the way, houses the official Virginia Division of Tourism's Welcome Center, where you can obtain information and literature about all state attractions.

Admission: Free.

Open: Tours given Apr–Nov, daily 9am–5pm; Dec–Mar, Mon–Sat 9am–5pm, Sun 1–5pm. **Bus:** 15 or 16.

MUSEUM OF THE CONFEDERACY, 1201 E. Clay St. Tel. 804/649-1861.

In case you missed the Civil War, you can find out all about it at the Museum of the Confederacy. The museum houses the largest Confederate collection in the country, much of it contributed by veterans (in the early days they often served as guides) and their descendants. All the war's major events and campaigns are documented, and exhibits include period clothing and uniforms, a replica of Lee's headquarters, the role of blacks in the Civil War, Confederate memorabilia, weapons, and art.

Next door to the museum (same phone) is a mansion known as the **White House of the Confederacy** because it was the official residence of Jefferson Davis from 1861 to 1865. When the capital of the Confederacy moved to Richmond, the city government leased the 1818 mansion as a temporary home for Davis and his family. Thereafter, it became the center of wartime social and political activity in Richmond. By the spring of 1865 Confederate defeat was inevitable and the Davis family left the city. In 1894 a group of civic-minded Richmond women acquired the property and began a long restoration of both the museum and the White House.

Visitors begin a **tour** in the lower-level exhibit area, where there's a short briefing on the history of the building. Upstairs, the entrance hall is notable for its bronzed classical Comedy and Tragedy figures holding exquisite gas lamps. Formal dinners, luncheons, and occasional cabinet meetings were held in the dining room, a Victorian chamber with ornate ceiling decoration; some of the furniture in this room is original to the Davis family. Guests were received in the center parlor, interesting now for its "prisoner of war" knickknacks produced by captured Confederate soldiers and for an 1863 portrait of Davis. The Drawing Room contains an original 1818 Carrara marble mantel and a white carpet that is a reproduction of one in use during the war (Robert E. Lee, coming in from the field, once tracked mud on it). Upstairs are the bedrooms and the Oval Office in which Davis conducted the business of war.

Admission: Museum $4 adults, $3.50 senior citizens, $2.25 students and children 7–12, free for children under 7. Combination ticket (White House and museum), $7 adults, $5 seniors, $4.50 students, $3.50 children 7–12, free for children under 7.

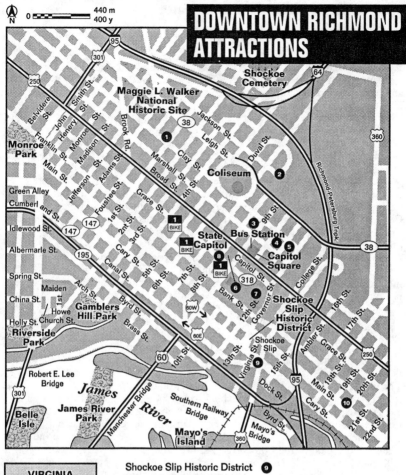

DOWNTOWN RICHMOND ATTRACTIONS

0   440 m
      400 y

VIRGINIA

RICHMOND

Richmond

Shockoe Slip Historic District **9**
Valentine Museum **4**
Virginia State Capitol **6**

ATTRACTIONS:
Edgar Allan Poe Museum **10**
Executive Mansion **7**
John Marshall House **3**
Maggie L. Walker National
     Historic Site **1**
Museum of the Confederacy **5**
Richmond Children's Museum **2**
St. Paul's Church **8**

Open: White House and museum, Mon–Sat 10am–5pm, Sun 1–5pm. **Bus:** 24 or 37.

VALENTINE MUSEUM, 1015 E. Clay St. Tel. 804/649-0711.

Named for Mann S. Valentine II, a 19th-century businessman and patron of the arts, this museum documents the history of Richmond from the 17th through the 20th century. It includes the elegant Federal-style Wickham-Valentine House, built in 1812 by attorney John Wickham, at the time Richmond's wealthiest citizen. He entertained Richmond's social elite here, along with such visiting notables as Daniel Webster, Zachary Taylor, John Calhoun, Henry Clay, and William Thackeray. Wickham is best known as a member of Aaron Burr's defense team in the latter's sensational 1807 trial for treason.

Wickham assembled the finest talents of his day to design and decorate his mansion. The architect was Alexander Parris, who also designed Boston's Faneuil Hall; master plasterers executed the exquisite ceilings; premier furniture makers like Charles Honoré Lannuier provided pieces; and there were paintings by Gilbert Stuart, Charles Saint-Mémin, and George Bridport (who worked on the U.S. Capitol), among others.

Highlights of the house include spectacular decorative wall paintings, perhaps the rarest and most complete set in the nation; the Oval Parlor, designated as "one of the hundred most beautiful rooms in America"; and the circular Palette Staircase. But it's not only the architectural and decorative grandeur that is re-created here. Slave and servant quarters have been restored to reveal the lives of the residents who supported the Wickhams' lavish life-style. Guided house **tours,** included in the price of admission to the museum, are given hourly.

In 1882, Valentine purchased the house and converted it into a private museum, willing it to the public when he died. (Valentine's fortune was based on the development and manufacture of a restorative tonic called Valentine's Meat Juice.) The museum opened in 1898 with a concentration on general history, later evolving to its current focus on Richmond. Exhibits cover social and urban history, decorative and fine arts, textiles, architecture, and more. An ongoing display, "New Nation, New City: Richmond Before the Civil War," explores the city's evolution from an unassuming Revolutionary War hamlet to one of the nation's foremost industrial centers and capital of the Confederacy. Downstairs, in the Children's Gallery, kids will enjoy seeing a replica of a one-room schoolhouse complete with rows of wooden desks and a pot-bellied stove, along with exhibits of historic dolls, toys, games, and photos of children. April through October, lunch in the garden is an option. Parking is free on the premises.

Admission: $3.50 adults, $3 seniors, $1.50 children 7–12, free for children under 7.

Open: Mon–Sat 10am–5pm, Sun noon–5pm (extended hours in summer). **Bus:** 24 or 37.

JOHN MARSHALL HOUSE, 818 E. Marshall St., at Ninth St. Tel. 804/648-7998.

This historic property is the restored home of a notable American patriot, John Marshall. From 1801 to 1835, he served as Chief Justice of the Supreme Court where he established the American system of judicial review and constitutional law. Earlier, he served in the Revolutionary Army and argued cases for George Washington (not only his commander during the war, but a close personal friend) and Thomas Jefferson, his cousin. He served as secretary of war under John Adams and had a brief term (in 1800) as secretary of state.

The house he built between 1788 and 1790, largely intact, is remarkable for many original architectural features—exterior brick lintels, interior wide-plank pine floors, wainscoting, and paneling. Original furnishings and personal artifacts have been supplemented by period antiques and reproductions. In the gracious dining room, the family's mahogany banquet table is set with original porcelain, silver, glassware, and a Waterford crystal épergne. Collections of 18th-century Chinese-export porcelain and Liverpool pitchers are displayed in a corner cupboard. The great hall (thought to have been Marshall's law office) is noteworthy for its arched doorway resembling that of Mount Vernon. A guided **tour** of the house takes about 20 minutes.

Admission: $3, free for children under 7.

Open: Apr–Sept, Tues–Sat 10am–5pm, Sun 1–5pm; Oct–Mar, Tues–Sat 10am–4:30pm, Sun 1–5pm. **Bus:** 41, 43, or 45.

ST. JOHN'S CHURCH, 2401 E. Broad St. Tel. 804/648-5015.

Originally known simply as the "church on Richmond Hill," St. John's dates to 1741, and the oldest marked tombstone in its graveyard to 1751. Edgar Allan Poe's mother and Declaration of Independence signer George Wythe are buried here. The congregation actually predates the church; it was established in 1611, and Alexander Whitaker, the first rector, ministered to the local tribes, instructed Pocahontas in Christianity, and baptized her.

The building was enlarged in 1772, and the second Virginia Convention met here in 1775 to discuss the rights of American subjects of the English king. Attending were Thomas Jefferson, George Wythe, George Mason, Benjamin Harrison, George Washington, Richard Henry Lee, and many other major historic personages. They introduced a bill for assembling and training a militia, and Patrick Henry made his famous declaration: "Is life so dear, or peace so sweet, as to be purchased at the price of chains or slavery? Forbid it, Almighty God! I know not what course others may take, but as for me, give me liberty or give me death." Later that year another convention at the church planned Virginia's defense and a temporary government.

On the 20-minute guided **tour** you'll see the original 1741 entrance and pulpit, the exquisite stained-glass windows, and the pew where Patrick Henry sat during the convention. From the last Sunday in May through the first Sunday in September, there's a living-history program at 2pm re-creating the second Virginia Convention.

Admission: $2 adults, $1 children 6–18, free for children under 6.

Open: Tours given Mon–Sat 10am–3:30pm, Sun 1–3:30pm; services Sun at 8:30 and 11am. **Bus:** 41 or 51.

RICHMOND NATIONAL BATTLEFIELD PARK, 3215 E. Broad St. Tel. 804/226-1981.

April 3, 1865: "As the sun rose on Richmond, such a spectacle was presented as can never be forgotten by those who witnessed it. . . . All of the horrors of the final conflagration, when the earth shall be wrapped in flames and melt with fervent heat, were, it seemed to us, prefigured in our capital. . . ."

Thus did an observer recall the coming of the Yankees and the disastrous final hours of the war that had raged for 4 bitter and bloody years around the Confederate capital of Richmond. As the political, medical, and manufacturing center of the South—the primary supply depot for troops operating on the Confederacy's northeastern frontier—Richmond was a prime military target. Seven major drives were launched against the city between 1861 and 1865.

A 100-mile tour of battlefields in the park begins at the **Chimborazo Visitor Center** at the park entrance on East Broad Street. A 12-minute slide show about the Civil War is shown throughout the day, and you can rent a 3-hour auto-tape tour with cassette player that covers the major 55-mile portion of the battlefield route. You can also view a 25-minute film here called *Richmond Remembers;* it documents the social and economic impact of the Civil War on the Confederate capital. Park rangers are on hand to answer all questions.

There are smaller visitor centers at **Fort Harrison,** about 8 miles southeast, and at **Cold Harbor,** about 10 miles northeast. The latter was the scene of a particularly bloody encounter in 1864 during which 7,000 of Grant's men were killed or injured in just 30 minutes. Programs with costumed Union and Confederate soldiers reenacting life in the Civil War era take place during the summer (inquire at Chimborazo). The Cold Harbor center is unstaffed (there are brochures, a bulletin board, electric map, and interpretive exhibits). Fort Harrison is staffed in summer only.

The Chimborazo Visitor Center occupies one of the Confederacy's largest hospitals: 76,000 patients were treated here during the war. It's convenient to combine visits to Shirley and Berkeley plantations with a battlefield tour; they're just slightly off the route.

Admission: Free.

Open: Daily 9am–5pm. **Closed:** New Year's, Thanksgiving, and Christmas days. **Bus:** 41 or 51.

EDGAR ALLAN POE MUSEUM, 1914–1916 E. Main St. Tel. 804/648-5523.

The Poe Museum consists of five buildings (enclosing an "Enchanted Garden") wherein the poet's rather sad life is documented. The museum centers on the Old Stone House, the oldest building in Richmond, dating to about 1736. Poe's connection with this building is thin; when Lafayette visited Richmond and was entertained here in 1824, the young Poe (age 15) was part of the Junior Volunteer Honor Guard. Today it is furnished in mid-18th-century style and contains a small but interesting museum shop. The other four buildings were added to house the growing collection which began in 1921.

Poe's real parents died when he was 2, and he was adopted by John and Frances Valentine Allan. The adoption was not legal, and only his middle name became Allan. As a young man Poe worked as a journalist in Richmond at the *Southern Literary Messenger*. A desk and chair such as he used at the *Messenger* are among the effects on display here, along with photographs, portraits, documents, and other memorabilia. Most fascinating is the Raven Room, in which artist James Carling's evocative illustrations of *The Raven* are displayed. Forty-minute **tours** are given throughout the day, and there's a 12-minute slide show about Poe's life. Free parking on the premises.

Admission: $4 adults, $2 students, free for children under 6.

Open: Sun–Mon 1:30–4pm, Tues–Sat 10am–4pm. **Bus:** 51 or 53.

MAGGIE L. WALKER NATIONAL HISTORIC SITE, 110½ E. Leigh St., between First and Second Sts. Tel. 804/780-1380.

Daughter of a former slave, Maggie Mitchell Walker was an unusually gifted woman who achieved success in the world of finance and business and rose to become the first woman bank president in the country. Originally a teacher, Walker, after her marriage in 1886, became involved in the affairs of a black fraternal organization, the Independent Order of St. Luke, which grew under her guidance into an insurance company, and then into a full-fledged bank, the St. Luke Penny Savings Bank. The bank continues today as the Consolidated Bank and Trust, the oldest surviving black-operated bank in the U.S. Mrs. Walker also became owner and editor of a newspaper and a department store.

This house, her residence from 1904 until her death in 1934, remained in the Walker family until 1979. The house has been restored to its 1930 appearance.

Admission: Free.

Open: Thurs–Sun 9am–5pm. **Closed:** New Year's and Christmas days. **Bus:** 50.

VIRGINIA MUSEUM OF FINE ARTS, The Boulevard and Grove Ave. Tel. 804/367-0844.

⭐ This is an art museum of which any city would be proud. It houses impressive collections of art nouveau, art deco, 19th- and 20th-century French paintings, contemporary American art, and art from India, Nepal, and Tibet. But even with none of the above, it would be well worth visiting to see the largest public Fabergé collection in the free world—more than 300 objets d'art created just before the turn of the century for Tsars Alexander III and Nicholas II. The Imperial jewel-encrusted Easter eggs evoke what art historian Parker Lesley calls the "dazzling, idolatrous realm of the last czars."

Other highlights include the Goya portrait *General Nicholas Guye,* a rare life-size marble statue of Caligula, Monet's *Iris by the Pond,* and six magnificent Gobelins *Don Quixote* tapestries. And that's not to mention works of de Kooning, Gauguin, van Gogh, Delacroix, Matisse, Degas, Picasso, Gainsborough, and others, or antiquities from China, Japan, Egypt, Greece, Byzantium, Africa, and South America.

The 90,000-square-foot West Wing houses two important collections. The Mellon Collection includes 18th- through 20th-century British, French, and American paintings, drawings, prints, and sculpture. On this same floor is the Sydney and Frances Lewis Collection of contemporary American painting and sculpture—Rothko, Gottlieb, de Kooning, Roy Lichtenstein, and Julian Schnabel, among others. My favorite part of the Lewis gift, however, is on the upper level—a decorative arts collection that includes Tiffany lamps, vases, and stained-glass windows; Lalique jewelry; Emile Gallé, Frank Lloyd Wright, and Hector Guimard furnishings; and other masterpieces of art nouveau, art deco, and modernism.

The museum also contains the 500-seat **Theatre Virginia** (see Section 4, "Evening Entertainment," below, for details) and a low-priced cafeteria overlooking a waterfall that cascades into a pool with a Maillol sculpture. Parking is free.

Admission: Suggested donation $3 adults, free for seniors and children.
Open: Tues–Sat 11am–5pm, Sun 1–5pm. **Bus:** 15 or 16.

SCIENCE MUSEUM OF VIRGINIA/ETHYL UNIVERSE THEATER, 2500 W. Broad St., three blocks east of the Boulevard. Tel. 804/257-6797 or 804/25-STARS for show times and ticket prices.

In addition to a distinguished art museum, Richmond boasts a worthy museum of science with a state-of-the-art planetarium. There are few DO NOT TOUCH signs in this museum's galleries; hands-on exhibits are the norm, making it an ideal attraction for youngsters.

Five large crystal-shaped structures on the rotunda floor create the setting for "Crystal World." Here you can venture inside a crystal, step into the center of a diamond, and see a crystal split a laser beam. In "Computer Works," the hows and whys of computer technology are explored in considerable depth. Visitors create programs, discuss their problems with a computer shrink, and play "assistant" for a computer magician. One wing features exhibits on aerospace, energy and electricity, chemistry, and physics. Elsewhere, you'll learn about optical illusions inside a giant kaleidoscope, try to get your bearings in a full-size distorted room, and crawl into a space capsule.

Not to be missed, of course, are the shows at the 300-seat Ethyl UNIVERSE Planetarium/Space Theater. It contains a projector for showing spectacular Omnimax films as well as the most sophisticated special-effect projection systems for multimedia planetarium shows. And the building itself merits attention. The Science Museum is housed in the former Broad Street Station, designed in 1919 by John Russell Pope (architect of the Jefferson Memorial, the National Archives, and the National Gallery of Art in Washington). In the Beaux Arts tradition, with a soaring rotunda, classical columns, vaults, and arches, it was created to evoke a sense of wonder—very fitting for a museum of science.

Admission: $3.50 adults, $3 children age 4–17 and senior citizens. Omnimax or planetarium shows $2 extra.

Open: Fri–Wed 9:30am–5pm, Thurs 9:30am–9pm. **Bus:** 1, 2, 3, or 4.

LEWIS GINTER BOTANICAL GARDEN AT BLOEMENDAAL, 7000 Lakeside Ave. Tel. 804/262-9887.

In the 1880s, self-made Richmond millionaire, philanthropist, and amateur horticulturalist Lewis Ginter built the Lakeside Wheel Club as a summer playground for the city's elite. The resort boasted a lake, nine-hole golf course, cycling paths, and a zoo. At Ginter's death in 1897 part of his vast fortune (he was one of the founders of the American Tobacco Company) went to his niece, Grace Arents. She converted the property to a hospice for sick children and named it Bloemendaal for Ginter's ancestral village in the Netherlands. An ardent horticulturist, she imported rare trees and shrubs and constructed greenhouses. A white gazebo and trellised seating areas were covered in rambling roses and clematis. Large beds on the front lawn were planted with shrubs and flowers. Grace died in 1926, leaving her estate to the city of Richmond to be maintained as a botanical garden and public park.

At the Visitors Center, pick up a brochure that suggests routes through the gardens and highlights significant aspects of the collection. If time allows, visit the green-shuttered Dutch-colonial house that Grace Arents remodeled and lived in until her death—interesting for its beautiful oak and wrought-iron front door and interior oak-beamed ceilings, paneling, leaded-glass skylight, and scalloped oak staircase. Ample free parking is available.

Admission: $2 donation.

Open: Daily 9:30am–4:30pm (Visitors Center closes at 4pm and also Sat–Sun Jan–Feb). **Bus:** 24. **Directions:** Take I-95N to Exit 16 to Route 1 (Brook Road) and turn left at Hilliard Road to Lakeside.

MAYMONT HOUSE AND PARK, just north of the James River between Rte. 161 and Meadow St. Tel. 804/358-7166.

In 1886, Maj. James Henry Dooley, a 25-year-old self-made millionaire, purchased a 100-acre dairy farm in Richmond on which to build a 33-room mansion surrounded by beautifully landscaped grounds. Now, more than a century later, his opulent estate is open to tourists, and the grounds comprise a park that any city might envy. The **mansion** is in the Neo-Romanesque style, with colonnaded sandstone facade, turrets, and towers. The architectural details of the formal rooms reflect various periods, most notably 18th-century French, as exemplified by the drawing rooms. The dining room has a stunning coffered rosewood ceiling; the library, a stenciled strapwork ceiling. A grand stairway leads to a landing from which rise two-story-high stained-glass windows. And the house is elaborately furnished with pieces from many periods chosen by the Dooleys—Oriental carpets, an art nouveau swan-shaped bed, marble and bronze sculpture, porcelains, tapestries, and Tiffany vases.

The same care that was lavished on the house was also given to the **grounds.** The Dooleys placed gazebos wherever the best views were to be enjoyed, laid out Italian and Japanese gardens, and planted horticultural specimens and exotic trees culled from the world over. At Mrs. Dooley's death in 1925, the property and grounds became Maymont Park. The hay barn today is the **Parsons Nature Center,** with outdoor animal habitats for birds, bison, beaver, deer, elk, and bear. At the **Children's Farm,** youngsters can feed chickens, piglets, goats, peacocks, cows, donkeys, and sheep. A collection of late 19th- and early 20th-century horse-drawn carriages—surreys, phaetons, hunting vehicles—is on display at the **Carriage House.** Carriage rides are a weekend afternoon option April through mid-December.

Guided **tours** of the house are given continuously between noon and 4:30pm Tuesday through Sunday. For information on tram rides through the park, call 804/358-7167. There's a parking lot off Spottswood Road, and another at Hampton Street and Pennsylvania Avenue.

Admission: Free (donations accepted).

Open: Apr–Oct, daily 10am–7pm; Nov–Mar, daily 10am–5pm. **Bus:** 3. **Directions:** Go south 2 miles to the end of Boulevard, and follow the signs to the parking area.

HOLLYWOOD CEMETERY, 412 S. Cherry, at Albemarle St. Tel. 804/648-8501.

Perched on the bluffs overlooking the James River not far from Maymont, Hollywood Cemetery is the serenely beautiful resting place of 18,000 Confederate soldiers, two American Presidents (Monroe and Tyler), six Virginia governors, Confederate President Jefferson Davis, and Confederate Gen. J. E. B. Stuart, the latter, one of 22 Confederate generals interred here. Designed in 1847, it was conceived as a place where nature would remain undisturbed. Its winding scenic roads, flowering trees, stone-bridged creeks, and ponds are largely intact today. The section in which the Confederates are buried is marked by a 90-foot granite pyramid, a monument constructed in 1869.

Admission: Free.
Open: Daily 8am–5pm. **Bus:** 11.

AGECROFT HALL, 4305 Sulgrave Rd. Tel. 804/353-4241.

Agecroft Hall is an authentic late 15th-century Tudor manor house built in Lancashire, England. In the 1920s, when the house was threatened with destruction, Mr. and Mrs. T. C. Williams, Jr., bought it, had it carefully taken down, every beam and stone numbered, and shipped it to Richmond for reconstruction in an elegant neighborhood overlooking the James. Today Agecroft serves as a museum portraying the architecture, interior decor, and life-style of a wealthy English family of the late Tudor and early Stuart eras. Typical of its period, the house has ornate plaster ceilings, massive fireplaces, rich oak paneling, leaded- and stained-glass windows, and a two-story Great Hall with a mullioned window 25 feet long. Furnishings authentically represent the period. Adjoining the mansion are a formal sunken garden, resembling one at Hampton Court Palace, and a formal flower garden, Elizabethan knot garden, and herb garden.

Visitors see a 12-minute slide show about the estate followed by a half-hour house **tour.** Plan time to explore the gardens as well.
Admission: $3 adults; $2.50 senior citizens, 50¢ students.
Open: Tues–Sat 10am–4pm, Sun 2–5pm. **Bus:** 13.

WILTON HOUSE, S. Wilton Rd. Tel. 804/282-5936.

Originally built some 10 miles down the James River in 1753 by William Randolph III, this stately Georgian mansion was moved to its present site in 1933. It was painstakingly dismantled, brick by numbered brick, and reconstructed on a bluff overlooking the James. Original floors, mantels, brasses, paneling, and window panes were all saved. Wilton's design has been attributed to a leading Williamsburg architect, Richard Taliaferro. It was part of a 2,000-acre plantation where the Randolphs entertained leading figures of the day. There is an entry in George Washington's diary for March 25 and 26, 1775, that he stayed at Wilton overnight. And Thomas Jefferson, whose mother was a Randolph, often visited his cousins at Wilton.

Many of the furnishings are original to the house and/or the Randolph family. William's secretary stands in the library, his desk in a bedroom upstairs, and 10 Randolph family portraits are on display. Visitors enter via the central hall, whose back door gives onto the river. The Willard tall-case clock, dated 1795, is in perfect condition. Both the parlor and adjoining dining room have elaborate paneling with handsome pilasters and denticulated cornices. Beautiful yellow silk Scalamandre draperies frame the dining-room windows, rose-colored silk in the parlor. Upstairs are the bedrooms and a nursery.

Admission: $3.50 adults, $3 seniors, $2 children over 6, free for children under 6.

Open: Sept–June Tues–Sat 10am–4:30pm, Sun 1:30–4:30pm; July, Tues–Sat 10am–4:30pm; Aug, by appointment only. **Closed:** National hols. **Bus:** 13. **Directions:** Take Route 147 west and turn south on Wilton Road at 5400 Cary Street.

PHILIP MORRIS MANUFACTURING CENTER, 3601 Commerce Rd. Tel. 804/274-3342 or 274-3329.

Smokers and nonsmokers alike will enjoy a tour of the Philip Morris factory in southern Richmond. At this $200-million showcase of state-of-the-art manufacturing technology, employees turn out over 500 million cigarettes a day to be distributed worldwide. Visitors are directed to a large exhibit area documenting the history of tobacco (from A.D. 300) and the history of Philip Morris. Next comes a short film in a screening room that also contains numerous smoking-related artifacts—everything from Eskimo pipes to old tobacco ads. Earphones are donned during the 20-minute tram ride through the manufacturing area. You'll also learn about growing, harvesting, and curing tobacco, and see some TV commercials for cigarettes; at the tour's end you'll get a free pack of your favorite Philip Morris brand.

Admission: Free.

Open: Mon–Fri 9am–4pm. **Directions:** Take I-95 south to Exit 8.

MORE ATTRACTIONS

RICHMOND CHILDREN'S MUSEUM, 740 N. Sixth St. Tel. 804/643-5436.

This unusual museum seeks to introduce children to the arts, nature, and the world around them with participatory exhibits, classes, and workshops. Amateur spelunkers can investigate stalagmites and stalactites in The Cave. Playworks invites children to try on the clothes and see what it feels like to be a member of the police force, a banker, or a shopkeeper.

Admission: $3 adults, $2 children 2–12.

Open: Tues–Fri 10am–4pm, Sat–Sun 1–5pm. **Bus:** 50.

SHOCKOE SLIP DISTRICT, from I-95 to 12th Street, between the James River and Main Street.

A historic district of century-old warehouses and cobblestone streets, Shockoe Slip is the hub around which the city of Richmond grew. When the capital of Virginia was moved to Richmond in 1780, the General Assembly met in Shockoe Slip at the corner of 14th Street and East Cary Street. In the 1800s tobacco merchants and grain shippers traded their goods here and loaded merchandise on barges in the Kanawha Canal. In 1865, when the city could no longer defend itself against the Union Army, the Confederate government ordered Shockoe warehouses ignited to keep their valuable contents out of enemy hands, and the business district was destroyed. Following the war the current buildings were constructed and the city's commercial activity centered here once more. However, the coming of the railroad reduced the importance of Shockoe's waterfront location, and the area faded in significance.

In the mid-1970s a major revitalization was begun, somewhat along the lines of San Francisco's Fishermen's Wharf—though much less extensive. Numerous restaurants and shops have emerged, there are organized walking tours of the area, and old factory buildings, mills, banks, and warehouses have been renovated (though kept intact for historic ambience, of course) to house additional shops, eateries, and trendy nightspots. The two major buildings, both at 13th and Cary, are **Commercial Block,** a converted 1870s barrel factory, and **Columbian Block,** the former grain and commodities exchange. The district is the scene of frequent events and festivals. Pick up a self-guided walking tour of the area at the Visitors Center.

Shockoe Bottom, by the way, is an area that predates even Shockoe Slip. Just to the east of the Slip, it, too, offers trendy restaurants and art galleries, as well as a farmer's market that operates daily on the corner of 17th Street and Main Street, occupying a site that has been used for this purpose for more than 2 centuries.

SIXTH STREET MARKETPLACE, along Sixth St. across Marshall, Broad, and Grace Sts. Tel. 804/648-6600.

Downtown Richmond has been the scene of a major urban-renewal effort in recent years, and its most notable manifestation is the Sixth Street Marketplace, which focuses on a glass-enclosed elevated pedestrian bridge spanning Broad Street between a Marriott hotel and a major department store. The center houses about 35 retail stores, a food court (in the historic Blues Armory, used to house Confederate troops during the Civil War), and several restaurants. Every Friday from May to October there's a street party with live bands and refreshments between 5 and 9pm. Parking validation programs are in effect for the lots on Fifth and Marshall and at Seventh and Marshall.

Admission: Free.
Open: Mon–Sat 10am–6pm, Sun 12:30–5:30pm.

MEADOW FARM AND CRUMP PARK, at Mountain and Courtney Rds., Glen Allen. Tel. 804/672-5106.

There's something for everyone at this little-publicized haven 12 miles north of downtown Richmond—nature, picnicking, and an opportunity to see 2 centuries of rural middle-class life.

In 1840 a country physician, Dr. John Mosby Sheppard, inherited a farmhouse built by his father and 150 acres of pasture and woodlands. There he raised his family, practiced medicine, and ran a subsistence farm of wheat, corn, tobacco, and other crops. Remarkably, the property stayed in the family until 1975, when it was donated to Henrico County as a public museum and park. History is interpreted at Meadow Farm by tour guides dressed in period clothing. An exhibit area that traces the family through several generations gets you started on your **tour** of the house and outbuildings. Those heady aromas following you through the house are from smoked ham, apple pie, and ginger cakes being prepared from authentic family recipes in the open-hearth kitchen below.

The rooms in the 1½-story house are comfortably furnished in Victorian style with many of the original pieces intact. Best seen from the bottom of the stairway is a "floating" balcony attached to a wall on one side only—an architectural enigma. There are several outbuildings on the property: a smokehouse, a farrier's shop with leather and wood bellows, a barn where tobacco is dried, and a fully furnished facsimile of Dr. Sheppard's medical office. The grounds are scrupulously maintained. There's also a goose pond, and the whole area is a bird sanctuary. Free parking is available.

Admission: Museum, $1 adults, 50¢ senior citizens and children 12 and under; grounds, free.
Open: Museum, Tues–Sun noon–4pm; grounds, daily dawn–dusk. **Closed:** Mid-Dec–Feb. **Directions:** Take I-95 north to Exit 36 (Route 295); exit Route 295 at Woodman Road South, follow it to Mountain Road, and then follow the signs.

WALKING TOUR — Court End

Start: Bell Tower, Capitol Square, near Franklin Street and Ninth Street.
Finish: John Marshall House, at Ninth Street and Marshall Street.
Time: Allow approximately 2 hours, not including museum visits.
Best Times: Any time.
Worst Times: Many museums and historic houses don't open till noon on Sunday; the John Marshall House is closed on Monday.

The Court End district of Richmond is rich in historic associations, with buildings and museums that detail the city's involvement in the American Revolution and the Civil War.

1. **Bell Tower,** built in 1824, is often the scene of lunchtime entertainment in summer. It houses a state Welcome Center, offering information about all Virginia attractions. Also in Capitol Square park is the:
2. **Virginia State Capitol,** designed by Thomas Jefferson, and modeled after the Roman Maison Carrée in Nîmes, France. To the east of the Capitol is the:
3. **Executive Mansion,** home to Virginia's governors since 1812. Head back across Ninth Street to:
4. **St. Paul's Church,** where Jefferson Davis was attending Sunday-morning services when he was handed a message from Gen. Robert E. Lee that Richmond could no longer withstand the Union attack. Going north along the park to Broad Street and turning right, you'll come to:
5. **Old City Hall,** an exuberant Victorian pile that stands out even more among the area's sleek modern and Classical Revival structures. Continue east on Broad Street to the:
6. **Virginia State Library,** at 11th Street and Capitol Square. It is the repository of the state archives, and makes available information on the state's history and culture. Continue east on Broad. Across the street, between 12th Street and College Street, is:
7. **Monumental Church,** built in 1812. Robert Mills, who designed the Washington Monument, was the architect. If the church is open (it's no longer a place of worship), go inside to admire the graceful interior. Turn north on College Street to East Marshall Street, where you'll find the:
8. **Egyptian Building,** an interesting curio, designed for use by the College of Medicine, forerunner of the Medical College of Virginia. Note the unusual iron fence: The posts are in the shape of mummies. Walk up 13th Street to two of Richmond's best-known Civil War sites:
9. **The Museum of the Confederacy and the White House of the Confederacy.** If you're going to visit inside, start with the museum, which has a unique collection of Confederate memorabilia. House tours are equally fascinating, as you peek into the domestic life of the Davis family. The:
10. **Maupin-Maury House** (1846), one block west on Clay Street, is not open to the public, but is marked with a bronze plaque. Matthew Fontaine Maury was an oceanographer who charted the depths of the Atlantic Ocean and made possible the laying of the Atlantic cable. Continuing west, the:
11. **Valentine Museum and Wickham House** present the history of Richmond. April through October visit the museum's garden cafe for lunch. Finally, turn left on 10th Street and then right on Marshall Street. At the corner of Ninth Street is the:
12. **John Marshall House,** built by the Chief Justice between 1788 and 1790, the last remaining 18th-century brick house on the block.

ORGANIZED TOURS

The **Historic Richmond Foundation,** 2407 East Grace Street (tel. 804/780-0107), offers a variety of well-planned guided tours, some in comfortable, air-conditioned 24-passenger vans, others on foot. Call for details, departure times, and prices.

A RIVERBOAT CRUISE Journey up the James on a 2-hour lunch cruise aboard the **Annabel Lee,** modern technology's answer to an 1850s riverboat. The fare, including a bountiful buffet lunch, is $13.95; children under 12 pay $7.50. After lunch, period-costumed waiters and waitresses don spangled derby hats and canes

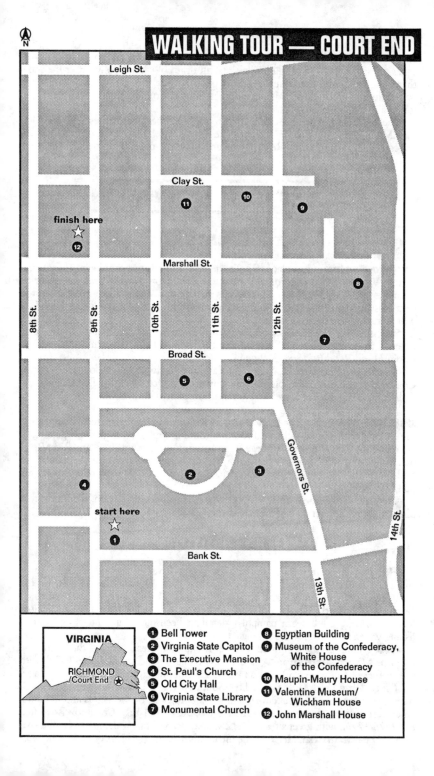

WALKING TOUR — COURT END

N

Leigh St.

Clay St.

⑪ ⑩ ⑨

finish here
☆
⑫

Marshall St.

⑧

8th St. 9th St. 10th St. 11th St. 12th St.

⑤ ⑥

Broad St.

⑦

Governors St.

② ③

④

start here
☆
①

14th St.

Bank St.

13th St.

VIRGINIA

RICHMOND
/Court End ★

① Bell Tower
② Virginia State Capitol
③ The Executive Mansion
④ St. Paul's Church
⑤ Old City Hall
⑥ Virginia State Library
⑦ Monumental Church
⑧ Egyptian Building
⑨ Museum of the Confederacy,
   White House
   of the Confederacy
⑩ Maupin-Maury House
⑪ Valentine Museum/
   Wickham House
⑫ John Marshall House

and, accompanied by a three-piece band, render patriotic and riverboat songs, show tunes, dance routines, and vaudeville skits, all of it upbeat and jolly. After the show there's dancing until the minute the boat docks.

Additional cruise options include dinner, Sunday brunch, James River plantation tours, and a 2-hour late-night party.

The *Annabel Lee* operates from April to mid-October. Departures are from 4400 East Main Street, just past the Intermediate Terminal (tel. 804/222-5700). Call for all prices and departure times. Reservations are a must, especially on weekends.

2. SPORTS & RECREATION

SPORTS

Auto Racing   The place to go is the **Richmond International Raceway,** at the Virginia State Fairgrounds, between Laburnam Avenue and the Henrico Turnpike (tel. 804/329-6796). Major races include the Pontiac 200 and 400 Winston Cup Nascar Races in February, and the Nascar Grand National and Miller High Life 400 Winston Cup in September.

Baseball   The **Richmond Braves,** farm team for the Atlanta Braves, play baseball from April through September at the Diamond, 3001 North Boulevard and Robin Hood Road (tel. 804/359-4444).

Hockey   Richmond's pro hockey team, the **Renegades,** belongs to the East Coast Hockey League and plays home games from October through March at the Coliseum, 601 East Lee Street and Seventh Street (tel. 804/780-4970).

COLLEGE SPORTS   The **University of Richmond** basketball team competes in the Colonial Athletic Association and plays from November through the beginning of March at the Robins Center, College Road between Boatwright Road and River Road (tel. 804/289-8388). The football team, the Spiders, plays from mid-September to mid-November at the UR stadium, McCloy Street and Douglasdale Street (tel. 804/289-8390).

Virginia Commonwealth University fields a basketball team, the Rams, that plays from November to mid-March at the Coliseum (tel. 804/367-1726).

RECREATION

Fishing   For freshwater fishing, the James River is a good place to catch smallmouth bass. One place to find river access is at **James River Park,** on the south bank between the Lee and Huguenot bridges. The **Virginia Department of Game and Inland Fisheries,** 1040 North Broad Street, Richmond, VA 23230 (tel. 804/367-1000), publishes a pamphlet detailing licensing requirements and public fishing waters; it's free for the asking.

Golf   Golf courses abound in the Richmond area. Among them are the **Belmont Park Recreation Center,** 1800 Hilliard Road (tel. 804/266-4929), with greens fees of $11 weekdays, $13 on weekends and holidays, when reservations are a good idea; **Pine Lake Golf Club,** 1100 South Providence Road (tel. 804/276-4641), with greens fees of $10 weekdays ($8 after 4:30pm), $12 on weekends and holidays, when reservations are suggested; and **Glenwood Golf Club,** Creighton Road (tel. 804/226-1793), with greens fees of $12 weekdays, $16 on weekends and holidays.

White-Water Rafting   Ride the rapids through the heart of Richmond with the **Richmond Raft Company,** East Main Street and Water Street (tel. 804/222-7238).

3. SAVVY SHOPPING

Downtown shopping focuses on the **Sixth Street Marketplace** (see Section 1, "Attractions," above). **Shockoe Slip,** the restored old warehouse district (see Section 1, "Attractions," above), has trendy shops.

In the Fan area is a mix of small stores and interesting cafés collectively known as **Carytown.** It extends for about nine blocks, and also includes a small strip mall, the **Cary Court Shopping Center,** 3122 West Cary Street. **Libby and Grove's "On the Avenues"** (5700 Grove and 400 Libbie) is an enclave of distinctive women's fashions and specialty shops in the fashionable West End, especially interesting if you're looking for decorative items—anything from needlepoint pillows to an abstract wall hanging.

The big suburban shopping malls, open Monday through Saturday from 10am to 9:30pm and on Sunday from 12:30 to 5pm, are the **Shops at Willow Lawn,** 5000 West Broad Street; **Regency Square,** Parham Road and Quioccasin Road; **Chesterfield Towne Center,** 11500 Midlothian Turnpike; and **Cloverleaf Mall,** 7201 Midlothian Turnpike.

SHOPPING A TO Z

ANTIQUES

THE ANTIQUES GALLERY, 3140 W. Cary St. Tel. 804/358-0500.
A big store with lots of merchandise—from pink carnival glass to Tiffany lamps and china.

ANTIQUE VILLAGE, U.S. 301, Richmond. Tel. 804/746-8914.
Located about 4 miles north of I-295, this complex of 16 shops is a treasure trove of Civil War relics, glassware, jewelry, and furnishings.

BOOKS

THE BOOK WAREHOUSE, in the Old Towne Shopping Center, 7801 W. Broad St. Tel. 804/755-3059.
This place is a book lover's dream—thousands of new books are discounted 50% to 90% off retail.

COKESBURY, 417-419 Grace St. Tel. 804/644-2921.
Just a block away from the Sixth Street Marketplace, Cokesbury specializes in hardback titles—a vast selection.

CHILDREN'S WEAR

LE PETIT BATEAU, 5804 Grove Ave., "On the Avenues." Tel. 804/288-0836.
A charming little shop with beautiful clothes for boys and girls, infants' layettes, and toys.

COOKWARE

THE COMPLEAT GOURMET, 3030 W. Cary St. Tel. 804/353-9606.

All you need in the way of kitchen gadgetry and utensils, baking tins, molds, spice jars and racks, potholders, oven mitts, and cast-iron and porcelain cookware.

GIFTS

GLASS WAREHOUSE, 3123 W. Cary St. Tel. 804/353-9171.

This fine shop features the works of American craftspeople, with exquisite perfume bottles, lamp shades, vases, paperweights, assorted hand-blown objets, and stained-glass lighting.

FESTIVAL FLAGS, 322 W. Broad St. Tel. 804/643-5247.

A truly unique gift could come from this maker of quality flags and banners. You can even have a custom design specially sewn—anything from a family crest to a "Happy Birthday" flag.

Z ROSA, 2225 W. Main St. Tel. 804/783-2900.

A beautiful selection of one-of-a-kind, museum-quality pieces of jewelry, tapestries, and folk art.

SECONDHAND CLOTHING

THE HALL TREE, 12 S. Thompson St., at Cary St. Tel. 804/358-9985.

It's always fun to browse through, and you just might find the Roaring '20s flapper dress or smoking jacket you've always wanted.

TOBACCO

THE TINDER BOX, 3 James Center. Tel. 804/343-1827.

This specialty store has a large selection of pipes, cigars, and other items that any smoker might want.

4. EVENING ENTERTAINMENT

Richmond is a major city, and there's usually quite a bit going on at night. Pick up a free copy of a magazine called **Style** at the Visitors Center. It provides details on theater, concerts, dance performances, and all other happenings. **Night Moves** appears twice monthly and provides information on music and entertainment.

Tickets can be reserved through **Ticketron** (tel. 804/780-3777, or toll free 800/448-9009) outlets in Standard Drug Stores in Richmond or at the Showcase in Sixth Street Marketplace, or through **Ticketmasters** (tel. toll free 800/736-2000).

THE PERFORMING ARTS
MAJOR PERFORMANCE HALLS

CARPENTER CENTER FOR THE PERFORMING ARTS, 600 E. Grace St., at Sixth St. Tel. 804/782-3900.

Built in 1928 by John Eberson, this former Loew's Theater was restored in 1983 to its Moorish splendor, complete with twinkling stars and clouds painted on the ceiling overhead. The center hosts national touring companies for dance, orchestral, and theatrical performances, including Broadway road shows. The **Richmond Ballet** (see "Dance," below), the **Virginia Opera** (tel. 804/643-6004), and the **Richmond Symphony** (tel. 804/788-1212) perform here as well.

DOGWOOD DELL, Byrd Park, Boulevard and Idlewild Ave. Tel. 804/780-8137.

In the summer months, Richmond goes outdoors to Byrd Park for free Festival of Arts music and drama performances under the stars in this tiered grassy amphitheater. Bring the family, spread a blanket, and have a picnic.

THE MOSQUE, Main and Laurel Sts. Tel. 804/780-4213.

Decorated with exotic mosaics and pointed-arch doorways, this 3,500-seat facility's offerings range from a production of *Peter Pan* to noted jazz pianist and composer George Shearing, who appeared here with the Richmond Symphony.

The **Richmond Forum** (tel. 804/330-3993) presents stimulating discussions of current topics. Past programs have included former NBC commentator and author Edwin Newman examining foreign affairs with four former secretaries of state—Dean Rusk, William Rogers, Edmund Muskie, and Alexander Haig—and, on a lighter note, Andy Rooney and Art Buchwald on "Humor and the Press."

RICHMOND COLISEUM, 601 E. Lee St. Tel. 804/780-4970.

The Coliseum hosts everything from the Ringling Bros. and Barnum & Bailey circus to rock concerts. It's the largest indoor entertainment facility in Virginia and can seat about 10,000 people. Major sporting events—wrestling, hockey, basketball—are also scheduled here.

THEATER

BARKSDALE THEATRE AT HANOVER TAVERN, U.S. 301N, across from Hanover Courthouse. Tel. 804/537-5333.

This is the nation's first dinner theater, occupying historic Hanover Tavern, where Patrick Henry once tended bar. Musicals, comedies, and dramas are performed Wednesday through Saturday evenings year round.

Prices: Dinner and theater, $24 Wed–Thurs, $25 Fri, $26 Sat; theater only, $11 Wed–Thurs, $12 Fri, $13 Sat.

SWIFT CREEK MILL PLAYHOUSE, Rte. 1, Colonial Heights. Tel. 804/748-5203.

Housed in a 300-year-old grist mill along Swift Creek, this dinner theater is about 11 miles south of Richmond on Route 1. During a recent season, productions included *Steel Magnolias, Big River,* and *A Walk in the Woods.* Performances are Wednesday through Saturday nights.

Prices: Dinner and theater, $22.50 Wed–Thurs, $23.50 Fri, $24.50 Sat; theater only, $13 Wed–Thurs, $14 Fri, $16 Sat.

THEATRE IV, 114 W. Broad St. Tel. 804/344-8040.

Noted principally for its productions for children, Theatre IV may be seen at the Empire Theater, at Broad Street and Jefferson Street, or the Virginia Museum of Art.

THEATRE VIRGINIA, Virginia Museum of Fine Arts, 2800 Grove Ave. Tel. 804/367-0831.

Located within the museum, this 535-seat house offers a good variety of theater. The 1990–91 season program included *Driving Miss Daisy, South Pacific, She Stoops to Conquer, Night of the Iguana,* and *A Walk in the Woods.* The season runs from October to the end of April.

Prices: Tickets, $10–$26; student-rush line, $5 a ticket (except Fri–Sat night). **Bus:** 15 or 16.

DANCE

The **Richmond Ballet** (tel. 804/359-0906) performs at both the Mosque and the Carpenter Center (see "Theater," above). Their productions run from mid-October through April. Among their program highlights in 1990–91 were *The Nutcracker,* Prokofiev's *Classical Symphony,* Agnes DeMille's *Rodeo,* and John Butler's *Carmina Burana.*

At the Virginia Museum of Art, an avant-garde musical series called **Fast Forward** (tel. 804/367-8148) includes dance performances.

THE CLUB & MUSIC SCENE

For quick reference, the clubs below are listed somewhat arbitrarily under categories like rock, blues, jazz, etc. Categories are not hard and fast, as you'll note from the accompanying descriptions.

COMEDY CLUBS

COMEDY CLUB AT MATT'S BRITISH PUB, 109 S. 12th St. Tel. 804/643-JOKE.

Acts here run the gamut of regional and national talents. Shows are on Friday and Saturday nights at 8 and 11pm, with local talent on Thursday night.
Admission: $5–$7.

RICHMOND COMEDY CLUB, 1216 E. Cary St. Tel. 804/745-3166.

The club is upstairs from the Shockoe Slip Café. Professional acts change weekly and show schedules vary, but usually it's Tuesday through Thursday at 8:30pm, on Friday at 8:30 and 11pm, and on Saturday at 7:30pm, 9:45pm, and midnight; there's an open microphone on Tuesday.
Admission: $2–$7; dinner and show specials, $14.95 Thurs, $16.95 Fri–Sat.

ROCK

THE BUS STOP, 1210½ E. Cary St. Tel. 804/788-9933.

This Shockoe Slip hot spot offers live music downstairs: Tuesday is Rocket Night with acoustic rock, and Wednesday through Saturday you'll find cutting-edge music. Upstairs, a dance club plays Top 40 tunes. Open Tuesday through Saturday from 9:30pm to 2am.
Admission: $2–$5.

FLOOD ZONE, 18th and Main Sts. Tel. 804/643-6006.

At this large concert hall you'll hear anything from reggae to rock to country. One of the top New Wave nightspots in Shockoe Bottom.
Admission: Varies with the performer; tickets may be cheaper if bought in advance.

THE METRO, 727 W. Broad St. Tel. 804/648-9543.

Live acts weekly. Wednesday through Saturday, dance to progressive sounds downstairs, progressive and funk upstairs. Monday is psychedelic night, a look back at the '60s. Open 11:30am to 2am.
Admission: $3–$9.

STONEWALL CAFE, Main and Lombardy Sts. Tel. 804/359-6324.

Sunday night features the Original Blues Jam; Monday, the Jazz Jam; Tuesday through Saturday you'll hear rock and R&B. For details on food service, see Section 4, "Dining," in Chapter 9. Entertainment is on nightly from 9:30pm to 1am.
Admission: $3 or less.

JAZZ

SAM MILLER'S WAREHOUSE, 1210 E. Cary St. Tel. 804/643-1301.

Jazz is king here, but Wednesday night is rock and roll, and Friday and Saturday there's a mix of R&R, blues, and jazz. Upstairs in the Captain Morgan Lounge there are live bands Thursday through Sunday. Music is on Wednesday through Sunday from 10pm to 1:30am.
Admission: $4 when live bands play.

TOBACCO COMPANY, 1201 E. Cary St. Tel. 804/782-9555.
There's live music, often a jazz trio, on the first floor Monday through Saturday from 8pm to 1am, plus dancing in the lower-level Club.
Admission: First floor, free; downstairs Club, $2 cover.

DANCE CLUBS

555 CANAL CLUB, in the Radisson Hotel, 555 Canal St. Tel. 804/788-0900.
While this is a good place to come for cocktails, it's also got a DJ who puts on light shows and spins classic rock and Top-40 tunes for dancing. Open daily 4pm to 2am.
Admission: Free.

THE SLIP AT SHOCKOE, 11 S. 12th St. Tel. 804/643-3313.
This downtown dance club is open for jazz in the afternoon; at night R&B and sophisticated dance tunes. There's a jazz DJ on offnights. Open on Wednesday from 5 to 9pm, on Thursday from 5pm to midnight, and on Friday and Saturday from 5pm to 2am.
Admission: $3.

BARS

MAIN STREET GRILL, 1700 E. Main St. Tel. 804/644-3969.
A small, convivial bar and grill, Main Street has Oldies Night on Thursday, and a variety of folk, Irish, and jazz tunes on weekends. Open on Tuesday and Wednesday 6am to 3pm, Thursday through Saturday from 6am to 2am, and on Sunday from 9am to 2:30pm.

MEMORIES LOUNGE, in the Commonwealth Park Hotel, 901 Bank St. Tel. 804/343-1111.
Just the place for a quiet drink and chat, with a soft piano playing in the background. Open Monday to Saturday 5pm to 2am.
Admission: $3 cover charge for Fri cabaret.

TRIPLETS, in the Richmond Marriott, 500 E. Broad St. Tel. 804/643-3400.
Jazz piano music to relax the customers during cocktail hour, Monday through Friday from 5 to 8pm. Open daily 11am to 11pm.

5. EASY EXCURSIONS FROM RICHMOND

JAMES RIVER PLANTATIONS

The historic James River plantations are midway between Richmond and Williamsburg (distance between the two cities is about 60 miles) on Route 5. Of all these tobacco planters' mansions, Berkeley and Shirley, described below, provide us with the most authentic feel for 18th-century plantation life. Among the others are:
Westover (tel. 804/829-2882), about 22 miles east of Richmond, is the beautiful

1730s Georgian manor house built by Richmond's founder, William Byrd II. The interior is only open to the public during Garden Week (last week in April), although visitors are permitted to walk around the grounds and gardens year round, daily from 9am to 5pm; admission is $2. **Evelynton,** adjacent to and originally part of the Westover estate, was named for Byrd's daughter, Evelyn. Her father refused to let her marry her chosen suitor, and she died shortly thereafter. According to legend, her ghost still roams both houses. The original Evelynton manor house was destroyed in the Civil War, and the present structure was built in 1935. It is open for tours daily from 9am to 5pm at $8 for adults, $4 for children 6 to 18, free for children under 6. **Sherwood Forest,** home to two Presidents (John Tyler and William Henry Harrison) is open by appointment only (tel. 804/829-5377). The 250-year-old frame house is still occupied by descendants of both presidents and remains a working plantation.

BERKELEY, Rte. 5, Charles City. Tel. 804/829-6018.

On December 4, 1619, 38 English settlers sent by the Berkeley Company put ashore after a 3-month voyage. They named their riverfront Virginia home Berkeley Plantation and Hundred, and fell on their knees in a prayer of thanksgiving—the first such official ceremony in the New World.

In 1691 Berkeley was acquired by the Harrisons, members in good standing of Virginia's aristocratic ruling class. Benjamin Harrison (III) made Berkeley into a prosperous commercial center. In 1726 his son, Benjamin Harrison (IV)—a leader in colonial affairs—built the three-story Georgian mansion still extant today and heralded as a "beau ideal" of the baronial dwellings that graced Virginia's "Golden Age." Benjamin Harrison (V) was a signer of the Declaration of Independence and thrice governor of Virginia. These were the days of fox hunts and fancy-dress balls. George Washington was a frequent guest, and every President through Buchanan enjoyed Berkeley's gracious hospitality. The next generation produced William Henry Harrison, the Indian fighter of the Northwest Territory called "Old Tippecanoe." Misrepresenting himself to the country as a humble frontiersman, he became our 9th President and wrote his inaugural address at Berkeley in the room in which he was born. Forty-seven years later his grandson, another Benjamin Harrison, would serve as the nation's 23rd President.

A few years after William Henry's death, Berkeley went out of the Harrison family, its owners by this time plagued by insurmountable debts. Like many other Richmond plantations, Berkeley was deserted (its owners having temporarily relocated to safer areas) by the time the Union army under General McClellan marched in. The Yankees trampled the gardens and chopped up the elegant furnishings for firewood. The rich carpeting was "completely covered with mud and soaked with human gore." It was during the Yankee occupancy that Gen. Dan Butterfield composed "Taps."

The Civil War occupation of Berkeley was not its first. During the Revolution the Harrisons also wisely fled before the British army under Benedict Arnold occupied their home, burned their family portraits, practiced target shooting on their cows, and went off with 40 of their slaves.

Returning to the Civil War—after it was over, most owners (including those of Berkeley) did not return to their slaveless, and therefore impossible-to-run, plantations. The gracious days of the Old South seemed gone forever. In 1907 John Jamieson, a New Yorker of Scottish birth who had served as a drummer boy in McClellan's army 50 years earlier, purchased the disfigured manor house and 1,400 acres. It was left, in 1927, to its present owner, his son, Malcolm, who is responsible for the complete restoration of the house and grounds to the glorious appearance of the early days of the Harrisons. Berkeley today is a working plantation, raising sheep and producing grains, soybeans, and other crops.

Twenty-minute guided **tours** of the house are given throughout the day by guides in Colonial dress following a 10-minute slide presentation. Allow at least another half hour to explore the magnificent grounds and gardens. Moderately priced lunches are served in a quaint restaurant on the grounds called the **Coach House Tavern** (tel. 804/829-6003), daily from 11am to 4pm. There are also picnic grounds on the premises. And if you're in town on the first Sunday of November, you can participate in the annual Thanksgiving celebration at Berkeley.

Admission: $8 adults, $4 children 13–18, $3 children 6–12, free for children under 6.

Open: Daily 8am–5pm. **Closed:** Christmas. **Directions:** From Richmond, take I-64E to the Laburnum exit, to Route 5E, a 30-minute drive.

SHIRLEY, Rte. 5, Charles City. Tel. 804/829-5121.

Another historic James River plantation, Shirley was founded in 1613 and has been in the same family since 1660. The present mansion, built by Edward Hill III or his son-in-law, John Carter (historians are not sure), dates to 1723. Since that time the Hills and the Carters—two very distinguished Virginia families—have occupied Shirley. Because of this continuous ownership, many original furnishings and family possessions remain at the estate.

The house survived the Revolution, the Civil War, and Reconstruction, as did the dependencies, including an 18th-century laundry (later used as a schoolhouse, where Robert E. Lee had lessons as a boy). You can visit the house on 35-minute **tours,** given throughout the day. Allow at least an extra 30 minutes to explore the grounds and dependencies.

Admission: $6 adults, $5 students 13–21, $3 children 6–12, free for children under 6.

Open: Daily 9am–5pm (last tour at 4:30pm). **Closed:** Christmas. **Directions:** From Richmond, take I-64E to the Laburnum exit, to Route 5E.

PETERSBURG

The last, decisive engagement of the Civil War took place in Petersburg, today a quiet southern town along the Appomattox River. In the 1860s it was a vital rail junction that Grant recognized as the key to his quest to take Richmond. Try as he could, Grant's army could not conquer the capital of the Confederacy, so in an inspired move, he went around Richmond and south of the James River to Petersburg, where North and South faced each other in a tragic 10-month confrontation.

Petersburg is just a 30-minute drive from Richmond, going south on I-95 for 23 miles. Begin at the **Visitors Center,** 425 Cockade Alley, Petersburg, VA 23804 (tel. 804/733-2400), where you can obtain a complimentary parking permit (valid for 1 day), maps, and literature.

In addition to the battlefield and Blandford Church, described below, visitors may wish to visit the **Siege Museum,** 15 West Bank Street (tel. 804/733-2400), which tells the story of everyday life in Petersburg up to and during the siege in displays and an exceptionally interesting film narrated by actor Joseph Cotten, whose family lived in Petersburg during the Civil War. The museum is in the old Merchant Exchange, a magnificent Greek Revival temple-fronted building. The **Trapezium House,** at Market Street and High Street (tel. 804/733-2400), is an amusing curiosity. It was built without any right angles, supposedly because its owner was frightened by tales of ghosts who lurked in them. **Centre Hill Mansion,** on Centre Hill Court, between Adams Street and Tabb Street (tel. 804/733-2400), is a nicely restored 1823 mansion, furnished with Victorian pieces. The army's **Quartermaster Museum** is located nearby at Fort Lee (tel. 804/735-1854), on Route 36; General Patton's Jeep is on display here. Visitors will also enjoy strolling through Petersburg's **Old Town,** browsing in small antique shops and watching progress on the restoration of the Appomattox Iron Works, a factory complex founded in 1872 that will include the original machinery and shops plus restaurants and stores.

PETERSBURG NATIONAL BATTLEFIELD PARK, Rte. 36, Petersburg. Tel. 804/732-3531.

At the Visitors Center, a multimedia presentation elucidates the story of the 10-month siege, which lasted from mid-June 1864 to early April 1865. The battlefield park encompasses some 1,530 acres. The 4-mile battlefield driving tour has wayside exhibits and audio stations; some stops have short walking tours. Most fascinating is the site of the Crater, literally a huge depression in the ground. It was made when a group of Pennsylvania militia, including many miners, dug a passage beneath Confederate lines and exploded 4 tons of powder, creating the 170- by 60-foot crater. The carnage was sickening; thousands of men on both sides died. Today the grassy site seems like some prehistoric earthworks, charged with a meaning we cannot comprehend. An extended 16-mile driving tour follows the entire siege line.

"The key to taking Richmond is Petersburg," Grant said, and he relentlessly kept up his attempts to capture the city, although the cost in men was brutal. Finally, on April 2, Grant's all-out assault smashed through Lee's right flank, and that night Lee evacuated Petersburg. One week later came the surrender at Appomattox Court House.

Admission: $3 per car.

Open: Visitors Center, daily 8am–5pm; battlefield park, daily 8am–dusk. **Directions:** Take Route 36 2½ miles east of Petersburg.

OLD BLANDFORD CHURCH, 319 S. Crater Rd., at Rochelle Lane. Tel. 804/733-2400.

Boasting one of the largest collections of Tiffany-glass windows in existence, Old Blandford Church is also where the first observance of Memorial Day took place. The church was built in 1735 but was abandoned in the early 1800s when a new Episcopalian church was built closer to the town center. During the Civil War, the building became a hospital for troops wounded in nearby battlefields, and many of them were later buried in the church graveyard. After the war, a group of Petersburg schoolgirls and their teacher, Nora Fontaine Maury Davidson, came here to decorate the soldiers' graves. The ceremony was witnessed by a visitor, Mary Logan, wife of Union Gen. John A. Logan, who was head of the Grand Army of the Republic, the major organization of Union army veterans. Under the Logans' initiative, the G.A.R. sponsored the idea of a national day of memorial, and it was first observed nationwide in 1868. The Tiffany windows were designed as a memorial to the Confederate dead. Former Confederate states were each asked to sponsor one of the windows; the 14th was commissioned by the local Ladies Memorial Association; and the artist himself, Louis Comfort Tiffany, gave the church the 15th window, a magnificent "Cross of Jewels" that is thrillingly illuminated at sunset. This gift, from a talented Northerner, has been prized as a symbol of the postwar reconciliation of North and South.

Admission: $2.

Open: Mon–Sat 10am–4pm, Sun 12:30–4pm. **Directions:** Take Bank Street east and turn right on Crater Road; it's about 2 miles south of downtown Petersburg.

WHERE TO STAY

MAYFIELD INN, 3348 W. Washington St. (P.O. Box 2265), Petersburg, VA 23804. Tel. 804/861-6775. 2 rms, 2 suites (all with bath). A/C **Directions:** From Richmond, take I-95 south to Exit 3W onto Washington Street (Route 1); the inn is about 3 miles from the exit.

$ Rates (including full breakfast): $60–$80 double. MC, V.

Built as a plantation around 1750 by a member of the House of Burgesses, this stately brick inn was moved to its present site on a 4-acre plot of land in 1969. General Lee is thought to have spent the night here before going on to Appomattox. The present owners, Jamie and Dot Caudle, acquired it in 1979 and spent 5 years restoring it and furnishing it with antiques and period reproductions. Much of the interior is original—seven fireplaces (all working), floors, windows, and shutters. Rooms are large and luxurious. The largest bedroom has a four-poster canopy bed, dormer windows, a love seat, and a small table with a pewter tea service cozily set in front of the fireplace. Hearty country breakfasts are served downstairs in a formal dining room. Guests can stroll in a lovely colonial herb garden, or lounge at a heated pool.

WHERE TO DINE

KING'S BARBEQUE, U.S. 1 South, Petersburg. Tel. 804/732-5861.
   Cuisine: AMERICAN. **Directions:** Follow U.S. 1 from Petersburg.
$ Prices: Entrees $3.95–$8.95. MC, V.
   Open: Daily 7am–9pm.
This Petersburg institution, open since 1946, offers some of the tastiest southern specialties in Virginia. An enormous clientele has led the owners to expand their white clapboard and brick restaurant three times. The setting is a vast room with Colonial-style Formica-top tables and Windsor chairs. At lunch or dinner you might order King's famous barbecue sandwich deluxe, beef ($4.50) or pork ($3.75), which comes with french fries, slaw, and coffee or tea. Side orders of barbecued beans, yam puffs, and fried potato cakes are highly recommended. Dinner platters include barbecue plates as well as crispy fried chicken, ham steak, and seafood items like salmon cakes and fried oysters. Homemade hot apple pie is a house specialty.

ASHLAND/DOSWELL

About 14 miles north of Richmond on I-95 is the small community of Ashland. Continue west about 8 miles to Scotchtown, plantation home of Patrick Henry during his most active political years. Hanover Tavern, built in 1723 and now home of the Barksdale Dinner Theatre (see Section 4, "Evening Entertainment," above) is 5 miles east of Ashland, at the intersection of Routes 54 and 301. And 7 miles farther north on I-95 is Kings Dominion theme park.

WHAT TO SEE & DO

SCOTCHTOWN, Rte. 2, Beaverdam, Va. Tel. 804/227-3500.
One of Virginia's oldest plantation houses, Scotchtown is a charming one-story white clapboard home, in a parklike setting of small dependencies and gardens. The house was built by Charles Chiswell of Williamsburg, probably around 1719. Patrick Henry bought the house in 1770, and a year later came to live here with his wife, Sarah, and their six children. They stayed until 1778. Sadly, Sarah was mentally ill during much of the time they lived here, and she was eventually confined to a room in the basement. The manor house has been beautifully restored and furnished with 18th-century antiques, some of them associated with the Henry family. In the study, Henry's mahogany desk-table still bears the ink stains made by him, and bookshelves still contain his law books. A walnut cradle used by several of his children is now in the guest bedroom. Scotchtown also has associations with another historical figure—Dolley Madison. Her mother was a first cousin to Patrick Henry, and Dolley and her mother lived here while their family was moving back to this area from North Carolina.
   Admission: $4 adults, $2 students.
   Open: Apr–Oct, Mon–Sat 10am–4:30pm, Sun 1:30–4:30pm. **Directions:** From Ashland, follow Route 54 west, then the signs for Scotchtown at Route 685 north.

KINGS DOMINION, Doswell, Va. Tel. 804/876-5000.
   If flying your own plane turns you on, head over to King's Dominion, a 400-acre

major theme park where a star attraction is Sky Pilot, a $2-million flight-trainer ride that simulates aerobatic flight maneuvers. Or run the rapids at White Water Canyon, a wet-and-wild ride simulating white-water rafting with all the thrills and excitement but without the danger of falling into the water and getting dragged away by a swirling current; you will, however, get soaking wet. Other attractions here include roller coasters, water slides, and a Wild Animal Safari area with over 100 free-roaming animals; it's viewed from a monorail.

In addition to 44 rides, Kings Dominion offers 10 live shows throughout the day (get a schedule when you come in). The most spectacular entertainment is offered at the park's outdoor amphitheater, the Showplace, featuring headliners like the Beach Boys, Bill Cosby, Patti LaBelle, and Conway Twitty.

Admission (including unlimited rides and attractions): $21.95 adults, $16.95 seniors, $13.95 children 3–6, free for children 2 and under. Headliner shows $4–$7 extra.

Open: Park, Mar–Apr, Sat–Sun 10am–8pm; May, Sat–Sun 10am–10pm; June, Mon–Fri 10am–8pm, Sat–Sun 10am–10pm; July–Aug, daily 10am–10pm; Sept–Oct, Sat–Sun 10:30am–8pm. International Street, Mar–Apr, Sat–Sun 9am–8pm; May, Sat–Sun 9am–10pm; June, Mon–Fri 9:30am–8pm, Sat–Sun 9am–10pm; July–Aug, Mon–Fri 9:30am–10pm, Sat–Sun 9am–10pm; Sept–Oct, Sat–Sun 9:30am–8pm. **Closed:** Nov–Feb. **Directions:** Take Route 30 exit off I-95.

WHERE TO DINE

HOMEMADES BY SUZANNE, 102 N. Railroad Ave., Ashland. Tel. 804/ 798-8331.
  Cuisine: AMERICAN. **Directions:** At intersection of Route 54 and railroad tracks.
$ Prices: Lunch special $5. MC, V.
  Open: Mon 11am–6pm, Tues–Fri 9am–6pm, Sat 10am–2pm.
A spacious tea room/garden welcomes visitors with the heady aroma of fresh-baked fare. Display cases show off the day's specials—homemade pies, cream puffs with real whipped cream, and huge chocolate-chip cookies. Sandwiches are delicious, whether they're stuffed with chicken salad, sliced fresh roast turkey, or pulled pork barbecue with slaw. Sandwich specials are accompanied by hearty soups.

CHAPTER 11

WILLIAMSBURG, JAMESTOWN & YORKTOWN

1. WILLIAMSBURG
2. JAMESTOWN
3. YORKTOWN

The 18th-century town of Colonial Williamsburg, the earliest permanent English settlement in North America at Jamestown, and the Yorktown battlefield where Washington's decisive victory over General Cornwallis's forces turned the colonists' dream of a new nation into a reality—these three sites are major tourist meccas of historic Virginia.

The area is renowned not only for its historic sites. The multi-million-dollar theme park Busch Gardens, The Old Country brims with entertainment and thrilling rides, and Water Country USA offers summertime fun with watery rides and attractions. And there's also world-class shopping in the numerous factory outlet stores near Williamsburg. You'll find the Historic Triangle, past and present, a wonderful place to explore.

1. WILLIAMSBURG

150 miles S of Washington, D.C.; 50 miles E of Richmond

GETTING THERE By Plane Patrick Henry Airport in Newport News is 14 miles from Williamsburg; limousine service is available. But most flights to the area come into Norfolk International Airport or Richmond International Airport, both of which are about 45 miles from town.

By Train There is rail transport via Amtrak's *Colonial* directly to Williamsburg. The train station, at Boundary Street and Lafayette Street (tel. 804/229-8750), is within walking distance of the historic area.

By Bus There is bus service via Greyhound/Trailways. The bus depot (tel. 804/229-1460) is at the train station, Boundary Street and Lafayette Street.

By Car I-64 is the principal highway leading to Williamsburg. U.S. 60 and Virginia Routes 5 and 31 also give good access. From Washington, follow I-95 south to its junction with I-64, near Richmond.

ESSENTIALS The **telephone area code** is 804.

HISTORY & BACKGROUND

"I know of no way of judging the future," said Patrick Henry, "but by the past." That particular quotation couldn't be more apt as an introduction to Williamsburg. For one thing, Patrick Henry played a very important role here when, as a 29-year-old backcountry lawyer, he spoke out against the Stamp Act in the House of Burgesses in 1765. Many considered him an upstart and called the speech traitorous; others were inspired to revolution.

Another reason the quote is so apt: if you can judge the future by the past, you'll never have a better opportunity of doing so. Williamsburg is unique even in history-revering Virginia. It's gone beyond restoring and re-creating important sites of the past. It's a completely reconstructed 18th-century town where women wear long dresses and ruffled caps, men don powdered wigs, Colonial fare is served in restaurants, blacksmiths' and harnessmakers' shops line cobblestone streets, and the local militia drills on the village green. Most of the year (except May 15 to July 4) a British flag flies over the Capitol.

To understand how it all came about, we must travel back almost 300 years to 1699. In that year, following the destruction of the State House by fire (the fourth one to burn down), and following nearly a century of famine, fevers, and battles with neighboring tribes, the beleaguered Virginia Colony abandoned the mosquito-infested swamp that was Jamestown for a planned colonial city 6 miles inland. They named it Williamsburg for the reigning British monarch, King William of Orange.

Royal Governor Francis Nicholson laid out the new capital. He also planned public greens and allotted every house on the main street a half acre of land. Most of the houses were wood frame (trees being abundant) and painted white; kitchens were outside because of the risk of fire and the heat they generated in summer. People used their land allotment for growing vegetables and raising livestock. Cities were much more rural in the 18th century.

A residence for the royal governor was completed in 1720. The town prospered and soon became the major cultural and political center of Virginia. The government met here four times a year, and during these "Publick Times" rich planters and politicos (one and the same in most cases) converged on Williamsburg and the population, normally about 1,800, doubled. Shops displayed their finest imported wares, and there were balls, horse races, fairs, and auctions.

In the years from 1699 to 1780 (when the offices of the new Commonwealth were moved to Richmond to be safer from British attack), Williamsburg played a major role as a seat of royal government and later as a hotbed of revolution. Here occurred many of the incitive events leading up to the Declaration of Independence. Thomas Jefferson and James Monroe studied at the College of William and Mary. Jefferson was also the second and last occupant of the Governor's Palace before the capital moved to Richmond (Patrick Henry was the first). During the Revolution, Williamsburg served as the wartime capital for 4 years and was variously the headquarters of Generals Washington (he planned the siege of Yorktown in George Wythe's house), Rochambeau, and Cornwallis.

A REVEREND & A ROCKEFELLER

After 1780 Williamsburg was no longer an important political center. For the next 150 years or so, it remained a quaintly charming Virginia town, unique only in that it changed so little. As late as 1926 the colonial town plan was virtually intact, including numerous original 18th-century buildings. The Reverend W. A. R. Goodwin, rector of Bruton Parish Church, saw the significance of Williamsburg's enduring heritage and envisioned a restoration of the entire town to its colonial appearance. He inspired John D. Rockefeller, Jr., with his dream of creating a tangible symbol of our early history. During his lifetime Rockefeller contributed some $68 million to the project, and set up an endowment to help provide for the permanence of the restoration and its educational programs.

WILLIAMSBURG REBORN

Today the Historic Area covers 173 acres of the original 220-acre town. A mile long, it encompasses 88 preserved and restored houses, shops, taverns, public buildings, and outbuildings that survived to the 20th century. More than 500 additional buildings and smaller structures have been rebuilt on their original sites after extensive archeological, architectural, and historical research. Williamsburg set a very high standard for other Virginia restorations. Researchers investigated international archives, libraries, and museums, and sought out old wills, diaries, court records, inventories, letters, and other documents. The architects carefully studied every aspect of 18th-century buildings, from paint chemistry to brickwork. And archeologists recovered thousands of artifacts while excavating 18th-century sites to reveal original foundations. The Historic Area also includes 90 acres of gardens and greens, and 3,000 surrounding acres serve as a "greenbelt" against commercial encroachment.

ORIENTATION
ARRIVING

Since cars are not allowed—except in a limited way—into the Historic Area between 8am and 6pm daily (during daylight savings time, till 9pm), drivers must park at the Colonial Williamsburg Visitor Center (see below) and take a shuttle bus (see "Getting Around," below, for details) to 10 stops at historic sites.

TOURIST INFORMATION

The entire operation is overseen by the Colonial Williamsburg Foundation, a nonprofit, educational organization whose activities include an ongoing restoration. To serve the annual one million visitors, they've created the **Colonial Williamsburg Visitor Center** off U.S. 60 Bypass, just east of Route 132 (P.O. Box B), Williamsburg, VA 23187 (tel. 804/220-7645). You can't miss it; bright-green signs point the way from all access roads to Williamsburg. Stopping here is a must. Open 365 days a year from 8am to 5pm January to March, till 8pm the rest of the year, the center offers maps and guidebooks, tours, and information on lodgings, dining, and evening activities. If you'd like to peruse information-filled brochures prior to arrival, call or write the center. The center shows a 35-minute orientation film, *Williamsburg—the Story of a Patriot,* continuously throughout the day.

The center also has two **reservations services** for Colonial Williamsburg Foundation operations: one for hotel reservations and the other for reservations at the four colonial taverns run by the foundation. In summer it's essential to make these reservations well ahead of time.

Most important, the center is where you buy your **block tickets** for the dozens of attractions that make up Colonial Williamsburg (see "What to See and Do," below).

Note: All Historic Area attractions are open 9am to 5pm daily, year round.

CITY LAYOUT

The 99-foot-wide **Duke of Gloucester Street** is the principal east-west artery of the Historic Area. The Capitol building terminates the eastern end of the street, and the Wren building of the College of William and Mary is at the western end. The other two major streets are **Francis Street** and **Nicholson Street.** Merchant Square shops and services are between the Historic Area and the college. The Visitors Center is north of the Historic Area.

GETTING AROUND

Bus service from the Visitor Center begins at 8:30am and serves the Historic Area with departures every 10 minutes until 10pm.

WHAT TO SEE & DO

SEEING THE HISTORIC AREA

TICKETS   There are three types of general admission tickets available. All entitle you to see the orientation film at the Visitor Center and use the Historic Area transportation system. A **Basic Admission Ticket** (providing admission to most Historic Area attractions) costs $21 for adults, $12.50 for children 6 to 12 (children under 6 are admitted free). With this ticket the Governor's Palace requires an additional ticket, as do Carter's Grove, Bassett Hall, the Abby Aldrich Rockefeller Folk Art Center (closed for a major expansion until mid-1992), the Patriot Tour, and the DeWitt Wallace Decorative Arts Gallery. The **Royal Governor's Pass** ($24.50 for adults, $14.75 for children) includes all Historic Area attractions except Carter's Grove, Bassett Hall, and the Patriot Tour. Our advice is to shell out the $28 ($17 for children) for the **Patriot's Pass,** good for 1 year of unlimited free admissions at all Colonial Williamsburg attractions plus a 1-hour guided walking tour. There's so much to see and do that you don't want to have to pick and choose, probably omitting attractions that interest you in the process. And the attractions that charge supplements with the Basic Admission Ticket are must-sees, so you'd probably be paying the same amount anyway.

The Capitol

✪ Virginia legislators met in the H-shaped Capitol at the eastern end of Duke of Gloucester Street throughout most of the 18th century (1704–80). America's first representative assembly, it was modeled on an English bicameral legislature with an upper house (His Majesty's Council of State consisted of 12 members appointed by the king for life) and a lower house (the House of Burgesses, elected by the freeholders of each county; by 1776 there were 128 burgesses). All civil and criminal cases (the latter punishable by mutilation or death) were tried in the General Court, and since juries were sent to deliberate in a third-floor room without heat, light, or food, there were very few hung juries. Blackbeard's pirate crew faced trial here, and 13 of them were sentenced to hang for their crimes. The General Assembly met when called by the governor, with sessions lasting anywhere from a few days to several months, depending on the amount of business at hand. The burgesses represented the people of Virginia and considered petitions from their electors and royal orders. They initiated legislation and bills, then sent them to the Council for approval or rejection. As 1776 approached there were increasing petitions and resolutions against acts of Parliament considered infringements on the rights of self-government. The House of Burgesses became a training ground for patriots and future governors such as George Washington, Thomas Jefferson, Richard Henry Lee, and Patrick Henry. The basis of Henry's argument—no taxation without representation—became the motto of the Revolution. In other historic moments at the Capitol, George Washington was praised

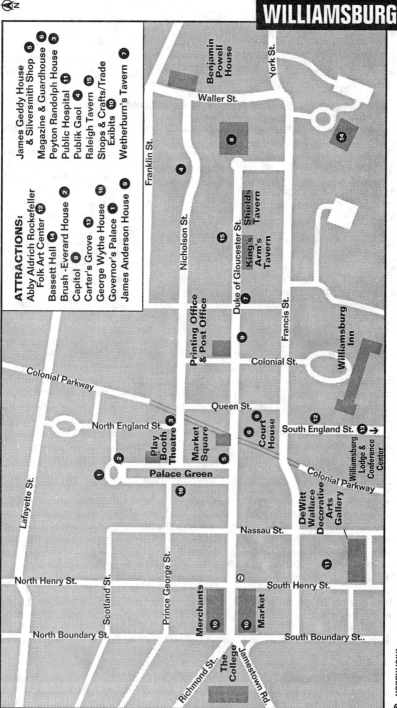

WILLIAMSBURG

ATTRACTIONS:

Abby Aldrich Rockefeller Folk Art Center ⑫
Bassett Hall ⑭
Brush-Everard House ②
Capitol ⑧
Carter's Grove ⑬
George Wythe House ⑯
Governor's Palace ①
James Anderson House ⑨

James Geddy House & Silversmith Shop ⑤
Magazine & Guardhouse ⑥
Peyton Randolph House ③
Public Hospital ⑪
Publik Gaol ④
Raleigh Tavern ⑮
Shops & Crafts/Trade Exibits ⑩
Wetherburn's Tavern ⑦

Benjamin Powell House

Waller St.

York St.

Franklin St.

Nicholson St.

Shields Tavern

King's Arm's Tavern

Duke of Gloucester St.

Francis St.

Printing Office & Post Office

Williamsburg Inn

Colonial St.

Colonial Parkway

Queen St.

North England St.

Play Booth Theatre

Market Square

Court House

South England St.

Williamsburg Lodge & Conference Center

Palace Green

Colonial Parkway

Lafayette St.

DeWitt Wallace Decorative Arts Gallery

Nassau St.

Scotland St.

Prince George St.

North Henry St.

South Henry St.

Merchants

Market

North Boundary St.

South Boundary St.

Richmond St.

Jamestown Rd.

The College

for his role in the French and Indian War and George Mason's Virginia Declaration of Rights (the prototype for the Bill of Rights) was passed.

The original Capitol burned down in 1747, was rebuilt in 1753, and succumbed to fire again in 1832. The reconstruction is of the 1704 building, complete with Queen Anne's coat-of-arms adorning the tower and the Great Union flag flying overhead. **Tours** (about 25 minutes) are given throughout the day.

The Governor's Palace

✪ Another complete reconstruction, this stately Georgian mansion, residence and official headquarters of royal governors, is today meticulously furnished in authentic Colonial pieces. The inventory of Royal Governor Lord Botetourt, who died at the palace in 1770, itemized over 16,500 objects contained in the 61-room complex, and shed light on the staff and facilities needed to maintain such an elaborate household. As at other Williamsburg sites, where authentic period pieces were not available, reproductions have been crafted to exacting standards by artisans thoroughly schooled in 18th-century methods, so it is Lord Botetourt's palace that visitors view today. The final 5 years of British rule is the period portrayed. Though the sumptuous surroundings, nobly proportioned halls and rooms, 10 acres of formal gardens and greens, and vast wine cellars all evoke the splendor of the official residence of the king's representative, research has indicated that by the 1760s the royal governor was a functionary of great prestige but limited power. He was more apt to behave like a diplomat in a foreign land than an autocratic colonial ruler.

The palace's residents included seven royal governors—from Alexander Spotswood, who supervised construction and moved in in 1714, to the Earl of Dunmore, who fled the premises in the face of armed resistance to royal authority just before dawn on June 8, 1775, thus ending British rule in Virginia. After independence, the state's first elected governors, Patrick Henry and Thomas Jefferson, lived here.

Tours, given continuously throughout the day, wind up in the gardens, where you can explore at your leisure the elaborate geometric parterres, topiary work, bowling green, pleached allées, and a holly maze patterned after the one at Hampton Court. Plan at least 30 minutes to wander these stunning grounds and visit the kitchen and stable yards.

The Palace is open daily. Admission for Basic Ticket holders is $13.

The Raleigh Tavern

Reconstructed on its original site in 1932, using data from inventories of past proprietors and information gleaned from archeological excavations, the Raleigh occupies a central location on the north side of Duke of Gloucester Street. After the Governor's Palace, it was the social and political hub of the town, especially during Publick Times when Williamsburg turned into a thronging metropolis. Colonists gathered here in 1769 to draw up a boycott of British goods—one of many meetings where grievances against the Crown were aired—and regular clients included some of our most esteemed forefathers. George Washington frequently noted in his diary that he "dined at the Raleigh." And Thomas Jefferson wrote ruefully in a letter the morning after the night before, "Last night, as merry as agreeable company and dancing with Belinda in the Apollo [the Raleigh's ballroom] could make me, I never could have thought the succeeding Sun would have seen me so wretched." However, he was often here on less frivolous business, such as a meeting in 1774 with Patrick Henry, Richard Henry Lee, and Francis Lightfoot Lee to discuss revolution. Patrick Henry's troops gave their commander a farewell dinner at the Raleigh in 1776. In 1859 the tavern was destroyed by fire.

This most famous of Williamsburg taverns was named for Sir Walter Raleigh, who was instrumental in Britain's efforts to colonize the New World. Its facilities include two dining rooms (George Washington often rented the smaller one for private dinners); the famed Apollo ballroom, scene of elegant entertainments; a club room that could be rented for private meetings, be they political conclaves or card games; a billiards room; and a bar where ale and hot rum punch were the favored drinks. The bedrooms upstairs offered nothing in the way of privacy. In fact it is believed that the expression "politics makes strange bedfellows," originated in the custom of renting bed space, especially during Publick Times when a smelly pig farmer might sleep next to a wealthy planter. In the tavern bakery you can buy 18th-century confections like gingerbread and Shrewsbury cake, and cider to wash it down.

Wetherburn's Tavern

Though less important than the Raleigh, Wetherburn's also played an important role in Colonial Williamsburg. George Washington occasionally favored the tavern with his patronage. And like the Raleigh, it was mobbed during Publick Times and frequently served as a center of sedition and a rendezvous of Revolutionary patriots. Henry Wetherburn ran a tavern here from 1738 until his death in 1760. In subsequent years it was reincarnated as a school for young ladies, a boardinghouse, and a store. The heart of yellow pine floors are original, so you can actually walk in Washington's footsteps; windows, trim, and weatherboarding are a mixture of old and new; and the outbuildings, except for the dairy, are reconstructions. A long, detailed inventory from Wetherburn's day listing the contents of the tavern room by room provided an excellent blueprint for furnishings.

Scene of auctions, lectures, balls, business dealings, and political meetings, the Wetherburn lodged 38 or more men in its 19 ropespring beds for 7½ pence a night (extra for horse bedding). A dozen slaves served guests and saw to the cooking, gardening, cleaning, and horse grooming. Gambling and drinking went on all night, not just in the gaming room but in the dining rooms and bedrooms—this in spite of licensing regulations condemning both activities. Twenty-five-minute **tours** are given throughout the day.

The George Wythe House

On the west side of the Palace Green is the elegant restored brick home of George Wythe (pronounced "With")—foremost classics scholar in 18th-century Virginia, noted lawyer and teacher (his students included Thomas Jefferson, Henry Clay, and John Marshall), and member of the House of Burgesses. A close friend of Royal Governors Fauquier and Botetourt, Wythe nevertheless sided with the patriots during the Revolution; he was the first Virginia signer of the Declaration of Independence. (On principle, Wythe did not sign the Constitution, because it did not contain the bill of rights or antislavery provisions he had fought for.) In 1777 he was elected Speaker of the House of Delegates, in 1778 one of the three judges of Virginia's High Court of Chancery, and in 1779 he became the first professor of law at an American college—William and Mary. During a 1782 case he helped establish the concept of judicial review.

Thomas Jefferson called Wythe "my faithful and beloved Mentor in youth, and my most affectionate friend through life."

The house, in which he lived with his second wife, Elizabeth Taliaferro (pronounced "Tolliver"), was Washington's headquarters prior to the siege of Yorktown and Rochambeau's after the surrender of Cornwallis. Domestic crafts typical of the time—spinning, weaving, open-hearth cooking, etc.—are demonstrated by artisans in the outbuildings. Products from the shops are sold at stores in the Historic Area. Craft displays are open 5 to 7 days a week from 9am to 5pm, with evening tours of candlelit shops available; visitors carry lanterns.

At Anthony Hay's cabinetmaking shop, fine furnishings, harpsichords, and spinets are produced of cherry, walnut, and mahogany using foot- and hand-powered tools. Thomas Jefferson was among the patrons of the original Hay. A music teacher instructs students in period instruments—harpsichord, cello, flute, oboe, violin, viola, recorder, etc.—at his shop; you can enjoy a concert of period music here.

The wigmaker operates out of the King's Arms Barber Shop. Here you'll see the cone-shaped mask that men donned in order to breathe while their wigs were powdered with pulverized starch and plaster.

Shops & Crafts/Trade Exhibits

✪ The 18th-century crafts practiced on the grounds of Wythe House (see above) are among numerous similar exhibits throughout the Historic Area. Such goings-on were a facet of everyday life in this preindustrial era. Several dozen crafts are practiced in cluttered shops by over 100 master craftspeople. They're an extremely skilled group, many having served up to 7-year apprenticeships both here and abroad. The program is part of Williamsburg's efforts to present an accurate picture of colonial society, portraying the average man and woman as well as more illustrious citizens.

James Geddy's silversmith shop adjoined his house (details below) and was right across from the master bedroom so that he could hear any hankypanky going on at night (silver items are valuable).

Sharing headquarters are the printer and bookbinder, together turning out reproductions of 18th-century books and newspapers. They operate out of a working post office where your letters receive a hand-stamped postmark patterned after one used here in 1770. On these premises printer William Parks (a colleague of Benjamin Franklin) published the first issue of the *Virginia Gazette* in 1736.

Tubs, buckets, barrels, kegs, and other containers made of staves are produced at the cooper's shop.

The workshop of colonial coachmaker Elkanah Deane is today utilized by a maker of saddles and harnesses.

A blacksmith turns out toasting forks, hinges, wagon tires, and many other wrought-iron objects both decorative and functional.

A shoemaker produces shoes and boots for the whole family. In a 12-hour day, an 18th-century shoemaker could turn out two pairs. The shop is on the site of a 1773 shoemaking establishment.

Exact replicas of weapons carried by colonial Virginians—English flintlock muskets, rifles, and fowling pieces used to shoot ducks and geese—are fashioned at Ayscough House.

The milliner (in the 18th century, carrying all fashion wear, not just hats) explains the styles of the day for men, women, and children.

A constant need for wheelbarrows, coach wheels, and wheeled carts provided ample work for the 18th-century wheelwright.

At building trades demonstrations you'll see housewrights creating hand-hewn beams, boards, and shingles, and brickmakers slapping clay into wooden molds.

Windmills were essential to grinding grain (a colonial mill could grind 200 pounds of cornmeal in an hour), but, as you'll learn here, the miller's trade was a dangerous one.

Basketmaking, candlemaking, 18th-century cooking, and laundering are among the domestic crafts demonstrated.

And always interesting in a morbid way is the apothecary shop, where sore feet were treated with leeches between the toes, a headache with leeches across the forehead, and a sore throat with leeches on the neck.

The James Anderson House

Originally owned by the secretary to Royal Governor Robert Dinwiddie, this historic building was later a tavern operated by Mrs. Christiana Campbell; George Washington frequently stayed the night. Blacksmith James Anderson acquired the property in 1770 and set up shop. During the Revolution he was Virginia's official armorer.

Today the building is used for exhibits excavated in Williamsburg archeological digs and found in colonial wells. A display of 88 unearthed objects is shown in conjunction with an adjoining bedroom, which was reconstructed using these objects as guidelines. They include fragments of scissors, candlesticks, coins, medicine bottles, tobacco pipes, turkey bones and oyster shells (clues to meals), Delftware, shoes, and a sword hilt. Also on display is a map of Williamsburg drawn up by a French cartographer in 1782. Taped narrations explain it all. Behind the house is a reconstruction of Anderson's blacksmith shop where a corps of workmen at seven forges turn out nails, farm tools, and tradesmen's tools.

The Publick Gaol

They didn't coddle criminals in the 18th century. Punishments included not only public ridicule (stocks and pillories), but also lashing, branding, mutilation, and hanging, the latter invoked even for such lightweight crimes as burglary, forgery, and horse stealing. Those who escaped more severe punishments and were sentenced to prison found it no picnic. In winter the dreary cells were bitterly cold; in summer, stifling. Beds were rudimentary piles of straw; leg irons, shackles, and chains were used frequently; and the daily diet consisted of "salt beef damaged, and Indian meal." In its early days (before the construction of a "Lunatick Hospital" in 1773) the gaol doubled as a madhouse, and during the Revolution redcoats, spies, traitors, and deserters swelled the prison population.

The gaol opened in 1704 (frontier colonies couldn't get along without one; of course, neither could we); debtors cells were added in 1711 (though the imprisoning of debtors was virtually eliminated after a 1772 law made creditors responsible for their upkeep), and keeper's quarters were added in 1722. The thick-walled red-brick building served as the Williamsburg city jail through 1910. The building today is restored to its 1720s appearance.

The Peyton Randolph House

The Randolphs were one of the most prominent—and wealthy—families in colonial Virginia, and Peyton Randolph was one of its most distinguished members. His father, Sir John Randolph, was a highly respected lawyer, Speaker of the House of Burgesses, and Virginia's representative to London where he was the only colonial-born Virginian ever to be knighted. When he died he left his library to a 16-year-old Peyton, "hoping he will betake himself to the study of law." When Peyton Randolph died in 1775, his cousin, Thomas Jefferson, purchased his books at auction; they eventually became the nucleus of the Library of Congress. Peyton Randolph did follow in his father's footsteps, studying law in London after attending the College of William and Mary. He served in the House of Burgesses from 1744 to 1775, the last 9 years as Speaker of the House. Known as the great mediator, he was unanimously elected president of the First Continental Congress in Philadelphia in 1774, and though he was a believer in nonviolence who hoped the colonies could amicably settle their differences with England, he was a firm patriot.

The house (actually, two connected homes) dates to 1715. It is today restored to reflect the period around 1770. Robertson's Windmill, in back of the house, is a post mill of a type popular in the 18th century. The house is open to the public for self-guided tours with period-costumed interpreters in selected rooms.

The Brush-Everard House

One of the oldest buildings in Williamsburg, the Brush-Everard House was occupied without interruption from 1717—when armorer and gunsmith John Brush built it as a residence-cum-shop—through 1946. Charged not only with maintaining and repairing weaponry, Brush also had to take part in various ceremonies requiring gun salutes, such as royal birthdays. At one of these he wounded himself slightly and applied—without success—to the House of Burgesses for damages. Little else is known about him. He died in 1726. The most distinguished owner was Thomas Everard, clerk of York County from 1745 to 1771 and two-time mayor of Williamsburg. Though not as wealthy as Wythe and Randolph, he was in their elite circle. He enlarged the house, adding the two wings that give it a U shape. Today the home is restored and furnished to its Everard-era appearance. The smokehouse and kitchen out back are original.

After an introductory talk in the library, visitors can tour the house on their own.

The James Geddy House & Silversmith Shop

This two-story L-shaped 1762 home (with attached shops) is an original building. Here visitors can see how a comfortably situated middle-class family lived in the 18th century. Unlike the fancier abodes you'll visit, the Geddy House has no wallpaper or oil paintings; a mirror and spinet from England, however, indicate relative affluence.

The Geddy dynasty begins with James Sr., an accomplished gunsmith and brass founder who advertised in the *Virginia Gazette* of July 8, 1737, that he had "a great Choice of Guns and Fowling Pieces, of several Sorts and Sizes, true bored, which he will warrant to be good; and will sell them as cheap as they are usually sold in England." He died in 1744, leaving his widow with eight children. His enterprising oldest sons, David and William, took over, offering their services as "Gunsmiths, Cutlers, and Founders," and on the side they did a little blacksmithing and engraving and sold cures for "all Diseases incident to Horses." A younger son, James Jr., became the town's foremost silversmith; he imported and sold jewelry, and was a member of the city's Common Council involved in furthering the patriot cause. At a foundry on the premises, craftsmen cast pewter, bronze, and brass items at a forge.

The Magazine & Guardhouse

The magazine is a sturdy octagonal brick building constructed in 1715 to house ammunition and arms for the defense of the British colony. It has survived intact to the present day. In Colonial Williamsburg every able-bodied freeman belonged to the militia from the ages of 16 to 60, and did his part in protecting hearth and home from attack by local tribes, riots, slave uprisings, and pirate raids. The high wall and guardhouse were built during the French and Indian War to protect the magazine's 60,000 pounds of gunpowder.

Today the building is stocked with 18th-century equipment—British-made flintlock muskets, cannons and cannonballs, barrels of powder, bayonets, and drums, the latter for communication purposes.

A 20-minute horse-drawn carriage ride around the Historic Area departs from a horse post at the Courthouse of 1770, just across the street; cost is $6 per person.

Carter's Grove

✪ To my mind, Carter's Grove—a magnificent plantation home that has been continuously occupied since 1755 on a site that was settled over 3½ centuries ago—is one of the most intriguing historical attractions in Virginia. The estate is reached via a stunningly scenic one-way, 7-mile wilderness road traversing streams, meadows, woodlands, and ravines. A re-creation of a colonial carriage pathway, the road is dotted with markers indicating old graveyards, Indian encampments, plantation sites, and other points of interest.

The history of Carter's Grove takes us back to the earliest days of the colonies—and beyond. Nomadic Paleo Indian hunters used the site as far back as 8,000 years ago. Searching for traces of lost plantation outbuildings on the banks of the James, archeologists have discovered here the "lost" 17th-century village of Wolstenholme Towne, site of a 20,000-acre tract settled in 1619 by 220 colonists who called themselves the Society of Martin's Hundred. The early town was short-lived; the great Indian uprising of March 22, 1622, destroyed most of the settlement and left only about 60 living inhabitants, who fled to Jamestown. At least half of the original town has been lost to us through erosion by the James River, but archeologists have found the remnants of a fortified compound and lookout tower, dwellings, a corral for penning livestock, graves, a cannon, and other structures (all on view).

Over a century after the abandonment of Wolstenholme Towne, Robert "King" Carter (Virginia's wealthiest planter) purchased the property for his daughter, Elizabeth. (Today 790 acres remain of the original 1,400-acre tract he purchased.) Between 1751 and 1754 Elizabeth's son, Carter Burwell, built the beautiful 2½-story, 200-foot-long mansion that is considered "the final phase of the evolution of the Georgian mansion." The West Drawing Room—with its exquisite 1750 fireplace mantel and carved frieze panel—is often called the "Refusal Room"; legend has it that southern belle Mary Cary refused George Washington's proposal of marriage in this room and Rebecca Burwell said "no" to Thomas Jefferson. In 1781 British cavalryman Banastre Tarleton headquartered at Carter's Grove and is said to have ascended the magnificent carved walnut stairway on his warhorse while hacking at the balustrade with his saber.

Despite Tarleton's abuse, Carter's Grove remains one of the best-preserved old houses in America. The Burwells occupied it through 1838, after which there were several owners. Rockefeller interests acquired the property in 1963, and since 1969 it has been owned and administered by the Colonial Williamsburg Foundation.

A fascinating Carter's Grove site is the reconstruction of the slave quarters. Though wattled circular enclosures to house chickens and a cabin's stick-and-mud chimney reflect African traditions, by the 1770s (the period here portrayed) most slaves were at least second-generation Virginians. Some 24 slaves would have lived in these few pine-log cabins, sleeping on straw pallets placed on dirt floors. There are few possessions or furnishings, except in the foreman's (or senior slave's) house, wherein an actual bed, a chair and table, a mirror, and a piece of Delft china indicate favored status.

At the reception/orientation center, housed in a red cedar building, visitors can view a 14-minute slide presentation on Carter's Grove, and an exhibit area displays historic photographs and documents. Allow at least 3 hours to see Carter's Grove. The house is open mid-March to late November and during Christmas season, Tuesday through Sunday from 9am to 4 or 5pm; the country road (take South England Street and follow the signs to get on it) is open from 8:30am to 4:30pm; it only goes one way, so you must return to Williamsburg via Route 60. Admission for Basic Ticket holders is $8 for adults, $5 for children.

Bassett Hall

Though colonial in origin (built between 1753 and 1766 by Col. Philip Johnson), Bassett Hall was the mid-1930s residence of Mr. and Mrs. John D. Rockefeller, Jr., and it is restored and furnished to reflect their era. The mansion's name, however, derives from the ownership of Burwell Bassett, a nephew of Martha Washington who lived here from 1800 to 1839.

The Rockefellers purchased the 585-acre property in the late 1920s and moved into the restored two-story dwelling in 1936. In spite of changes they made, much of the interior is original, including woodwork, paneling, mantels, and yellow-pine flooring. During their years here the Rockefellers entertained such royal notables as Britain's Queen Elizabeth and Emperor Hirohito of Japan. The house was bequeathed to the Colonial Williamsburg Foundation along with its furnishings in 1979.

Much of the furniture is 18th- and 19th-century American in the Chippendale, Federal, and Empire styles. There are beautifully executed needlework rugs made by Mrs. Rockefeller herself, and six early 19th-century prayer rugs adorn the morning room. Hundreds of examples of ceramics and china are on display, as are collections of 18th- and 19th-century American and English glass, Canton enamelware, and folk art.

Forty-minute **tours** of the house are given between 10am and 5pm daily by reservation only (tel. 804/229-1000, extension 4119; or write to Bassett Hall Reservation Office, P.O. Box C, Williamsburg, VA 23187). Tours conclude in the garden, which you can explore at your leisure.

The Abby Aldrich Rockefeller Folk Art Center

Note: This attraction will be closed for a major expansion through mid-1992.

The works of folk art displayed at Bassett Hall (above) are just a small sampling of enthusiast Abby Aldrich Rockefeller's extensive collection. This delightful museum contains more than 2,600 folk-art paintings, sculptures, and art objects. Mrs. Rockefeller was a pioneer in this branch of collecting in the 1920s and 1930s. Folk art is of interest not only aesthetically but as visual history; since colonial times untutored artists have creatively recorded everyday life.

The Folk Art Center collection includes household ornaments and useful wares (hand-stenciled bed covers, butter molds, pottery, utensils, painted furniture, boxes), mourning pictures (embroideries honoring departed relatives and national heroes), family and individual portraits, shop signs, carvings, whittled toys, calligraphic drawings, weavings, quilts, and paintings of scenes from daily life.

The Public Hospital

Opened in 1773, the "Public Hospital for Persons of Insane and Disordered Minds" was America's first lunatic asylum. Before its advent, the mentally ill were often thrown in jail or confined to the poorhouse. From 1773 to about 1820, treatment—or, one might say, mistreatment—involved solitary confinement and a grisly course of action designed to "encourage" patients to "choose" rational behavior (it was commonly assumed that patients willfully and mistakenly chose a life of insanity). So-called therapeutic techniques included the use of powerful drugs to exhaust or stimulate, submersion in cold water for extended periods, bleeding, blistering salves, and an array of restraining devices. On a self-guided tour you'll see a 1773 cell, with its filthy straw-filled mattress on the floor, ragged blanket, and manacles. Patients were totally idle and without distraction of any kind—a condition that might drive anyone crazy.

During what is called the Moral Management Period (1820–65), patients were seen to have an emotional disorder and were treated with kindness. The high point of the Moral Management Period was the administration of John Minson Galt II, from mid-1841 to his death in 1862. Galt created a carpentry shop, a shoemaking shop, a games room, and sewing, spinning, and weaving rooms. He conducted reading and music classes and organized evening lectures, concerts, and social gatherings. An 1845 cell seen on the tour has a comfortable bed with a patchwork quilt, a rug, table, and chair. However, for all his good intentions, Galt admitted that "practice invariably falls short of theory." His rate of cure was not notable.

After Galt's death, the hospital was administered by nine different superintendents—a factor mitigating against any real continuity in treatment. Confidence in reform and government intervention on behalf of the unfortunate diminished in this age of Social Darwinism when the survival of the fittest was the new ethic. Though some of the improvements initiated during the Moral Management Period were extended, restraining devices once more came into vogue. This final period, when patients were essentially warehoused with little hope of cure, is known as the Custodial Care Period.

The self-guided tour sets one thinking about our often equally ineffective methods of treating the mentally ill today. The Public Hospital is open daily.

The DeWitt Wallace Decorative Arts Gallery

✪ Adjoining the Public Hospital is a 62,000-square-foot museum housing some 8,000 17th- to 19th-century English and American decorative art objects. In its galleries you'll see period furnishings, ceramics, textiles, paintings, prints, silver, pewter, clocks, scientific instruments, mechanical devices, and weapons.

The $14 million in funding for this project, provided by DeWitt and Lila Acheson Wallace, represents the largest gift in the history of Colonial Williamsburg, apart from the support of John D. Rockefeller, Jr., and his family. In the upstairs Masterworks Gallery, an 18th-century governor's chair is flanked by a coronation portrait of King George III of England and a Charles Willson Peale study of George Washington. Surrounding the atrium are some 150 objects representing the highest achievement of American and English artisans from the 1640s to 1800.

At the east end of the museum, a 6,000-square-foot area with four galleries around a skylit courtyard is used for changing exhibits. On the first level you'll see small exhibits of musical instruments, objects related to European conquest and expansion in the New World, and 18th-century dining items. A small café here offers light fare, beverages, and a limited luncheon menu.

The Lila Acheson Wallace Garden, on the upper level, centers on a pond with two fountains, a trellis-shaded seating area at one end, a 6-foot gilded bronze statue of *Diana* by Augustus Saint-Gaudens at the other. The garden is surrounded by a 19-foot-high, plum-colored brick wall embellished (in season) with flowering vines.

Admission for Basic Ticket holders is $7.50, though a combination ticket for the DeWitt and Bassett Hall is $12.

NEARBY ATTRACTIONS

BUSCH GARDENS/THE OLD COUNTRY, 1 Busch Gardens Blvd., Williamsburg. Tel. 804/253-3350.

At some point you'll need a break from early American history, especially if you have kids in tow. That's the time to head over to Busch Gardens, a 360-acre family amusement park. True, it, too, is historically themed, with attractions in eight authentically detailed 17th-century European hamlets, but no mental effort is required to enjoy the rides, shows, and festivities.

One of the most popular rides is the terrifying Big Bad Wolf, a suspended roller coaster that culminates in an 80-foot plunge into the "Rhine River." Another "scream machine," the serpentine Loch Ness Monster with two interlocking 360° loops and a 130-foot drop is one of the fastest coasters in America. And not to be missed is the Enchanted Laboratory, a fascinating production utilizing computer-animated special effects in recounting the misadventures of a wizard's apprentice.

Many rides and attractions—including an entire kiddie area called Grimm's Hollow—are geared to younger visitors. Kids also love the Anheuser-Busch Clydesdale horses in Scotland, and crafts exhibits and medieval games at Threadneedle Faire.

Your one-price admission entitles you not only to unlimited rides but to top-quality musicals, bird shows, ice-skating revues, and more. Get a show schedule when you come in. Worth the price of entry alone are the headliner shows at the 5,200-seat Royal Palace Theater in France, featuring artists like Crystal Gayle, John Schneider, and the Oak Ridge Boys.

The 7,150-foot-long Eagle One monorail takes visitors to the Anheuser-Busch Hospitality Center for a brewery tour and complimentary beer.

Admission: $22.95 for unlimited rides, shows, and attractions (children 2 and under, free). Nominal charge for headliner concert tickets. Two-day tickets available, and discount nighttime tickets offered in summer. Parking is $3 in a 7,000-car lot.

Open: Early Apr to mid-May, Sat–Sun 10am–7pm; mid-May to mid-June and in

early Sept, daily 10am–7pm; mid-June to Aug, Sun–Fri 10am–10pm, Sat 10am–
midnight; early Sept to Oct, Fri–Tues 10am–7pm. **Directions:** From Williamsburg,
take Route 60E for about 3 miles.

WATER COUNTRY USA, Rte. 199. Tel. 804/229-9300.
  In June 1984 Virginia's first water theme park—40 acres of wet-and-wild
attractions—opened its floodgates. A highlight is Surfer's Bay, a man-made wave pool
the size of five Olympic swimming pools that produces a perfect 3½-foot wave every 4
seconds. The Jet Stream, a water flume, propels you down a 450-foot slide at up to 25
m.p.h. toward the splashdown pool. You can experience the thrills of white-water
tubing on the Run-a-Way Rapids, enjoy tandem tubing thrills on the Amazon, or
"surfboggan" at the Rampage. And there are high-diving and sea lion shows. The
younger set (under 12) can frolic safely at Polliwog Pond. There's a shop on the
premises, should you need to purchase swimwear, and the use of a bathhouse with
complete changing facilities is included in your admission price.
  Admission (including parking): $15.95 adults, $13.95 children 4–12, free for
children 3 and under. $7.95 after 3pm or for spectator ticket for those who don't plan
to get wet.
  Open: Daily. Early May to June 14, 10am–7pm; June 15–Aug 14, 10am–8pm;
Aug 15 to the second weekend in Sept, 10am–7pm. **Directions:** Take Route 199 to
its intersection with I-64 and follow the signs.

COOL FOR KIDS

Colonial Williamsburg offers several tours geared specifically to youngsters.
Tickets to all children's programs cost $5. Inquire at the Visitors Center.
  For kids ages 4 to 6, **Once Upon a Town tours** explore the lives of 18th-century
tots. For ages 7 to 11, there's the **Welcome Little Patriots tour** at the DeWitt
Wallace Decorative Arts Gallery, including a weapons display and many other period
objects. The **Young Apprentice Tour,** led by a costumed historical interpreter,
allows children 10 to 12 to participate in 18th-century trades and domestic crafts and
learn about their counterparts of the period. And for the whole family, there's
Stepping into the Past: Families at Work and Play in Colonial Virginia,
exploring family life in the 18th century.

SHOPPING

In the Historic Area

Duke of Gloucester Street is the center for 18th-century wares created by
craftspeople plying the trades of our forefathers. The goods offered include
hand-wrought silver jewelry from the Sign of the Golden Ball, hats from the Mary
Dickenson shop, pomanders to ward off the plague from McKenzie's Apothecary,
hand-woven linens from Prentis Store, books bound in leather and hand-printed
newspapers from the post office, gingerbread cakes from the Raleigh Tavern Bake
Shop, and everything from foodstuffs to fishhooks from Greenhow and Tarpley's, a
general store.
  Not to be missed is **Craft House,** also run by the Colonial Williamsburg
Foundation. There are two locations, one in Merchants Square, the other near the
Abby Aldrich Rockefeller Folk Art Center. Featured at Craft House are exquisite
works by master craftspeople and authentic reproductions of Colonial furnishings.
There are also reproduction wallpapers, china, toys, games, maps, books, prints, and
souvenirs aplenty.
  Merchants Square "shoppes" offer a wide range of merchandise: antiquarian
books and prints, 18th-century-style floral arrangements, candy, toys, handcrafted
pewter and silver items, needlework supplies, and Oriental rugs. It's not all of the "ye

olde" variety, however; you can also find a Baskin-Robbins ice-cream parlor, a drugstore that offers Excedrin in lieu of leeches, a camera shop, and clothing stores.

On Richmond Road

Shopping in the Historic Area is fun, but the biggest merchandising draw in town is out on Richmond Road (Route 60W) where the famed Williamsburg Pottery Factory and numerous factory outlet shops are located. Head out on Richmond Road, stopping first at the **Williamsburg Pottery Factory** (tel. 804/564-3326), 5 miles west of Williamsburg (you can't miss it). Open daily from 8am to 8pm in summer, till 6pm in spring and fall, and from 9am to 5pm in January and February, this is a 200-acre shopping complex with over 31 buildings selling merchandise from all over the world. It's all bought in large volume and sold at competitive prices. Pick up a shopping cart and a map in the parking lot and charge in.

It would be easier to describe what you can't buy here than what you can. Shops on the premises sell Christmas decorations, garden furnishings, lamps, art prints, dried and silk flowers, luggage, linens, baskets, hardware, glassware, cookware, candles, toys, crafts, clothing, food, jewelry, plants (there's a large greenhouse and nursery)— you name it. There's plenty of quality and plenty of kitsch. And of course, you can buy pottery here.

Continue a bit farther along Route 60 and you'll come to the **Pottery Factory Outlets**—the discount offerings of 20 major manufacturers under one roof. They include Black & Decker, Van Heusen, Cannon, Manhattan, Fieldcrest, Oneida, Kid City, Pfaltzgraff, and Cabin Creek Furniture.

Proceed farther along Route 60 until you see signs for the **Williamsburg Soap & Candle Company** (tel. 804/564-3354) across the road, your first stop en route back to town. It's open daily from 9am to 5pm, with extended hours in summer. Here you can see a narrated slide presentation on candle making while watching the process through viewing windows that look out on the factory. You can, of course, buy candles of every description here. There are interesting shops adjoining, and a cozy, country-style restaurant is on the premises.

Continuing toward town, the next stop is the **Williamsburg Doll Factory & Museum** (tel. 804/564-9703), for limited-edition porcelain collector's dolls. You can observe the dollmaking process and even buy parts to make your own. Other items sold here are stuffed animals, dollhouses and miniatures, clowns, and books on dolls. Open daily from 9am to 5:30pm.

Finally, if you still have the money and stamina, you can peruse the discounted wares (20% to 70% off) at dozens of factory-owned stores and outlets under a cross-shaped roof at **Outlets Ltd. Mall** (tel. 804/565-3378), a little farther east on Route 60. Open Monday through Saturday from 9am to 9pm and on Sunday from 9am to 6pm. There are no fountains or skylights at this mall, but it's a pleasant shopping environment.

The above are the Route 60 highlights; there's actually quite a bit more, which you'll see as you drive along.

WHERE TO STAY

As one of the great tourist attractions in the world, Williamsburg can accommodate vast numbers of visitors. The listings below lead off with hotels operated by the Colonial Williamsburg Foundation (inquire about packages at all of these), followed by a selection of nearby accommodations.

COLONIAL WILLIAMSBURG FOUNDATION HOTELS

Several accommodations choices within or adjacent to the Historic Area are operated by the Colonial Williamsburg Foundation: the Williamsburg Inn (including the

Colonial Houses and Taverns, and Providence Hall), the Williamsburg Lodge, the Motor House, the Cascades, and the nearby Governor's Inn. For reservations at any of these Colonial Williamsburg Foundation-owned properties, call the **Visitor Center reservations service** (tel. toll free 800/HISTORY).

Very Expensive

WILLIAMSBURG INN, Francis St. (P.O. Box B), Williamsburg, VA 23187. Tel. 804/229-1000, or toll free 800/HISTORY. Fax 804/220-7096. 102 rms. A/C TV TEL

$ Rates: $165–$235 single or double. Children 18 and under stay free in parents' room. AE, MC, V. **Parking:** Free.

One of the nation's most distinguished hotels, this rambling white-brick Regency-style inn has played host to hundreds of VIP guests, including heads of state from 17 countries and U.S. Presidents Truman, Eisenhower, Nixon, Ford, and Reagan.

The lobby lounge is graced with Federal-style furnishings and two working fireplaces. Complimentary high tea is served every afternoon in the Regency Lounge and the East Lounge. Rooms are exquisitely furnished in Regency reproductions, and guests are pampered with remote-controled TVs; French-milled soap, hairdryers, and terry-cloth robes in the bath; and fresh flowers. A special reduced-price ticket to the Historic Area is sold at the concierge desk daily. All guests staying in official Colonial Williamsburg hotels are invited to a special 2-hour guided walking tour of the Historic Area.

In addition to accommodations in the main inn building, there are some 84 rooms close by in the Historic Area in the perfectly charming **Colonial Houses and Taverns.** Tastefully furnished with 18th-century antiques and reproductions, they are variously equipped with canopied beds, kitchens, living rooms, fireplaces, and/or sizable gardens. Breakfast for two at Shields' Taverns is included in the rates, which range from $99 to $211.

Adjacent to the inn and golf course in a modern building called **Providence Hall,** rooms are furnished in contemporary style with balconies or patios overlooking a beautiful wooded area. Complete services are provided by the inn. Rates, from $89 to $165, offer exceptionally good value.

Dining/Entertainment: The inn's Regency Lounge offers cocktails and entertainment nightly. The Regency Dining Room is a very elegant venue for breakfast, lunch, and dinner. The menu features classic American cuisine at its finest. Dinner entrees ($23 to $29) run the gamut from Maine lobster and scallops (with new potatoes, artichokes, and carrots in a sherry-basil cream) to rack of lamb provençal (with eggplant and pepper timbale) and vegetables. Regency Sunday brunch ($19.75) is served from noon to 2pm.

Services: Nightly bed turndown with chocolates, concierge, room service 7am to midnight, babysitting.

Facilities: Croquet, Tazewell Club Fitness Center in the lodge available for inn guests, two golf courses, lawn bowling, two outdoor pools, eight tennis courts.

Expensive

WILLIAMSBURG LODGE, S. England St. (P.O. Box B), Williamsburg, VA 23187. Tel. 804/229-1000, or toll free 800/HISTORY. Fax 804/220-7685. 315 rms. A/C TV TEL

$ Rates: $69–$116 single or double in Main and South wings, $85–$164 single or double in Tazewell and West wings. Children under 18 stay free in parents' room. Extra person $12. AE, MC, V. **Parking:** Free.

If there's no room at the inn, or in your budget, consider the adjacent Williamsburg Lodge, offering all the sports facilities of the inn and a pleasantly rustic interior. The flagstone-floored lobby is indeed lodgelike, with raw pine paneling and a large working fireplace. And there's a covered veranda with rocking chairs overlooking two swimming pools and a golf course. Accommodations are contemporary but warm and homey, with pretty print bedspreads, thick shag rugs, arched windows, and pine furnishings. West Wing rooms have window walls overlooking duck ponds or the Colonial Parkway. They're furnished in oak, cane, and bamboo, and 12 have working fireplaces. The Tazewell Wing is built around a central landscaped courtyard with informal lounge areas on all three floors. Guest rooms are attractively furnished with reproductions inspired by pieces in the Abby Aldrich Rockefeller Folk Art Center.

Dining/Entertainment: The attractive Bay Room overlooks a garden and fountain. On Friday and Saturday nights it features a Chesapeake Bay Feast, and on Sunday an omelet brunch buffet is the draw. The Garden Lounge has drinks and musical entertainment from early afternoon.

Facilities: All inn facilities are available to lodge guests. The Tazewell Health Club is in the lodge.

Moderate

THE CASCADES, Rte. 123, off U.S. 60 Bypass (P.O. Box B), Williamsburg, VA 23187. Tel. 804/229-1000, or toll free 800/HISTORY. 96 suites. A/C TV TEL
$ Rates: $39–$98 single or double. Children under 18 stay free in parents' room. Extra person $8. AE, MC, V. **Parking:** Free.
A good choice for families, the Cascades, on the Visitors Center grounds, offers suites only, each with a bedroom furnished with a king-size bed, a separate study/sitting room with a work desk, and a sitting area. A pull-down bed is useful for extra sleeping space. The look is contemporary. The Cascades Restaurant and cafeteria is conveniently nearby, with outdoor tables for good-weather dining. All the facilities listed below for the Motor House are easily accessible to Cascades guests.

Budget

GOVERNOR'S INN, Rte. 132 (Henry St.) (P.O. Box B), Williamsburg, VA 23187. Tel. 804/229-1000, or toll free 800/HISTORY. 200 rms. A/C TV TEL
$ Rates: $46–$75. AE, MC, V. **Parking:** Free. **Closed:** Jan–Feb.
Least expensive of the Colonial Williamsburg hotels, the Governor's Inn was recently taken over by the foundation and completely renovated and redecorated. Furnishings are clean and bright. A new wing was added as well as an outdoor swimming pool. It's near the Visitors Center on Route 123, an extension of Henry Street.

MOTOR HOUSE, Rte. 123, off U.S. 60 Bypass (P.O. Box B), Williamsburg, VA 23187. Tel. 804/229-1000, or toll free 800/HISTORY. Fax 804/220-7941. 219 rms. A/C TV TEL
$ Rates: $29–91 single or double. Children under 18 stay free in parents' room. Extra person $8. AE, MC, V. **Parking:** Free.
Set on 20 wooded acres with picnic tables under the pines, the Motor House offers a lot for your money: You're right behind the Visitors Center; rooms are cheerful, attractive, and equipped with all the modern amenities; facilities include a jogging path, golf putting green, miniature golf course, shuffleboard, playground, horseshoes, volleyball, badminton, a nice-size swimming pool and sun deck, and a toddler's pool. And the Cascades restaurant and cafeteria are steps away.

NEARBY ACCOMMODATIONS

To be sure of getting a room, you're well advised to reserve in advance. The **Williamsburg Hotel/Motel Association** (tel. 804/220-3330, or toll free 800/

446-9244) will make reservations for you in any price range. It's a free service. Their listings include most of the accommodations mentioned below.

Expensive

HOSPITALITY SUITES WILLIAMSBURG, 415 Richmond Rd., Williamsburg, VA 23185. Tel. 804/229-4020. 300 rms, 9 suites. A/C MINIBAR TV TEL

$ Rates: $62–$109 single or double; $100–$150 one-bedroom suite; $135–$185 two-bedroom suite. AE, CB, DC, DISC, MC, V. **Parking:** Free.

Just two blocks from Colonial Williamsburg opposite William and Mary College, this 2½-story red-brick Colonial-style property is entered via a spacious lobby charmingly decorated with 18th-century reproduction furnishings; it has a working fireplace. The hotel is built around a central atrium courtyard with a fountain. An elegant blend of 18th-century, country French, and Oriental pieces make the guest rooms very plush.

Dining/Entertainment: The Colony dining room specializes in colonial fare. A typical menu might include peanut soup, roast beef, roast potatoes, spoon bread, pumpkin fritters, and English trifle for dessert. S.F. Drake's lounge has live entertainment and dancing on weekend nights and holidays.

Services: Concierge.

Facilities: Outdoor pool, gift shop; golf and tennis can be arranged nearby.

KINGSMILL RESORT, 1010 Kingsmill Rd., Williamsburg, VA 23185. Tel. 804/253-1703, or toll free 800/832-5665. Fax 804/253-8246. 300 units. A/C TV TEL **Directions:** From I-64, take Exit 57A (Busch Gardens) and follow Route 199W to Kingsmill Road.

$ Rates: "Value season" (mid-Nov to mid-Mar), $85–$100 studio; $122–$135 one-bedroom; $207–$235 two-bedroom; $292–$335 three-bedroom. "Prime season (mid-Mar to mid-Nov), $110–$138 studio; $165–$186 one-bedroom; $275–$324 two-bedroom; $385–$462 three-bedroom. Golf, tennis, and weekend packages available. AE, CB, DC, DISC, MC, V. **Parking:** Free.

Nestled in a peaceful setting on beautifully landscaped grounds between the James River and Wareham's Pond, the gray clapboard Kingsmill resort complex is just 5 minutes from Colonial Williamsburg. It's very much like a country club, with 2,900 acres of resort facilities, including the world-famous River Course, home of the Anheuser-Busch Golf Classic; the Plantation Course designed by Arnold Palmer; and the Bray Links Par Three (complimentary to guests). Kingsmill accommodations—studios and one-, two-, and three-bedroom units—are in tastefully furnished villas overlooking the James River (most expensive), golf-course fairways, or tennis courts. They're in individually owned and furnished condos, so decors vary from handsome Colonial reproductions to sophisticated contemporary settings. Most have complete kitchens and living rooms with fireplaces. Daily housekeeping service, including fresh linens, is included.

Dining/Entertainment: All five dining rooms feature panoramic views of the James. The Riverview Room is softly lit and elegant, with fresh flowers on pink tablecloths; jackets are required for men at dinner. In the less formal Bray dining room, breakfast, lunch buffets, and à la carte evening meals are reasonably priced. Other casual dining spots are Moody's Tavern, the Peyton Grille, and the Pettus Grille at the golf clubhouse.

Services: Concierge, complimentary shuttle to Colonial Williamsburg and Busch Gardens.

Facilities: Golf, tennis (15 courts), indoor and outdoor pools, racquetball courts, Nautilus exercise room, saunas, Jacuzzi, billiards, marina, gift shop, pro shop.

Moderate

COURTYARD BY MARRIOTT, 470 McLaws Circle, Williamsburg, VA

23185. Tel. 804/221-0700, or toll free 800/321-2211. Fax 804/221-0741. 142 rms, 9 suites. A/C TV TEL **Directions:** From Williamsburg, follow Route 60E for about 2 miles.

$ Rates: $54–$80 single; $79–$90 double; $83–$106 suite. Children under 18 stay free in parents' room. AE, CB, DC, DISC, MC, V. **Parking:** Free.

Housed in a four-story cream stucco building, in an attractively landscaped setting of trees and shrubs, the Courtyard is an attractive hostelry with a pleasant, plant-filled lobby, and a good-size pool. The very nice guest rooms are decorated in pastel tones of pink, beige, and mauve. Furnished with substantial oak pieces, they feature large desks, separate seating areas, clock radios, and in-room coffee or tea. Suites have full sofa-bedded living rooms with extra phones and TVs, plus wet bars with small refrigerators.

Dining/Entertainment: The lobby restaurant offers breakfast and lunch buffets and an à la carte dinner menu.

Services: Concierge.

Facilities: Indoor/outdoor pool, Jacuzzi.

Budget

A boon to budget travelers is the **Williamsburg Hotel Group,** 1408 Richmond Road, Williamsburg, VA 23185 (tel. toll free 800/444-4678). Under their auspices are 10 centrally located hotels (most of them inexpensive, a few more moderate), so one call to the above toll-free number puts you in line for over 1,300 rooms. Five of the properties—**Friendship Inn,** 1413 Richmond Road (tel. 804/229-8551); **Econo Lodge Midtown,** 1408 Richmond Road (tel. 804/229-2981); **Williamsburg TraveLodge,** 1408 Richmond Road (tel. 804/220-2367); **Rodeway Inn,** 1408 Richmond Road (tel. 804/220-9304); and **Carolyn Court,** 1446 Richmond Road (tel. 804/229-6666)—are adjacent to one another in a compound about a mile from the Historic Area. On-premises facilities include three outdoor pools and one indoor pool, a picnic area, games room, wading pool, children's playground, and four restaurants. The complex occupies many attractively landscaped acres.

Rates at these properties mostly range from $30 to $45 single, $40 to $55 double, from November to March, about $10 to $20 higher across the board April to mid-June and in September and October, reaching a peak of $50 to $75 single, $55 to $80 double, from mid-June through the first week in September.

Two additional choices include the following:

THE CEDARS, 616 Jamestown Rd., Williamsburg, VA 23185. Tel. 804/ 229-3591. 9 rms (3 with bath). A/C

$ Rates (including continental breakfast): $55 single or double without bath, $60–$70 single or double with bath. Extra person $5. $125 cottage. No credit cards.

This charming three-story Georgian-style guesthouse, within walking distance of the Historic Area, is only 70 years old, though it seems of an earlier period because it's built of 200-year-old bricks from an old plantation. All rooms are attractively furnished, some with canopied or four-poster beds. They're painted in Williamsburg colors or papered in pretty floral prints. You can also rent a cozy cottage with a fully equipped kitchen; it accommodates up to six. Hostess Gloria Melton is a delightful person and very knowledgeable about local attractions and restaurants. Adjoining rooms with a connecting bath are available for families.

MOTEL 6, 3030 Richmond Rd., Williamsburg, VA 23185. Tel. 804/565-3433. 169 rms (all with bath). A/C TV TEL

$ Rates: $25.95 single; $6 each additional adult. Children under 18 stay free in parents' room. AE, DC, DISC, MC, V.

The only catch to snagging one of the low-priced rooms here is that you usually have to reserve far in advance. A nice swimming pool and sun deck are out back, and a woodsy location is a plus.

WHERE TO DINE

Williamsburg abounds in restaurants catering to the tourist horde. In addition to the restaurants in the Colonial Williamsburg accommodations (see "Where to Stay," above), the Colonial Williamsburg Foundation runs four very popular reconstructed colonial taverns.

COLONIAL WILLIAMSBURG FOUNDATION TAVERNS

If you're planning on dinner at one of these restaurants, make your reservations first thing in the morning—if not a day or two before—by calling the Information Center (tel. 804/229-2141). In the spring-to-fall season it's a good idea to reserve even prior to arrival (you can do so up to 60 days in advance). All are reconstructed 18th-century "ordinaries" or taverns, and aim at authenticity in fare, ambience, and costuming of the staff. All offer al fresco dining in good weather on brick patios under grape arbors. Low-priced children's menus are available.

CHOWNING'S TAVERN, Duke of Gloucester St. Tel. 804/229-2141.
Cuisine: COLONIAL. **Reservations:** Essential.
$ Prices: Appetizers $1.25–$8.25; entrees $12.95–$18.95; fixed-price dinner $19.95. AE, MC, V.
Open: Lunch daily 11:30am–3:30pm; dinner, three seatings nightly 5–8:30pm; refreshments served to 1am.

Chowning's Tavern dates to 1766 when Josiah Chowning announced the opening of a tavern "where all who please to favour me with their custom may depend upon the best of entertainment for themselves, servants, and horses, and good pasturage." It's very charming, with low beamed ceilings, raw pine floors, and sturdy country-made furnishings. There are two working fireplaces, and at night one dines by candlelight.

At lunch there's Welsh rarebit—melted Cheddar cheese blended with beer and seasonings on homemade toast, perhaps followed by buttered apple pie à la mode (made with apples from the Shenandoah Valley). At dinner, bypass the à la carte entrees, and order a fixed-price dinner—plantation vegetable soup, salad with chutney dressing, sautéed backfin crabmeat and ham topped with butter and laced with sherry, vegetable, baked potato, homemade bread, and deep-dish apple pie with Cheddar cheese.

CHRISTINA CAMPBELL'S TAVERN, Waller St. Tel. 804/229-2141.
Cuisine: COLONIAL. **Reservations:** Essential.
$ Prices: Brunch entrees $6.25–$7.75; fixed-price dinner $16. AE, MC, V.
Open: Brunch daily 10am–2:30pm; dinner daily 5:30–9:30pm.

Christina Campbell's Tavern, close to the Capitol, is "where all the best people resorted" circa 1765. George Washington was a regular (in 1772 he recorded in his diary that he dined here 10 times over a 22-month period). After the capital moved to Richmond, business declined and operations eventually ceased. In its heyday, however, the tavern was famous for seafood, and today that is once again the specialty. Campbell's is an authentic reproduction with 18th-century furnishings, blazing fireplaces, and flutists and balladeers to entertain diners.

Brunch, definitely not an 18th-century concept, is served here. Choices include a traditional southern breakfast—mulled apple cider, Virginia ham, fried chicken, scrambled eggs, spiced apples, and coffee, which should keep you going until dinner. Other possibilities are a seafood salad served with spiced peach and fried cabbage or pecan waffles with country sausage and warm maple syrup. The fixed-price dinner includes clam chowder, southern fried chicken, Virginia ham, vegetables, and pumpkin fritters.

KINGS ARMS TAVERN, Duke of Gloucester St. Tel. 804/229-2141.
Cuisine: COLONIAL. **Reservations:** Essential.
$ Prices: Appetizers $1.25–$5.95; entrees $15.45–$19.95; fixed-price dinner $18.45. AE, MC, V.
Open: Lunch daily 11:30am–2:30pm; dinner, with three nightly seatings, 5:15–9:30pm.

The Kings Arms Tavern, on the site of a 1772 establishment, is actually a re-creation of the tavern and an adjoining home. Outbuildings—including stables, a barbershop, laundry, smokehouse, and kitchen—have also been reconstructed. The original proprietress, Mrs. Jane Vobe, was famous for her fine cooking, and her establishment's proximity to the Capitol made it a natural meeting place during Publick Times.

Today the 11 dining rooms (8 with fireplaces) are all painted and furnished following authentic early Virginia precedent. The Queen Anne and Chippendale pieces are typical appointments of this class of tavern, and the prints, maps, engravings, aquatints, and mezzotints lining the walls are genuine examples of Colonial interior decorations. Balladeers wander the rooms during dinner and entertain.

Though the atmosphere is quainter by candlelight, prices are lower at lunch. Midday fare includes items like Smithfield ham and Old English Cheddar cheese on manchet (wheat) bread with Dijon mustard and dill pickle garnish. At dinner there's a fixed-price offering, a nut-soup to nut-pie meal beginning with Virginia peanut soup and continuing with an entree of pan-fried boneless breast of chicken and Smithfield ham in grape sauce, vegetables, salad, Sally Lunn bread, and pecan pie.

SHIELDS TAVERN, Duke of Gloucester St. Tel. 804/229-2141.
Cuisine: COLONIAL. **Reservations:** Essential.
$ Prices: Appetizers $1.75–$6.95; entrees $14.95–$18.25. AE, MC, V.
Open: Breakfast daily 8:30–10am; lunch daily 11:30am–3:30pm; dinner daily 5:30–9:30pm.

With 11 dining rooms and a garden under a wisteria-covered arbor that seats 200, Shields is the largest of the Historic Area's tavern/restaurants. It's named for James Shields who, with his wife, Anne, and family, ran a much-frequented hostelry on this site in the mid-1700s. Using a room-by-room inventory of Shields's personal effects—and as a result of detailed archeological investigation—the tavern has been furnished with items similar to those used in the mid-18th century and many of the rooms have working fireplaces. A specially designed rotisserie unit in the kitchen allows chefs here to approximate 18th-century roasting techniques.

Shields is the only tavern open for breakfast—a simple affair offering homemade breads, sweet-potato muffins, juice, and coffee. Luncheon entrees range from sautéed filet of perch with cole slaw and red potatoes to a ploughman's lunch of bread, cheese, ham, pickled onions, grapes, and an apple. Dinner might begin with cream of crayfish soup, continue with an entree of baked pork chop with Virginia apple stuffing, and conclude with cranberry-apple pie. And at either meal you might try a Shields sampler platter of 18th-century foods like meat pasties, Indian corn pudding, and sillabub. Menus here change daily. Gambols—music, games, and other diversions—take place on the lower level from 9pm to midnight.

OTHER HISTORIC AREA RESTAURANTS

Expensive

TRELLIS CAFE, RESTAURANT & GRILL, Duke of Gloucester St., Merchant Sq. Tel. 804/229-8610.

Cuisine: AMERICAN. **Reservations:** Suggested at dinner.
$ Prices: Appetizers $3.50–$7.50; entrees $14–$23; fixed-price dinner $18–$30. AE, MC, V.
Open: Mon–Sat 11:30am–9:30pm, Sun 11:30am–3pm and 5–9:30pm.

★ *The New York Times* has called the Trellis "the best restaurant in this part of Virginia." Evocative of California's delightful wine-country restaurants in both decor and exciting, contemporary cuisine, it is entered via a grapevine-covered trellis. Inside, the Garden Room is the plushest setting, with apricot velvet furnishings. The Trellis Room is country-contemporary in feel, with forest-green upholstered pine furnishings and walls minimally adorned with vineyard baskets full of dried flowers and antique French farm implements. In the Grill Room, you can watch food being prepared over an open hearth using Texas mesquite wood. Very cozy is the Vault Room, with tables under an arched ceiling of narrow heart-of-pine beams. In the Café Bar walls are hung with antique wine-motif prints. And if the weather is fine, you might dine al fresco on the planter-bordered brick terrace.

The extensive and varied menu offers diners choices at several price levels. Selections change seasonally. Luncheon entrees ($6 to $9) might include a sandwich of lemon-marinated chicken breast seared over mesquite wood served on hot, crusty French bread. At dinner the light menu served in the Café Bar and outdoor terrace features items like a hearty serving of Chesapeake chowder or Trellis quiche. Other menus list more serious (and pricier) entrees, such as grilled rainbow trout with sautéed fresh lump crabmeat and pan-seared pork medallions with sautéed apples and roasted shallots. There's a well-chosen wine list, and at least two premium wines are always offered by the glass. For dessert, the chocolate temptation is not to be believed.

Moderate

LE CLOS DES MARCHANDS, 433 Prince George St., Merchants Sq. Tel. 804/220-3636.
Cuisine: FRENCH. **Reservations:** Suggested for dinner.
$ Prices: Appetizers $1.95–$6.95; entrees $10.95–$18.95. MC, V.
Open: Lunch daily 11:30am–2:30pm; dinner daily 5:30–9:30pm.

This charming little eatery offers "honest French fare" at reasonable prices. Parisian-born owner Danielle Bourderau oversees the kitchen, turning out traditional daily specialties like blanquette de veau, bouillabaisse, boeuf bourguignon, and navarin d'agneau. Lace-café-curtained windows, seating in bentwood chairs at marble-top pedestal tables, French music, and a checkerboard floor create a bistro ambience. Everything here is made from scratch, even the fresh-baked baguettes. At lunch you can get a sandwich, perhaps chicken breast with homemade herb mayonnaise or a niçoise pan bagnat stuffed with tuna, sliced egg, salad, and anchovies. Other choices include a salade niçoise and crêpes filled with salmon mousse. At dinner, begin with escargots de Bourgogne, or goat cheese profiteroles on tomato coulis. Couscous with lamb, merguez sausage, and chicken is an excellent entree choice. And for dessert there's homemade ice cream. Premium French wines are available by the glass.

Inexpensive

A GOOD PLACE TO EAT, 410 Duke of Gloucester St., Merchants Sq. Tel. 804/229-1000, ext. 2002.
Cuisine: AMERICAN.
$ Prices: Breakfast $2.50–$4.50; lunch/dinner $5–$11. No credit cards.
Open: Sept to mid-June, daily 7:30am–8pm; mid-June to Aug, daily 7:30am–10pm.

This is an especially good place for family meals. The food is high quality for a cafeteria operation—burger meat is prepared from the best cuts of chuck and round, breads and cakes are fresh baked, even the ice cream is homemade. And the setting is rather attractive. There's a big indoor dining room with terra-cotta-tile floors, imitation-oak Formica tables, and many hanging plants. Better yet is the outdoor seating at umbrella tables on a geranium-bordered brick patio.

Stop by for an inexpensive breakfast of scrambled eggs and ham with homemade biscuits, a croissant, or a sweet-potato muffin and coffee. At lunch or dinner you can get a turkey sandwich, hamburger, or chef's salad. Leave room for a sundae with homemade ice cream and fresh whipped cream.

Picnic Fare & Where to Eat it

There are benches throughout the restored area (lots of grass, too), and if you have a car you can drive to nearby scenic picnic areas off Colonial Parkway. **The Cheese Shop,** 424 Prince George Street in Merchants Square, between North Boundary Street and North Henry Street (tel. 804/220-0298), is a good place to purchase the fixings. Open Monday through Saturday from 10am to 6pm.

NEARBY RESTAURANTS
Moderate

LE YACA, Rte. 60E, in the Village Shops at Kingsmill. Tel. 804/ 220-3616.
   Cuisine: FRENCH. **Reservations:** Suggested.
$ **Prices:** Appetizers $3–$5.50; entrees $10–$20; fixed-price dinner $16–$39. AE, CB, DC, MC, V.
   Open: Lunch Mon–Sat 11:30am–2pm; dinner Mon–Sat 6–9:30pm.

Centered on a large open hearth on which a leg of lamb is often roasting, creating a tantalizing aroma, Le Yaca is charmingly provincial, with glossy oak floors, rough-hewn beams overhead, and romantic soft lighting from oil candles and shaded lamps. Pale-peach walls are hung with lovely prints of Paris scenes. At lunch a create-your-own-salad table has all you might desire of 15 scrumptious French salads including, perhaps, pasta salad with smoked duck, cucumber in fresh cream, potato salad with lamb, carrots rapé, seafood and rice, and tomato vinaigrette; fresh-baked bread and butter is included. A fixed-price dinner might begin with a heavenly cream of onion soup, an entree of fresh sea scallops in tangy chablis butter, an array of fresh vegetables, salad, and for dessert, a marquise au chocolate—rich chocolate truffles afloat on crème anglaise.

Inexpensive

OLD CHICKAHOMINY HOUSE, 1211 Jamestown Rd., at Rte. 199. Tel. 804/229-4689.
   Cuisine: TRADITIONAL SOUTHERN.
$ **Prices:** Breakfast $3–$6.25; lunch $3.95–$7.50. V.
   Open: Daily 8:30am–2 or 3pm.

The Old Chickahominy House is a reconstructed 18th-century house with mantels from old Gloucester homes and wainscoting from Carter's Grove. Floors are bare oak, and walls, painted in traditional Colonial colors are hung with gilt-framed 17th- and 18th-century oil paintings. Three adjoining rooms house an antique/gift shop. The entire effect is extremely cozy and charming, from the rocking chairs on the front porch to the blazing fireplaces within.

Authentic southern fare is featured at breakfast and lunch. The house specialty in the morning is the plantation breakfast—real Virginia ham with two eggs, biscuits, cured country bacon and sausage, grits, and coffee. At lunch, Miss Melinda's special is a cup of Brunswick stew with Virginia ham on hot biscuits, fruit salad, homemade pie, and tea or coffee. After dining it's fun to roam through the warren of antique-filled rooms. Also check out the Shirley Pewter Shop next door.

PIERCE'S PITT BAR-B-QUE, Rochambeau Dr. (I-64 access road, F-137). Tel. 804/565-2955.
   Cuisine: SOUTHERN.
$ Prices: Most items under $3; barbecue dinner $4.95. No credit cards.
   Open: Sun–Thurs 11am–8pm, Fri–Sat 11am–9pm.

A mecca for local barbecue aficionados, Pierce's offers the traditional no-frills setting. Doc Pierce, founder of the restaurants, sets high standards. Boston butts are cooked on an open pit over oak and hickory wood. From the open pit the pork butts are pulled by hand into bite-size chunks, then spiced with a secret sauce. Also on the menu—Brunswick stew and barbecued chicken, plus homemade side dishes like cole slaw, beans, french fries, onion rings, and hush puppies. There's usually a line at the counter where you place your order, but it's worth the wait.

2. JAMESTOWN

9 miles SW of Williamsburg

GETTING THERE   By Car   From Williamsburg, follow the Jamestown Road, Route 31S, or the Colonial Parkway.

ESSENTIALS   For **information** about Jamestown Settlement, write P.O. Box JF, Williamsburg, VA 23187 (tel. 804/229-1607). See below for **block-ticket** information combining admissions with Yorktown Victory Center.

The story of Jamestown, the first English settlement in the New World, is documented here in museum exhibits and living-history interpretations. The exploits of Capt. John Smith, leader of the colony; his legendary rescue from execution by the Indian princess Pocahontas; and a vivid picture of life in 17th-century Virginia are all part of the first chapter of American history, re-created near the original site of the first colony. Archeologists have excavated more than 100 building frames, evidences of manufacturing ventures (pottery, winemaking, brick making, and glass blowing), early wells, and old roads, as well as millions of artifacts of everyday life—tools, utensils, ceramic dishes, armor, keys, and the like.
   Allow a full day for your visit, and consider packing a picnic lunch. Other than a cafeteria at Jamestown Settlement, there are no restaurants, but there are scenic picnic areas along the parkway (the nicest is called Great Neck).

WHAT TO SEE & DO
JAMESTOWN SETTLEMENT

This indoor/outdoor museum, operated by the Commonwealth of Virginia, is open daily except New Years and Christmas days. The outdoor exhibit areas are closed in January and February. Basic hours of 9am to 5pm daily are extended to 7pm June 15 through August 15. Admission is $7 for adults, $3.50 for children 6 to 12 (under 6, free).
   If you're also planning to visit the Yorktown Victory Center (it doesn't have to be the same day), purchase a money-saving **combination ticket** to both museums at $9.60 for adults, $4.80 for children.
   A fast-food restaurant is on the premises and parking is free.
   After purchasing tickets, you can browse in a changing-exhibit gallery just off the lobby and then enter an orientation **theater** to watch a 20-minute film that provides an introduction to Jamestown.
   Beyond the theater, three large permanent **museum** galleries feature artifacts, documents, decorative objects, dioramas, and graphics relating to the Jamestown

period. The English Gallery focuses on Jamestown's beginnings in the Old World. A Powhatan Indian Gallery explores the origins and culture of the Native Americans who lived near Jamestown. The Jamestown Gallery deals with the history of the colony during its first century of existence.

Leaving the museum complex, visitors come directly into the **Powhatan Indian Village,** representing the culture and technology of a highly organized chiefdom of 32 tribes that inhabited coastal Virginia in the early 17th century. There are several mat-covered lodges, or "longhouses," which are furnished as dwellings, as well as a garden and a ceremonial dance circle. Historical interpreters tend gardens, tan animal hides, and make bone and antler tools, flint-knap projectile points, and pottery.

Triangular **James Fort** is a re-creation of the one constructed by the Jamestown colonists on their arrival in the spring of 1607. Inside the wooden stockade are 18 primitive wattle-and-daub structures with thatched roofs representing Jamestown's earliest buildings. Interpreters are engaged in activities typical of early 17th-century life, such as agriculture, animal care, carpentry, blacksmithing, and meal preparation.

A short walk from James Fort are reproductions of the three **ships** that transported 104 colonists to Virginia in 1607. Visitors can board and explore the largest ship, the 110-foot *Susan Constant,* and talk with an interpreter about the 4½-month voyage from England. The *Godspeed* retraced the 1607 voyage from England to Virginia in 1985. The smallest ship, the *Discovery,* is often open to visitors in the summer and for special events. It is used for demonstrations of 17th-century sailing techniques.

JAMESTOWN ISLAND

When you leave the Settlement, go back to the Colonial Parkway and turn right. You'll soon come to the Ranger Station entrance gate where a $5-per-car admission is charged to visit Jamestown Island. The gate is open daily from 8:30am to 4:30pm in winter, with extended hours spring through fall. If any of the occupants of your car is a senior citizen—62 or over—the car is admitted free.

Exploration of the actual site of the first permanent English settlement in America begins at the **Visitor Center** here (tel. 804/229-1733). Open daily except Christmas (from 9am to 5pm in winter, with extended hours spring through fall), it contains an information desk, an exhibit area, and a theater in which a 12-minute orientation film is shown every half hour. Allow at least 2 hours for this attraction.

Exhibits document the 92 years when Jamestown was capital of Virginia. An area focusing on possessions brought from England features artifacts of the home. From the Visitor Center, a footpath leads through the actual site of **"James Cittie,"** where reconstructed rubbly brick foundations of 17th-century homes, taverns, shops, and statehouses are enhanced by artists' renderings and recorded narratives. Spring through fall there are frequent half-hour guided tours of the site, and in summer there are living-history programs. Most complete are the remains of the tower of one of the first brick churches built in Virginia (1639). Directly behind the tower is the **Memorial Church,** a 1907 gift of the Colonial Dames of America. It houses remnants of early Jamestown churches.

The footpath continues to the seawall, believed to be the site of the original James Fort and the May 13, 1607, landing site. There are many **monuments and memorials** throughout James Cittie, including a memorial cross marking some 300 shallow graves of colonists who died during the "Starving Time," the winter of 1609–10.

At the **Dale House,** near the statehouse ruins, there are demonstrations of 17th-century pottery making.

A fascinating **5-mile loop drive** (beginning at the Visitor Center parking lot) winds through 1,500 wilderness acres of woodland and marsh that have been allowed to return to their natural state in order to approximate the landscape as 17th-century settlers found it. Markers and large paintings interpret aspects of the daily activities of the colonists—tobacco growing, lumbering, silk production, pottery making, farming, etc. There is a 3-mile loop if your time is limited.

Before leaving Jamestown Island, stop at the remains of America's first factory, the **Glasshouse,** a 1608 glassworks on the shore of the James where settlers attempted to make glass of coarse river sand. Nearby is a thatch-roofed reproduction of the original building with a working 17th-century-style furnace. Inside, costumed artisans create simple glass objects. Open daily from 8:30am to 5pm in winter, to 5:30pm in spring and fall, to 6pm in summer.

3. YORKTOWN

14 miles NE of Williamsburg

GETTING THERE   By Car   From Williamsburg, drive to the eastern end of the Colonial Parkway.

ESSENTIALS   The **telephone area code** is 804. The **information office** is at the battlefield, Route 238 at Colonial Parkway, Yorktown, VA 23690 (tel. 804/887-1776).

Yorktown was the setting for the last major battle of the American Revolution. Here, on October 19, 1781, George Washington wrote to the president of the Continental Congress, "I have the Honor to inform Congress, that a Reduction of the British Army under the Command of Lord Cornwallis, is most happily effected." Though it would be 2 years before a peace treaty was signed, and sporadic fighting would continue, the Revolution, for all intents and purposes, had been won.

Though tourist attention focuses to a large degree on the town's role as the final Revolutionary battlefield, Yorktown is also of interest as one of America's earliest colonial towns.

HISTORY

BEFORE THE REVOLUTION

Though a number of settlers lived and farmed in the area by the 1630s, Yorktown's history really dates to 1691 when the General Assembly at Jamestown (then Virginia's capital) passed the Port Act creating a new town on the site. To encourage the development of the town, 50 acres were purchased from Benjamin Read for 10,000 pounds of "merchantable sweet-scented tobacco and cask," then broken into 85 half-acre lots, and sold for 180 pounds of tobacco each. By the end of the century Yorktown was on the way to becoming a principal mid-Atlantic port and a center of tobacco trade.

In the 18th century Yorktown was a thriving metropolis with a population of several thousand planters, innkeepers, seamen, merchants, craftsmen, indentured servants, and slaves. After the waterfront officially became part of the town in 1738, Water Street, paralleling the river, was lined with shops, inns, and loading docks.

THE VICTORY AT YORKTOWN

The siege began on September 28, 1781, when American and French troops under Washington occupied a line encircling the town within a mile of the army led by Cornwallis. The allied army of 17,000 men, spread out in camps extending 6 miles, dug siege lines and bombarded the redcoats with cannonfire. British defeat was inevitable.

Cornwallis compounded his tactical errors by evacuating almost all his positions except for Redoubts (forts) 9 and 10 in order to concentrate his troops closer to town and better defend it. Washington was thus able to move his men to within 1,000 yards of British lines. By October 9 the allies were ready to respond to British artillery. But they didn't wait to respond. The French were the first to fire. Two hours later George Washington personally fired the first American round. By October 10 the British were nearly silenced. On October 11 the allies moved up about another 500 yards.

On October 14 the French stormed Redoubt 9 while the Continentals made short work of Redoubt 10. Both columns began their assaults at 8pm. The Americans were through by 8:10pm; the French, whose target was stronger, by 8:30pm.

On October 16, following a last-ditch and fruitless attempt to launch an attack on the allies, a desperate Cornwallis tried to escape with his troops across the York River to Gloucester Point, but a violent storm scattered his ships. On October 17 at 10am a British drummer appeared on the rampart. He beat out a signal indicating a desire to discuss terms with the enemy. A cease-fire was called, and a British officer was led to American lines where he requested an armistice. On October 18 commissioners met at the house of Augustine Moore (see "What to See and Do," below) and worked out the terms of surrender.

On October 19, 1781, at 2pm the French and Continental armies lined Surrender Road, each stretching for over a mile on either side. The French were resplendent in immaculate white uniforms, their officers plumed and decorated; the Americans were in rags and tatters. The British army (about 5,000 British soldiers and seamen), clad in new uniforms, marched between them out of Yorktown to a band playing a tune called "The World Turned Upside Down." General Charles O'Hara of the British Guards represented Cornwallis who, pleading illness, did not surrender in person.

The battle marked the end of British rule in America and made a permanent place for Yorktown in the annals of American history.

AFTER THE REVOLUTION

Though it is doubtful that Yorktown would have recovered from the destruction and waste that accompanied the Siege of 1781, it received the coup de grace in the "Great Fire" of 1814 and declined steadily over the years, becoming a quiet rural village. In fact, like Williamsburg, it changed so little that many of the picturesque old streets, buildings, and battle sites have survived intact to this day. Today most of Yorktown— including the surrounding battlefield areas—is part of the 9,300-acre Colonial National Historical Park.

WHAT TO SEE & DO

YORKTOWN VICTORY CENTER

✪ First stop is the Yorktown Victory Center (tel. 804/887-1776), open daily except New Year's and Christmas days from 9am to 5pm. Set on 21 acres overlooking part of the battlefield of 1781, it offers an excellent orientation to Yorktown attractions, including a film, a living-history program, and museum exhibits. Admission is $5 for adults, $2.50 for children 6 to 12 (under 6, free); or you can purchase a **combination ticket** for this and Jamestown Settlement at $9.60 for adults, $4.80 for children 6 to 12 (under 6, free).

Visitors follow a timeline walkway, **"Road to Revolution,"** to the main building. Exhibits located in pavilions along the way illustrate the relationship between the Colonies and Britain beginning in 1750. The timeline ends inside the main building with an exhibit on the first battles of the war and a 12-foot-tall copy of the Declaration of Independence.

Aspects of the American Revolution are explored in three **gallery exhibits.** "Witnesses to Revolution" focuses on ordinary individuals who recorded their observances of the war and its impact on their lives. "At Water's Edge: The Towns of York and Gloucester" shows those towns' roles as port and urban centers in the 18th century. "Yorktown's Sunken Fleet" uses artifacts recovered from British ships sunk during the siege of Yorktown to describe shipboard life.

In the outdoor **Continental army camp,** costumed interpreters re-create the lives of men and women who took part in the American Revolution. There are presentations on weaponry, military drills and tactics, medicine, and cookery.

The Road to Yorktown, an evocative 28-minute documentary film produced by David Wolper (of *Roots* fame), follows the movements of Generals Washington and Rochambeau and documents the final grueling days of the Revolution.

YORKTOWN BATTLEFIELD VISITOR CENTER

After you've seen the Yorktown Victory Center, head over to **National Park Service Visitor Center** (tel. 804/898-3400), starting point for self-guided auto tours of the battlefield and a full-service information center. Here, too, there's an orientation film. This 16-minute documentary called *Siege at Yorktown* is about the formal surrender of the British and their German mercenary allies.

Museum displays include Washington's actual military headquarters tent, a replica (which you can board and explore) of the quarterdeck of H.M.S. *Charon,* additional objects recovered from the York River in the excavations, exhibits about Cornwallis's surrender and the events leading up to it, and dioramas detailing the siege. Upstairs, an "on-the-scene" account of the Battle of Yorktown is given by a 13-year-old soldier in the Revolutionary army, his taped narrative accompanied by a sound-and-light show.

National Park Service Rangers are on hand to answer questions. Spring and fall weekends, and daily in summer, they give free **tours** of the British inner defense line. The center is open daily except Christmas from 9am to 5pm, with extended hours spring through fall.

TOURING THE BATTLEFIELD

The National Park Service Visitor Center is the starting point for the 7.7-mile Red Arrow route and the 10.2-mile Yellow Arrow route auto tours of the battlefield. You'll be given a map indicating both routes and detailing major sites. At each stop there are explanatory historical markers (sometimes taped narratives as well), but for the most interesting experience, rent a cassette player and tape at the Visitor Center. Narrated by "British and American colonels" whose polite hostilities to each other are most amusing, the taped commentary further elucidates the battlefield sites. You won't stay in your car the whole time; it's frequently necessary to park, get out, and walk to redoubts and earthworks. A lot of the drive is very scenic, winding through woods and fields abundant with birdlife; the Yellow route is especially beautiful. If you purchase the cassette, listen to the introduction in the parking lot; it will tell you when to depart. Auto tour highlights include:

The Grand French Battery This was a large artillery area in the French section of the first siege line. Here French soldiers manning cannons, mortars, and howitzers fired on British and German mercenary troops.

The Moore House When Lord Cornwallis realized the inevitability of his defeat, he sent a message to General Washington: "Sir, I propose a cessation of hostilities for twenty-four hours, and that two officers may be appointed by each side, to meet at Mr. Moore's house, to settle terms for the surrender of the posts of York and Gloucester." General Washington granted Cornwallis just 2 hours to submit general terms. On the afternoon of October 18, 1781, two British commissioners, Col. Thomas Dundas and Maj. Alexander Ross, met in "Mr. Moore's house" with

American Col. John Laurens and French representative the Viscount de Noailles. Negotiations went on late into the evening, the British protesting terms of Article III, which required them to march out of Yorktown "with shouldered arms, colors cased [that means flags furled], and drums beating a British or German march." They finally agreed to the humiliating exit, and negotiations wound up just before midnight. Washington made a few adjustments, the Articles of Capitulation were signed by Cornwallis and his senior naval officer, and the document was delivered back to Washington.

The Moore House has a long history. In the early 1700s Lawrence Smith constructed the two-story white frame building that would become Moore House when the property went to his daughter, Lucy, and her husband, Augustine Moore. Though surviving the battle of Yorktown unscathed, Moore House suffered considerable damage during military action in the Civil War. Shellfire destruction was aggravated by soldiers stripping away siding and other usable wood for fuel. The house was pretty much abandoned (sometimes even used as a cow barn) until John D. Rockefeller, Jr., purchased it in 1931 and the National Park Service restored it to its Colonial appearance. It is today furnished with appropriate period pieces, some of which are believed to have been in the house during the surrender negotiations. It's open spring and fall weekends from 1 to 5pm; in summer, daily with extended hours. Twenty-minute living-history tours are presented daily in summer.

Surrender Field   Here your imagination, stoked by visions from orientation films, can evoke the British march out of Yorktown. William Conrad narrates the story of the surrender scene from a pavilion overlooking the field. Surrender cannons encircle the pavilion below.

Along the Yellow Arrow route you'll come to the sites of Washington's and Rochambeau's headquarters, a French cemetery and Artillery Park, and allied encampment sites.

TOURING THE TOWN

Self-guided walking tours of Old Yorktown—including some places of interest not related to the famed battle—are available at the Battlefield Visitor Center. Begin your ramble close to the center at:

The Victory Monument   News of the allied victory at Yorktown reached Philadelphia on October 24, 1781. On October 29 Congress resolved "that the United States . . . will cause to be erected at York, in Virginia, a marble column, adorned with emblems of the alliance between the United States and his Most Christian Majesty; and inscribed with a succinct narrative of the surrender of Earl Cornwallis to his excellency General Washington, Commander in Chief of the combined forces of America and France. . . ."

All very well in theory, but due to financial difficulties no action was taken for a century. Finally, on October 18, 1881, the cornerstone for the monument was laid by Masons as an appropriate opening to the Yorktown Centennial Celebration. The highly symbolic 98-foot marble shaft overlooking the York River was completed in 1884. The podium is adorned with 13 female figures hand in hand in a solemn dance to denote the unity of the 13 colonies; beneath their feet is the inscription ONE COUNTRY, ONE CONSTITUTION, ONE DESTINY, a moving post–Civil War sentiment. The column itself symbolizes the greatness and prosperity of the nation, and its stars represent the "constellation" of states in the Union in 1881. Atop the shaft is the figure of Liberty.

Cornwallis Cave   According to legend, Cornwallis lived here in two tiny "rooms" during the final days of the siege when he hoped to withdraw to the river and escape overland to New York. The two rooms were carved out by various occupants of the cave—which may at one time have included the pirate Blackbeard—and Confederate soldiers later enlarged the shelter and added a roof. A taped narrative at the entrance tells the story. The cave is at the foot of Great Valley, right on the river.

The Dudley Digges House   You can only view the restored 18th-century white weatherboard house on Main Street and Smith Street from the outside—it's a private residence, not open to the public. Its dormer windows set in the roofline, and surrounding outbuildings, are typical of Virginia architecture in the mid-1700s. Owner Dudley Digges was a Revolutionary patriot who served with Patrick Henry, Benjamin Harrison, and Thomas Jefferson on the Committee of Correspondence. After the war he was rector of the College of William and Mary.

The Nelson House   Scottish merchant Thomas Nelson made three voyages between Great Britain and Virginia before deciding to settle in Yorktown in 1705. He proceeded to sire a dynasty and by 1707 he had acquired two lots, along with a number of slaves, and built himself a house at Main Street and Nelson Street. Between 1711 and 1723 he obtained title to several other lots and became co-operator of a ferry, charter member of a trading company, builder of the Swan Tavern, trustee of York's port land, and a large-scale planter. By 1728 he had added 600 acres, a private warehouse and wharf, and a mill to his holdings. He died in 1745 leaving a vast estate, which his descendants—who included several prominent Revolutionary leaders, one of them a signer of the Declaration of Independence—further enlarged.

   Though damaged (cannonballs remain embedded in the brickwork), the house survived the Battle of Yorktown (Cornwallis seized it for a command post during part of his occupation) and Nelson's descendants continued to occupy the house through 1907. The National Park Service acquired the house in 1968 and restored it to its original appearance.

   It is open daily in summer and during the December holiday season (check at the Visitor Center for a schedule). Ranger-guided tours take 30 to 45 minutes.

The Sessions House   Just across from the Nelson House, this is the oldest house in Yorktown, built in 1692 by Thomas Sessions. At least five U.S. Presidents have visited the house, today a private residence off-limits to the public. You may, however, stare at it.

The Customhouse   Dating to 1721, this sturdy brick building at the corner of Main and Read was originally the private storehouse of Richard Ambler, collector of ports. It became Gen. J. B. Magruder's headquarters during the Civil War. Today it is maintained by the Daughters of the American Revolution as a museum, open on weekends only (call 804/898-4788 for exact hours).

Grace Episcopal Church   Located on Church Street near the river, Grace Church originally dates to 1697 and has been an active house of worship since then. Its first rector, the Rev. Anthony Panton, was dismissed for calling the secretary of the colony a jackanapes. Gunpowder and ammunition were stored here during the siege of Yorktown. And during the Civil War the church served as a hospital. It's open to visitors daily from 9am to 5pm. The original communion silver, made in England in 1649, is still in use. Thomas Nelson (II) is buried in the adjacent graveyard.

The Swan Tavern   For over a century the Swan Tavern, at the corner of Main Street and Ballard Street (tel. 804/898-3033), was Yorktown's leading hostelry. Originally owned by Thomas Nelson, it was in operation 20 years before Williamsburg's famous Raleigh. The Swan was demolished in 1863 by an ammunition explosion at the courthouse across the street, rebuilt, and destroyed again by fire in 1915. Today it is reconstructed as per historical research, and the premises house a fine antique shop. Call for hours.

WHERE TO DINE

Consider a **picnic** lunch in a large tree-shaded area at the Victory Center, or at a waterfront picnic area with tables and grills at the foot of Comte de Grasse Street near the cofferdam. There's another gorgeous picnic area called **Ringfield,** 7 miles from Williamsburg on the Colonial Parkway.

NICK'S SEAFOOD PAVILION, Water St. Tel. 804/887-5269.

Cuisine: AMERICAN/SEAFOOD. **Reservations:** Recommended, especially in summer for dinner.

$ Prices: Appetizers $2–$5; entrees $8–$25. AE, CB, DC, MC, V.

Open: Lunch Mon–Fri 11:30am–2pm; dinner Mon–Thurs 4:30–11pm, Fri–Sat 4–11pm.

Behind its weathered clapboard exterior, Nick's interior is an exuberant surprise. Several spacious dining rooms are bedecked with reproductions of classic stone statuary, mosaic tiles, plants, fountains, and oil paintings. Soft-shell crabs sautéed in butter, broiled tuna or mahi mahi, and broiled lobster are menu standbys, along with nonseafood entrees ranging from pork tenderloin to pheasant and quail dishes. There's baked Alaska for dessert.

CHAPTER 12

NORFOLK, VIRGINIA BEACH, & THE EASTERN SHORE

1. NORFOLK
2. VIRGINIA BEACH
3. THE EASTERN SHORE

Norfolk, home to a major naval base, is a bustling, cosmopolitan metropolis with a thriving downtown centered around the Waterside, "a festival marketplace." About 20 minutes southeast, you'll find Virginia Beach, a classic resort, with a magnificent white sand beach. Drive across the 17-mile Chesapeake Bay Bridge-Tunnel and shift into a more relaxed mode as you traverse the rural Delmarva Peninsula to Chincoteague Island, on Virginia's peaceful Eastern Shore. And nature-lovers will delight in the pristine Assateague Wildlife Refuge.

---

1. NORFOLK

190 miles SE of Washington, D.C.; 93 miles E of Richmond

GETTING THERE   By Plane   The **Norfolk International Airport,** bordering the Botanic Gardens at Norview Avenue, 1½ miles east of I-64 (tel. 804/857-3351), serves the Norfolk/Virginia Beach metropolitan area. There is no bus service into Norfolk, but taxis, rental cars, and limousines are at the airport.

By Train   The nearest **Amtrak** station is 21 miles away in Newport News, at 9304 Warwick Boulevard near Mercury Boulevard (tel. 804/245-3589, or toll free 800/872-7245). An Amtrak Thruway bus connection carries passengers to Norfolk.

By Bus   The **Greyhound/Trailways** terminal is at 120 East Main Street (tel. 804/622-7181).

By Car   From I-95 (Richmond), take I-64 or Route 60E. From north or south, Routes 13 and 17 lead to Norfolk. If you're coming from Virginia Beach, the Norfolk Expressway (Route 44) goes directly to downtown.

ESSENTIALS   The **telephone area code** is 804. Norfolk's **Convention & Visitors Bureau** is located at 236 East Plume Street, Norfolk, VA 23510 (tel. 804/441-1852, or toll free 800/368-3097).

Getting Around The **Tidewater Regional Transit System (TRT)** (tel. 804/623-3222) bus system serves Norfolk. Fare is 80¢, with an additional 35¢ per zone. Exact change is required.

The **Shopper's Shuttle Trolley** operates downtown and to Waterside; fare is 50¢.

A **TRT trolley tour** makes seven stops at attractions downtown and in outlying neighborhoods; visitors can get off at any stop and reboard a later trolley. It operates daily May to the beginning of September, hourly from 10am to 5pm; throughout September, from noon to 4:30pm. Fare is $1.50 for adults, 75¢ for seniors and children under 12. Tickets may be purchased at the TRT kiosk at Waterside.

You can also take an easy, **drive-it-yourself tour** of Norfolk attractions by following the blue-and-gold NORFOLK TOUR signs. At each of the stops is a box with a free, handy listing of all other attractions on the tour and directions for getting to them.

One of the nation's most important seaports, Norfolk sits at the mouth of the Elizabeth River, where it flows into Chesapeake Bay. The cities of Portsmouth and Norfolk, south of the harbor, are linked by a bridge-tunnel to Newport News and Hampton.

Today this city is known as Norfolk-by-the-Sea, and its image is one of historic charm, unlike its bawdy past when downtown sailor bars and burlesque houses were notorious. Those places have been demolished, and in their stead are high-rise offices, condominiums, marinas, shops, and entertainment. Interspersed in this newly revitalized downtown are reminders of Norfolk's past such as historic houses and the old City Hall (now converted into a museum and memorial to World War II hero Gen. Douglas MacArthur).

WHAT TO SEE & DO

CHRYSLER MUSEUM OF ART, Olney Rd. and Mowbray Arch. Tel. 804/622-1211.

Facing the Hague Inlet of the Elizabeth River, this imposing Italian Renaissance museum houses encyclopedic collections spanning almost 4,000 years of art history. A 1989 renovation project added a dazzling glass roof over the interior atrium, bathing the courtyard below in sunlight.

Originally built in 1932, and called the Norfolk Museum of Art, the museum was renamed in 1971 when Walter P. Chrysler, Jr., gave a large portion of his collection to the city of Norfolk. Chrysler began to collect art at the age of 13, with the purchase of a small landscape by Renoir. His magnificent collection spans artistic periods from ancient Egypt to the 1980s. The 8,000-piece glass collection, one of the finest and most comprehensive in the world, includes 200 Tiffany pieces. Adjoining is an outstanding collection of art nouveau furniture, including works by Guimard, Jouant, de Faure, and Gallé. Other first-floor galleries exhibit ancient Indian, Islamic, Oriental, African, and pre-Columbian art.

Most second-floor galleries are devoted to painting and sculpture, with Italian baroque and French holdings particularly strong. Among the artists represented are Gauguin, Picasso, Renoir, Matisse, Braque, Bernini, and Rouault. American art holdings include 18th- and 19th-century paintings by Charles Willson Peale, Benjamin West, John Singleton Copley, and Thomas Cole. And the 20th century is documented in works by Thomas Hart Benton, Calder, Kline, Warhol, Rauschenberg, and Rosenquist, among others. A permanent gallery is devoted solely to photography, showcasing everyone from Walker Evans to Diane Arbus.

Admission: $3.

Open: Tues–Sat 10am–4pm, Sun 1–4pm. **Closed:** New Year's, Independence, Thanksgiving, and Christmas days.

DOUGLAS MACARTHUR MEMORIAL, MacArthur Sq., between City Hall Ave. and Plume St., at Bank St. Tel. 804/441-2965.

When he arrived in Australia after suffering a crushing defeat at the hands of Japanese invaders in the Philippines, General MacArthur uttered the immortal words "I shall return." Here those words, which became a rallying cry for Americans fighting in the Pacific Theater of World War II, are engraved on a bronze plaque, along with excerpts from his other speeches, at the general's final resting place.

Visitors view a film that uses news footage to document the major events of MacArthur's life. And 11 galleries are filled with memorabilia ranging from historic World War II surrender documents to the general's famous corncob pipe.

The MacArthur Memorial is housed in Norfolk's old city hall, an imposing domed structure with a columned front portico.

Admission: Free.

Open: Mon–Sat 10am–5pm, Sun 11am–5pm. **Closed:** New Year's, Thanksgiving, and Christmas days.

THE WATERSIDE, Waterside Dr., between the Omni Hotel and Town Point Park. Tel. 804/627-3300.

A $23-million steel-and-glass pavilion that opened in 1983, the Waterside, which bills itself as a "festival marketplace," is the showpiece for Norfolk's revitalized downtown waterfront. Built by the Rouse Organization—also noted for Baltimore's Inner Harbor, Boston's Faneuil Hall, and New York's South Street Seaport—the Waterside houses over 30 international food outlets as well as several full-service restaurants. Shops offer a mix of souvenirs, jewelry, fashions, gift items, Virginia products, and crafts that make for pleasurable browsing.

And a short stroll along the busy waterfront and adjacent marina will bring you to the dock where cruise ships offer harbor tours (see below).

Town Point Park's amphitheater, just west of the Waterside, features a full schedule of free special events throughout the year—concerts, children's theater, magic shows, puppetry, and more.

Admission: Free.

Open: Summer, Mon–Sat 10am–10pm, Sun noon–8pm; winter, Mon–Sat 10am–9pm, Sun noon–6pm.

NORFOLK BOTANICAL GARDENS, Airport Rd. Tel. 804/441-5385.

A quiet haven with more than 12 miles of floral pathways, the gardens can be seen on foot, by trackless train, or by canal boat. From early April to mid-June the grounds are brilliantly abloom with a massive display of azaleas. The Statuary Vista is a beautiful setting for Moses Ezekiel's heroic-size statues (originally intended for the Corcoran Gallery in Washington) of great painters and sculptors—Rembrandt, Rubens, Dürer, and daVinci, among others. Notable, too, are the rose garden, with a terrace, overlooks, and a sculpture garden; a classic Japanese

---

IMPRESSIONS

Duty, Honor, Country. These three hallowed words reverently dictate what you ought to be, what you can be, what you will be. . . . The code which those words perpetuate embraces the highest moral law and will stand the test of any ethics or philosophies ever promulgated for the uplift of mankind.
    —GEN. DOUGLAS MACARTHUR, MAY 12, 1962

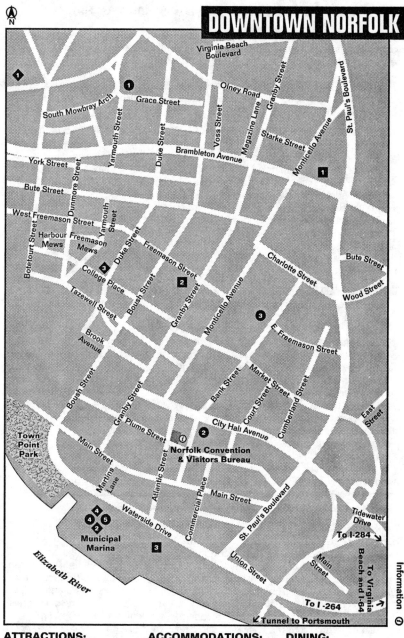

DOWNTOWN NORFOLK

Virginia Beach Boulevard
Olney Road
Grace Street
South Mowbray Arch
Granby Street
St. Paul's Boulevard
Yarmouth Street
Duke Street
Voss Street
Magazine Lane
Starke Street
Monticello Avenue
Brambleton Avenue
York Street
Bute Street
West Freemason Street
Dunmore Street
Yarmouth Street
Harbour Mews
Freemason Mews
Botetourt Street
Freemason Street
Duke Street
Boush Street
Granby Street
Charlotte Street
Bute Street
Wood Street
College Place
Tazewell Street
Monticello Avenue
E. Freemason Street
Brook Avenue
Boush Street
Granby Street
Bank Street
Market Street
Court Street
Cumberland Street
East Street
Plume Street
City Hall Avenue
Norfolk Convention & Visitors Bureau
Town Point Park
Main Street
Martins Lane
Atlantic Street
Commercial Place
Main Street
St. Paul's Boulevard
Tidewater Drive
Waterside Drive
Municipal Marina
Elizabeth River
Union Street
Main Street
To I-284
To Virginia Beach and I-64
To I-264
Tunnel to Portsmouth

Information

ATTRACTIONS:
Chrysler Museum of Art ❶
Douglas MacArthur Memorial ❷
Moses Myers House ❸
Trolley Tour ❹
The Waterside ❺

ACCOMMODATIONS:
Holiday Inn-Waterside Area ◼1
Madison Hotel ◼2
Omni International Hotel ◼3

DINING:
Elliot's ❶
Il Porto ❷
Le Charlieu ❸
Phillip's Waterside ❹

hill-and-pond garden; a fragrance garden; and an Italian Renaissance garden with terraces, statuary, a fountain, and reflecting pool. Behind the pool is the coronation court where the Azalea Queen is crowned each April.

Admission: $2 adults, $1 seniors.

Open: Daily 8:30am–sunset. **Directions:** Take I-64 to the Norview/Airport exit, pass two lights, and turn left onto Azalea Garden Road at the third light. It's about 4 miles from downtown Norfolk.

NAVAL BASE TOUR, 9809 Hampton Blvd. Tel. 804/444-7955 or 804/623-3222.

Norfolk has the world's largest naval installation, and visitors can take a guided bus tour of the base, enhanced by informed commentary by naval personnel. From the bus you'll see huge aircraft carriers, bulbous submarines, and training centers. The bus passes Admiral's Row, a strip of Colonial Revival houses built at the turn of the century for the Jamestown Exposition. On weekends from 1 to 4:30pm there may be visits to selected ships, admission free.

Admission: $3 adults, $1.50 children. Tickets may be purchased at the TRT kiosk at Waterside or at the Naval Base on Hampton Boulevard.

Open: Daily Apr–Oct 10am–2pm. **Directions:** Follow Hampton Boulevard north from downtown.

MOSES MYERS HOUSE, 323 E. Freemason St. Tel. 804/622-1211.

This handsome, early Federal brick town house set in a pretty garden was home to five generations of Myerses from 1792 to 1930. Moses Myers and his wife, Eliza, came to Norfolk in 1787. They were one of the first Jewish families to settle here, and special programs in observance of Jewish holidays are among the museum's annual events. Some 70% of the furniture and decorative arts collections displayed throughout the house is original to the first generation of the family. Two Gilbert Stuart portraits of Mr. and Mrs. Myers hang in the drawing room, which has some distinctive Empire pieces. The fireplace surround has unusual carvings depicting a sun god—with the features of George Washington.

A block away from the Moses Myers House is the **Willoughby-Baylor House,** at 601 East Freemason Street, built in 1794 and furnished with Georgian and Federal pieces. Admission, hours, and phone are the same for both museums.

Admission: $2 adults, $1 children, free for children under 6.

Open: Apr–Dec, Tues–Sat 10am–5pm, Sun noon–5pm; Jan–Mar, Tues–Sat noon–5pm.

HARBOR CRUISES

The *Carrie B* (tel. 804/393-4735), a reproduction of a 19th-century Mississippi riverboat, offers daytime and sunset cruises of Norfolk's harbor from the Waterside. Depending on the tour, you can see the shipyard with nuclear subs and aircraft carriers, the naval base, and the site of the Civil War battle between the *Monitor* and the *Merrimac.* In April and May and from Labor Day to October, 90-minute cruises leave at noon and 2pm; from June 1 to Labor Day, there are cruises at noon, 2pm, and 4pm. Tickets cost $11 for adults, $6 for children under 12. A 2½-hour sunset cruise, June 1 to Labor Day, leaves at 6pm; costing $14 for adults, $7 for children.

Also departing from the Waterside, the *Spirit of Norfolk* (tel. 804/627-7771) is like an oceangoing cruise ship, complete with dancing, good food, and entertainment. Offerings include a Fun & Sun Lunch Cruise from noon to 2pm ($16.95 Monday through Friday, $18.50 on Saturday), Sun brunch cruises from 1 to 3pm ($18.50), evening cruises with a show, dancing, and buffet dinner ($27.95 Sunday through Thursday, $31.95 on Friday and Saturday), and a midnight party cruise from midnight to 2am, with live bands, dancing, and cocktails ($13.20).

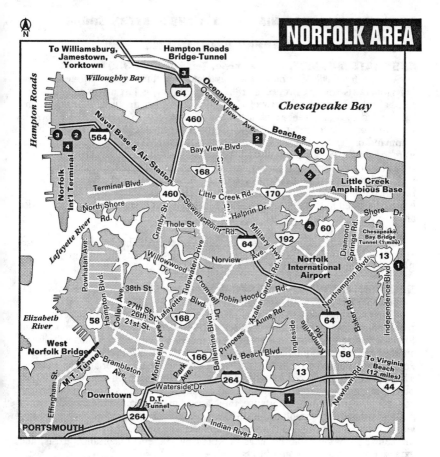

NORFOLK AREA

ACCOMMODATIONS:
Best Western Center Inn **1**
Econo Lodge, East Ocean View **2**
Econo Lodge, West Ocean View Beach **3**
Norfolk Hampton Inn **4**

DINING:
Ship's Cabin ❶
Uncle Louie's ❷

ATTRACTIONS:
Adam Thoroughgood House ❶
Naval Base Ship Visitation ❷
Naval Base Tour ❸
Norfolk Botanical Gardens ❹

NEARBY ATTRACTIONS

CASEMATE MUSEUM, Fort Monroe. Tel. 804/727-3391.

A must for Civil War buffs, the Casemate Museum at Fort Monroe, where Jefferson Davis was imprisoned in 1865 after the war, is just across the Hampton Roads Bridge-Tunnel, in the city of Hampton. Located at the tip of a peninsula and surrounded by a moat, the stone fort was built between 1819 and 1834. Robert E. Lee, a second lieutenant in the Army Corps of Engineers in 1831, was second in command of the detachment that constructed the fort. The "casemates," or rooms, were originally designed as storage for seacoast artillery. After 1900 they were modified to serve as living quarters for the soldiers and their families stationed at the fort. Visitors can view displays of military memorabilia, and enter the sparsely furnished room where Davis was held prisoner. The accusation against Davis—that he had participated in the plot to assassinate Lincoln—was eventually found to be false and Davis was released in 1867.

Admission: Free.

Open: Daily 10:30am–4:30pm. **Closed:** New Year's, Thanksgiving, and Christmas days. **Directions:** From Norfolk, take I-64 across the Hampton Roads Bridge-Tunnel and follow the Fort Monroe signs.

HAMPTON UNIVERSITY MUSEUM, Hampton University, Hampton. Tel. 804/727-5308.

Hampton University, founded in 1868 to provide an education for newly freed African-Americans, boasts among its graduates Booker T. Washington, who himself founded Tuskegee Institute in Alabama. This museum is housed in Academy Building, an 1881 red-brick landmark on the waterfront in the historic section of the campus. Four other landmarks are nearby, including the imposing Memorial Chapel (1886). The museum is noted for its African collection, comprising more than 2,700 art objects and artifacts representing 887 ethnic groups and cultures. Rivaling the African collection in quality and importance, the Native American collection includes works from 93 tribes; it was established in 1878 when the federal government began sending young Native Americans from western reservations to be educated at Hampton. The museum also has notable holdings in works by Harlem Renaissance artists, and extensive Oceanic and Asian objects.

Admission: Free.

Open: Sept–May, Mon–Fri 8am–5pm, Sat–Sun noon–4pm; June–Aug, Mon–Fri 8am–5pm. **Directions:** From Norfolk, take I-64 across the Hampton Roads Bridge-Tunnel to County Street, Exit 68; then follow signs to the university.

MARINERS' MUSEUM, 100 Museum Dr., Newport News. Tel. 804/595-0368.

In a pleasant 550-acre park setting, with a lake, picnic areas, and walking trails, the Mariners' Museum is dedicated to preserving the culture of the sea and its tributaries. Handcrafted ship models, scrimshaw, maritime paintings, decorative arts, working steam engines, and more are displayed in the spacious galleries. Particularly interesting in the Antique Boats Gallery are three antique Chris-Crafts from 1923, 1934, and 1935. The Chesapeake Bay Gallery tells the story of the area's early history. Other notable pieces are a Native American dugout canoe (ca. 1630) and a U.S. Coast Guard channel buoy. An 18-minute film narrated by actor James Earl Jones tells about maritime activity the world over. From time to time, costumed historical interpreters, including a wood carver and marlinspike ropeworker, give demonstrations.

Admission: $4 adults, $3.50 seniors, $1.50 children 6–16, free for children under 6.

Open: Mon–Sat 9am–5pm, Sun noon–5pm. **Directions:** From I-64, take Exit 62A and follow J. Clyde Morris Boulevard west to its intersection with Warwick Boulevard where Museum Drive meets it.

WHERE TO STAY

All the downtown hotels recommended below are within walking distance of the Waterside, and the others are no more than 15 minutes away.

DOWNTOWN

Expensive

OMNI INTERNATIONAL HOTEL, 777 Waterside Dr., Norfolk, VA 23510. Tel. 804/622-6664, or toll free 800/THE-OMNI. Fax 804/625-8271. 419 rms, 23 suites. A/C TV TEL

$ Rates: $89–$139 single or double. Children under 16 stay free in parents' room. Weekend and other packages available. AE, CB, DC, DISC, MC, V. **Parking:** Valet parking $8.50 per day; self-parking $3 per day in adjacent Dominion Tower garage.

Overlooking busy Norfolk Harbor, the Omni is next door to the Waterside. Its three-story atrium lobby is enhanced by stunning floral arrangements, and in the sunken Lobby Bar, 30-foot windows overlook the river. Guest rooms are decorated in restful pastel tones. The Omni Club Level, on the 10th floor, offers a private express elevator and such special amenities as complimentary continental breakfast, afternoon hors d'oeuvres, free daily newspaper, and nightly turndown with chocolates.

Dining/Entertainment: The Riverwalk Café offers American fare at all three meals. The Lobby Bar features piano music Monday through Thursday and dancing on Friday and Saturday nights. Omni's dinner theater, Wednesday through Saturday night, costs $21.95 and includes a four-course dinner.

Services: 24-hour room service, in-room movies, concierge, multilingual staff.

Facilities: Business center, florist, gift and sundries shop, hair salon, outdoor pool; health club nearby.

Moderate

MADISON HOTEL, 345 Granby St., Norfolk, VA 23510. Tel. 804/622-6682, or toll free 800/522-0976. 116 rms, 8 suites. A/C TV TEL

$ Rates: $45–$85 single or double. Rates $55 and above include full breakfast. Children stay free in parents' room. Weekend and other packages available. AE, CB, DC, DISC, MC, V. **Parking:** Free sheltered parking on property.

Built in 1906 at the corner of Granby Street and Freemason Street as the Southland Hotel, the Madison was the first hostelry in Norfolk to provide indoor plumbing for its guests. The lobby reflects the hotel's status as Norfolk's grande dame landmark, with crystal chandeliers, polished walnut columns, wing chairs, and a medallion-printed carpet. The original 180 rooms have been renovated and decorated in Colonial style with pale floral-print fabrics and mahogany furnishings. All rooms have clock radios.

Dining/Entertainment: Dolley's Restaurant serves daily breakfast and lunch buffets. The main restaurant and lounge, Bentley's, is open for drinks and dinner nightly.

Services: Room service, airport limo, hotel limo available for special needs.

Facilities: Complimentary use of health and racquetball club across the street.

Inexpensive

HOLIDAY INN—WATERSIDE AREA, 700 Monticello Ave., Norfolk, VA 23510. Tel. 804/627-5555. 340 rms, 4 suites. A/C TV TEL

$ Rates: Summer $48–$85 single or double; winter, $39–$70 single or double. Children under 18 stay free in parents' room. Weekend and other packages available. AE, CB, DC, DISC, MC, V. **Parking:** Free parking adjacent to hotel.

Directly across the street from the Scope Convention Center, this refurbished 12-story Holiday Inn is about six blocks from the Waterside. Accommodations are nicely appointed with blue quilted spreads and matching draperies; rooms with king-size beds have desks, and all rooms have remote-control TVs (with free Showtime and ESPN) concealed in armoires. Their Chesapeake Dining Room serves all three meals buffet style; Harvey's Lounge offers complimentary hors d'oeuvres Monday through Friday, and live entertainment. Room service and complimentary shuttle to airport and Waterside are available and there is a gift shop, florist, outdoor pool, and barbershop on the premises.

NEARBY ACCOMMODATIONS

Inexpensive

BEST WESTERN CENTER INN, One Best Sq., Norfolk, VA 23502. Tel. 804/461-6600, or toll free 800/237-5517. 152 rms. A/C TV TEL **Directions:** From I-64, take Exit 80 (downtown Norfolk) onto I-264 and exit at North Military Highway/Route 13; at the red light turn left into Best Square and follow the service road to the inn entrance.

$ Rates: $52–$62 single; $60–$70 double; $100–$120 suite. Weekend and other packages available. AE, CB, DC, DISC, MC, V. **Parking:** Free.

You'll realize this Best Western is something special from the moment you see the tasteful two-story gray clapboard complex, set around a nicely landscaped courtyard and garden with park benches and old-fashioned street lamps. All rooms face the courtyard and Olympic-size pool, and second-floor rooms have balconies. Accommodations have a summery look, with bamboo furnishings and lavender, pink, and blue spreads and matching draperies. Complimentary continental breakfast is available in the lobby. Next door to the inn are Best Center shops and restaurants; the Military Circle shopping mall is also nearby. Barry's Restaurant has a good reputation; a lounge adjoins.

Complimentary airport shuttle is offered, and there is a health club, sauna, Jacuzzi, indoor and outdoor pools, gift shop, coin-op laundry, and conference center.

Budget

ECONO LODGE, 9601 Fourth View St., Norfolk, VA 23503. Tel. 804/480-9611, or toll free 800/446-6900. Fax 804/480-1307. 70 rms (including 22 efficiencies). A/C TV TEL **Directions:** From I-64, take Exit 71 to the corner of Route 60 (Ocean View Avenue) and Fourth View.

$ Rates (including continental breakfast): $41.95–$47.95 single; $45.95–$57.95 double. Children under 18 stay free in parents' room. Extra person $5. AE, CB, DC, DISC, MC, V. **Parking:** Free.

This Econo Lodge, one of the nicest representatives of this chain we've encountered, is across the road from the Chesapeake Bay beach and Harrison fishing pier. The rooms are large, many decorated in tones of green and gold, and all have refrigerators. Efficiencies have full kitchen facilities; microwave ovens are available for a small extra charge. A coin-op laundry, sauna, Jacuzzi, and pool are on the premises.

If this Econo Lodge is full, there are four others in the area, including the Econo Lodge at 1111 East Ocean View Beach Avenue, Norfolk, VA 23503 (tel. 804/480-1111).

NORFOLK HAMPTON INN, 1450 Military Hwy., Norfolk, VA 23502. Tel. 804/466-7474, or toll free 800/HAMPTON. 130 rms. A/C TV TEL **Directions:** From I-64, take Exit 78 and follow Military Highway south to its intersection with Princess Anne Road.

$ Rates: $43–$49 single; $48–$54 double. Children 18 and under stay free in parents' room. AE, CB, DC, DISC, MC, V. **Parking:** Free.

Cost-conscious travelers will find that the Hampton gives good value. In addition to comfortable rooms decorated in soft contemporary tones of mauve and green, with light oak furniture, the motel offers many complimentary amenities, among them continental breakfast in the lobby, local phone calls, in-room movies, and newspapers. There's an outdoor swimming pool.

WHERE TO DINE

DOWNTOWN

Expensive

LE CHARLIEU, 112 College Place. Tel. 804/623-7202.
   Cuisine: FRENCH. **Reservations:** Recommended, especially on weekends.
   $ Prices: Appetizers $3.95–$6.50; entrees $10.95–$19.95. AE, CB, DC, MC, V.
   Open: Lunch Mon–Fri 11:30am–2pm; dinner Mon–Sat 5:30–10pm.
Occupying the first floor of a town house, Le Charlieu is beautifully appointed with crystal chandeliers, gilt-framed oil paintings, and cozy tables with pink cloths and flowers setting off gleaming-white china. Owner/chef Richard Tranchard hails from Lyons.

At lunch, hors d'oeuvres include a tasty avocado stuffed with shrimp, homemade pâté, and smoked salmon with capers. Special main dishes—a fish, a meat, and a quiche—priced at $6.95, change daily.

At dinner, start with smoked rainbow trout or a hearty dish of mussels with spinach and cheese. Roast duck with Grand Marnier, roast pheasant with pecans and bourbon sauce, and rabbit in madeira sauce are chef's specials. The dessert tray is a symphony of fresh-baked treats, and the wine card lists over 200 vintages.

Moderate

IL PORTO, The Waterside. Tel. 804/627-4400.
   Cuisine: ITALIAN. **Reservations:** Suggested, especially on weekends.
   $ Prices: Appetizers $4.25–$5.25; entrees $8.75–$12.50. AE, MC, V.
   Open: Lunch daily 11:15am–4pm; dinner Sun–Thurs 4–11pm, Fri–Sat 4pm–midnight.
Il Porto has been at the Waterside since the marketplace opened, and has expanded several times. Its continuing popularity is due to its great waterfront views and delicious Italian specialties. The candlelit interior evokes the Mediterranean with terra-cotta-tile floors, stucco walls, a copper-hooded fireplace, and red-and-white-checked tablecloths. In good weather you can dine outdoors overlooking the harbor.

For a light lunch, have an antipasto (entree-size portion is $6.45) of assorted Italian cold meats, cheeses, and marinated vegetables on salad greens. At dinner, start off with mussels in white wine and parsley. Homemade pastas run the gamut from lasagne, manicotti, or linguine with clam sauce, to the house special lobster, scallops, fish, and shrimp sautéed in herb butter and tossed with broccoli and pasta. Children's plates of spaghetti and meatballs, lasagne, or veal parmigiana are $5.25. At night a pianist plays ragtime.

PHILLIPS WATERSIDE, 333 Waterside Dr. Tel. 804/627-6600.
   Cuisine: SEAFOOD. **Reservations:** Suggested.
   $ Prices: Appetizers $2.75–$5.95; entrees $8.95–$16.95. AE, CB, DC, DISC, MC, V.
   Open: Summer, daily 11:30am–11pm; winter, daily 11:30am–10:30pm (bar open until 1:30am).

This extravaganza of a restaurant at the Waterside is itself a festival. It seats some 400 diners in a series of dining rooms with blue wrought-iron chairs and tables amid old brick archways, aquariums, stained-glass lamps, a gazebo, nautical items, and hanging plants. Blue tents cover the Deckside Lounge, where there's live entertainment and light fare at night. In the Main Lounge there may be piano bar sing-alongs. But the center of attention is good seafood. At lunch, grilled tuna, broiled mahi-mahi, and a crabcake sandwich are each under $6. At dinner, she-crab soup, fresh local oysters, and spiced shrimp are favorite starters. Proceed to crab-stuffed red snapper, a fried or broiled seafood platter, or crab cakes. And finish up with a hot-fudge brownie.

Inexpensive

ELLIOT'S, 1421 Colley Ave. Tel. 804/625-0259.
  Cuisine: AMERICAN.
$ Prices: Appetizers $1.75–$4.95; entrees $8.95–$15.45. AE, CB, DC, DISC, MC, V.
  Open: Sun–Mon 11am–10pm, Tues–Thurs 11am–11pm, Fri–Sat 11am–midnight.

Many are the fans of Elliot's, which encompasses five former stores and an airy glass-enclosed patio in Norfolk's trendy Ghent district. An eclectic art deco decor features old photos and advertising signs on the walls, ceiling fans, hanging plants, and etched-glass partitions. Pink and green tiles delineate the bar. Specialties include mile-high nachos with chicken chili and a delicious hot artichoke dip. Fresh-catch selections come broiled, blackened, or with a choice of special sauces. There are also burgers, croissant sandwiches, and sautéed vegetable dishes. And a children's menu is a plus for families. For dessert, you can't beat a homemade fudge brownie topped with ice cream and chocolate sauce. A selection of domestic and imported beers is available—or have a carafe of house wine.

NEARBY RESTAURANTS

Expensive

SHIP'S CABIN, 4110 E. Ocean View Ave. Tel. 804/480-2526.
  Cuisine: SEAFOOD. **Reservations:** Recommended.
$ Prices: Appetizers $5.50–$6.75; entrees $11.95–$19.95. AE, DC, MC, V.
  Open: Dinner only, daily 6–10pm.

This fine seafood restaurant is in the Ocean View section, about a 15-minute drive north of downtown Norfolk. It does resemble a ship's cabin, with dark wood-paneled walls, ceiling fans, brass lamps, and exposed timbers. The bayside dining room overlooks the beach and Chesapeake Bay. The menu changes often, depending on availability of seafood items. Oysters bingo is the house special appetizer—fresh-shucked Eastern Shore oysters sautéed in butter, white wine, and shallots. Main dishes might include broiled flounder with duchesse potatoes, shrimp scampi, and seafood fra diablo, plus some nonseafood items like New York strip steak and chicken breast parmesan. All entrees come with fresh-baked breads, house salad, vegetable, and potato. For dessert, pull out all the stops with chocolate decadence, a rich cake made with Ghirardelli chocolate and surrounded with raspberry purée.

Moderate

UNCLE LOUIE'S, 132 E. Little Creek Rd., Ward's Corner. Tel. 804/480-1225.
  Cuisine: AMERICAN. **Reservations:** Recommended for dinner.
$ Prices: Appetizers $4.50–$5.95; entrees $5.95–$13.95. AE, DC, MC, V.
  Open: Mon–Thurs 11am–11pm, Fri–Sat 11am–midnight, Sun 10am–10pm; brunch Sun 10am–2pm (deli open daily 8am–8pm).

A sophisticated art deco setting, and a multipage menu that includes everything from bagels and lox to braised tuna filets Paul Bocuse, puts Uncle Louie's in a class by itself. Portions are hefty. Breakfast fare, served all day, includes three-egg omelets served with two potato pancakes and a bagel or three cheese blintzes with sour cream. Sunday brunch features challah French toast, eggs Benedict, and eggs Créole. For lunch, huge deli sandwiches come with a choice of cole slaw or potato salad. Dr. Brown's sodas are a perfect accompaniment. Soups, pastas, and smoked-fish platters are among the offerings, and chicken-fried steak with pan gravy, mashed potatoes, and a fresh vegetable costs just $5.95. The mud pie here comes topped with coffee ice cream, pecans, chocolate syrup, and whipped cream. Louie's bar, open till 2am, also serves tropical bar drinks.

LIGHT FOOD

DOUMAR'S, 19th to 20th Sts. and Monticello Ave. Tel. 804/627-4163.
   Cuisine: AMERICAN.
$ Prices: Sandwiches 80¢–$2.45. No credit cards.
   Open: Mon–Thurs 8am–11pm, Fri–Sat 8am–12:30am.
A Norfolk institution since the 1930s, Doumar's features carhops, curb service, and a 1950s-style menu. The specialties here are ice-cream cones and barbecued sandwiches. According to owner Al Doumar, cones were invented by his great uncle, Abe Doumar, at the St. Louis Exposition and World's Fair in 1904. Uncle Abe's original cone-making machine is still in use at Doumar's, where the sweet wafflelike cones are made. Barbecue plates with french fries and slaw are served only after 4pm; before then you can have a barbecue, burger, hot dog, or other sandwich, sundae, milkshake, or a vanilla, chocolate, strawberry, or butter-pecan cone.

EVENING ENTERTAINMENT

Norfolk is a lively town. For a rundown on evening events, pick up a free copy of *Port Folio,* an entertainment weekly available at the Visitors Bureau, most hotel lobbies, and the Waterside. In addition to entertainment at hotel lounges, and the Omni Dinner Theater mentioned above, you may be in town during performances of several outstanding companies. The **Virginia Stage Company** puts on seven productions annually, October through April, at the restored Wells Theatre, Monticello Avenue and Tazewell Street (tel. 804/627-1234). The Center Theater, Virginia Beach Boulevard and Llewellyn Avenue (tel. 804/627-9595), is home to the **Virginia Opera** and the **Savoyard Gilbert & Sullivan Society.**

   SCOPE, Brambleton Avenue and St. Paul's Boulevard (tel. 804/441-2161), seats 12,000 for major events—including the circus, ice shows, and concerts. Part of the SCOPE complex, **Chrysler Hall,** Charlotte Street and St. Paul's Boulevard (tel. 804/441-2161), is home to the **Virginia Symphony** and the annual Pops series conducted by Skitch Henderson.

---

2. VIRGINIA BEACH

18 miles SE of Norfolk, 110 miles E of Richmond,
207 miles S of Washington, D.C.

GETTING THERE   By Plane   Virginia Beach is serviced by **Norfolk International Airport** (tel. 804/857-3351), about 30 minutes (15 miles) from the oceanfront resort area. For airport limousine service, call 804/857-1231.

By Train   The nearest **Amtrak** station is in Newport News, at 9304 Warwick Boulevard (tel. 804/245-3589, or toll free 800/872-7245). An Amtrak Thruway bus connection carries passengers to Virginia Beach.

By Bus The **Greyhound/Trailways Bus Terminal** is at 1017 Laskin Road (tel. 804/422-2998).

By Car From the west, following I-64 to Route 60 brings you to Shore Drive. U.S. 13 and 17 lead to Virginia Beach from north and south. The Virginia Beach–Norfolk Expressway, Route 44, runs straight to the heart of the oceanfront resort area.

ESSENTIALS Orientation Virginia Beach, at the southeastern tip of the state, is bordered by the Chesapeake Bay and the Atlantic Ocean. The oceanfront **resort area,** where you'll find most of the big hotels and the boardwalk, extends from Rudee Inlet (approximately 2nd Street) north to 42nd Street. The two main north-south streets paralleling the boardwalk are **Atlantic Avenue** and **Pacific Avenue.** There's no real downtown in Virginia Beach; major shopping and movie theaters are at the malls, as are many restaurants.

Information For information in planning your trip, or assistance while you're in Virginia Beach, contact the **Visitor Information Center,** Expressway 44 and Parks Avenue, Virginia Beach, VA 23451 (tel. 804/425-7511, or toll free 800/446-8038).

Getting Around In spring and summer, **trolleys** (50¢ fare) run on Atlantic Avenue from 1st Street to 42nd Street. Routes from the Dome Civic Center, 19th Street and Pacific Avenue, go south on General Booth Boulevard (to the Virginia Marine Science Museum), to Lynnhaven Mall via Expressway 44, and to the Waterside in Norfolk ($1.90 one way). Call 804/428-3388 for more details.

A **boardwalk train** runs from June 15 to Labor Day and costs $1.

Although the beachfront is lined with big hotels that effectively block off ocean views from Atlantic Avenue, the boardwalk boasts immaculate landscaping, wood benches, small parks, and attractive white Colonial-style street lamps. Noticeable improvements along Atlantic Avenue (still in progress at this writing) include spacious brick walkways instead of narrow sidewalks, flags and banners that have replaced overhanging commercial signs, and an unobstructed view skyward as all cables and wires are now buried under the street.

Vacationers flock here in the summer to enjoy sun, surf, and sand. Also in Virginia Beach: the Virginia Marine Science Museum, the most popular museum in the state, and several historic sites, including the First Landing Cross, where the Jamestown settlers first came ashore.

WHAT TO SEE & DO
HISTORIC ATTRACTIONS

The history of Virginia Beach goes back to 1607, when the British settlers who would go on to found Jamestown came ashore at Cape Henry, on the northern tip of Virginia Beach. Now part of Fort Story, the site of the **first landing** is marked by a cross and plaque where the colonists under Capt. Christopher Newport "set up a Crosse at Chesupioc Bay and named that place Cape Henry" for Henry, Prince of Wales. Also at this site is a monumental relief map showing the French and British naval engagement off Cape Henry during the Revolutionary War and a statue of the French commander. Now known as the **Battle of the Capes,** this decisive battle effectively trapped Cornwallis at Yorktown and helped end British dominion in America. When Cornwallis surrendered, George Washington expressed his gratitude to the French Admiral de Grasse: "I wish it was in my power to express to Congress how much I feel myself indebted to the Count de Grasse and his fleet." Near the plaque commemorating the battle, visitors can enter the old **Cape Henry Lighthouse,** the first lighthouse built by authorization of Congress, in 1791. It lit the entrance to

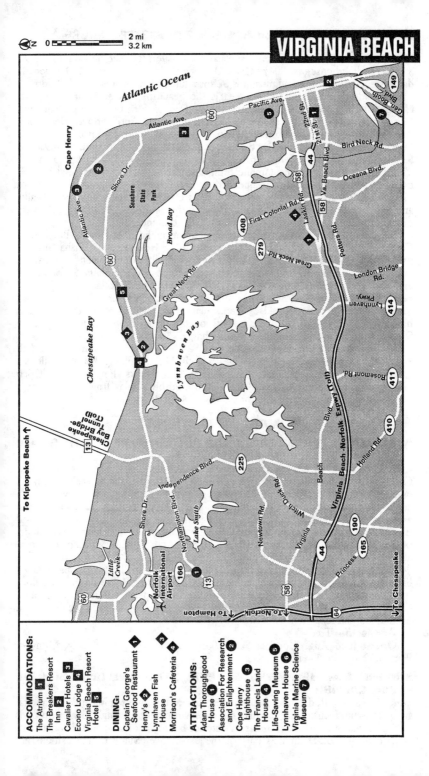

VIRGINIA BEACH

0 2 mi
   3.2 km

Atlantic Ocean

Cape Henry

Atlantic Ave.
Pacific Ave.
Atlantic Ave.
Shore Dr.
Seashore State Park
Broad Bay
Great Neck Rd.
Chesapeake Bay
Lynnhaven Bay
22nd St.
21st St.
Gen. Booth Blvd.
Bird Neck Rd.
Oceana Blvd.
First Colonial Rd.
Laskin Rd.
Va. Beach Blvd.
Potters Rd.
London Bridge Rd.
Lynnhaven Pkwy.
Rosemont Rd.
Virginia Beach - Norfolk Expwy. (Toll)
Holland Rd.
Beach Blvd.
Chesapeake Bay Bridge-Tunnel (Toll)
To Kiptopeke Beach ↑
Independence Blvd.
Shore Dr.
Northampton Blvd.
Lake Smith
Little Creek
Norfolk International Airport
Newtown Rd.
Witch Duck Rd.
Virginia Beach Blvd.
Princess
↓To Hampton ↓To Norfolk ↓To Norfolk
To Chesapeake↓

ACCOMMODATIONS:
The Atrium 1
The Breakers Resort Inn 2
Cavalier Hotels 3
Econo Lodge 4
Virginia Beach Resort Hotel 5

DINING:
Captain George's Seafood Restaurant 1
Henry's 2
Lynnhaven Fish House 3
Morrison's Cafeteria 4

ATTRACTIONS:
Adam Thoroughgood House 1
Association For Research and Enlightenment 2
Cape Henry Lighthouse 3
The Francis Land House 4
Life-Saving Museum 5
Lynnhaven House 6
Virginia Marine Science Museum 7

Chesapeake Bay until 1881. There is no charge for visitors to enter the grounds of Fort Story. The lighthouse (tel. 804/422-9421) is open mid-March through October 31, daily from 10am to 5pm; admission is $2 for adults, $1 for students and seniors.

The oldest brick home in America is the beautiful **Adam Thoroughgood House,** 1636 Parish Road, near the intersection of Pleasure House Road and Northampton Boulevard (tel. 804/627-2737). It is open April through December, Tuesday through Saturday from 10am to 5pm and on Sunday from noon to 5pm; January through March, Tuesday through Saturday from noon to 5pm. Admission is $2 for adults, $1 for students. Probably constructed about 1680 by one of Adam Thoroughgood's grandsons (architectural historians believe its namesake never occupied the house), this picturesque medieval English-style cottage sits on 4½ acres of lawn and garden. The interior has exposed wood beams and whitewashed walls, and although the furnishings did not belong to the Thoroughgood family, they are original to the period and reflect the family's English ancestry.

Two 18th-century historic houses are open to the public in the Virginia Beach area. Costumed docents provide tours of the **Lynnhaven House,** 4405 Wishart Boulevard (tel. 804/460-1688), from the fourth week of April through the end of October, Tuesday through Sunday from noon to 4pm; admission is $2 for adults, $1 for seniors and students, free for children under 6. The **Francis Land House,** 3131 Virginia Beach Boulevard (tel. 804/340-1732), built as a plantation manor in 1732, now looks toward a busy highway instead of the farmland that once surrounded this elegant home. It is open year round, Wednesday through Saturday from 9am to 5pm and on Sunday from noon to 5pm; no admission charge.

Virginia Beach's **Life-Saving Museum,** 24th Street and Atlantic Avenue (tel. 804/422-1587), housed in a small white 1903 clapboard building that was built as a Coast Guard station, recalls rescue missions and shipwrecks along the coast. Open Tuesday through Saturday from 10am to 5pm and on Sunday from noon to 5pm; admission is $2 for adults, $1.50 for seniors, 75¢ for children.

MORE ATTRACTIONS

ASSOCIATION FOR RESEARCH AND ENLIGHTENMENT, 67th St. and Atlantic Ave. Tel. 804/428-3588.

The international headquarters carrying on the work of the late psychic Edgar Cayce has a host of free activities daily. You can see a movie that tells about Cayce's psychic talent, which first manifested when, as a young man, he found he was able to enter into an altered state of consciousness and answer questions on any topic. His answers, or "discourses," now called readings, number some 14,256 and have stood the test of extensive research. The movie is shown daily at 4pm; there are guided tours of the building daily at 11:15am, group ESP testing from 1 to 2pm, and a daily lecture at 3pm (see the receptionist for the day's topic). The A.R.E. Bookstore on the first floor has an excellent selection of titles in the fields of holistic health, parapsychology, life after death, dreams, and even cooking. The Meditation Room on the third floor has a spectacular view of the ocean and is painted with special colors chosen because Cayce readings suggest that they can assist higher thoughts. Outside the center is a Meditation Garden.

Admission: Free.

Open: June–Aug, Mon–Sat 9am–10pm, Sun 1–10pm; Sept–May, Mon–Sat 9am–5:30pm, Sun 1–6pm.

VIRGINIA MARINE SCIENCE MUSEUM, 717 General Booth Blvd. Tel. 804/425-FISH.

Just across Rudee Inlet from the resort area, this entertaining and educational museum focusing on Virginia's marine environment is fittingly located on Owls Creek salt marsh. It even has an outdoor boardwalk that makes the marsh, its waterfowl, and other animals part of the experience. Many of the exhibits are interactive, and visitors can view live sea animals in their natural living conditions. A magnificent 50,000-gallon aquarium represents the area from the Chesapeake Bay beach to the first island of the Bay Bridge-Tunnel. You can walk along the banks of a river and look at the turtles and freshwater fish in the Coastal Plains River Room, and in the weather room, create a hurricane, forecast the weather, or just make some waves. One of the most popular areas is the Touch Tank, which simulates the shallow waters of the bay; here visitors can pick up a horseshoe crab and other bay animals. Instructors are on hand at each exhibit to answer questions. Daily programs include fish feedings, guided tours, and special presentations.

Admission: $4 adults, $3.60 seniors, $3.25 children 4–12, free for children under 4.

Open: Daily 9am–5pm. **Closed:** New Year's and Christmas days. **Directions:** From the resort area, follow Pacific Avenue south; across Rudee Inlet the street becomes General Booth Boulevard; the museum is less than a mile past the inlet bridge.

OUTDOOR RECREATION

Water Sports

Virginia Beach offers a wonderful variety of water sports, starting, of course, with its fine white sand beach.

Fishing Deep-sea fishing aboard a party boat can provide an exciting day's entertainment for both novices and dedicated fishermen. Party boats leave from the **D and M Marina,** 3311 Shore Drive, Lynnhaven Inlet (tel. 804/481-7211), and the **Virginia Beach Fishing Center,** 200 Winston Salem Avenue, Rudee Inlet (tel. 804/422-5700).

You may not fish from the sandy beach south of 42nd Street from Memorial Day to Labor Day from 10am to 5pm, but you can drop a line from numerous piers. The **Virginia Beach Fishing Pier,** between 14th Street and 15th Street, oceanfront (tel. 804/428-2333), open April through October, has bait for sale and rods for rent. **Lynnhaven Inlet Fishing Pier,** Starfish Road off Shore Drive, Chesapeake Bay (tel. 804/481-7071), open 24 hours a day in summer, rents rods and reels and sells crab cages.

Swimming During the summer season there are lifeguards on duty along the resort strip from 2nd Street to 42nd Street; they also handle raft, umbrella, and beach-chair rentals.

Surfing Surfers can call the **Eastern Surfing Association Hotline** (tel. 804/456-2163) for events and schedules. Surfing areas are subject to change without notice; for the latest information on where to surf, call 804/428-9133.

Land Sports

Biking and Jogging You can walk, jog, or run on the boardwalk, or bicycle on the boardwalk bike path. Rent a bike at **North End Cyclery Ltd.,** three blocks from the oceanfront at 406 Laskin Road (tel. 804/428-4235); **Tom's Bike Rental** (tel. 804/422-6096) will deliver to various locations. There are biking and hiking trails in **Seashore State Park,** 2500 Shore Drive (tel. 804/481-4836).

Golf Virginia Beach has nine public golf courses within the city limits. Among them are the **Hell's Point Golf Course,** 2700 Atwoodtown Road (tel. 804/721-3400), designed by Rees Jones and cited by *Golf Digest* magazine as one of America's best new courses, and the **Red Wing Lake Municipal Golf Course,** 1080 Prosperity Road (tel. 804/425-6300).

Tennis The city has some 200 public tennis courts, most of which are lighted and free. If you call the city's **Parks Department** (tel. 804/471-2027), they'll be glad to steer you to the one closest to you. The **Owl Creek Municipal Center,** 928 South Birdneck Road (tel. 804/422-4716), which has a pro shop, children's play area, 12 hard-surface and 2 tournament courts, is the major facility.

WHERE TO STAY

Rates at Virginia Beach hotels rise steeply during the summer season; so a hotel that's expensive in the summer can be surprisingly affordable in spring and fall, and downright inexpensive in winter. Therefore, we've listed both summer and winter rates for the hotels recommended below, but categorized the hotels according to their summer rate.

EXPENSIVE

CAVALIER HOTELS, 42nd St. at the Oceanfront, 42nd On-the-Hill, Virginia Beach, VA 23451. Tel. 804/425-8555, or toll free 800/446-8199, 800/582-8324 in Virginia. Fax 804/428-7957. 259 rms and 21 suites oceanfront, 120 rms and 2 suites on the hill. A/C TV TEL

$ Rates: Summer, $80–$120 single or double; winter, $50–$80 single or double. Children under 18 stay free in parents' room. Extra person $20. Weekend and other packages available. AE, CB, DC, DISC, MC, V. **Parking:** $10 per night in garage.

⭐ This resort consists of two hotels—the original Cavalier on the hill, built in 1927, and the Cavalier on the ocean, which opened in 1973. Eighteen acres of nicely landscaped lawns surround both properties, and guests may use facilities at either hotel.

The older property has all the gracious features you'd expect in a fine old resort, including an enclosed veranda with white wicker furnishings, potted plants, and great ocean views; it evokes memories of the days when Scott and Zelda Fitzgerald danced here and lunches were black tie. The lobby is a gracious entry, complete with Colonial-style furnishings and crystal chandeliers. Guest rooms have all been refurbished, some exquisitely so, with European-style bathrooms in black and white tile, with pediment sinks, whirlpool baths, lighted makeup mirrors, bidets, and hairdryers. Furnishings in these individually decorated rooms employ Williamsburg-quality Chippendale reproductions, Colonial-print fabrics, gilt-framed artworks, and museum-quality decorative objects. The heated indoor Olympic-size pool is magnificently tiled and illuminated by a grand skylight.

The oceanfront hotel has contemporary-style rooms, very nicely decorated in pastels, with a shell motif appearing on wall sconces and fabrics. Some rooms here have oceanfront balconies and Jacuzzi baths.

Dining/Entertainment: The elegant Orion rooftop restaurant in the oceanfront hotel is open for cocktails and dinner; the dining room on the lobby floor serves all three meals. The dining room in the hotel on the hill is open seasonally.

Services: Valet parking, room service, concierge, shuttle service between hotels, baby-sitting.

Facilities: Indoor, outdoor, and kiddie pools; 20-station aerobic fitness course; health club; putting green; four tennis courts; croquet, volleyball, shuffleboard, basketball, bike rentals, and two playgrounds; gift shop; children's activities program in season.

VIRGINIA BEACH RESORT HOTEL, 2800 Shore Dr. (Rte. 60), Virginia Beach, VA 23451. Tel. 804/481-9000, or toll free 800/468-2722, 800/422-4747 in Virginia. 295 suites. A/C TV TEL

$ Rates: Summer, $119–$224 (penthouse) single or double; winter $64–$149 single or double. Extra person $10. Weekday and other packages available. AE, DC, MC, V. **Parking:** Free.

Situated 3½ miles east of Chesapeake Bay Bridge-Tunnel on 4 acres of Chesapeake Bay beachfront property, this self-contained luxury resort is about 3 miles from the oceanfront resort area. All suites have balconies with bay views, and separate sleeping and living areas, all furnished with sophisticated, contemporary light-wood pieces in pleasing pastel hues. Kitchen areas are equipped with refrigerator and microwave. Utensils are available for a $5 charge, or you may bring your own.

Dining/Entertainment: The Tradewinds Restaurant next to the pool offers wonderful water views and good American fare; the Café by the Bay is for more casual dining.

Services: Room service (6:10am to 11pm), turndown on request.

Facilities: Beach, tennis club on site, indoor/outdoor pools, health club, sauna, jet-ski rental, volleyball, children's activities, gift shop, meeting facilities, coin-op laundry.

MODERATE

THE ATRIUM, 21st St. and Arctic Ave., Virginia Beach, VA 23451. Tel. 804/491-1400, or toll free 800/443-7040, 800/443-7044 in Virginia. Fax 804/491-7751. 90 suites. A/C TV TEL

$ **Rates:** Summer, $95–$120 single or double; winter, $39–$59 single or double. Children under 12 stay free in parents' room. Extra person $6; cots $5. AE, CB, DC, DISC, MC, V. Weekend and other packages available. **Parking:** Free.

Just 1½ blocks from the oceanfront, the six-story Atrium is an attractive family resort with a stepped-glass facade that permits brilliant light to illuminate the lobby-level pool all day long. Many of the suites have balcony views facing the pool as well as views of the surrounding resort area. Bright, modern, and spacious accommodations have separate bedrooms, complete kitchen facilities, and separate living rooms with sleeper sofas. Every suite has two color TVs. There are coin-op laundry facilities on three floors.

THE BREAKERS RESORT INN, 16th St. at the Oceanfront, Virginia Beach, VA 23451. Tel. 804/428-1821, or toll free 800/237-7532, 800/468-1354 in Virginia. 57 rms and efficiencies. A/C TV TEL

$ **Rates:** Summer, $100–$130 single or double; winter, $30–$65 single or double. Weekend and other packages available. AE, MC, V. **Parking:** Free.

One of the more reasonable priced oceanfront hostelries, the Breakers is a small family-operated hotel. A white boxlike nine-story building, its rooms are comfortably furnished with contemporary pieces. All have oceanfront balconies and refrigerators; some rooms with king-size beds contain Jacuzzis. Efficiency apartments have a bedroom with two double beds, a living room with a Murphy bed, and a sitting area. Kitchens are fully equipped. Additional amenities: an outdoor heated pool, coffee shop for poolside dining, and free bicycles.

BUDGET

ECONO LODGE, 2968 Shore Dr. (Rte. 60), Virginia Beach, VA 23451. Tel. 804/481-0666, or toll free 800/446-6900. 41 rms. A/C TV TEL

$ **Rates:** Summer, $50–$80 single or double; winter, $40–$50 single or double. Extra person $5. AE, CB, DC, DISC, MC, V. **Parking:** Free.

This Econo Lodge is attractive with gray clapboard siding and blue doors. About 2 miles east of the Chesapeake Bay Bridge-Tunnel, it's just a short walk from the Chesapeake Bay beach, or you can take a dip in the motel's own heated outdoor pool. Standard motel accommodations all have microwaves and refrigerators. VCRs and tapes are available for rental. Complimentary coffee and doughnuts are served in the reception area every morning.

WHERE TO DINE

MODERATE

CAPTAIN GEORGE'S SEAFOOD RESTAURANT, 1956 Laskin Rd. Tel. 804/428-3494.

Cuisine: SEAFOOD. **Reservations:** Accepted only for 6 or more. **Directions:** From the resort area, follow 31st Street (Laskin Road) west for about 3 miles.

$ **Prices:** Buffet $17.95 Mon–Fri, $18.95 Sat–Sun. AE, MC, V.

Open: Mon–Fri 5–10pm, Sat 4:30–10pm, Sun noon–10pm.

There's always a crowd at this immensely popular all-you-can-eat-buffet restaurant. Part of a chain with restaurants throughout the Tidewater, Captain George's features lavish spreads of fresh, first-quality fare in very simpatico surroundings. There are several spacious dining rooms, two of them with magnificent stained-glass domed ceilings. Polished-brass chandeliers, a brass rail setting off a raised seating area, crossed harpoons, ropes, pulleys, and ship's figureheads provide a festive nautical atmosphere.

An array of delicious salads and fresh vegetables accompanies the entrees, which are uniformly excellent. These might include large Alaskan snow crab legs, soft-shell crabs (in season), steamed shrimp, crab imperial, deviled crab, seafood casserole, prime rib, and southern fried chicken. Homemade cornbread, rolls, and other breads are part of the spread. Everything is fresh and made from scratch, including desserts—rice puddings, peach cobblers, cakes, pastries, and fresh fruits.

LYNNHAVEN FISH HOUSE, 22350 Starfish Rd. Tel. 804/481-0003.

Cuisine: SEAFOOD. **Reservations:** Recommended. **Directions:** From the resort area, take Route 60 (Shore Drive) to the Lynnhaven Fishing Pier, near the bridge-tunnel.

$ **Prices:** Appetizers $4.95–$7.95; entrees $13.95–$22.95. AE, CB, DC, DISC, MC, V.

Open: Daily 11:30am–10:30pm.

The Lynnhaven Fish House is a Virginia Beach institution, specializing in fresh Chesapeake Bay fish. Its spacious, airy dining room has wraparound windows overlooking the bay. At lunch, a good bet is a half dozen fresh-shucked clams on the half shell with cocktail sauce ($5.90). Other choices include a crabcake sandwich, shrimp salad on croissant, seafood pasta salad, or seafood stir-fry.

The dinner menu starts off with oysters Rockefeller, and selections from the chowder pots. Fresh fish of the day (flounder, sea trout, salmon, mako shark, red snapper, tuna, swordfish, or rainbow trout) are offered broiled, grilled, steamed, or poached, and you have a choice of nine sauces to enhance the flavor. There are also crabmeat, scallop, shrimp, and oyster dishes. All dinners come with a choice of baked potato, sweet potato, french fries, or black beans and rice; cole slaw, house salad, or Caesar salad; and a bread basket. For dessert, there's moist carrot cake, lavishly frosted, or a refreshing peach Melba.

HENRY'S, 3319 Shore Dr. (Rte. 60). Tel. 804/481-7300.

Cuisine: SEAFOOD. **Reservations:** Not accepted Fri–Sat in summer. **Directions:** From the resort area, take Route 60 west for about 5 miles.

$ **Prices:** Appetizers $2.25–$5.95; entrees $8.95–$16.95. DISC, MC, V.

Open: Summer, daily 11am–2am; brunch Sun 9am–2pm. Winter, Mon–Sat 5pm–midnight; brunch Sun from 10am.

You'll feel as though you're aboard ship in any one of the casual dining rooms or outdoor decks of this bilevel waterfront dining complex. At the front door, an 8,000-gallon cylindrical aquarium rises two stories and holds marine life native to this area. Gray tile floors, blond-wood tables, white easy chairs, and lots of mirrors create an appealing contemporary setting. Fresh fish is prepared six different ways—grilled, broiled, fried, blackened, Cajun, or poached—and there are usually over a dozen varieties of fresh fish on the menu. Seafood platters, sautéed combinations, and Henry's famous lump crab cakes are all eminently recommendable. Dessert treats include deep-dish apple pie à la mode.

INEXPENSIVE

MORRISON'S CAFETERIA, 1532 Laskin Rd. Tel. 804/422-4755.
   Cuisine: AMERICAN.
$ Prices: Entrees $3.20–$5.50. AE, MC, V.
   Open: Sun–Thurs 11am–8pm, Fri–Sat 11am–8:30pm.
This chain has spread far and wide throughout the Southeast, so you may already be familiar with Morrison's casual atmosphere and amazingly low prices. Decorated tastefully with Colonial-style and Audubon prints, hanging plants, and light woods, Morrison's offers daily specials like a roast turkey platter with dressing and two vegetables for $3.10. Options also include salads and fresh-baked breads, cakes, and pies.

3. THE EASTERN SHORE

182 miles NE of Richmond, 83 miles N of Virginia Beach and Norfolk,
85 miles SE of Washington, D.C.

GETTING THERE   By Bus   While there is no direct public transportation to Chincoteague, you can take a Greyhound/Trailways bus (tel. 804/824-5935) from Richmond, Virginia Beach, or Norfolk to T's Corner Exxon Station, in Oak Hall at the Route 175/Route 13 intersection, which is also headquarters for Mears Taxi Service, which can run you the 15 miles to Chincoteague.

By Car   From Norfolk take I-64E, or from Virginia Beach take Route 60W, and follow the gull signs to the Chesapeake Bay Bridge-Tunnel, a beautiful 17.6-mile drive across and under the bay ($9 per car). From the Cape Charles end of the bridge, take Route 13N about 60 miles, turn right onto Route 175E, and continue about 15 miles to Chincoteague Island.

ESSENTIALS   Orientation   Virginia's Eastern Shore is a peaceful 70-mile-long peninsula dropping south of the Maryland border between the Chesapeake Bay and the Atlantic Ocean. A small island connected to the Eastern Shore by a bridge, Chincoteague is also the gateway to the pristine barrier island of Assateague, home of the wild Chincoteague ponies. The **telephone area code** is 804.

Information   For information about the Eastern Shore, contact the **Eastern Shore Tourism Commission,** U.S. 13 South (P.O. Box R), Melfa, VA 23410 (tel. 804/787-2460). In Chincoteague there is a **visitors center** in the traffic circle on Maddox Boulevard, about a quarter mile before you come to the Assateague bridge. You can stop in during the season daily 9am to 5pm or write them at P.O. Box 258, Chincoteague, VA 23336 (tel. 804/336-6161).

Getting Around   There is no public transportation on the Eastern Shore. This is good biking terrain; bikes can be rented at **T&T Biking Rentals,** Maddox Boulevard, Chincoteague (tel. 804/336-6330).

Miles of uncrowded beaches, countless waterways, abundant wildlife, and down-home cooking and hospitality welcome visitors to the tranquil Eastern Shore.

Whether you'd like to take a day cruise to quaint Tangier Island in the Chesapeake Bay, browse the little villages, meander along traffic-free back roads, or go birdwatching on the beach of the wildlife refuge, you'll enjoy the gentle pace of this serene area. With its many motels, inns, and restaurants, and proximity to Assateague Island, Chincoteague makes a natural base for exploring the Eastern Shore.

Chincoteague Island, a small fishing village just 7 miles long and 1½ miles wide, is famous for its oyster beds and clam shoals. Marguerite Henry's children's book, and later film, *Misty of Chincoteague* aroused wide interest in the annual pony penning and swim. The island is connected via a small bridge to the barrier island of Assateague, site of the National Seashore Park and Chincoteague Wildlife Refuge. First settled by the English in the late 1600s, Chincoteague remained a fairly isolated fishing community until construction of the Chesapeake Bay Bridge-Tunnel.

WHAT TO SEE & DO
ASSATEAGUE ISLAND

A barrier island protecting Chincoteague Island from the Atlantic Ocean, Assateague Island boasts over 37 miles of pristine **beaches** on its east coast, the northern part of which is in Maryland. At the Virginia end, lifeguard-protected beaches at Toms Cove have bathhouses and toilet facilities.

The **Chincoteague National Wildlife Refuge** in the Virginia part of Assateague Island is open March 15 to October 31, daily from 5am to 10pm; November 1 to March 14, daily from 6am to 6pm. Owned and managed by the U.S. Fish and Wildlife Service, the refuge accepts the annual entrance passes issued at national parks; otherwise, admission is $3 per car, or $1 per person on foot or bicycle. For information about the refuge and visitor-center seasons, write or call: Refuge Manager, Chincoteague National Wildlife Refuge, P.O. Box 62, Chincoteague, VA 23336 (tel. 804/336-6122). Another visitor center, at Toms Cove, is managed by the National Park Service (tel. 804/336-6577).

Birdwatchers know Assateague Island as a prime Atlantic Flyway habitat where sightings of peregrine falcons, snow geese, great blue heron, and snowy egrets have been made. The annual Waterfowl Week, generally held around Thanksgiving, takes place when a large number of migratory birds use the refuge. **Wildlife tours** of the refuge can be booked in advance with Island Cruises, P.O. Box 83, Chincoteague, VA 23336 (tel. 804/336-5593 or 336-5511).

In addition to the beach, fishing, and the naturalist activities associated with the refuge, outdoor activities on Assateague also include shell collecting (most productive at the tip of the Toms Cove spit of land), hiking, and biking along the path that leads from Chincoteague to the Refuge visitors center, then follows Wildlife Drive (best place to encounter the ponies) to the Toms Cove visitors center. In spring or fall, when visitors are few, the refuge offers miles of undisturbed marsh, lake, and ocean vistas punctuated by breathtaking vignettes featuring shorebirds, ponies, and other wildlife. Bring a camera, you won't regret it.

IN CHINCOTEAGUE

On Maddox Boulevard, between the traffic circle and the bridge to Assateague, are two small marine-themed museums. The **Oyster Museum** (tel. 804/336-6117), open Memorial Day weekend to Labor Day, daily from 11am to 5pm (admission is $2.50 for adults, $1 for children 12 and under), tells all about this vital industry; and the **Refuge Waterfowl Museum** (tel. 804/336-5800), open Memorial Day to Labor Day, daily from 10am to 5pm (admission is $2.50 for adults, $1 for children 12 and under), has an interesting variety of antique decoys, boats, traps, art, and carvings by outstanding craftspeople.

In mid-July the **Chincoteague Fireman's Carnival,** a fun fest with rides, live

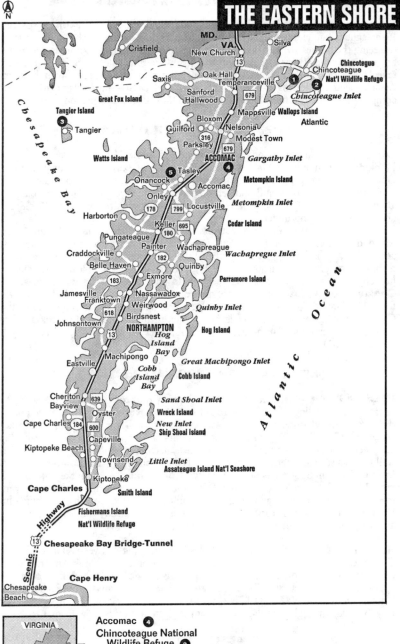

THE EASTERN SHORE

Chesapeake Bay

Atlantic Ocean

MD.
VA.

Crisfield
Silva
New Church
Chincoteague
Chincoteague Nat'l Wildlife Refuge
Oak Hall
Saxis
Temperanceville
13
Great Fox Island
Sanford
Hallwood
679
Chincoteague Inlet
Tangier Island
Bloxom
Mappsville Wallops Island
Atlantic
Tangier
Guilford
Nelsonia
Parksley
316
Modest Town
Watts Island
679
Gargathy Inlet
ACCOMAC
Tasley
Metompkin Island
Onancock
Accomac
Onley
178
Locustville
Metompkin Inlet
Harborton
799
Keller
695
Cedar Island
Pungateague
180
Craddockville
Painter
Wachapreague
Wachapregue Inlet
Belle Haven
182
Quinby
183
Exmore
Parramore Island
Jamesville
Nassawadox
Franktown
Weirwood
Quinby Inlet
618
Birdsnest
Johnsontown
NORTHAMPTON
Hog Island
13
Hog Island Bay
Machipongo
Eastville
Cobb Island Bay
Great Machipongo Inlet
Cobb Island
Cheriton
639
Sand Shoal Inlet
Bayview
Oyster
Wreck Island
Cape Charles
184
New Inlet
600
Ship Shoal Island
Capeville
Kiptopeke Beach
Townsend
Little Inlet
Kiptopeke
Assateague Island Nat'l Seashore
Cape Charles
Smith Island
Fishermans Island
Nat'l Wildlife Refuge
Highway
13
Chesapeake Bay Bridge-Tunnel
Scenic
Cape Henry
Chesapeake Beach

VIRGINIA

Eastern Shore

Accomac ④
Chincoteague National Wildlife Refuge ②
Onancock ⑤
Oyster Museum ①
Refuge Waterfowl Museum ①
Tangier Island ③

entertainment, and food, is climaxed by the famous **ponies' swim** across the Assateague Channel to Chincoteague Memorial Park. There is no charge for parking or seeing the ponies swim. The ponies are herded to the carnival grounds where the first colt to come ashore is given away and many are then sold at auction. The swim takes place on the last Wednesday in July; the remaining ponies swim back to Assateague the following Friday. It's all in a good cause—proceeds go to the fire company's ambulance fund. Telephone 804/336-6519 for information.

A CRUISE TO TANGIER ISLAND

Cruises to tiny Tangier Island, a picturesque village of 750 souls, leave from the Hopkins General Store, 2 Market Street (tel. 804/787-8220), near the town wharf in Onancock, a town about 12 miles south on Route 13 from the Chincoteague turnoff at Route 175. The Tangier Island ferry operates June through September, daily at 10am, returning at 3pm. Adult fare is $16 round-trip; children ages 6 to 11, $8; no charge for ages 5 and under.

There are no cars on the narrow streets, which seems appropriate to this unspoiled island, discovered by Capt. John Smith in 1608. In fact, we've been told that the local accent actually harks back to Elizabethan English. This is no glitzy resort. Entertainment consists of walking around the island, perhaps chatting with local baymen, and just enjoying the serenity and fresh sea air. In any case, you'll want to eat at the **Chesapeake House,** where sumptuous dinners are served for $11, family style from 11:30am to 5pm daily. You can also stay overnight on Tangier Island at the Chesapeake House for a reasonable $35, which includes dinner and breakfast. For details and reservations, the address is simply Tangier Island, Tangier, VA 23440 (tel. 804/891-2331).

MORE EASTERN SHORE ATTRACTIONS

IN ONANCOCK While you're in the very pretty port town of Onancock going to or from the ferry, linger for a bit in **Hopkins & Bro. store,** built in 1842 and one of the oldest general stores on the East Coast. The **Blue Crab Bay Co.,** 57 Market Street (tel. 804/787-3602), has gourmet souvenirs of your visit to the Chesapeake Bay area: herb seasonings for shellfish, smoked fish, herring-roe mousse, and more. Also well worth a stop in Onancock is the stately Federal mansion that is now headquarters for the Eastern Shore Historical Society, **Kerr Place,** on Market Street (tel. 804/787-8012), open March through December, Tuesday through Sunday from 9am to 4pm (closed holidays); admission is $3. Built in 1799 by Scottish merchant John Shepherd Kerr, this two-story brick manor house is beautifully furnished with 18th- and 19th-century antiques.

IN ACCOMAC Another back-road destination, lying between Onancock and Chincoteague, is the historic town of Accomac, on Route 605. This sleepy little town has handsome Victorian houses and an unusual **debtor's prison,** open by appointment only (tel. 804/787-2462). **Accomack Vineyards,** on Route 607 in Painter, Va. (tel. 804/442-2110), is open for tours and free tastings July 4 to Labor Day, Tuesday through Saturday from 10am to 4pm and on Sunday from 1 to 5pm.

WHERE TO STAY

Numerous motels, B&B inns, and campgrounds offer accommodations along Route 13 and adjoining highways. If you're looking for a longer-term rental on Chincoteague Island, contact **Virginia Cottages,** Route 1 (P.O. Box 547), East Side Drive, Chincoteague, VA 23336 (tel. 804/336-3720, or toll free 800/45PONIES); they have fully furnished cottages in various locations, including some on the waterfront, in spring, summer, and fall. For shorter stays, consider these Chincoteague Island accommodations:

MOTELS
Moderate

REFUGE MOTOR INN, Beach Rd. (P.O. Box 378), Chincoteague, VA 23336. Tel. 804/336-5511. Fax 804/336-6134. 68 rms. A/C TV TEL
$ Rates: $40–$105 single or double Mon–Fri, $50–$105 single or double Sat–Sun. AE, CB, DC, DISC, MC, V. **Parking:** Free.

Located between the traffic circle and the bridge to Assateague, this very attractive motor inn with weathered gray siding nestles on beautifully landscaped grounds shaded by tall pines. The care and attention lavished on decor and facilities at this family-owned spot are evident everywhere. Furnishings are charming. Some rooms have Colonial-style pieces, bleached pine headboards, decoys, handmade wall hangings, and all the elements of country style. All rooms have refrigerators. First-floor rooms facing the back have sliding doors to private patios where guests can use outdoor grills. There's an observation sun deck on the roof, a health club with sauna, glass-enclosed pool and Jacuzzi, children's center and a pony enclosure, rental bikes, coin-op laundry facilities, and a lobby gift/craft shop. The inn is headquarters for daily wildlife tours through the Chincoteague Refuge.

WATERSIDE MOTOR INN, 544 S. Main St. (P.O. Box 347), Chincoteague, VA 23336. Tel. 804/336-3434. Fax 804/336-1878. 45 rms. A/C TV TEL **Directions:** At the bridge entering Chincoteague, turn right; the motel is on the right, about half a mile from the bridge.
$ Rates: Summer, $70–$103 single or double; winter, $46–$78 single or double. Children under 12 (limit of two children) stay free in parents' room. Extra person $5. AE, DC, DISC, MC, V. **Parking:** Free on-site parking.

All the accommodations at this three-story property have private balconies overlooking Chincoteague Channel, guaranteeing some breathtaking sunset views. Gray clapboard siding with blue-and-white trim has a properly nautical look. Rooms are decorated in tones of blue, beige, and green in comfortable, contemporary style. All have coffee makers and refrigerators. The Waterside also offers a Jacuzzi, exercise room, and swimming pool, and it's located right on a fishing and crabbing pier.

Budget

BEACH ROAD MOTEL, 105 Maddox Blvd. (P.O. Box 557), Chincoteague, VA 23336. Tel. 804/336-6562. 19 rms, 1 cottage. A/C TV TEL **Directions:** Turn left at the bridge, and drive seven blocks to Maddox Boulevard.
$ Rates: $32–$54 single or double. Extra person $5. MC, V. **Parking:** Free. **Closed:** After Thanksgiving to early Mar.

This owner-operated motel offers very nice rooms in a one-story white masonry building with blue doors. The rooms are immaculate, with all the basics, including refrigerators. The cottage is actually a mobile home, and has a separate bedroom and full kitchen facilities. There is an outdoor pool on the property.

COUNTRY B&B INNS
Expensive

CHANNEL BASS INN, 100 Church St., Chincoteague, VA 23336. Tel. 804/336-6148. 10 rms and suites (all with bath). **Directions:** From the bridge into Chincoteague, turn left onto North Main Street and right onto Church Street; the inn is less than half a block from the corner of Main Street.

$ Rates: $108–$162.75 per room, double occupancy. AE, CB, DC, MC, V.
Parking: Free. **Closed:** Mid-Dec to mid-Feb.

The Channel Bass Inn is a bastion of luxury and elegance with a first-class restaurant. Visitors from Washington make the trip to Chincoteague just to have dinner here. (Casual attire is fine, but dinner reservations are required.) The inn's 10 rooms are individually decorated in exquisite taste; everything is top quality, from the Egyptian cotton towels to the ensemble bed linens. Spacious accommodations feature four-poster beds, Erté prints on the walls, bamboo or mahogany furnishings, live plants, and comfortable wing chairs. Owner/chef James Hanretta offers 3-day cooking vacations, Monday through Wednesday; classes, limited to just three people per session, involve demonstration and full participation with the noted chef. The rate of $800 includes 3 nights' lodging, meals, and instruction.

Dining/Entertainment: In this renowned dining room, tables are elegantly appointed with Wedgwood china, sterling-silver flatware, and crystal stemware. Tables are nicely spaced, and only 18 people can dine here on a given evening. Dinner for two, with wine, may be $200, with entrees in the $30 to $39 range—and well worth the price. A meal might begin with a beautifully seasoned crab stew, followed by an entree of shrimp provençal on saffron rice or backfin crab soufflé. Breakfast, which must be ordered by 10pm the previous night, is not included in the rates. Continental breakfast is served on weekdays, full breakfast on weekends. Among the morning specialties are Hanretta's souffléed pancakes, served with fresh strawberries and whipped cream ($16), and omelets with a choice of tasty fillings, including shrimp with sauce espagnole and crabmeat imperial ($24 to $25).

Moderate

THE LITTLE TRAVELLER BED & BREAKFAST, 112 N. Main St., Chincoteague, VA 23336. Tel. 804/336-6686. 7 rms (1 with bath). A/C.
Directions: From the bridge into Chincoteague, turn left onto North Main Street and continue about 1½ blocks; the inn is on the right.

$ Rates (including full breakfast and afternoon tea): $55–$99 single or double. No credit cards. **Parking:** Free. **Closed:** Dec–Mar, and Mon–Thurs in Apr and Nov.

This B&B consists of two white clapboard houses joined by a one-story garden room with a lovely brick patio and fountain in the back. Originally there was one house, built before the Civil War by two young men. They eventually married sisters, who did not enjoy living under the same roof, so they split the house and moved the front half next door. Today both houses have been handsomely restored and are furnished mainly in Federal style, but also with 17th-, 18th-, and 19th-century pieces collected by hospitable owners Jim and Priscilla Stam. In the two first-floor sitting rooms are a TV, a telephone for guest use, and a fireplace. A full breakfast, which is served in Miss Molly's Inn, under the same ownership and right across the street, might include fresh fruit or juice, an egg dish, crunch cake, and coffee or tea.

MISS MOLLY'S INN BED & BREAKFAST, 113 N. Main St., Chincoteague, VA 23336. Tel. 804/336-6686. 7 rms (1 with bath). A/C.
Directions: From the bridge into Chincoteague, turn left onto North Main Street and continue about 1½ blocks to the inn, on the left.

$ Rates (including full breakfast and afternoon tea): $59–$105 single or double. No credit cards. **Parking:** Free. **Closed:** Dec–Mar, and Mon–Thurs in Apr and Nov.

This charming white Victorian (1886) house, with a wide, wicker-furnished front porch, is named for the daughter of the builder, J. T. Rowley, known as "the clam king of the world." Miss Molly, who lived in this house until the age of 84, was a resident when Marguerite Henry stayed here while she was writing *Misty of Chincoteague*. All rooms are an agreeable mix of Victorian and earlier antiques, with lace curtains, pretty coverlets, wicker pieces, Tiffany-style lamps, and bibelots adorning mantels and dresser tops. The parlor and dining room have exceptionally fine Victorian pieces—marble-top tables, a curved sofa, original newel-post lamps, and Oriental carpets. A full breakfast is served daily.

CAMPGROUNDS

MADDOX FAMILY CAMPGROUND, Maddox Blvd. (P.O. Box 82), Chincoteague, VA 23336. Tel. 804/336-3111. 550 campsites. **Directions:** From the bridge, turn left onto North Main Street, right on Maddox Boulevard, which runs into Beach Road; at the traffic circle, turn right to the campgrounds.

$ Rates: $15.75 tent site; $18.45 site with water and electricity; $21.70 site with full hookup. Rates cover four people; additional people over age 3 pay $3 per night. MC, V.

A good-size property, well located near the traffic circle and half a mile away from the bridge to Assateague, the camp has 550 sites spread across 200 acres of woods. Some sites have views of the Assateague Lighthouse. On the campground are a swimming pool, playground, pavilion, grocery store with RV supplies, rec hall, laundry room, bath houses, dump station, and propane filling station. Shuffle board, a duck pond, horse shoes, crabbing, and birdwatching are on site.

NEARBY CAMPGROUND

CHERRYSTONE CAMPGROUND, P.O. Box 545, Cheriton, VA 23316. Tel. 804/331-3063.

$ Rates: $15 for a tent site; $19 for site with water and electricity; $20.50 for a full hookup. Rates cover two people; additional adults pay $31; children over 3 pay $1. Children under 3 are free. AE, DISC, MC, V.

Eleven miles north of the Bay Bridge Tunnel, about 40 miles south on Route 13 of the Route 175 Chincoteague turn-off, Cherrystone is an outstanding family vacation campground. It is on the Chesapeake Bay and offers four piers for fishing and crabbing. The Bait & Tackle Shop rents rowboats, motorboats, surf bikes, clam rakes, and bicycles. The list of its facilities includes two Olympic-size pools, a wading pool, laundry, mini-golf, rental trailers, camping cabins, rec hall, grocery, modern tiled bath houses, volleyball, tennis, and more. With over 700 sites on 300 acres of wooded waterfront property, Cherrystone is an appealing mix of seaside resort and rustic campground.

WHERE TO DINE

MODERATE

LANDMARK CRAB HOUSE, N. Main St., on the bay, Landmark Plaza. Tel. 804/336-5552.

Cuisine: SEAFOOD. **Reservations:** Suggested.

$ Prices: Appetizers $3.95–$5.95; entrees $9.95–$15.95. AE, DC, DISC, MC, V.

Open: Dinner only, Mon–Sat 5–9pm, Sun 1–10pm. **Closed:** Mon in winter.

A Chincoteague institution for fresh local seafood, the Crab House sits at the end of a pier, and is surrounded by decking; wraparound windows provide panoramic views of small fishing vessels tied up for the evening in the channel. The gorgeous Victorian bar, dating to 1897, was brought here from Chicago. The wood-paneled dining room has a nautical motif with ship figureheads, ship models, lanterns, and mounted fish. For an appetizer, you can't beat Chincoteague oysters on the half shell or a bucket of oyster steamers. Trips to the salad bar come with all entrees. A children's menu features fish, chicken, clam strips, and hamburger, all with french fries and salad bar. Landmark specials include half a pound of steamed shrimp with fresh broccoli and hollandaise sauce, soft-shell crabs, and crab imperial. Landlubbers can choose from fresh fried or teriyaki chicken, filet mignon, or New York strip steak. There's a small wine list, and an international variety of beers are available. On Friday, Saturday, and holiday evenings there's piano music in the lounge.

VILLAGE RESTAURANT, Maddox Blvd. Tel. 804/336-5120.
  Cuisine: AMERICAN. **Reservations:** Suggested Sat–Sun.
$ Prices: Appetizers $2.50–$5.95; entrees $9.95–$16.95. AE, DISC, MC, V.
  Open: Dinner only, daily 5–10pm.
Entered via a cozy bar and lounge, the Village Restaurant is gardenlike, with floral wallpaper, hanging plants, ceiling fans, white trellises, and a white gazebolike dining area in the back of the restaurant. Green-shaded lamps provide soft lighting. Seating is in comfortable Windsor chairs. Appetizers include calamari, stuffed mushroom caps, oyster stew, and oysters or clams on the half shell. Seafood entree choices are uniformly excellent, whether you choose fried oysters, stuffed flounder, or crab imperial. The house seafood platter is piled with fish filet, crab cake (delicious), shrimp, scallops, oysters, clams, and lobster tail. There are nonseafood main dishes like stuffed veal, chicken stir-fry, and filet mignon. All entrees are served with salad, home-baked bread, and a choice of potato, rice, or vegetable of the day. Oven-fresh desserts include an exceptionally light and delicate cheesecake.

INEXPENSIVE/MODERATE

ETTA'S FAMILY RESTAURANT, East Side Dr. at Assateague Channel. Tel. 804/336-5644.
  Cuisine: AMERICAN. **Reservations:** Accepted.
$ Prices: Appetizers $2–$5.50; entrees $8.95–$15.95. DISC, MC, V.
  Open: Summer, Wed–Mon 7am–9pm; winter, Fri–Mon 8am–8pm.
Etta's is an unpretentious eatery where service is friendly and food is hearty. It's right next to Memorial Park, and its windows give diners the best view in town of the pony swim. Everything is cooked to order here, so you may have a bit of a wait for such down-home breakfasts as steak and eggs or creamed chipped beef on toast. Lunch sandwiches include hot beef with gravy, soft-shell crab, and fried oyster ($2.50 to $4.75). Dinnertime, appetizers of creamy crab soup or oyster stew precede entrees like fresh flounder, homemade crab cakes, and fried combination seafood platters. A children's menu ($4.50) has chopped steak, chicken, and fried clam strips.

SHUCKING HOUSE CAFE, N. Main St. on the bay, Landmark Plaza. Tel. 804/336-5145.
  Cuisine: AMERICAN.
$ Prices: Appetizers $1.50–$4.50; entrees $10.95–$11.95; sandwiches $3.50–$4.95. AE, DC, DISC, MC, V.
  Open: Daily 8am–3pm.
Adjoining the Landmark Crab House and under the same owners, the Shucking House Café has a cathedral ceiling, windows overlooking the channel, and seating in red-leather-upholstered booths and small tables. Breakfast options include scrapple and biscuits or blueberry pancakes. The lunch menu features soups, chowders, sandwiches, and seafood entrees such as crabcake platter, fried scallops, and seafood au gratin. Beer and wines are available.

INDEX

GENERAL INFORMATION

DESTINATIONS

KEY TO ABBREVIATIONS: *B* = Budget; *B&B* = Bed & Breakfast; *E* = Expensive; *I* = Inexpensive; *M* = Moderate; *VE* = Very Expensive; *$* = Special Value; * = an Author's Favorite

NOW, SAVE MONEY ON ALL YOUR TRAVELS!
Join Frommer's™ Dollarwise® Travel Club

Saving money while traveling is never easy, which is why the **Dollarwise Travel Club** was formed 32 years ago to provide cost-cutting travel strategies, up-to-date travel information, and a sense of community for value-conscious travelers from all over the world.

In keeping with the money-saving concept, the annual membership fee is low—$25 for U.S. residents and $35 for residents of Canada, Mexico, and other countries—and is immediately exceeded by the value of your benefits, which include:

1. Any TWO books listed on the following pages;
2. Plus any ONE Frommer's City Guide;
3. A subscription to our quarterly newspaper, *The Dollarwise Traveler;*
4. A membership card that entitles you to purchase through the Club all Frommer's publications for 33% to 40% off their retail price.

The eight-page **Dollarwise Traveler** tells you about the latest developments in good-value travel worldwide and includes the following columns: **Hospitality Exchange** (for those offering and seeking hospitality in cities all over the world); and **Share-a-Trip** (for those looking for travel companions to share costs).

Aside from the various Frommer's Guides, the Gault Millau Guides, and the Real Guides you can also choose from our Special Editions, which include such titles as *Caribbean Hideaways* (the 100 most romantic places to stay in the Islands); and *Marilyn Wood's Wonderful Weekends* (a selection of the best mini-vacations within a 200-mile radius of New York City).

To join this Club, send the appropriate membership fee with your name and address to: Frommer's Dollarwise Travel Club, 15 Columbus Circle, New York, NY 10023. Remember to specify which single city guide and which two other guides you wish to receive in your initial package of member's benefits. Or tear out the pages, check off your choices, and send them to us with your membership fee.

FROMMER BOOKS
PRENTICE HALL TRAVEL   Date_____
15 COLUMBUS CIRCLE
NEW YORK, NY 10023

Friends: Please send me the books checked below.

FROMMER'S™ COMPREHENSIVE GUIDES
(Guides listing facilities from budget to deluxe, with emphasis on the medium-priced)

☐ Alaska	$14.95	☐ Italy	$19.00
☐ Australia	$14.95	☐ Japan & Hong Kong	$17.00
☐ Austria & Hungary	$14.95	☐ Morocco	$18.00
☐ Belgium, Holland & Luxembourg	$14.95	☐ Nepal	$18.00
☐ Bermuda & The Bahamas	$17.00	☐ New England	$17.00
☐ Brazil	$14.95	☐ New Mexico	$13.95
☐ California	$18.00	☐ New York State	$19.00
☐ Canada	$16.00	☐ Northwest	$16.95
☐ Caribbean	$17.00	☐ Puerta Vallarta (avail. Feb. '92)	$14.00
☐ Carolinas & Georgia	$17.00	☐ Portugal, Madeira & the Azores	$14.95
☐ Colorado (avail. Jan '92)	$14.00	☐ Scandinavia	$18.95
☐ Cruises (incl. Alaska, Carib, Mex, Hawaii, Panama, Canada & US)	$16.00	☐ Scotland (avail. Feb. '92)	$17.00
		☐ South Pacific	$20.00
☐ Delaware, Maryland, Pennsylvania & the New Jersey Shore (avail. Jan. '92)	$19.00	☐ Southeast Asia	$14.95
		☐ Switzerland & Liechtenstein	$19.00
☐ Egypt	$14.95	☐ Thailand	$20.00
☐ England	$17.00	☐ Virginia (avail. Feb. '92)	$14.00
☐ Florida	$17.00	☐ Virgin Islands	$13.00
☐ France	$15.95	☐ USA	$16.95
☐ Germany	$18.00		

0891492

FROMMER'S CITY GUIDES

(Pocket-size guides to sightseeing and tourist accommodations and facilities in all price ranges)

☐ Amsterdam/Holland	$8.95	☐ Minneapolis/St. Paul	$8.95
☐ Athens	$8.95	☐ Montréal/Québec City	$8.95
☐ Atlanta	$8.95	☐ New Orleans	$8.95
☐ Atlantic City/Cape May	$8.95	☐ New York	$12.00
☐ Bangkok	$12.00	☐ Orlando	$12.00
☐ Barcelona	$12.00	☐ Paris	$8.95
☐ Belgium	$7.95	☐ Philadelphia	$11.00
☐ Berlin	$10.00	☐ Rio	$8.95
☐ Boston	$8.95	☐ Rome	$8.95
☐ Cancún/Cozumel/Yucatán	$8.95	☐ Salt Lake City	$8.95
☐ Chicago	$9.95	☐ San Diego	$8.95
☐ Denver/Boulder/Colorado Springs	$8.95	☐ San Francisco	$12.00
☐ Dublin/Ireland	$10.00	☐ Santa Fe/Taos/Albuquerque	$10.95
☐ Hawaii	$12.00	☐ Seattle/Portland	$12.00
☐ Hong Kong	$7.95	☐ St. Louis/Kansas City	$9.95
☐ Las Vegas	$8.95	☐ Sydney	$8.95
☐ Lisbon/Madrid/Costa del Sol	$8.95	☐ Tampa/St. Petersburg	$8.95
☐ London	$12.00	☐ Tokyo	$8.95
☐ Los Angeles	$8.95	☐ Toronto	$8.95
☐ Mexico City/Acapulco	$8.95	☐ Vancouver/Victoria	$7.95
☐ Miami	$8.95	☐ Washington, D.C.	$12.00

FROMMER'S $-A-DAY® GUIDES

(Guides to low-cost tourist accommodations and facilities)

☐ Australia on $40 a Day	$13.95	☐ Israel on $40 a Day	$13.95
☐ Costa Rica, Guatemala & Belize		☐ Mexico on $45 a Day	$18.00
on $35 a Day	$15.95	☐ New York on $65 a Day	$15.00
☐ Eastern Europe on $25 a Day	$16.95	☐ New Zealand on $45 a Day	$16.00
☐ England on $50 a Day	$17.00	☐ Scotland & Wales on $40 a Day	$18.00
☐ Europe on $45 a Day	$19.00	☐ South America on $40 a Day	$15.95
☐ Greece on $35 a Day	$14.95	☐ Spain on $50 a Day	$15.95
☐ Hawaii on $70 a Day	$18.00	☐ Turkey on $40 a Day	$22.00
☐ India on $40 a Day	$20.00	☐ Washington, D.C., on $45 a Day	$17.00
☐ Ireland on $40 a Day	$17.00		

FROMMER'S CITY $-A-DAY GUIDES

☐ Berlin on $40 a Day	$12.00	☐ Madrid on $50 a Day (avail. Jan '92)	$13.00
☐ Copenhagen on $50 a Day	$12.00	☐ Paris on $45 a Day	$12.00
☐ London on $45 a Day	$12.00	☐ Stockholm on $50 a Day (avail. Dec. '91)	$13.00

FROMMER'S FAMILY GUIDES

☐ California with Kids	$16.95	☐ San Francisco with Kids	$17.00
☐ Los Angeles with Kids	$17.00	☐ Washington, D.C., with Kids (avail. Jan	
☐ New York City with Kids (avail. Jan '92)	$18.00	'92)	$17.00

SPECIAL EDITIONS

☐ Beat the High Cost of Travel	$6.95	☐ Marilyn Wood's Wonderful Weekends	
☐ Bed & Breakfast—N. America	$14.95	(CT, DE, MA, NH, NJ, NY, PA, RI, VT)	$11.95
☐ Caribbean Hideaways	$16.00	☐ Motorist's Phrase Book (Fr/Ger/Sp)	$4.95
☐ Honeymoon Destinations (US, Mex &		☐ The New World of Travel (annual by	
Carib)	$14.95	Arthur Frommer for savvy travelers)	$16.95

(TURN PAGE FOR ADDITONAL BOOKS AND ORDER FORM)

- ☐ Paris Rendez-Vous $10.95
- ☐ Swap and Go (Home Exchanging). $10.95
- ☐ Travel Diary and Record Book. $5.95
- ☐ Where to Stay USA (from $3 to $30 a night). $13.95

FROMMER'S TOURING GUIDES

(Color illustrated guides that include walking tours, cultural and historic sites, and practical information)

- ☐ Amsterdam. $10.95
- ☐ Australia $12.95
- ☐ Brazil. $10.95
- ☐ Egypt. $8.95
- ☐ Florence. $8.95
- ☐ Hong Kong $10.95
- ☐ London $12.95
- ☐ New York $10.95
- ☐ Paris $8.95
- ☐ Rome. $10.95
- ☐ Scotland. $9.95
- ☐ Thailand. $12.95
- ☐ Turkey $10.95
- ☐ Venice $8.95

GAULT MILLAU

(The only guides that distinguish the truly superlative from the merely overrated)

- ☐ The Best of Chicago $15.95
- ☐ The Best of Florida $17.00
- ☐ The Best of France $16.95
- ☐ The Best of Germany $18.00
- ☐ The Best of Hawaii. $16.95
- ☐ The Best of Hong Kong $16.95
- ☐ The Best of Italy. $16.95
- ☐ The Best of London $16.95
- ☐ The Best of Los Angeles $16.95
- ☐ The Best of New England $15.95
- ☐ The Best of New Orleans. $16.95
- ☐ The Best of New York $16.95
- ☐ The Best of Paris $16.95
- ☐ The Best of San Francisco $16.95
- ☐ The Best of Thailand. $17.95
- ☐ The Best of Toronto $17.00

☐ The Best of Washington, D.C. $16.95

THE REAL GUIDES

(Opinionated, politically aware guides for youthful budget-minded travelers)

- ☐ Amsterdam $9.95
- ☐ Berlin. $11.95
- ☐ Brazil. $13.95
- ☐ California & the West Coast $11.95
- ☐ Czechoslovakia $13.95
- ☐ France $12.95
- ☐ Germany $13.95
- ☐ Greece. $13.95
- ☐ Guatemala $13.95
- ☐ Hong Kong $11.95
- ☐ Hungary. $12.95
- ☐ Ireland $12.95
- ☐ Italy. $13.95
- ☐ Kenya. $12.95
- ☐ Mexico. $11.95
- ☐ Morocco $12.95
- ☐ New York $9.95
- ☐ Paris $9.95
- ☐ Peru. $12.95
- ☐ Poland $13.95
- ☐ Portugal $10.95
- ☐ San Francisco $11.95
- ☐ Scandinavia $14.95
- ☐ Spain $12.95
- ☐ Turkey $12.95
- ☐ Venice $11.95
- ☐ Women Travel $12.95
- ☐ Yugoslavia $12.95

ORDER NOW!

In U.S. include $2 shipping UPS for 1st book; $1 ea. add'l book. Outside U.S. $3 and $1, respectively.

Allow four to six weeks for delivery in U.S., longer outside U.S. We discourage rush order service, but orders arriving with shipping fees plus a $15 surcharge will be handled as rush orders.

Enclosed is my check or money order for $_____

NAME _____

ADDRESS _____

CITY _____ STATE _____ ZIP _____

0891492